# The social history of Canada

MICHAEL BLISS, GENERAL EDITOR

# The woman suffrage

# movement in Canada

CATHERINE L. CLEVERDON

WITH AN INTRODUCTION BY RAMSAY COOK

UNIVERSITY OF TORONTO PRESS

Copyright, Canada, 1950

by University of Toronto Press

Second edition 1974

© University of Toronto Press 1974

Toronto and Buffalo

Printed in Canada

ISBN (casebound) 0-8020-2108-5

ISBN (paperback) 0-8020-6218-0

LC 73-82587

CN ISSN 0085-6207

Social History of Canada 18

This book has been published with the assistance of a grant from the
Canada Council.

# An introduction

BY RAMSAY COOK

BY 1910 THE DEBATE over woman suffrage in both Great Britain and
the United States had reached a new peak of intensity. In Britain
Mrs Pankhurst was preparing to lead her Women's Social and
Political Union in a new, more radical assault on that most privileged
of men's clubs, Parliament. That same year the state of Washington
became the fifth American state to grant the vote to women, and the
stage was set for the movement's final victories.[1] In Canada, too, the
tide seemed to be turning. The annual report of the Canadian
Suffrage Association observed confidently that 'at last Canadian
women of all classes are awakening to the importance of this great
worldwide movement, and showing signs of giving more serious
thought to it.'[2]

One sign of that growing awareness was a spirited controversy
over women's rights in the letters column of the Toronto *Globe* in
February and March 1910. Allan Studholme, the Labour member
for Hamilton East, had given notice of his intention to sponsor a
resolution supporting woman suffrage at the forthcoming session of
the Ontario legislature. Mrs Clementina Fessenden, of Hamilton,
initiated the controversy by declaring her total opposition to Mr
Studholme's proposal. 'The question,' she asserted, 'is not one of
inferiority, but of fitness; because the spheres of men and women
are different, owing to natural causes; therefore their share in the
public management of the state should be different.'[3] At once the
arguments and counter-arguments began to appear with even an
occasional intrepid male joining the debate. By the time the editor
announced that the discussion was closed, after nearly a month of
exchanges, the suffragists had carried the day: they wrote more
letters, offered more imaginative arguments, and, on the whole,
seemed more in touch with the spirit of the Canada of 1910. Yet, in
a striking way, Mrs Fessenden had been proven right about the two
spheres. The argument had been confined to the woman's page,
surrounded by homemakers' hints, new fashions, and endless
advertisements advocating elixirs for every imaginable woman's
complaint: Burdock's Blood Bitters, Dr Pierce's Pleasant Pellets,
Pe-Ru-Na, and even Madame du Barrie's Positive French Method of
Developing the Bust.[4] The suffrage controversy never once slipped
over into man's sphere: the debate over Laurier's naval policy and
the story of Sir George Foster's libel suit against the Reverend J.A.
Macdonald, the *Globe*'s editor, filled the headlines and exhausted

the space of the editorial columns. Here was proof, probably unintentional, of the different spheres.

Yet, within the next decade, most Canadian women were granted equal voting rights with men. But Canadian historical writing, for the most part, has continued to reflect the two spheres philosophy. This has meant that the history of woman suffrage has been largely ignored in the standard accounts of our past and has attracted little attention from research students — at least until recently. The major exception is Catherine L. Cleverdon's study, *The Woman Suffrage Movement in Canada.* Written nearly a quarter of a century ago, it remains the authoritative, indeed the only complete account of the suffragist struggle in Canada. The origin of the book is interesting, and best told in Dr Cleverdon's own words:

It was written as a doctoral dissertation at Columbia University, where my adviser was Professor J.B. Brebner, an ex-patriate Canadian. Originally I had intended to write on Queen Victoria's political influence, for my first love was English history. However, a book on this very subject appeared in England in the early 1940s & so that door was closed. Because of the war I couldn't go to England for research in any case, so my English history professor suggested my doing something in Canadian history. I told him I knew nothing about Canadian history. He said, 'Well, start reading.' so I did, jotting down subjects that might do for a thesis as I went along. After making quite a list of them & checking them out to make sure no one had written anything on them, I was left with a short list of topics. Women suffrage seemed the most interesting of those available.[5]

Though the circumstances explaining the topic's choice were somewhat accidental, Miss Cleverdon obviously set out on her research with energy and skill. Since she had accepted a school-teaching position, a common necessity in the days before the graduate fellowship horn of plenty, only vacations were available for research. Consequently she took those free periods to work in Canada, using the resources of the Public Archives and the Library of Parliament. So, too, she contacted as many of the living leaders of the suffrage movement as she could trace and interviewed them. The long list of names in Appendix B attests to her success in finding many of the most important participants in the movement: Dr

Augusta Stowe-Gullen, Dr Grace Richie-England, Mrs E.M. Murray, Mrs Lillian Beynon Thomas, Mrs Irene Parlby, and Mrs Nellie McClung. She also became acquainted with women in Canadian public life in the 1940s, collecting views on the small role that women had actually found for themselves after the suffrage had been gained. Professor Brebner recognized the originality and thoroughness of the resulting thesis and urged his student to prepare it for publication. In 1950 the University of Toronto Press published the first edition.

The merits of the book were obvious enough. The research was careful, the writing clear, and the organization effective. The author's sympathies with the suffragists were evident, but she let their opponents speak too. The book was well received, one reviewer remarking that it might even help to disprove the claim that Canadian history was dull.[6] Another, worried about the problem of reviewing a book written not only by a woman but by an American woman, nevertheless concluded that 'she seems to have sized us up very well; her book is both enjoyable and informative.'[7]

However, the book's impact was slight and its sales small and slow. It went out of print, unfortunately, just at the time that the 'new feminism' of the nineteen-seventies might have produced a revival of interest in it. Its success in stimulating further research in the history of Canadian women was also negligible. Apart from a number of interesting, but usually unscholarly biographies, the subject received almost no further attention from Canadian historians. Women had the vote, now they had a history. Meanwhile Laurier's naval policy was in need of further analysis.

It would be interesting to speculate on the reasons for this striking lack of interest in the history of women in Canada. Certainly it was not a peculiarly Canadian phenomenon. Moreover, there is always the fact that the Canadian historical profession, at least until recently, has been so small that any subject that is covered by one whole book is lucky. There were, and are, many that have none. And since even that small profession was dominated by men, it is not surprising that what work was done on the history of women was done by amateurs. Finally, it is obviously of some significance that the book appeared in 1950 when Canadian society was entering a period of calm, complacency, and conformity. It was not that women had achieved equality, as a little pamphlet[8] by Anne Francis made plain in the same year. It was rather that once again, as in the 1920s, with a war over, Canadians turned more toward their private affairs and away from public crusades. Prosperity and the Liberal ascendency, ably seconded by the Bomb and the Cold War, set the climate of a country interested in economic growth, educational expansion, large families, and split-level suburbs. The 'minorities' — French Canadians, women, unorganized workers, native peoples,— were quiescent, and ideology appeared to have come to an end.

The election first of John Diefenbaker and later Jean Lesage marked the end of those peaceful post-war years. In Canada, as elsewhere, the sixties were marked by a renewal of social and political unrest, accompanied by the rediscovery of ethnic, class, regional, and sexual inequalities. The French Canadians led the way but others were not far behind. The period was also characterized by an unprecedented number of royal commissions — even for Canada.[9] Most publicized, and expensive, was the Royal Commission on Bilingualism and Biculturalism, appointed in 1965. Hardly less significant, as a barometer of the times, was the one that came two years later: The Royal Commission on the Status of Women. When its *Report* was released in September 1970 it seemed to confirm the contention of those anti-suffragists of half a century ago who had always claimed that granting votes to women would change nothing. 'The last fifty years,' the *Report* remarked sombrely, 'since woman suffrage was introduced, have seen no appreciable change in the political activities of women beyond the exercise of the right to vote. ... The voice of government is still a man's voice.'[10] Once again, the voice of the woman was heard in the land demanding that same equality which their grandmothers and mothers thought they had won.[11]

The 'new feminism' has had at least one important result for students of Canadian history: it has revived interest in the history of Canadian women. A few graduate students are beginning to pick up the story where Miss Cleverdon left off.[12] Undergraduates ask to write term papers on women; publishers scurry to reprint the 'classics' of past struggles — though they are few enough. The long overdue republication of Dr Catherine Cleverdon's *The Woman Suffrage Movement in Canada* is part of this new climate of interest in the study of the history of women in Canada.

While the strengths of Miss Cleverdon's book are plain enough, the historian of the 1970s will doubtless ask some questions about the history of Canadian women that would not have seemed especially relevant to a writer in the 1940s. Of particular interest is the socio-economic context of the suffragist movement and the character of its ideology. Further, discussion of these areas, though occasionally repetitive of Miss Cleverdon's own text, may help to explain more fully the rise of the movement and provide clarification of the reasons for its limited impact upon Canadian society. It is obvious that the demand that the franchise be given to women arose as a result of some quite substantial changes in woman's status and from an accompanying change in attitudes about woman's role, capacities, and responsibilities.

By the 1880s a growing number of commentators on Canadian society were remarking that many women were no longer willing or able to accept domestic life as their only legitimate concern. 'The future historian of the nineteenth century,' wrote the Reverend Benjamin Fish Austin, principal of Alma Ladies' College, Brantford, Ontario, in 1890, 'will find no more prominent or distinguishing feature stamped upon it than the enlarged opportunity of labour and usefulness afforded to women, and the marvellous march of women to the front in almost every field of human activity.[13] The reverend gentleman was referring chiefly to the increasing though still small number of young women attending universities not merely to obtain drawing room culture credits, but as entry into some professions, notably medicine and even more into school-teaching, where women were beginning to outnumber men. He seemed less aware that even larger numbers of women were engaged in factories at low pay and for long hours.[14] Still, Austin's anthology did include a well-documented account of the special problems of women in the industrial world. 'In the factories of our province [Ontario],' Minnie Phelps wrote, 'there are 7,594 women, 247 girls between the ages of 12 and 14 years; 1,588 between the ages of 14 and 18 years. These women, working side by side of the male laborers, battling with the same physical struggles, full of the same high aspirations, the value of the world's market of exchange being equal, find they receive from one-third to one-half less wages, doing the same work with as much skill as their brother workers.' Her conclusion, significantly, was that these injustices would not be remedied until women became voters.[15]

It was naturally the educated, reasonably well-paid, professional woman in late nineteenth-century Canada who provided leadership for the suffragist movement. Dr Emily Howard Stowe, Canada's first woman medical doctor and founder of the first suffragists' group (disguised as 'The Toronto Woman's Literary Club'), symbolized the new woman.[16] 'The New Ideal of Womanhood,' which novelist Agnes Maule Machar, herself one of the 'new women,' was writing about in 1879, demanded that women be allowed access to an education equal to that provided men. She had no hesitation in contending that equal educational opportunity should lead to equal employment opportunity. Once women had demonstrated their capacity in all spheres of employment, the last arguments against woman suffrage would vanish.[17]

Professional women, then, doctors, teachers, novelists, and journalists, provided much of the leadership for the suffrage movement. But there was another group of women who, though sometimes more traditional than their sisters in the world of work, provided both leaders and followers for the suffragists. These were married, middle-class women, frequently well educated but rarely professionals. Their material well-being ensured that servants, labour saving devices, and commercial foods made housekeeping and motherhood less demanding responsibilities than they had once been. 'Women will continue to be wives, mothers, homemakers,' Professor Carrie Derrick, president of the Montreal Suffrage Association, wrote, 'but they will no longer be content with the dull routine of homes from which nearly all productive employments have been removed to shop or factory.'[18]

Many of these women turned to social and charitable activities, responding to the urgings of an awakening Christian social conscience. There were church groups and missionary societies for the more orthodox. For those interested in applied Christianity there were the Woman's Christian Temperance Union, founded in the late seventies, and later the University Settlements and City Missions organized to serve, and evangelize, immigrants and underprivileged urban slum families.[19] This 'new woman' was clearly depicted in one of the most revealing novels of the nineties: Agnes Maule Machar's *Roland Graeme: Knight.* When the daughter of a prosperous manufacturer announced her intention of organizing a working women's club, her mother could only sigh: 'When I was young, girls

thought tract distribution and collecting for missions good enough
for them. Now, they must have all sorts of new fangled ideas.'[20]

It was women like these who banded together for an endless
variety of purposes – religious, charitable, literary, and social.
Marjorie MacMurchy provided an accurate, if impressionistic, snap-
shot of the Canadian club woman: 'Married, not single. She is
middle-aged. She is a woman of household occupations and yet with
some leisure. ... The need of this middle-aged married woman for
work and social co-operation, her impulse to help others and to
accomplish something worth doing in the world outside, are forces
which have created women's organizations.'[21]

Both professional women and club women, for the most part
middle-class and urban (though farm women were increasingly
organization-minded, too), came together in 1893 to found the
National Council of Women of Canada. Lady Aberdeen, the
governor-general's busy wife and leading spirit in the new organization, was conscious of a fear, expressed by members of both sexes,
that the National Council would become a subversive challenge to
woman's primary responsibility in the home. In fact, of course, it
had no such intention. 'There is one thing of which I should like to
remind you,' Lady Aberdeen told a Montreal audience, 'and that is
that in attempting this work we are most anxious to have it
remembered that we do not desire to overlook the fact that woman's
first duty and mission is to her home. ... People sometimes speak as
if ... woman's first mission in itself prevented her from taking part in
public work. They forget that a woman, if she is to do her duty truly
to her sons and daughters must keep touch with the world, its
thoughts, its activities, its temptations.'[22] These were sentiments
which the vast majority of Canadian women – suffragist or anti-
suffragist – shared fully: home and the family remained the primary
female preoccupation. Even among suffragists there was never a hint
of suspicion that these very institutions – marriage and the
family – might themselves be serious obstacles to equality. A radical
like Francis Marion Beynon could think of no more effective
description of woman's desired role in society than

a new spirit of national motherhood – mothers whose love for their
own children teaches them love for all children; mothers who will
not boast of their weakness but seek for strength to fight for their

own and their neighbors' children; mothers who are more concerned with raising the moral and intellectual standard of the community in which they live than in applying the latest suggestions of the beauty doctor.[23]

Indeed, it has been argued that it was the apparent evidence of the disintegration of traditional family life that turned many women toward public affairs and suffragism.[24] Certainly suffragists realized, with much greater perception than opponents like Goldwin Smith, Stephen Leacock, and Henri Bourassa, that in an industrial and urban society there were no longer air-tight compartments; family, home, work, education, politics, and health were increasingly integrated. Consequently the suffragist could turn the old 'woman's place is in the home' argument against an opponent. Sonia Leathes made the case most effective at the National Council of Women meeting in 1913 when she pointed out how much individual, family, and state concerns had coalesced.

It is on this account that women today say to the governments of the world: you have usurped what used to be our authority, what used to be our responsibility. It is you who determine today the nature of the air which we breathe, of the food which we eat, of the clothing which we wear. It is you who determine when, and how long, and what our children are to be taught and what their prospects as future wage earners are to be. It is you who condone or stamp out the white slave traffic and the starvation wage. It is you who by granting or refusing pensions to the mothers of young children can preserve or destroy the fatherless home. It is you who consider what action shall be considered a crime and how the offender, man, woman or child shall be dealt with. It is you who decide whether cannons or torpedos are to blow to pieces the bodies of the sons which we bore. And since all of these matters strike at the very heart strings of the mothers of all nations, we shall not rest until we have secured the power vested in the ballot: to give or to with-hold our consent, to encourage or to forbid any policy or course of action which concerns the people — our children every one.[25]

This speech is extremely revealing. Above all it illustrates the extent to which the organizations — public and private — of urban-industrial society drew women inexorably into public life. Only the most hidebound or blind traditionalist could fail to recognize that this was so. Even in Quebec, where home and family were more completely sanctified than in the rest of the country, the process was obvious to those who wanted to face reality. 'La femme en faisant ainsi sa part de la lutte pour la vie doit inévitablement subir à l'influence du dehors,' Mme Henri Gérin-Lajoie observed in 1896, 'l'air ambiante, du milieu où elle se trouve, elle respire quelques-unes des émanations troublants qui séjournent dans notre atmosphère. Soit-on s'étonner alors qu'elle fasse de sa cause, de la cause de la femme une fraction de la question sociale.'[26] Of course, most of the leading politicians, churchmen, and intellectuals from Sir Lomer Gouin to Maurice Duplessis, Mgr L.-A. Paquet to Cardinal Villeneuve, Henri Bourassa to abbé Lionel Groulx, persisted in defending the inviolability of the traditional home?[27] But the process went on despite them. Mgr Paquet, for example, recognized that the process of industrial-urban growth was destroying the traditional structure of society, drawing women into the world of work, and consequently encouraging feminism and other nefarious doctrines. He could only condemn the entire process.[28] Bourassa, too, recognized the process and sometimes accepted it, but not when it encouraged a feminism which threatened the very existence of the nation. 'En cent cinquante ans, leurs flancs généreux nous ont donné un peuple de trois millions; et ce qui vaut mieux encore, leurs coeurs de chrétiennes ont prodigué les traditions de foi, d'endurance et de bon sens qui nous ont permis de lutter contre la brutalité conquérante, de déjouer les calculs des assimilateurs et de résister à l'absorption.'[29] To vote and to propagate were apparently incompatible.

Mrs Leathes' speech revealed another important and sometimes underestimated aspect of the suffragist movement in Canada. This is the significant role played by the National Council of Women of Canada in popularizing the cause of votes for women. It is true that at its foundation the organization eschewed questions of politics and religion, since these were obviously divisive.[30] Yet at no time was the question of woman suffrage ignored. Emily Stowe spoke on the subject at the first meeting in Ottawa in 1894. She was doubtless conscious of a certain hostility to her views, for she was led to remark: 'I am perfectly indifferent to what people think and say. I represent Truth, and I know that all truth will triumph.'[31] Moreover, the Dominion Women's Franchise Association held fairly regular sessions at the National Council's annual meetings. In 1906 a Standing Committee on Political Equality was established. Finally in 1910, a year in which the movement was in full sail, the council adopted a resolution favouring the enfranchisement of women.[32] The annual discussions at the National Council had contributed to making the suffragist cause respectable among middle-class, and often influential women. More important, however, the range of the council's interests – hours of work, conditions of labour, the liquor trade, patriotism, the arts, public playgrounds, international arbitration, health laws, the white slave trade, and so on – had gradually helped women to understand that politics was the only effective route to reform, and only voters counted in politics. Thus, while the National Council was slow in coming around to the suffrage side, its importance was great. When Mrs Leathes spoke of the large number of once private problems which had become public ones, she was speaking to an audience that understood and sympathized because these were the very questions that had been at the centre of the National Council's deliberations for fifteen years.

While the growing complexity of Canadian society explains the emergence of feminism, it is important to keep in mind that the country was not uniformly affected by industrial and urban growth and that certain cultural differences gave the suffrage movement some special regional characteristics. In the Maritimes, though women were granted votes in the early 1920s the movement was never as vigorous as in Ontario and the west. This reflects, it would seem, a stronger adherence to the traditional view of woman's place and a slower pace of industrial and urban development.[33]

In Quebec, feminism was an even more fragile growth, at least among French-speaking women. Prior to the 1920s it was largely restricted to English-speaking women in Montreal, though Joséphine Dandurand and Mme Gérin-Lajoie played prominent parts in attempting to have the laws of Quebec modified in the interests of women.[34] Few French-Canadian men were prepared to follow the avant garde views of Olivar Asselin in supporting woman suffrage;[35] Sir Wilfrid Laurier, after a lifetime of opposition, only came over to the suffragists' side in 1918. In doing so he could hardly claim widespread support in his province, or for that matter even among the French-speaking members of his caucus.[36] Both religious and cultural traditions were opposed to suffrage in Quebec. The importance placed upon the family in Roman Catholic thought was greater than in Protestant theology: the family was a central religious institution in Quebec. It was woman's calling to ensure the health and vigour of the family, whereas public life was man's special vocation.[37] Indeed, many French Canadians, men like abbé Groulx, condemned feminism as nothing more than the logical and undesirable conclusion of that Anglo-Saxon liberalism that found its roots in the Reformation.[38] On the cultural side, where English-Canadian women were deeply influenced by their sisters in the United States and Great Britain, French-Canadian women remained largely isolated from these currents. Whatever influence there was from France, where women were denied the vote until 1944, was obviously conservative.[39] Only a woman as independent-minded, as politically well connected, and as financially secure as Thérèse Casgrain could be expected to resist this combination of cultural and religious opposition to suffragism.[40]

Finally, there was the west, where the movement grew most rapidly and experienced its earliest successes. The pattern here is slightly at variance with Ontario because of the importance of agriculture and the large number of immigrants. Farm women had special problems: loneliness, isolation, and heavy work being the most obvious. But they also had an advantage: since they had to play the role of equal partner in pioneering conditions, their husbands could hardly fall back on the argument of the different spheres. Consequently, farmers' organizations were relatively quick in supporting the suffragist cause.[41] So, too, the presence of foreign immigrants, who quickly qualified for the vote, pointed to what some agrarian reformers saw as an obvious injustice. 'What an outrage to deny to the highest-minded, most cultured native born lady of Canada, what is cheerfully granted to the lowest-browed, most imbruted foreign hobo that chooses to visit our shores,' was E.A. Partridge's characteristically blunt way of stating the argument.[42] Farm women like Irene Parlby and Violet McNaughton quickly teamed up with urban feminists like Cora Hind, Nellie McClung, and Lillian Beynon Thomas to demand the vote.

While farm women joined their city sisters in the feminist cause, there were few signs of interest among working-class women. They probably had more pressing concerns: food, clothing, heat, medicine, education. One suffragist with an interest in working-class women recognized the problem:

Turn to that demoralized sight, the racked and poverty burdened woman dwelling in a city tenement, with her brood of ill-nurtured, sickly children. All trace of that softness and feminine delicacy, and the reflective deep souled mother-love of the Madonna obliterated in this poor, hard-used mortal. Teach her hygiene when there is no fresh air to be had, and barely a blink of the sun, not a mouthful of unpolluted water to drink, nor sufficient bread to eat, because taxes are too high, wages too low, and liquor too near her husband's temptation.[43]

Certainly political power might help to alter these debilitating conditions, but the conditions themselves weakened the will to demand anything but the next day's subsistence.

Moreover, there were certain contradictions between the middle-class suffragists' demand for political equality and the working woman's need for special protection.[44] If women required legislation controlling hours and conditions of labour different from that applied to men, was this not an explicit admission of inequality? The answer to the dilemma, of course, was better working conditions and shorter hours for all, but that was not an easy position for women, whose husbands were sometimes employers, to accept. ('In legislating for the weak,' one doubter remarked, 'we may be doing an injustice to the strong.'[45]) In any case, for a variety of reasons working-class women did not play a prominent part in the suffragist movement. But that should be no surprise. After all, their husbands, who did have the vote, played only a small part in politics and only a minority saw any reason to change that condition.[46]

Many suffragists could claim a serious interest in the problems of labouring people, even if their own cause found little vocal support in that segment of Canadian society. Indeed, the suffragists were a part of a more general, middle-class reform movement that was concerned to remove a wide range of injustices and evils that afflicted the country. The most obvious features of this broad reform movement were its Protestant ethos (though the Roman Catholic church was certainly not unmoved by social questions), its revulsion at the materialism of 'Canada's Century,' its predominantly Anglo-Saxon nationalism, and its often naïve optimism. Combined, these elements made up that amorphous but potent phenomenon, the Social Gospel. It was not a homogeneous ideology; it had left, centre, and right tendencies, as well as Methodist, Presbyterian, Baptist, and Anglican variations.[47] J.S. Woodsworth, the Methodist heretic, was its best-known proponent, but the capacious social gospel tent had room for many others: Ben Spence, prohibitionist; Nellie McClung, feminist; R.C. Henders, agrarian; James Simpson, socialist; and many others. In some respects its most characteristic exponent was the Reverend Charles W. Gordon, Presbyterian, novelist, reformer, nationalist, and soldier. Oddly enough, his autobiography, *Postscript to Adventure,* reveals little of his association with the suffragist cause in Winnipeg. Yet he did support the Political Equality League of Manitoba and was an important participant in the Social Service Council of Canada, whose 1914 congress considered the whole gamut of progressive causes.[48] One of his speeches, delivered to some 800 people at a suffragists' meeting in 1912, revealed much about the righteous causes of the time. Gordon was reported as stating 'that he was not a prophet, but would predict five great coming events: first, the prevalence of the Anglo-Saxon tongue; secondly, the removal of the tariff; third, political equality; fourth, equal distribution of wealth according to skill and ability; and, fifth, restriction of liquor traffic to such an extent as to guarantee absolute sobriety.' And he emphasized that 'Divine love, in human embodiment, would never be attained until women were given the ballot.'[49]

The spirit of Christian, liberal optimism, the belief that someday, somehow, the Kingdom of God would be established on earth, motivated the reform movement in general and suffragism in particular. As one suffragist put her case in 1896: 'She followed Christ Her Master everywhere else, and she must follow Him too into the legislative halls, for "the government shall be upon his shoulders." And when she went it would be with her hand in His.'[50]

Examples of this type of Christian meliorism could be multiplied many times as reform causes became, increasingly, secular substitutes for Christianity. And an important ingredient in the reform mix was a large dash of liberal social darwinism. 'May the day soon dawn,' Augusta Stowe-Gullen exclaimed in 1909, 'when the artificial barriers which have evolved and fostered an antagonism and misunderstanding between the sexes be swept aside and the world, so full of needs, and replete with problems, demanding men and women strong to do and achieve, will be born unto them a finer type of manhood and womanhood united by a community of interests — their destiny, the evolution of mankind.'[51]

No doubt this conviction of being on the side of righteousness, supported by the inevitable processes of nature, was important to the suffragists. It provided a helpful psychological defence against the repeated rebuffs that the movement met. It was probably also inevitable that the suffrage cause should become part of the wider reform movement and be presented as one of the steps in the establishment of the Kingdom — 'when the world reinstates woman, in the place which God assigned her as the equal of man, the first step will be taken to introduce the millenium.'[52] The result was, however, that many who supported woman suffrage argued for it by claiming that it would result in a far better society. 'If we are ever to be freed from the demon rum in Canada,' wrote a male advocate of the suffragist cause, 'if we are ever to secure social purity, if we are ever to occupy the position we should occupy as a Christian country in working out the country's true destiny, and elevating the moral tone of Eastern immigrants who are to throng to our coasts, the rights of citizenship must be given to our women.'[53] Many suffragists, notably Nellie McClung, make similar promises for the future in which 'male statecraft' would be replaced by political equality.[54]

Yet in the long run the association of suffragism and the more general meliorism weakened the suffragist cause. For one thing these utopian claims made the suffragists vulnerable to conservative critics like Sir Andrew Macphail, who could point out sarcastically that 'it is hard for these intelligent super-women to understand in the first flush of their ignorance that there are some evils which cannot be cured, and are made worse by talking about them, especially when the talk must, of necessity, be a mere repetition of hearsay.'[55] What Macphail and other opponents of political equality sometimes succeeded in doing was to shift the argument away from the principle to the promised, but unprovable, results.

More seriously, perhaps, the very extent of the suffragists' claims ensured that the movement would ultimately be judged a failure.

When the promised utopia did not materialize, some women appear to have lost interest in politics. Others wondered if the struggle had really been worth all the effort. Yet the major goal of the suffragists had been achieved: voting rights. That this did not lead to a vast increase in the number of female office holders or to a radically reformed society should not have been astonishing. The number of women who were active suffragists had always been small. As for women as reformers, what the post-World War I years proved was what the suffragists had always admitted in their realistic moments: women and men were very much alike. A few of each sex were highly political and reform-minded; most were not. But that realization did not invalidate the essential claim of the suffragists that once democracy was accepted as a form of government there was no principle that could logically be called forth to deny women the right to vote. The demand for woman suffrage was merely 'a chapter in the great history of the emancipation of the individual, black or white, rich or poor, male or female, from social and political disabilities imposed upon him or her on account of birth alone.'[57]

Only those who feared the consequences of giving women the vote and those whose expectations were utopian should have been surprised by the outcome. Goldwin Smith, whose liberalism knew many bounds, feared that the 'revolution' would be at once 'unparalleled in importance and unprecedented in kind.'[58] Some of the more intemperate supporters of the cause viewed it as a part of humanity's march onward and upward 'until we have reached that full, that millennial day.'[59] But from the outset of the great suffragist debate there were always those who knew the truth, as well as the real justification for political equality. In 1879, one of them wrote:

Let no confident friend of the movement anticipate too great results from such success. That it will be followed by great disappointment to many — happy disappointment to those who fear, and unhappy to those who hope — there can be little doubt. It will effect far less change than is generally fancied; at first scarcely any. All social evils will not be voted down; nor the offices all filled with saints at the next election thereafter. It will not be found the panacea for all human, or all womanly, ills. It will scarcely be the *cure* of any.

It will simply be the opening of another door — the passage into a larger freedom. ... But to work out her complete womanhood vastly more is required than the right of suffrage.[60]

NOTES

1  George Dangerfield, *The Strange Death of Liberal England* (New York 1935) ch. 3; William L. O'Neill, *The Woman Movement: Feminism in the United States and England* (Chicago 1969) ch. 4
2  'Report of the Canadian Suffrage Association' in *Report of the National Council of Women of Canada* (Toronto 1910) xvii
3  Clementina Fessenden to *The Globe* (11 February 1910) 4
4  *The Globe* (19 February 1910) 12
5  C.L. Cleverdon to Ramsay Cook, 13 March 1973
6  F.H. Underhill, *Canadian Historical Review* XXXI 4 (December 1950) 442
7  Norman Ward, *Canadian Journal of Economics and Political Science* XVI 4 (November 1950) 543
8  Anne Francis, *The Rights of Women,* Behind the Headlines X 4 (September 1950)
9  For a lively journalistic account see Peter C. Newman, *The Distemper of Our Times* (Toronto 1969).
10  *Report of the Royal Commission on the Status of Women* (Ottawa 1970) 355
11  See, for example, Maxine Nunes and Deanna White, *The Lace Ghetto* (Toronto 1972), *Women Unite: An Anthology of the Canadian Women's Movement* (Toronto 1972); *Manifeste des femmes québecoises* (Montréal 1971).
12  Carol Lee Bacchi-Ferraro, 'The Ideas of Canadian Suffragists, 1890-1920' (unpublished MA thesis, McGill University 1970)
13  B.F. Austin, ed., *Woman: Her Character, Culture and Calling* (Brantford 1890) 23
14  Statistics on the increasing number of women in the labour force are not readily available, nor has much been written on this aspect of Canadian social history. For the figures after 1891 see M.C. Urquhart and K.A. Buckley, *Historical Statistics of Canada* (Toronto 1965) series C8-35, 59. For Ontario at an earlier date see Jean Scott

Thomas, 'The Conditions of Female Labour in Ontario,' *University of
Toronto Studies in Political Science* first series III, ed. W.J. Ashley.
Though attempting to demonstrate more than is possible in a short
essay, Christina Maria Hill's 'Women in the Canadian Economy' in
Robert Laxer, ed. *(Canada) Ltd: The Political Economy of Depen-
dency* (Toronto 1973) 84-106, represents a provocative attempt to
look at the status and problems of Canadian working women in an
historical context; see also D. Suzanne Cross, 'The Neglected Majority: The Changing Role of Women in 19th Century Montreal,'
*Histoire Sociale–Social History* VI 12 (November 1973) 202-23.
15  Minnie Phelps, 'Women as Wage Earners' in Austin, *Woman: Her
Character, Culture and Calling* 51
16  Edith M. Luke, 'Woman Suffrage in Canada,' *The Canadian Magazine*
V (1895) 328-36; Joanne L. Thompson, 'The Influence of Dr Emily
Howard Stowe on the Woman Suffrage Movement in Canada,' *Ontario History* (December 1962) 253-66
17  'Fidelis', 'The New Ideal of Womanhood,' *The Canadian Monthly and
National Review* III (November 1879) 674. See also Principal Grant,
'Education and Co-Education,' ibid. 509-18.
18  Carrie M. Derrick, 'The Common Cause,' *The Montreal Daily Herald*
(26 November 1913) 6
19  Mrs S.G.E. McKee, *Jubilee History of the Ontario Woman's Christian
Temperance Union, 1877-1927* (Whitby, nd); 'City Mission Work,'
*The Christian Guardian* (20 December 1899) 10; Catharine Vance,
*Not By Gods but by People: The Story of Bella Hall Gauld* (Toronto
1968)
20  Agnes Maule Machar, *Roland Graeme: Knight* (Montreal 1892) 194
21  Marjorie MacMurchy, *The Woman – Bless Her* (Toronto 1916) 14
22  *Montreal Daily Herald* (1 December 1893) 1
23  Francis Marion Beynon, 'Answers to an Anti-Suffragist,' *The Grain
Growers' Guide* (1 October 1913) 10
24  Terrence R. Morrison, 'The Child and Urban Social Reform in Late
Nineteenth Century Ontario' (unpublished PhD thesis, University of
Toronto 1971) ch. 4
25  *Report of the National Council of Women of Canada* (Toronto 1913)
74. The speech was reprinted as 'Votes for Women,' *The University
Magazine* XIII 1 (February 1914) 68-78. Recently, some 'new feminists' and scholars, especially in the United States, have criticized the
suffragists for failing to realize the extent to which marriage and the

family were obstacles to equality. See William O'Neill, *Everyone was Brave* (Chicago 1971) and Aileen S. Kraditor, *Up from the Pedestal* (Chicago 1968) 21-4. This criticism, of course, rests largely on hindsight. It could be argued that historically, at least in Canada, women achieved what they did *because* of their refusal to attack the family.

26 Mme Gérin-Lajoie, 'Le Mouvement féministe,' *Report of the National Council of Women of Canada* (Montreal 1896) 289.

27 Jennifer Stoddard, 'The Woman Suffrage Bill in Quebec' in Marylee Stephenson, *Women in Canada,* ed. (Toronto 1973) 90-106. This article, while useful as a summary of the debate, is analytically weak in explaining anti-suffragism in Quebec.

28 Mgr L.-A. Paquet, 'Féminisme,' *Le Canada Français* I 4 (décembre 1918) 245-6

29 Henri Bourassa, 'Déplorable ignorance des Canadiennes françaises,' *Le Devoir* (31 mars 1913)

30 Rosa Shaw, *Proud Heritage* (Toronto 1957)

31 *Report of the National Council of Women of Canada* (Ottawa 1894) 178

32 *Report of the National Council of Women of Canada* (Toronto 1910) 97ff

33 T.W. Acheson, 'The National Policy and the Industrialization of the Maritimes, 1880-1910,' *Acadiensis* (spring 1972) 3-28

34 Madame Dandurand, *Nos Travers* (Montreal 1901) 218-29

35 *Montreal Daily Herald* (26 November 1913) 6

36 See Senator Raoul Dandurand's speech on the enfranchisement of women in *Senate of Canada, Debates, 1918* 369.

37 Henri Bourassa, 'Le Rôle social de la femme: conception française et tradition anglaise,' *Le Devoir* (23 avril 1913)

38 Lionel Groulx, *Dix Ans d'Action française* (Montreal 1926) 75

39 Micheline D. Johnson, 'History of the Status of Women in the Province of Quebec' in *Studies of the Royal Commission on the Status of Women* 8 (Ottawa 1971)

40 Thérèse Casgrain, *Une Femme chez les hommes* (Montreal 1971)

41 June Menzies, 'Votes for Saskatchewan Women' in Norman Ward and Duff Spafford, eds., *Politics in Saskatchewan* (Toronto 1968) 78-92

42 *Grain Growers' Guide* (22 September 1909) 6

43 J.M. to *The Globe* (25 February 1910) 10

44 Viola Klein, *The Feminine Character: History of an Ideology* (New York 1949) 15

45  *Report of the National Council of Women of Canada* (Toronto 1896) 426

46  Martin Robin, *Radical Politics and Canadian Labour, 1880-1930* (Kingston 1968)

47  Richard Allen, *The Social Passion* (Toronto 1971)

48  *Social Service Congress, Ottawa, 1914* (Toronto 1915)

49  *Grain Growers' Guide* (22 May 1912) 27

50  *Report of the National Council of Women of Canada* (Toronto 1896) 545

51  *Report of the National Council of Women of Canada* (Toronto 1909) 27

52  Mrs Dr Parker, 'Women in Nation-Building' in Austin, ed., *Woman: Her Character, Culture, and Calling* 462-3

53  Thomas Webster, 'The Citizenship of Women,' *The Methodist Magazine* XXXIX 2 (February 1894) 157. Webster, a Methodist minister, wrote what must have been one of the earliest defences of women's rights using some Canadian examples. See his *Woman Man's Equal* (Cincinnati 1873).

54  Nellie L. McClung, *In Times Like These* (Toronto 1972) 19

55  Sir Andrew Macphail, 'On Certain Aspects of Feminism,' *The University Magazine* XIII 1 (February 1914) 87

56  Ann Anderson Perry, 'Is Woman Suffrage a Fizzle?' *Maclean's Magazine* XLI (3 February 1928) 6-7, 58-9, 63; Charlotte Whitton, 'Is the Canadian Woman a Flop in Politics?', *Saturday Night* (26 January 1946) 6-7

57  Leathes, 'Votes for Women,' 69

58  'A Bystander,' 'The Woman's Rights Movement,' *The Canadian Monthly and National Review* I 3 (March 1972) 249

59  Dr Augusta Stowe-Gullen, 'Women in the Study and Practise of Medicine,' in Austin, ed., *Woman: Her Character, Culture and Calling* 124

60  'M', 'The Woman Question,' *The Canadian Monthly and National Review* II (May 1897) 579

FURTHER READING
The most complete printed bibliography on the history of Canadian
women is the excellent essay by Veronica Strong-Boag entitled 'Cousin Cinderella' in Marylee Stevenson, ed., *Women in Canada* (Toronto 1973) 262-90. The same volume contains a bibliography of more
contemporary social science materials: Margrit Erlicher and Lynn
Primrose, 'A Bibliography of Material on Canadian Women' 291-326.
Veronica Strong-Boag's edition in the Social History of Canada series
of Nellie L. McClung's *In Times Like These* (Toronto 1972) is the
best available statement of the suffragist argument, and the introduction offers a balanced assessment of Mrs McClung. The anti-suffragist
case may be found in Goldwin Smith, *Essays on Questions of the
Day* (New York & London 1893); Andrew Macphail, *Essays in
Fallacy* (New York & London 1910); and Henri Bourassa, *Femmes-
hommes ou hommes et femmes* (Montréal 1925).
   The largest body of material on Canadian women is probably in
the form of biography and autobiography. *The Clear Spirit*, ed. Mary
Q. Innis (Toronto 1966), contains several useful biographical
sketches. Among the numerous other books, the best include Nellie
L. McClung's *Clearing in the West* (Toronto 1935) and *The Stream
Runs Fast* (Toronto 1945); Mrs George Black, *My Seventy Years*
(Toronto & New York 1938); Emily Carr, *Growing Pains* (Toronto
1946); Judy LaMarsh, *Memoirs of a Bird in a Gilded Cage* (Toronto
1967); Thérèse Casgrain, *Une Femme chez les hommes* (Montreal
1971); Claire Martin, *Dans un Gant de fer* (Montreal 1965-6). The
essays on women in Jean LeMoyne's *Convergences* (Montreal 1969)
are fundamental to any understanding of the role of women in
Quebec Society.
   There are several books which help to place the Canadian suffragist movement in a wider context. Robert Craig Brown and
Ramsay Cook's *Canada 1896-1921: A Nation Transformed*
(Toronto 1974) is one place to start. Robert Wendell Carr's introduction to John Stuart Mill's *The Subjection of Women* provides an
excellent analysis of the intellectual currents surrounding the suffragists' arguments. Trevor Lloyd's *Suffragettes International*
(London 1971) is a brief, sprightly introduction to the subject. William O'Neill's brilliant, opinionated *Everyone was Brave* (Chicago
1969) and Aileen S. Kraditor's *The Ideas of the Woman Suffrage*

*Movement, 1890-1920* (New York 1965) are important accounts of
the feminist movement in the United States, while George Dangerfield's *Strange Death of Liberal England* (New York 1935) and
Constance Rover's *Woman Suffrage and Party Politics in Great
Britain* (Toronto & London 1967) present the British story.

# The woman suffrage movement in Canada

CATHERINE L. CLEVERDON

Lord Chancellor Sankey, of His Majesty's Privy Council, at Temple Bar,
1929, on his way to deliver judgment re the status of women as
'persons' under the British North America Act

TO JESS

IN THIS, AS ALWAYS, MY MAINSTAY

# PREFACE

GREAT BRITAIN'S two sturdy North American offspring—
the United States and Canada—have traversed sharply
contrasting routes in reaching their goal of nationhood.
The southerly and more assertive member of the family
chose a picturesque shortcut. Beset with excitement, even
violence, at frequent intervals along the way, it has afforded
a paradise to the historian and tale-spinner. The more cir-
cumspect northern member chose a longer and less scenic
route, arrived safely in the course of time—and then lamented
audibly over the lack of colour in the journey.

Perhaps this feeling, so common to Canadians, that their
country's story is too prosaic to interest anyone accounts for
a curious omission in its historical literature. Whatever the
reason, there has never been a full account of a significant
chapter in the development of Canadian democracy: the winning of political equality by the feminine half of the nation.
This is in marked contrast with Great Britain and the United
States where women's efforts to attain equality have provided
the basis for extensive writings. It is true that no Canadian
suffragist was ever known to throw herself under the pounding
hoofs of a race horse, nor even to empty a bag of flour upon
the head of an unfriendly lawmaker. But if Canadian feminists robbed their story of colour by waging a wholly dignified
campaign, their painstaking and often costly struggle for political freedom surely merits its page in the dominion's history.

That the first effort to fill this void should be made by an
American rather than a native writer may appear regrettable,
even presumptuous, to some Canadians. Some justification
may perhaps be found in the possibility that, where the story
has an element of conflict between rival factions, an outsider

may be less open to the charge of "playing favourites." However, if a second plea is needed, this particular outsider would like to proffer one of a different kind—that she can claim a sense of kinship with the Canadian scene from the fact that of her grandparents three were born on Canadian soil.

President Roosevelt's well-worn phrase, "the good neighbor policy," is vested with a concrete, personal meaning for me as a result of this Canadian venture. Dependent, as I was, for material upon many Canadians, I found them helpful, hospitable, and generous to an incredible degree. On several occasions irreplaceable documents were lent without question, both by libraries and individuals. With true *noblesse oblige*, Byrne Hope Sanders permitted me to read the manuscript of her biography of Judge Emily Murphy months before it appeared in print. Patience matched generosity as scores of Canadians penned long replies to endless questions, granted interviews, and supplied introductions to others who could help. These contacts sometimes resulted in friendships which have given me a lasting interest in the country which has become my second home.

Generosity of another sort it was my good fortune to encounter when the Canadian Social Science Research Council made available a very liberal grant-in-aid towards publication of this work; and again, when the University of Toronto Press agreed to assume the quite considerable balance of the production costs. To both go my sincerest thanks for their openhanded aid in surmounting the financial hurdle.

I should like to acknowledge gratefully the long-suffering patience of the staffs of the Library of Parliament and the Public Archives at Ottawa. No requests, even for materials buried in the most inaccessible vaults, were ever refused. A special word of appreciation is due Mr. Robert Hamilton of the Library of Parliament for keeping me posted on events which occurred long after research days were officially ended.

To Professors J. B. Brebner and R. L. Schuyler of Columbia University, New York, goes my gratitude for their excellent advice and kindly encouragement at every stage; and, though editors are traditionally the targets of unkind (if usually unspoken) thoughts by authors, I should also like to express my thanks to Miss Eleanor Harman, associate editor of the University of Toronto Press, for her many skilful criticisms and suggestions.

Finally, to my sister, Jessie C. Mintkeski, just simply— many thanks. There are too many reasons to enumerate.

*Bronxville, New York*                                    C. L. C.
*October 15, 1949*

# LIST OF ABBREVIATIONS

*Canada: H. of C. Debates.*—Debates of the House of Commons of the Dominion of Canada.

*Canada: H. of C. Journals.*—Journals of the House of Commons of the Dominion of Canada.

*Canada: Senate Debates.*—Debates of the Senate of the Dominion of Canada.

*Journals* for all provincial legislatures appear with the name or initials of the province first, then *Journals*, then the year of the session; e.g. *Manitoba: Journals, 1916.*

*N.B.: Synoptic Reports.*—Synoptic Reports of the Proceedings of the Legislative Assembly of New Brunswick.

*N.S.: Debates.*—Debates and Proceedings of the House of Assembly of the Province of Nova Scotia. Not kept after 1916.

*Ontario: Debates.*—Ontario: Parliamentary Debates. Bound volumes of the *Globe's* reports of the provincial legislative sessions.

A. S.-G., Scrap Books.—The six volumes of scrap books dealing with the suffrage movement owned by Dr. Augusta Stowe-Gullen, Toronto.

L. W. R. Minute Books.—Minute Books of the League for Women's Rights, Montreal.

N. B. Minute Books.—The Minute Books of the New Brunswick Branch of the Dominion Women's Enfranchisement Association.

P. E. L. Minute Book.—The Smaller Minute Book of the Political Equality League of Manitoba.

L. C. W. Montreal, *Annual Reports.*—The *Annual Reports* published by the Local Council of Women, Montreal.

N. C. W., *Year Books.*—National Council of Women, publ., *Women Workers of Canada.* Known familiarly as *Year Books.*

*Canadian Annual Review.*—J. Castell Hopkins, ed., *The Canadian Annual Review of Public Affairs.*

J. B. McBride, "Memorandum."—J. B. McBride, K.C., "Memorandum as to Women's Rights in Alberta."

Murphy Papers.—Emily F. Murphy Papers, in the possession of Miss Evelyn Murphy, Edmonton, Alta.

*Privy Council Proceedings.*—Record of the Proceedings in the Privy Council, No. 121 of 1928, On Appeal from the Supreme Court of Canada: In the Matter of a Reference as to the meaning of the word "persons" in Section 24 of the British North America Act, 1867.

# CONTENTS

# ILLUSTRATIONS

# THE WOMAN SUFFRAGE
# MOVEMENT IN CANADA

# REFERENCE LIST OF DATES FOR THE ACHIEVEMENT
# OF POLITICAL EQUALITY

| *Province* | *Suffrage* | *Eligibility to hold office* |
|---|---|---|
| Manitoba | January 28, 1916. | January 28, 1916. |
| Saskatchewan | March 14, 1916. | March 14, 1916. |
| Alberta | April 19, 1916. | April 19, 1916. |
| British Columbia | April 5, 1917. | April 5, 1917. |
| Ontario | April 12, 1917. | April 24, 1919. |
| Nova Scotia | April 26, 1918. | April 26, 1918.* |
| Dominion of Canada | Relatives of members of armed forces—September 20, 1917. All women—May 24, 1918. | July 7, 1919. Reaffirmed and made permanent by the Dominion Elections Act, 1920. |
| New Brunswick | April 17, 1919. | March 9, 1934. |
| Prince Edward Island | May 3, 1922. | May 3, 1922. |
| Newfoundland | April 13, 1925. | April 13, 1925. |
| Quebec | April 25, 1940. | April 25, 1940. |

*Separate act.

The dates given are those for the granting of Royal Assent.

# *I*

# INTRODUCTION

## *Chivalry and Justice*

IN PRESIDING over a radio forum on December 11, 1938, dealing with the *Position of Women in Canada*, B. K. Sandwell, distinguished editor of *Saturday Night*, noted that men's attitude toward women has been about the same through all ages: that the business of women is "to keep house and keep quiet." Continuing in this vein, Dr. Sandwell reflected:

Now keeping quiet obviously includes making no protest against injustices that may be committed against the class which is told to keep quiet. . . . The persons who have to keep quiet become the wards . . . of the persons who are allowed to make a noise. On the assumption that the persons who are allowed to make a noise are perfectly fair and just, this is a very good arrangement; and men of course have always admitted that they are perfectly fair and just to women. But women have lately begun to maintain that men do not know enough about women to be perfectly fair and just . . . and that the only way to get fairness and justice is to allow women to make a noise also by voting and holding office in much the same way as men do.[1]

The campaign of Canadian women to win the right to make this particular "noise" covers slightly more than half a century, if Quebec be included, and outside of Quebec, rather closely parallels similar efforts by the women of Great Britain and the United States.

In fairness to Canadian men, however, it should be stated at the outset that the task of the women advocates of political

---

[1]C.B.C. National Forum, *The Position of Women in Canada*, Dec. 11, 1938. The entire programme may be found in the Canadian Pamphlet Collection (C.P.C. No. 1004) of the Parliamentary Library at Ottawa.

equality was made doubly onerous by the apathy, if not out-right hostility, which they encountered quite widely among members of their own sex. Suffrage forces constituted but a small minority of Canadian women throughout the entire campaign (except possibly on the Prairies), and drew their most active recruits in general from that small segment of the feminine population which had a fair degree of economic inde-pendence. Outstanding suffragists were most frequently pro-fessional and self-employed women, or wives of men with com-fortable incomes.

A student of the general growth of democracy in the dominion has written: "Democracy, as measured by the fran-chise, came to Canada almost by stealth, certainly not as an army with banners."[2] This general observation applies also to the feminine side of the story. Lacking completely the flam-boyance, bitterness, and even violence of the English cam-paign, the Canadian effort to extend democracy to women has been aptly characterized by one of its own pioneers as "a struggle, never a fight."[3] To the women of Quebec, where the struggle came nearest to being a fight and where memories of countless bitter disappointments are still fresh, this general statement may seem unjust; but from the broader viewpoint of the nation as a whole, it appears to be well founded. At no stage of the campaign was there anything remotely resembling militant tactics, even if the patience of women was sometimes severely tested by legislative hostility or indifference. Per-suasion, not force, was the lever which gradually caused the gates of political freedom to swing open for Canadian women.

Since Canada, like the United States, employs the federal form of government, it has been necessary to consider separ-ately the acquisition of the franchise in the federal and pro-

[2]W.L. Morton, "The Extension of the Franchise in Canada: A Study in Democratic Nationalism," *Canadian Historical Association Report*, 1943 (Toronto), p. 73.

[3]Anne Anderson Perry, "Winning the Franchise," *Grain Growers' Guide* (Winnipeg), July 7, 1920. A letter to the author from Senator Cairine Wilson, dated Mar. 22, 1943, also bears out this contention: "The story of the struggle for the franchise is a fascinating one, but apart from the Province of Quebec, I do not think has been quite as sensational in Canada as in other parts of the world."

vincial spheres. But in contrast to the United States, where the Constitution leaves to the states the determination of both federal and state electors,[4] granting of the provincial franchise to women in the five western provinces of Canada was not deemed by the federal government to have included the right to vote in dominion elections. Accordingly separate enfranchisement acts were passed by the dominion parliament in 1917 and 1918. These in turn did no more than bestow the *federal* franchise upon women of the eastern provinces. Provincial voting privileges had to be won later through separate enactments in each province.

Political equality was ordinarily first attained on the local level. By 1900 many provinces permitted women to vote for school trustees and for municipal officials, although these privileges were often restricted to unmarried women. With the turn of the century, suffragists concentrated on winning the provincial and dominion franchises. Aided immeasurably by the first world war, their efforts achieved complete success between 1916 and 1922,[5] except in Quebec. From 1918 until 1940 the women of that province endured the anomaly of participating in federal elections, while being forced to keep silent in provincial affairs.

Opponents of the suffrage movement faced the women with a formidable array of arguments, some of which, while carrying great weight at the time, seem nonsensical today. Such for example was the claim that women were organically too weak to participate in the broils and excitements of elections. Closely allied to this was the reasoning that since women took no share in the defence of the nation, they were not entitled to a voice in its councils. There were even some hardy souls among opponents in the earliest days who contended that women did not have the mental capacity to comprehend political problems; this argument, however, was discarded at an early stage.

A contention which carried great weight in the eighties

[4]Article I, section 2. This privilege of the states has, of course, been limited to some extent by amendments XIV, XV, and XIX.
[5]This does not include Newfoundland.

and nineties was that woman suffrage was contrary to Biblical teachings. A fervent exponent of this view was Hon. John Dryden, minister of agriculture in Ontario in 1893. Attacking a proposed suffrage measure then before the House, Dryden quoted Scripture: "The man was not made for the woman, but the woman for the man," and again, "Thy desire shall be to thy husband and he shall rule over thee." From these and other excerpts, he concluded that woman's place was to be "in submission to man."[6] In this stand he was supported by countless others (both men and women), who no doubt were deeply sincere.

Even more terrifying than flying in the face of Biblical teachings was the fear of many, again including women, that enfranchisement would unsex and degrade women, destroy domestic harmony, and lead to a decline in the birthrate. Such an appalling prospect moved the great American historian, Francis Parkman, to write an essay graphically setting forth the unhappy effects not only upon domestic life, but upon women's delicate constitutions and upon the laws of the nation "if the most impulsive and excitable half of humanity had an equal voice in making the laws."[7] Goldwin Smith, a signer of John Stuart Mill's first woman suffrage petition many years before in England, added his voice to Parkman's lament. By 1895 conservative old age was upon the former apostle of liberalism, and from the study of his stately Toronto home (the property of his wife), he sent forth thundering denunciations of this latest menace to the welfare of society.[8]

Women were told that they did not need the ballot, for they could accomplish as much, if not more, by "loving persuasion." This argument was given special prominence in French-speaking Quebec, where year after year flowery ora-

---

[6]Hon. John Dryden, *Womanhood Suffrage*, a speech delivered by the Minister of Agriculture in the Ontario legislature, May 10, 1893; (C.P.C. No. 1487), Parliamentary Library.

[7]Francis Parkman, *Some of the Reasons Against Woman Suffrage* (C.P.C. No. 3990), Parliamentary Library. This essay appears to have been written in the United States c. 1895, but was republished in pamphlet form in Canada in 1912 "at the request of an Association of Women."

[8]*Globe* (Toronto), April 11, June 3, 1895.

tions by the legislators referred to woman's position as the *reine du foyer*. Of course the argument failed completely to take into consideration the growing number of unmarried women wage earners who had no close male relatives to persuade lovingly—or otherwise.

The crowning argument of the opposition right down to the day of final surrender was that women did not want the vote and would not use it if they had it. There was considerable evidence to support this contention, particularly in the Maritime Provinces and Quebec. Writing from British Columbia, where the movement began almost as early as in Ontario, Mrs. Rose Henderson surveyed the Canadian scene in 1918, when all but three provinces had enfranchised women, and concluded that it was the world war rather than a desire generally expressed by women themselves which had won them political equality. "Certainly a few women put up a determined fight but the masses of women at no time, and in no place were with them, so that it would be wrong to conclude that woman's political emancipation came about solely through her own efforts and desire for freedom."[9]

In this fifty-year debate the heavy battery of arguments was on the side of the women. Their plan of attack upon the conservative forces was two-fold: first to demolish the contentions set forth by their opponents and then to submit an array of evidence for their own side of the case. The work of demolition was undertaken with such a weighty mixture of statistics and satire that by the turn of the century the opposing camp was left with only two guns still firing and even they with less power than formerly. Quebec, as might be expected, clung to the theory that woman would be dragged from her pedestal and contaminated by politics, and as already mentioned, reluctant governments everywhere persevered in the belief that, apart from a few "cranks," women did not want the vote.

Many prominent men, as well as women, gave their best efforts to refuting anti-suffrage arguments. One of the dough-

[9]*British Columbia Federationist* (Vancouver), Sept. 27, 1918.

tiest champions was Dr. James L. Hughes of Toronto, who in 1895 put forth a pamphlet in which he blasted forty-two stock objections to enfranchisement and listed twenty-seven arguments in favour of the proposal. Dr. Hughes presented such a staggering weight of testimony supporting equality of the sexes from both the Old and New Testaments, as well as written endorsements from leading churchmen of Toronto, that he ended any further serious debate on the religious aspect of the question.[10]

Attacking the proposition that woman suffrage would increase divorce and lower the birthrate, Mrs. Sonia Leathes of Toronto drew facts from statistics compiled by the Royal Divorce Commission in England to prove that Norway, one of the very few countries which had enfranchised women, had one of the lowest divorce rates in the world. And in New Zealand, where women had been voting since 1893, the records showed the highest marriage rate of any English country, the highest birthrate, except for two Australian states where women also voted, and the lowest infant mortality in the world.[11]

For those who claimed that women would not use the vote, the suffragists produced not only masses of statistics from countries and states where women were enfranchised, but also the personal testimony of distinguished statesmen such as Sir Joseph Ward, premier of New Zealand, and Sir William Lynne, premier of New South Wales.[12] They hastened to add, too, that if not all women would use the vote, neither did all men, yet no one asserted that the latter should be disfranchised in consequence. A clear illustration of this was brought out during a debate on an Ontario franchise bill in 1916, when a member reminded Premier Hearst, who had a special fondness

[10]James L. Hughes, *Equal Suffrage* (Toronto, 1895; C.P.C. No. 756), Parliamentary Library. Dr. Hughes was superintendent of education in Toronto at this time and president of the local Toronto Suffrage Association for several years in the early 1900's.
[11]From an undated, unidentified clipping (c. 1909) in Dr. Augusta Stowe-Gullen's collection of Scrap Books. Scrap Book VI, 29. Hereafter cited as A. S.-G., Scrap Books.
[12]*Ibid.*, VI, 38, 48.

for this argument, that in the last election the premier's own constituency had polled only 3,662 votes out of a possible 7,045.[13] Mrs. Nellie McClung demonstrated the inconsistency of the average male in this respect by a story about an old fellow who appeared at the polls for the first time in fifteen years. When asked what got him out, he replied: "You bet I came out today to vote against givin' these fool women a vote; what's the good of giving them a vote? they wouldn't use it!"[14] In more serious vein, Dr. Margaret Gordon, one of the outstanding suffragists of Toronto, wrote to N. W. Rowell, Opposition leader in Ontario in 1911, to remind him that the average person, man or woman, is too busy with his own daily pursuits to take much interest in public questions. Still, she asked, was that a good reason to deny justice to public-spirited minorities? "To deny the vote to an unrepresented section of the community because they do not ask for it is equivalent to a refusal to grant the protection of the law to the persons and property of those who do not expressly ask for it. . . ."[15]

Probably no campaigner took greater delight in tearing apart a foolish argument than Mrs. Nellie McClung. To those who foresaw domestic discord following close upon the heels of enfranchisement she countered: "If a husband and wife are going to quarrel they will find a cause for dispute easily enough and will not be compelled to wait for election day."[16] That group which professed to see man's chivalry to women destroyed by the ballot were informed that "Chivalry is a poor substitute for justice, if one cannot have both. Chivalry is something like the icing on cake, sweet but not nourishing."[17]

To weaken or destroy the arguments of their opponents was not enough: this the women well knew. Some more positive justification for their stand must be furnished to a sceptical public. The basic plea of the suffrage forces was for

[13]*Globe*, Mar. 25, 1916.
[14]Nellie L. McClung, *In Times Like These* (Toronto, 1915), p. 70.
[15]From an unidentified clipping dated Nov. 2, 1911, in A. S.-G., Scrap Books, VI, 37.
[16]Nellie L. McClung, *op. cit.*, p. 67.
[17]*Ibid.*, p. 54.

simple justice. Women were forced to pay taxes and obey laws; why not give them a share in making them? The old cry, "No taxation without representation," which had once rung out with such startling consequences in the neighbour country, now re-echoed in Canada in a milder way.

The forces advocating woman suffrage contended that the state, like the home, needed women's point of view and influence in order to create a more perfectly balanced way of life. The homemakers of the nation would take a special interest in laws to protect their homes and families, and find particular scope for their talents in such matters as health, education, and child protection. In 1941 Dr. Gordon Bates, Director of the Health League of Canada, prophesied that if there were enough women in parliament, the health ministry would become more important than that of finance.[18] It was also argued that women would influence moral questions, especially prohibition; and certainly there was a close working alliance between woman suffrage and prohibition forces at all stages of the campaign. Some optimists even went so far as to claim that if women voted, war would be abolished; a prediction which unhappily has not been fulfilled.

In the nineteenth and twentieth centuries women have emerged from their homes into the industrial and commercial worlds, either voluntarily or through pressure of economic necessity. Flooding the labour market, they forced down not only their own wages, but also the general wage level. This fact, clearly perceived by labour unions, was the main reason for their general support of the suffrage cause. Failure of legislatures to pass protective legislation for women in industry so long as laws were exclusively man-made became a powerful argument for extending the franchise to women.[19]

Frankly admitting that many women were not interested in public questions, suffragists contended that exercising the

[18]*Daily Star* (Montreal), Mar. 19, 1941.
[19]See the brief submitted by the League for Women's Rights (Montreal) to the Rowell-Sirois Commission in 1938 for an excellent statistical presentation of this viewpoint. *Canada: Royal Commission on Dominion-Provincial Relations. Briefs.* (Winnipeg, 1937-1938). The League's brief is listed as number 70.

vote would train them to a higher sense of social and civic responsibility, broaden their interests, and generally make them better and more useful citizens.

The last great argument for political equality came with Canada's entrance into the world war in 1914 and, quite fittingly, was used more by men than by women. This, of course, was women's magnificent contribution to the war effort, both in war relief and in filling the places vacated by men on the farm and in the factory. The average Canadian was unstinting in praise and generous enough to admit that women had earned their right to help chart the nation's future course.

While it was true that the nerve centre of the suffrage movement in each province was a small group of devoted workers, usually operating in the principal city, these determined little bands had the assistance of some very powerful allies. The latter included nationwide women's organizations, farm and labour groups, a substantial number of the Protestant clergy, and the most influential sections of the press.

Of the women's organizations, the first to throw its support to the cause of political equality was the Woman's Christian Temperance Union, which began to appear in Canada on a local scale in the seventies and achieved national status in 1885. Though suffrage was only a corollary to its main objective, the W.C.T.U. was often at work in this field many years before any full-fledged woman suffrage organization appeared on the scene. It is no mere coincidence that suffrage leaders from one end of the country to the other often served an apprenticeship as workers in the temperance field. Tirelessly, W.C.T.U. workers petitioned local, provincial, and federal governments, and frequently organized delegations to recalcitrant legislatures, sometimes alone, more often in co-operation with a woman suffrage association. Referring to the early 1900's, a past president of the Union wrote: "Of course the programme wound up with a Franchise message.

That was as much an integral part of every convention in those days as the opening and closing exercises."[20]

The most influential woman's organization in Canada for over half a century has been the National Council of Women. Founded by Lady Aberdeen in 1893 for the purpose of "applying the Golden Rule to society, custom and law," it has achieved important reforms in many fields such as laws for the protection of women and children, prison reforms, and better treatment for unfortunate classes. It never was a suffrage organization and made that very clear at the outset, but since women's organizations of all types were welcome to join the National Council and the many Local Councils established in cities across Canada, it was natural that suffrage groups should become affiliated with it. The Dominion Women's Enfranchisement Association, founded in 1889, was a member society of the National Council from its beginning and each year submitted its report on woman suffrage activities. Moreover, the D.W.E.A. often held sectional conferences at the Council's annual meetings which aroused interest among women who had previously been apathetic or hostile to the movement.

In 1904 the National Council established a Standing Committee on Suffrage and Rights of Citizenship, presided over until 1921 by the eminent suffragist, Dr. Augusta Stowe-Gullen of Toronto. Under her leadership, this committee served the political equality movement with unswerving fidelity, correlating suffrage news from all over the dominion, giving publicity to every small gain made, and lamenting quite audibly when there were no gains to report. Finally, at the Halifax conference in 1910, the National Council, by a vote of 71 to 51, endorsed woman suffrage.[21] It would be difficult to overestimate the value of this support, because of the universal respect in which the National Council was held.

---

[20]S. G. E. McKee, *Jubilee History of the Ontario Woman's Christian Temperance Union: 1877-1927* (Whitby, 1927), *passim*. The quotation will be found on p. 81. Hereafter cited as S. McKee, *Jubilee History*.

[21]The National Council of Women, *Women Workers of Canada* (Ottawa, 1910), pp. 97-104. Hereafter cited as N.C.W., *Year Book*.

Following this handsome gesture, the Council turned to more active agitation. When the Borden government in 1917 passed the highly controversial Wartime Elections Act, enfranchising only those women who had close relatives in the armed services, an outcry against the injustice of the measure could be heard from one end of the country to the other. While not openly expressing its displeasure, the National Council that same year passed a resolution to petition the federal government to grant the federal franchise immediately to all women,[22] and this may have been no small factor in deciding Sir Robert to do so at the next session of parliament. During the 1920's, the National Council also gave loyal support to the effort to have women declared eligible for the senate, a struggle which culminated successfully following an appeal to the Privy Council in 1929.[23]

Among the rural women of Canada, the Women's Institutes filled the same need for organization answered by the Local Councils in towns and cities. These associations of country women early began to discuss woman suffrage and to agitate for its adoption. In certain provinces where the rural population was predominant, as for example in the Prairie Provinces and New Brunswick, the Women's Institutes were particularly effective.

It was not only women's organizations which allied themselves with the movement. The women of the Prairie Provinces found their staunchest backers in the vigorous farmers' associations of Manitoba, Saskatchewan, and Alberta, all three of which openly endorsed suffrage in 1911 and 1912. These farmers did more than pay lip service as they joined their women in petitions and delegations, and carried the idea of equality into their own organizations by admitting women to full membership.[24]

Organized labour also gave its support, although never with the concerted power and drive of the prairie farm assoc-

[22]*Ibid.* (1917-18), p. 51.
[23]The Wartime Elections Act and the appeal to the Privy Council are both treated more fully in Chapter V.
[24]See Chapter III.

iations. As early as 1912 a labour convention at Kamloops, B.C., drew up a resolution demanding woman suffrage,[25] and the well-organized British Columbia Federation of Labor officially endorsed it in 1912.[26] The *British Columbia Federationist*, mouth-piece of west coast labour, carried on a campaign for woman suffrage in its somewhat red-tinged columns from 1914 to 1916. Representatives of organized labour frequently joined the almost annual pilgrimages of Toronto women to their provincial government. Mrs. A. V. Thomas, suffrage leader in Winnipeg, recalls that labour oranizations were usually very co-operative in that city.[27] And in Fredericton, the sponsor of a suffrage bill in 1913 pointed out that it was backed not only by the local suffrage society and the W.C.T.U., but also by the Carpenters' and Joiners' Brotherhood of Saint John.[28] A distinct exception to this general rule was reflected in the attitude of the Catholic Syndicates of the province of Quebec. Efforts by the League for Women's Rights to win their support in 1933 and 1938 met with no success.[29]

Other very influential allies were to be found among the Protestant clergy in several of the English-speaking provinces. Individual clergymen from one end of the country to the other not only gave their approval to the campaign in sermons, but frequently joined the women in their petitions and delegations.[30] But the story again was entirely different in Quebec where the Roman Catholic Church, under Cardinal Villeneuve's leadership, steadily opposed woman suffrage.

The last great auxiliary of the women in their struggle for

[25]J. Castell Hopkins, ed., *The Canadian Annual Review of Public Affairs* (Toronto, 1902), pp. 86-7. Hereafter cited as *Canadian Annual Review*.
[26]*Ibid.* (1912), pp. 273-4.
[27]Letter to the author from Mrs. A. V. Thomas, April 21, 1944.
[28]*Daily Telegraph* (Saint John), Feb. 22, 1913.
[29]*Gazette* (Montreal), Nov. 29, 1933. An entry dated Sept. 12, 1938, in the Minute Books of the League for Women's Rights. Hereafter cited as L.W.R. Minute Books.
[30]For some specific instances of this support see the *Daily Telegraph*, June 4, 1917. *Globe* (Toronto), Feb. 28, 1894. *Manitoba Free Press* (Winnipeg), Jan. 28, 1914. Rev. R. J. Hutcheon, *Man's World* (Toronto, 1911), a pamphlet in the Canadian Suffrage Association Series. Helen Gregory MacGill, "Story of Women Suffrage in British Columbia" (n.p., n.d.), p. 2. The latter is a type-written copy of an address made by Judge MacGill, in the possession of the City Archives, Vancouver.

the franchise was the press, or at least fairly substantial sections of it. Since in seven of the nine provinces Liberal administrations accorded the franchise to women, it is not surprising to find that newspapers supporting the Liberal party were more likely to be friendly to the suffrage cause than those of Conservative sympathies, especially in the period just preceding the actual enactment of franchise legislation. Support of the "party line," however, was not the motive which caused editors like John W. Dafoe of the *Manitoba Free Press* or George Chipman of the *Grain Growers' Guide* to give handsome endorsement to political equality. It was their own inner conviction, bred from the western pioneers' traditional faith in democracy.

Seldom did an English language paper definitely oppose the project openly. Unfriendliness was more likely to be shown by complete indifference. While portions of the French language press, such as *Le Droit* (Ottawa) and *L'Action Catholique* (Quebec) were bitterly opposed and had no hesitancy about saying so, this attitude was not uniform among French newspapers. On the contrary, *La Presse* (Montreal) financed radio time for propaganda work by the League for Women's Rights for five years during the early 1930's[31] and *Le Devoir* (Montreal) took a very liberal stand in those lively spring days of 1940 when political rights were at long last bestowed upon the women of Quebec.

Certain English papers like the *Morning Chronicle* of Halifax and the Victoria *Daily Times*, after many years of indifference became warm advocates; but some of the dominion's outstanding journals championed the cause when it was least popular. Papers such as the *Manitoba Free Press*, the Saint John *Telegraph*, the Montreal *Gazette*, *Daily Star*, and *Herald*, and the Toronto *Globe*, *World*, and *Citizen* not only gave suffrage bills and activities complete coverage in their news columns but often extended strong editorial support. In the Prairie Provinces the widely circulated farmers'

[31]Annual Report of the League for Women's Rights for 1936-37, contained in L.W.R. Minute Books.

weekly, the *Grain Growers' Guide*, was a loyal and steadfast
ally. Had it not been for this journalistic assistance, the road
to political emancipation would have been much harder.

In the development of the woman suffrage movement in
Canada, the play of external influences has been strongly felt.
There is evidence that Canada sent delegates to women's
rights conventions in the United States as early as 1852 and
1854.[32] It was attendance at a similar meeting in 1876 which
inspired Dr. Emily Howard Stowe to initiate the first suffrage
society in her own country. As years went by, Canadian
groups were ever more frequently represented at suffrage gatherings south of the border, one of the most interesting being
the gigantic suffrage parade in Washington, D.C., on the eve
of Wilson's inauguration (March 3, 1913).

Outstanding personalities in the women's rights movement
from both England and the United States visited Canada in
considerable numbers on "recruiting" missions. They were
most cordially received and invariably addressed capacity
audiences. Dr. Stowe brought both Dr. Anna Howard Shaw
and Susan B. Anthony to Toronto in 1889. As a result of the
enthusiasm generated by these two key figures of the American movement, the almost moribund Toronto Suffrage Association took a vigorous new hold upon life. Dr. Shaw (who
returned many times, always to find a warm welcome) and
Miss Anthony were but the first two of a number of distinguished Americans who crossed the border and left their
imprint upon the Canadian movement.[33] Across the Atlantic
came representatives not only of the moderate wing of the
English movement like the brilliant and charming Mrs. Philip
Snowden, but also several of the militants, including the two
Pankhursts, Miss Barbara Wylie, and Mrs. Borrmann Wells,
all of whom had served prison sentences. While they had no

---

[32]From an address by Professor Carrie M. Derick, printed in the Montreal *Daily
Star*, Nov. 29, 1933. See also Ida Husted Harper *et al.*, eds., *The History of
Woman Suffrage*, I (N.Y., 1922), 375-6. Hereafter cited as I. Harper *et al.*,
*Woman Suffrage*.
[33]Others included Julia Ward Howe, Mrs. May Wright Sewell, Mrs. Mary S.
Howell (who did organizing work for the Dominion Women's Enfranchisement
Association throughout Ontario in 1889), and Senator Helen Robinson of Colorado

wish to adopt militant methods themselves, many Canadian women openly expressed sympathy and admiration for the Englishwomen.

Debates in both the federal and provincial legislatures abound in references to suffrage activities and statistics from Great Britain and the United States. Indeed, both advocates and adversaries availed themselves liberally of facts from abroad. Provincial premiers, reluctant to grant the franchise to women, argued, as Roblin of Manitoba once had, that the mother country itself had not yet taken such a drastic step. On the other side, the platform of the Manitoba Liberals in 1914 almost resembled a brief history of the suffrage movement, so heavily did it draw upon outside sources to support its suffrage plank.[34]

Newspapers, too, were an important highway over which ideas derived from the British and American woman suffrage movements made their way into Canada. Sometimes journals used their control of news sources to block progress in Canada as when, in the spring of 1913, the Victoria *Daily Times* featured stories of militant riots in England. A similar campaign was conducted by the Halifax *Morning Chronicle* during much of 1912 and 1913, and the effect upon the already conservative "Bluenoses" may well be imagined. However, for every one of these examples of unfavourable publicity in the Canadian press, there were more than a dozen items calculated to stimulate friendly interest. Nowhere was this more evident than in the pages of the *Grain Growers' Guide*, whose principal fount of inspiration was the states of the American West which had granted the vote to women. The same Victoria *Daily Times* which regaled its readers with suffragette atrocities in Great Britain also faithfully reported news of the much less colourful American campaigns, particularly those in the states of Washington and California. These are but scattered examples of scores of columns of news of woman suffrage activities abroad which were almost daily reading fare for Canadians

[34]*Platform of the Manitoba Liberals, 1914* (Winnipeg, 1914), pp. 52-5.

from coast to coast, and which, in the aggregate, doubtless
wielded great influence.

In explaining the amazing amount of interest manifested
by Canadians in woman suffrage during the first world war,
after two or three decades of very general indifference, W. L.
Morton holds the republic's influence heavily responsible.
"By 1914 two things had happened. Democracy had become
respectable, . . . and the progressive Movement in the United
States had infiltrated unacknowledged into Canada. Growing
friendliness with the United States and increasing national
confidence undoubtedly contributed much to these developments."[35]

In tracing the events which culminated in the complete
political emancipation of Canadian women, this history will
follow generally the chronological pattern. Ontario is the
notable exception. She was the unquestioned pioneer in the
field of political equality. Although destined to witness the
earlier triumphs of the cause in the four provinces to her west,
Ontario laid the solid foundations.

[35]W. L. Morton, *op. cit.*, pp. 79-80.

# 2

# ONTARIO

## *The Pioneer*

THE MOVEMENT for woman suffrage in Canada was initiated largely because of the vision and courage of Dr. Emily Howard Stowe of Toronto. Early in the 1860's Mrs. Stowe was faced with the problem of supporting an invalid husband and three children. She returned for a few years to her former vocation of teaching, and by careful management of her slender income saved enough money to permit the realization of her consuming ambition, which was to enter the medical profession. Rebuffed by Canadian medical schools on account of her sex, Mrs. Stowe entered the Women's New York Medical School. She graduated in 1868. Returning to Canada, she and her family settled in Toronto where she practised medicine successfully until her death in 1903. As Canada's first woman physician, Dr. Stowe was confronted with prejudice which must often have tried her sorely, but she never manifested any of the bitterness or intolerance she so frequently met in others. Instead, she devoted her entire life to making the path easier for those who followed.

Largely owing to Dr. Stowe's efforts, the University of Toronto opened its doors to women in 1886, and professional schools began to let down the bars. Dr. Stowe also strove to secure factory and health laws, a better Married Women's Property Act, and above all, the political enfranchisement of women, for she rightly felt that this would act as a powerful lever in opening the door to other reforms.[1]

Shocked by the apathy of Canadian women towards matters ordinarily lumped together as "women's rights," the doctor somehow found time not only to care for her family and prescribe for the sick, but also to lecture in several large Ontario towns on subjects of interest to women, and to write an occasional letter of protest to the press. After attending a meeting of the American Society for the Advancement of Women in 1876, she decided that the hour had come when some similar organization should appear on Canadian soil. Such a body would not only teach Canadian women what their rights were, but would also help secure these rights. In November 1876 Dr. Stowe and a small energetic group of Toronto women launched what they chose to call the Toronto Women's Literary Club. The time was not considered opportune for the bold use of the word "suffrage," the mere mention of that term producing violent reactions in many quarters; hence the camouflage of a "literary club."[2]

This little organization, which met weekly under the presidencies of both Dr. Stowe and Mrs. Donald McEwen, entertained its members with a mixture of light and heavy fare. After listening to a prepared paper on working conditions for women or some similar topic, discussion followed, but before the evening was over there were usually musical selections, and on one occasion at least, "a very beautiful reading of Tennyson's 'Lady Clara Vere de Vere.'"[3] During the six years of its existence the Literary Club was very active in educating its members and the public. Its most effective means of publicity appeared in 1881. In that year the *Canada Citizen*, a Toronto weekly devoted to the prohibition cause, placed a column at the disposal of the Club, and Mrs. S. A.

---

[1]A. S.-G., Scrap Books, III, 61. *Globe* (Toronto), May 1, 1903. *Sunday World* (Toronto), Mar. 3, 1912.

[2]Hilda M. Ridley, *A Synopsis of Woman Suffrage in Canada* (n.p., n.d.), pp. 5-6. Hereafter cited as H. Ridley, *Woman Suffrage*. I. Harper *et al.*, *Woman Suffrage*, III, 832. A. S.-G., Scrap Books, I, 9, 108. Edith M. Luke, "Woman Suffrage in Canada," *Canadian Magazine*, V (Toronto, 1895), 328-9. Hereafter cited as E. Luke, "Woman Suffrage."

[3]A. S.-.G., Scrap Books, III, 2-6.

Curzon, one of the cleverest of the members, became associate editor. The *Citizen* thus has the distinction of being the first Canadian paper to support woman suffrage.

The Club's work was more than educational. It organized in 1881 the first deputation to wait on the provincial government in the cause of woman suffrage. The Club also succeeded in getting the Ontario legislature to pass a law in 1882 permitting unmarried women with property qualifications to vote on municipal by-laws.[4] (It need scarcely be said that when concessions were made to women, privileges for unmarried women almost always preceded those for married women, on the assumption that the innovation would be less likely to destroy domestic harmony.) This was a small concession, to be sure, but it was at least an opening wedge.

By 1883 the Literary Club appears to have felt that its educational programme had been rooted deeply enough to permit the formation of a new organization openly devoted to woman suffrage. With this object in view, the Club was disbanded and a request sent to the Toronto City Council for the use of the Council Chamber to hold a meeting on the night of March 9. If the city fathers were surprised by the request, they gallantly concealed the fact, and granted the ladies' wish.[5] About one hundred and thirty men and women accepted the invitation, and marked enthusiasm was the keynote of the gathering. Two resolutions were carried unanimously, one endorsing the principle of equal suffrage, and the other proposing the immediate formation of a society to achieve that goal. Mrs. Donald McEwen headed a slate of officers which included men as well as women, and about forty of those present immediately enrolled as members. The new society cast aside subterfuge and called itself the Toronto Women's Suffrage Association.[6]

[4] *Statutes of Ontario, 1882*, ch. 23, s. 15.

[5] This early action by the Toronto City Council was typical of its attitude throughout the struggle in Ontario. Its unfailing and courteous co-operation stands in sharp contrast to the behaviour of the provincial legislature, where contemptuous mockery was frequently meted out to those who advocated or sponsored measures for woman suffrage.

[6] *World* (Toronto), Mar. 12, 1883. *Globe*, Mar. 7, 1883. A. S.-G., Scrap Books, III, 3, contains a pamphlet announcing formation of the new society, listing the officers, and soliciting membership.

In its first years the Suffrage Association made notable progress. The University of Toronto was opened to women students, and the Ontario Medical College for Women established in October 1883 as the result of a public meeting held on June 13, under the auspices of the Association. Dr. Augusta Stowe-Gullen, Dr. Emily Stowe's brilliant daughter, was appointed the first woman member of the faculty of the new medical school.[7] And there was some activity in the political field.

Although little progress had been made, the Ontario legislature had not entirely neglected woman suffrage in the two decades preceding 1890. The right to vote for school trustees had been granted to both married and single women with property as far back as 1850, though there is evidence to indicate they did not make much use of the privilege.[8] Attempts were made in 1875 and 1877 to extend the municipal franchise to women. The first of these, which limited the proposal to unmarried women, failed of passage by the narrow margin of 33 to 31. During discussion of a manhood suffrage bill in 1875, W. Robinson had the courage to say he "should like to see the females given the right to vote," a sentiment which drew hearty laughter from his fellow lawmakers.[9] In 1882 unmarried women with property qualifications were granted the right to vote on municipal by-laws; in 1884 they were granted the full municipal franchise. In 1884, too, the motion for the admission of women to the University of Toronto was passed; it took effect in 1886.[10]

The Ontario legislators now felt they had gone far enough

[7]E. Luke, "Woman Suffrage," pp. 330-1. *Mail and Empire* (Toronto), Oct. 3, 1932. Augusta Stowe-Gullen, *A Brief History of the Ontario Medical College for Women* (Toronto, 1906). The Medical College for Women closed in 1906, after the co-educational principle had been so well established at the University of Toronto as to make a separate medical school for women no longer necessary.

[8]I. Harper *et al.*, *Woman Suffrage*, III, 831. A. S.-G., Scrap Books, V, 90. In Ontario the right to be elected as trustees was included in the school franchise.

[9]*Ontario: Parliamentary Debates, 1875*, pp. 32, 80; *1877*, pp. 29-30. These volumes are to be found in the Library of Parliament at Ottawa. They are not official reports, but rather newspaper clippings, mostly from the *Globe*, which have been bound for each year down through 1910. Hereafter cited as *Ontario: Debates.*

[10]*Statutes of Ontario, 1884*, ch. 32. *Ontario: Journals of the Legislative Assembly, 1884*, p. 114. Hereafter cited as *Ontario: Journals.*

in the dangerous matter of privileges for women, which might end Heaven alone knew where. However, three things brought the troublesome problem to their attention with increasing urgency as the 1880's advanced. The first of these was a bombardment of petitions from city, town, and county councils, as well as from private persons, in 1884, 1887, and 1888. There were no fewer than 57 petitions in 1884, and more than that in 1888, praying both for municipal franchise for married women and provincial franchise for all.[11] Although there is no ready clue to this epidemic of petitions, there are at least two possible explanations. There may have been a repercussion of interest from the stiff though unsuccessful fights put up by suffragists in the United States to win political equality in the states of Oregon (1884) and Rhode Island (1887). More likely, however, the epidemic originated in local temperance activities, even though the provincial W.C.T.U. did not officially espouse woman suffrage until 1891. While petitions do not force legislative action, these paper cloudbursts must have kept the lawmakers aware of the rising tide, whether they welcomed it or not.

Now, too, a sturdy champion appeared in the halls of the legislature itself. John Waters, a Liberal member, gave warning in 1885, when introducing the first proposal to give women the provincial franchise, that he would introduce a woman suffrage bill in every session until he got it passed or as long as he sat in the House. He meant what he said, for the *Journals* record no fewer than nine measures sponsored by Waters between 1885 and 1893, some to give the municipal franchise to married women, but most to extend the provincial vote to unmarried women. The rather sparse accounts of debates on these measures indicate that they were usually treated with scorn and derision, at least until 1889, and were invariably turned down by substantial majorities.[12]

A third factor destined to upset legislative complacency

[11]*Ibid.*, *1884, 1887, 1888, passim.*
[12]See *Ibid.*, *1885, 1886, 1887, 1888, 1889, 1890, 1892, 1893.* The *Debates* for the same years give brief accounts of the reception accorded these ill-fated measures.

was the reappearance early in 1889 of a strong and vigorous suffrage organization. Between 1884 and 1889 the Toronto Women's Suffrage Association ceased to function regularly. Though no reason for the inactivity appears on the surface, one may imagine that many women were satisfied with the gains already made and lost the momentum of their first enthusiasm. More than one veteran leader has told the author that these "breathing spells" were a natural reaction to a heavy expenditure of energy, and lasted until some new set of incidents or leaders appeared to rekindle the crusading spirit.

The revival in 1889 was the result of a small meeting at the home of Dr. Stowe, at which it was decided that any effort towards favourable legislative action must be based upon increased publicity. A committee engaged the great American suffragist, Dr. Anna Howard Shaw, and she lectured to a capacity audience in Association Hall on the night of January 31. As a direct result of the enthusiasm she created, the Dominion Women's Enfranchisement Association was established with Dr. Stowe as president. This post Dr. Stowe retained until her death in 1903. As its name would indicate, the new organization hoped to become the nucleus of a nation-wide network of societies, a hope that was only partially fulfilled. However, several branches were formed in Ontario during the first year with the assistance of Mrs. Mary Howell of Albany, New York, a capable lecturer and organizer.[13]

The first endeavour of Dr. Stowe and her colleagues was a delegation to the provincial government on February 8, a few days after the formation of the Association. In co-operation with the Toronto W.C.T.U., they urged the passage of the Waters bill of 1889. Introduced by Mayor Clarke of Toronto, the women pleaded their case before Attorney-General (and Premier) Mowat, who, as on two previous occasions (1881 and 1883), assured them of his sympathy with

[13]E. Luke, "Woman Suffrage," p. 332.　*Mail and Empire*, Feb. 1, 1889. *Globe*, Feb. 1, 1889.　A. S.-G., Scrap Books, III, 12-16.

their objective, but would promise no help. The women remained long enough in the House to hear their champion, Mr. Waters, introduce his bill and make an eloquent plea for its passage. A few weeks later this bill was killed on second reading, but not before it had been subjected to a full-dress debate in which the levity of previous parliamentary discussions was conspicuously absent.[14] Apparently the delegation had accomplished something.

Stung by the defeat of the Waters bill, the women redoubled their efforts. Quantities of literature explaining and justifying their purpose were distributed, Dr. Anna Shaw was recalled several times to lecture, and on the evening of December 2, 1889, a climax was reached with the appearance of Susan B. Anthony, most famous of American suffragists, upon the lecture platform in Toronto. The city's newspapers commented enthusiastically the following day upon the stirring address delivered before a vast audience of men and women by the key figure in the American suffrage movement. Favourable publicity such as this was bound to give strong impetus to the cause.[15]

Feeling themselves strong enough now for the attempt, the members of the Association held their national convention on June 12 and 13, 1890. Delegates came from affiliated clubs and distinguished guests from the United States. Men as well as women attended in large numbers; indeed, the closing session was presided over by an eminent Toronto lawyer, James Beatty, Q.C., and J. W. Garvin, president of the newly formed Woodstock branch of the Association, was a very active delegate.[16]

In 1891 the D.W.E.A. received the help of a very powerful ally. The local W.C.T.U. had given assistance in the 1889 delegation to the government, but the provincial temperance organization had repeatedly shied away from the thorny

[14]*Ontario: Debates, 1889*, pp. 14, 31-3. A. S.-G., Scrap Books, III, 16-21; V, 83.

[15]*Ibid.*, III, 30. E. Luke, "Woman Suffrage," p. 332.

[16]*Ibid.*, pp. 333-4. H. Ridley, "Woman Suffrage," p. 9. A. S.-G., Scrap Books, III, 30-2. *World*, June 13, 1890. *Mail and Empire*, June 13, 1890.

question of suffrage. At its fourteenth annual convention in Toronto, however, the Ontario W.C.T.U. had Dr. Anna Shaw as its principal speaker. "Her marvelous address alternately rocked the audience with laughter and reduced it to tears. . . . The next day the Convention endorsed woman's franchise without any attached tags."[17]

Two important advances were made by women in 1892. For the first time in Toronto's history, three women were elected to the school board, one of them Dr. Augusta Stowe-Gullen. During her four years on the board she was the unfailing champion of Toronto's 460 women (out of 500) teachers and successfully opposed an attempt to lower the salaries of women principals. The other forward-looking step was the passage of an act permitting women to study and practise law. At first they were allowed to act only as solicitors, but in 1895 permission to act as barristers was also granted.[18] This progressive measure was the result of a successful struggle by Ontario's pioneer woman lawyer, Clara Brett Martin, who accomplished for women in the legal profession what Dr. Stowe-Gullen had already achieved in medicine.

Following Waters's last two unsuccessful attempts in the sessions of 1892 and 1893, legislative activity died out completely for ten years, except when the legislature was reminded of the unpleasant subject by petitions or delegations. Such periods of apathy, as we have already noted, were an experience common to all provinces. Inasmuch as Canada was affected by American influences, a further clue to the lethargy may be that no state enfranchised its women between 1896 and 1910.

Before inactivity settled in, however, the D.W.E.A. joined forces with the W.C.T.U. in March 1894, to approach Sir Oliver Mowat, and again received nothing but polite sympathy. On this occasion the 150 delegates were headed by two men, F. S. Spence representing the prohibitionists, and

[17]S. McKee, *Jubilee History*, p. 28.
[18]*Statutes of Ontario, 1892*, ch. 32; *1895*, ch. 27.

Dr. J. L. Hughes speaking for the D.W.E.A. Although Dr. Stowe-Gullen had prepared a speech, through either design or oversight she was not called upon to make it. However, the doctor left a draft of her address for the government to read.[19]

To gain publicity, the women staged a Mock Parliament in February 1896, in which men's and women's roles were reversed. To a delegation of men "humbly praying that our down-trodden sex be granted the first right of a citizen, the ballot," the lady premier replied in words which were a classic imitation of Sir Oliver's, and amid gales of laughter from the audience, the men retired with downcast looks.[20]

Between 1896 and 1905 there was little agitation for woman suffrage, except by the W.C.T.U. which was interested in getting passed both provincial and dominion prohibition laws. A provincial plebiscite in 1894 and a dominion plebiscite in 1898 had given the prohibition forces overwhelming victories, but the resulting legislation (or lack of it) proved so disappointing that it seemed clearer than ever that women must have the ballot before success could be achieved. The president of the W.C.T.U. voiced this idea emphatically in her annual address of 1904. "If we dropped every other Department in our organization, and worked for woman's enfranchisement, we should be farther ahead in ten years than we will be in fifty years without it."[21] The W.C.T.U. deluged the legislature with petitions in 1901 and helped turn the Liberals out of office in 1905, but of suffrage legislation there was none, except for one feeble and unsuccessful attempt in 1903 to secure the municipal franchise for married women.[22]

In 1905, however, the D.W.E.A. sprang into action with renewed energy. Dr. Stowe-Gullen had succeeded her mother as president of the organization in 1903 and, until her own resignation in 1911, furnished a leadership unparalleled in the annals of the Canadian suffrage movement. The Liberals

[19]A. S.-G., Scrap Books, V, 84-6. *Ontario: Debates, 1894*, pp. 24-5.
[20]*Star* (Toronto), Feb. 18, 1896.
[21]S. McKee, *Jubilee History*, pp. 61-2.
[22]*Ontario: Debates, 1903*, p. 71.

were defeated early in 1905, and the hopes of the Association soared in the expectation that the new Conservative regime under Premier J. P. Whitney[23] might listen to its pleas with a friendlier ear. Anxious to learn with certainty the views of the new administration, a D.W.E.A.-W.C.T.U. delegation, accompanied by a group of outstanding Toronto men, including the mayor, approached Premier Whitney with the mild plea that married women be accorded the municipal franchise. In reply the new premier was most cordial, and indefinite. He believed personally that the request was reasonable, that men had no rights apart from women, that a nation could never rise to a higher level than its homes; but he concluded that the Infinite was at work and that woman had been assigned her place according to a divine plan. What place Premier Whitney and the "divine plan" assigned to women he did not elaborate at that interview, but his later actions made the point abundantly clear.[24] In later years, Dr. Stowe-Gulien remarked that she was always suspicious of any man who attempted to hide his own infirmities behind the Almighty.

During the 1905 session of the legislature agitation for woman suffrage revived, with an inundation of petitions (72 in all) from local governments requesting municipal voting privileges for married women.[25] Better still, a new champion, John Smith (Liberal) of Peel, rose to take the place vacated twelve years before by Waters. His debut in this thankless role was brief and bitter, for when he moved second reading of his bill on May 11, debate lasted about one full minute, and was intensely silly. Seeing the temper of the House, Smith withdrew his bill, which proposed to give the provincial

[23]Hon. J. P. Whitney remained in the office of premier from Feb. 8, 1905 to Sept. 25, 1914. After a brief interval of a week he was succeeded by another Conservative premier, Hon. William H. Hearst, who held office from Oct. 2, 1914 to Nov. 14, 1919.

[24]S. McKee, *Jubilee History*, p. 65. I. Harper *et al.*, *Woman Suffrage*, VI, 757. *Canadian Annual Review* (1905), p. 264.

[25]A record of these petitions may be found between April 13 and May 12 in *Ontario: Journals, 1905*. Once again it is reasonable to suppose that temperance groups had much to do with causing the commotion, especially since a new provincial administration had just come into power.

franchise to all women. His action was accompanied by laughter and applause.[26]

Undeterred, Smith reintroduced the same measure in 1906. On motion for second reading a debate arose, in the course of which Premier Whitney viciously attacked the sponsor and said that the sooner the bill was defeated the better. George W. Ross, leader of the Opposition, although opposed to suffrage himself, reproved the premier for his "ungallant manner." When Smith insisted upon a division, the bill was swamped by a vote of 66 to 9.[27] After this chilling blast from the legislature, the women derived some comforting warmth from the unanimous passage by a large public gathering presided over by Mayor Coatsworth of Toronto on November 20 of a resolution favouring extension of both provincial and federal franchises to women.[28]

In 1907 the D.W.E.A. wisely changed its name to the shorter and more effective Canadian Suffrage Association. One of its most active members was Mrs. Flora McDonald Denison who, for several years, edited a page in the Toronto *Sunday World* which was of great propaganda value. Mrs. Denison was an outstandingly successful business woman, and gave generously of her ample income for the promotion of the work of the Suffrage Association. She twice represented the Association at International Woman Suffrage Conferences (Copenhagen in 1906 and Budapest in 1913) and in 1908 undertook an organizing campaign in the Maritime Provinces. When Dr. Stowe-Gullen resigned from the presidency in 1911, Mrs. Denison took her place.[29] Two others whose work in the Association was exceptional were Dr. Margaret Johnston and Dr. Margaret Gordon. Dr. Johnston was president of the local Toronto Suffrage Association, organized in 1909, for

[26]*Ontario: Debates, 1905*, May 11. When John Smith died many years later, newspapers commented on his wonted silence on all subjects except woman suffrage.
[27]*Ibid., 1906*, p. 43. *Ontario: Journals, 1906*, pp. 58, 202, 253.
[28]*Star*, Nov. 21, 1906.
[29]Although Mrs. Denison did not become president of the Suffrage Association until 1911, she was active in its work for many years prior to that time, preferring to do much of her work behind the scenes. Her adherence to the suffrage cause may partially explain the resumption of intensive activity in 1905.

some time, and was active in the national organization. After a brief period as president of the local suffrage association, Dr. Gordon became president of the Canadian Suffrage Association in 1914, led it to victory in both the provincial and the federal field, and remained in office until the disbanding of the Association in 1925.[30]

With admirable determination, John Smith reintroduced his suffrage bill in the sessions of 1907 and 1908, only to have Premier Whitney leap to the attack, imploring the members to protect "the dignity of the House and the dignity of the women of this country." Supporting Smith was Allan Studholme, Labour member from East Hamilton.[31] Dr. Stowe-Gullen recalled that Mr. Studholme always wore a small black cap over his grey locks as he sat in the House, which made him the subject of unkind jests. Studholme's appearance may have been unprepossessing, but he fought a rugged battle for women through the next ten years, either by introducing measures of his own or vigorously supporting the bills of others.

In 1909 the suffragists were exceedingly busy, and though the franchise bill was defeated as usual,[32] there were signs of hope. Dr. Stowe-Gullen, supported by Dr. Gordon and Mrs. Mary Craigie, appeared in March before the annual convention of the Dominion Alliance, a national temperance organization composed of men, and successfully urged the endorsement of woman suffrage by that organization.[33] In the same month the Canadian Suffrage Association and the W.C.T.U. again joined forces to organize what may truthfully be called a "monster" delegation to the provincial government. This made all previous delegations fade into insignificance, for it had hundreds of members who represented fourteen different societies and its petition, presented by Dr. Stowe-Gullen to Premier Whitney, contained 100,000 signatures. Introduced

[30]H. Ridley, *Woman Suffrage*, pp. 11-12.
[31]*Ontario: Journals, 1907*, pp. 166, 298; *1908*, pp. 181, 273. *'Ontario: Debates, 1907*, p. 51; *1908*, p. 51. The quotation is from *1908*.
[32]This was the extremely liberal Fripp bill to give all women both provincial and municipal political rights; lost with no debate on the last day of the session. See *Ontario: Journals, 1909*, pp. 180, 318. *Ontario: Debates, 1909*, pp. 20, 33.
[33]A. S.-G., Scrap Books, V, 91.

by Controller Hocken of the Toronto City Council, six or seven speakers representing teachers, doctors, labour, clergy, and political groups, besides the usual suffrage and temperance organizations, presented their arguments so concisely and effectively that the *Globe* congratulated them. It said, "The women who are carrying on this agitation are certainly more advanced in political education than the average man now undertaking the responsibility of directing public affairs with his vote." Sir James, however, was, as usual, non-committal in his reply.[34]

In 1909 one of the most brilliant gatherings of women in the world, the International Council of Women, held its Fourth Quinquennial Meeting in Toronto from June 16 to 21. During these five eventful days suffrage seems to have been of principal interest in the reports submitted, the resolutions passed, and the mass meetings which were open to the public. The International Council reaffirmed its support of woman suffrage given at the Berlin Conference in 1904, but more important to Canadians was the public endorsement of Lady Aberdeen, President of the International Council and founder of the Canadian National Council. In the eyes of Canadian women, this gracious lady, who had done so much for the country while Lord Aberdeen had been governor general, could do no wrong. Her open stand must certainly have swayed thousands favourably. A further impetus to the movement was the reappearance of Dr. Anna Howard Shaw, who came as a convention delegate from the United States. This veteran had lost none of her ability. Great crowds heard her at Massey Hall on June 20 and at Convocation Hall the following evening. Evidence of her power was the resolution adopted unanimously that women ought to possess the vote in all countries where representative governments existed.[35]

[34]*Canadian Annual Review* (1909), p. 360. I. Harper *et al.*, *Woman Suffrage*, VI, 758. *Globe*, Mar. 25, 1909. *Evening Telegram* (Toronto), Mar. 24, 1909. The International Woman Suffrage Alliance, *Report of the Fifth Conference* (London, 1909), pp. 89-91.
[35]*Globe*, June 17, 21, 1909. *Canadian Annual Review* (1909), pp. 133-4, 136. International Council of Women, *Report of Transactions of the Fourth Quinquennial Meeting* (Toronto, 1909), pp. 107-8, 209, 218-21. N.C.W., *Year Book* (1910), p. xxvii.

Newspaper allies were always welcome. The Toronto *World* had shown friendliness in allowing the women to speak through Mrs. Denison's page, but on October 23, 1909 the editor threw his support unreservedly behind the movement. In a front page editorial captioned, "Canada Is Politically out of Joint," the *World* attributed the low tone of the nation's political life to the absence of women from politics and urged the province of Ontario to be the first to enfranchise women. The editor advised women to make their demands more articulate, and concluded by pointing out a sad truth which suffrage workers would have been ready to admit—that the task ahead was not so much to convince the men as to educate the unconverted masses of women.

This eventful year ended with the appearance on Toronto lecture platforms of two leading English suffragists, Mrs. Emmeline Pankhurst in November, and Mrs. Philip Snowden in the following month. Since Mrs. Pankhurst led the militant wing whose activities were so generally condemned by Canadians, it is a little surprising to find the staid and dignified *Canadian Annual Review* reporting that the militant leader "was found to have a bright, intelligent, gracious and feminine personality and to be an effective and eloquent speaker." Referring to Mrs. Pankhurst's address before the Canadian Club in Toronto, the *Review* reported that she "impressed 500 thinking men with a vivid sense of the seriousness of the movement, a keen realization of the sincerity of its advocate and her capacity as a leader, a sense of having listened to an appeal to reason as well as to sentiment." This was Toronto's first direct introduction to the English suffrage movement, and it must have allayed considerably the fears and prejudices of men and women whose only previous contact had been through headlines blazing stories of outrages.

Tangible results of Lady Aberdeen's stand on suffrage at the Toronto gathering were not long delayed. Early in 1910 the Toronto Local Council endorsed the movement; it was followed in June by the National Council, meeting at Halifax. Dr. Margaret Gordon made the motion, and with its passage the suffragists of Canada had behind them the support of the largest and most powerful women's organization in the country.[36] Woman suffrage, though still years away from actual fulfilment, had now at least the blessing of respectability.

Allan Studholme made his first attempt to introduce a suffrage bill in 1910, but his bill met with a more ignominious fate than most such measures, for it could find no seconder.[37] Having dealt this bothersome matter such a swift *coup de grâce*, the legislators received an unpleasant shock on the very day of prorogation. As the lieutenant-governor reached the close of his address, a young woman arose in the speaker's gallery and addressed herself directly to that exalted official. Thunderstruck, a silent House heard her proclaim:

There is just one thing you have forgotten. I object to this Parliament closing without doing justice to women. Women are just as much entitled to vote as men. I hope that at your future meetings you will do more justice to the cause of women. This is all I have to say at present. Thank you.

Before House officials had recovered sufficiently from their paralysis to eject the young woman by force, she had disappeared. Later it was revealed that she was Miss Olivia Smith of London, England, and had already suffered imprisonment for disturbing the British House of Commons.[38] The Ontario lawmakers showed more gallantry than their British counterparts and let the matter drop.

Stirred by the fate of the 1910 bill, the Toronto Suffrage Association determined to do its utmost for the bill which the undaunted Hamilton member promised to reintroduce in 1911. On March 4 a deputation of two hundred women wearing yellow daffodils (yellow was the suffrage colour) appeared at the Legislative Buildings. Sir James Whitney met them at the head of the grand staircase and listened to well-reasoned pleas by Dr. Gordon, Dr. Stowe-Gullen, Mrs. Denison, and several other leaders of important women's organizations in

[36]*Ibid.*, p. 96.
[37]*Ontario: Debates, 1910*, p. 38.
[38]*Ibid.*, pp. 37-8. *Canadian Annual Review* (1910), p. 313.

the city.   The premier seemed friendlier than he had been
two years earlier, but sent the women away with no assurance
of any change of heart on his part.[39]   The Association turned
to a letter-writing campaign, sending copies of resolutions and
other materials to the premier and to branch organizations
throughout the province.   The latter were offered both additional literature and the services of speakers, and were urged
to bring pressure on their members to support the pending
Studholme-Proudfoot bill.[40]

In spite of these efforts, the bill was overwhelmingly defeated on March 21.   In a three-hour debate the whole subject
was seriously threshed out.   Though some speakers, such as
A. G. MacKay, leader of the Opposition, professed themselves
unopposed to the general principle, the only staunch defender
was the sponsor of the bill.   Significant of women's changing
economic status was Studholme's key argument that women
needed the ballot to protect themselves in the economic field.
Forced, without protective legislation, to sell their labour
cheaply, they undercut the whole labour market.   Labour
organizations understood this and hence almost invariably
supported woman suffrage.   Premier Whitney raised the argument from the mundane sphere to ethereal realms when he
again allied himself with the Infinite: "This is a matter of
evolution and evolution is only a working out of God's laws.
For this reason we must not attempt to hurry it on."[41]

Mrs. Denison and Mrs. Sonia Leathes sent indignant
letters to the press which were printed in pamphlet form and
widely distributed by the Toronto Suffrage Association.   The
pitiful arguments of the lawmakers, especially those of the
premier, were ridiculed or torn to shreds by these two clever
women.   Mrs. Denison's tone softened, however, as she wrote
in admiration of the lone man who had dared to support
the suffrage cause.

[39]For accounts of the delegation, clippings from the Toronto *News, Telegram,*
and *Star,* Mar. 4, 1911 may be found in A. S.-G., Scrap Books, VI, 3.   Also
N.C.W., *Year Book* (1911), pp. xxviii-xxix.

[40]Copies of these letters are found on pp. 16 and 19 of A. S.-G., Scrap Books, VI.

[41]*Mail and Empire,* Mar. 21, 1911.   N.C.W., *Year Book* (1911), p. xxix.   *Globe,*
Mar. 22, 1911.   *Ontario: Journals, 1911,* pp. 97, 250.

EMILY HOWARD STOWE

AUGUSTA  STOWE-GULLEN

The restless members of the House did not seem to realize what the women did—that the small, bent figure, the white head, the hard-worked hands, and the imperfect enunciation were far more eloquent than the oratory of a Webster. What a 'sign of the times,' what a 'Star in the East,' that this scoffed-at man representing the workers should be the only one to stand for Ontario Womanhood![42]

As a lighter side of the campaign, Toronto Suffrage Headquarters, Ltd., a propaganda agency formed by Mrs. Denison, presented a play in April called *How the Vote Was Won*.[43] This short skit depicted the plight of a young man who was strongly anti-suffrage until an invasion of female relatives, all clamouring to be supported, made him see the light. It was produced with marked success in Toronto and eventually used at one time or another by almost every important suffrage group in Canada.

Intense disappointment over the fate of the Studholme-Proudfoot bill led to rumours, circulated by the Toronto *News*, that suffragist circles were about to begin a militant campaign. The *News* went so far as to quote an unidentified Miss Browne as saying that in the coming offensive, "Officer Phillips on the Yonge Street beat would be the first victim."[44] Any fears which this ominous statement may have raised in the stout heart of Officer Phillips or other Torontonians were promptly laid to rest when Dr. Johnston, as secretary of the local suffrage association, wrote a letter to the *News* (April 6, 1911) and emphatically denied any plans for militancy.

With provincial elections looming ahead for the winter of 1911-12, both Dr. Stowe-Gullen and Dr. Gordon wrote letters to Sir James Whitney and N. W. Rowell,[45] the new Liberal leader, in an effort to have a women's suffrage plank included in the platforms of either or both parties. Mrs. Denison carried the campaign a step further by getting in touch with

[42]*Star*, Mar. 25, 1911. *Globe*, Mar. 29 and 30, 1911.
[43]*News* (Toronto), April 4, 1911.
[44]An undated clipping from the *News* in A. S.-G., Scrap Books, VI, 30.
[45]Newton Wesley Rowell was elected leader of his party in 1911 and won a seat in the legislative assembly in the provincial election of that same year. Rowell's intense interest in the prohibition question made him a logical spokesman for the women's cause, first on the provincial stage and later in the federal arena, where he championed their fight to be regarded as "persons" in the eyes of the law. (See Chapter V.)

all candidates for the legislature and asking for an expression of their views on the question. Mrs. Denison received no more than twenty-five favourable replies from several times that many candidates, and neither party included such a plank.[46]

The year 1911 was concluded with a banquet to pay tribute to Dr. Stowe-Gullen upon her retirement as president of the Canadian Suffrage Association, and also to honour Mrs. Emmeline Pankhurst, who was again in Toronto while on a nation-wide lecture tour. Mrs. Denison, as the new president, spoke of Dr. Stowe-Gullen's services in the fields of medicine, education, and social reform, but stressed particularly the debt of gratitude owed her by Canadian women for her unremitting efforts in the sphere of political rights.[47] This retirement from the presidency did not by any means mark the end of Dr. Stowe-Gullen's suffrage campaign. She became honorary president of the national suffrage association, a vice-president of the National Council of Women, and remained in her position as chairman of the Council's very active citizenship committee.

By 1912 Toronto had a healthy crop of suffrage societies and organizations in sympathy with the movement. According to a count made by Mrs. Denison in February, at least eight were functioning.[48] Most of these were of strictly local significance, but one, the newly formed Political Equality League, led by Mrs. L. A. Hamilton, expanded in March 1914 to become the National Union of Woman Suffrage Societies of Canada. Like the older Canadian Suffrage Association, it aspired to create one large organization linking together and giving strength to the local suffrage efforts in each province, but once again the attempt met with only partial success.[49]

[46]*Mail and Empire*, Nov. 9, 1911. A. S.-G., Scrap Books, VI, 37, contains an unidentified clipping dated Nov. 2, 1911, giving both Dr. Gordon's letters in full.

[47]A. S.-G., Scrap Books, V, 140; unidentified clipping dated Dec. 13, 1911.

[48]*Sunday World* (Toronto), Mar. 3, 1912.

[49]N.C.W., *Year Book* (1915), pp. 123-5. The organization, which was affiliated with the British Dominion Woman Suffrage Union, changed its name in 1915 to the National Equal Franchise Union. Much of its energy between 1914-18 was consumed in war work. The obvious duplication involved in the creation of this second would-be national organization appears to have been the result of personal ambition and pique on the part of its founder. This, at least, is the view of Mr. and Mrs. Merrill Denison, both of whom knew her well.

Legislative activities took on a much more hopeful tone in the 1912 session. At the outset the women's hopes swelled when N. W. Rowell, the Opposition leader, rose to criticize the speech from the throne for omitting all reference to the suffrage question.[50] Bills to extend the provincial franchise to women were introduced in this session by McDonald, Whiteside, and Studholme. Those by McDonald and Whiteside included property qualifications, but Studholme's waived that requirement. The McDonald bill received the unanimous backing of the Liberals, but all three were eventually lost. Yet two things emerged from the mêlée to give the suffragists some confidence for the future: N. W. Rowell had declared himself in favour of woman suffrage and Premier Whitney had said that if it were ever granted, it would be to all women, though for the present he believed the issue to be "dull and dead."[51]

In December of this same year, Sir Robert Borden visited Toronto. Seizing the opportunity to impress their views upon the prime minister of the dominion, a delegation from the Canadian Suffrage Association, including Mrs. Denison and the three doctors, waited upon Sir Robert and made a plea for federal enfranchisement. His reply, which placed the whole problem squarely at the doors of the provinces,[52] was in striking contrast with the attitude he adopted in 1917 during debates on the Wartime Elections Act.

Three franchise bills livened the 1913 session, those by McDonald and Studholme for provincial voting and one by J. C. Elliott to extend the long-sought municipal franchise to married women. All collapsed under heavy majorities on second reading, but one hope still remained. As third reading was reached on the municipal bill, a Conservative member rose to move an amendment permitting married women to vote. There was momentarily an optimistic belief that the government was behind this motion. That brief hope died

---

[50]*Canadian Annual Review* (1912), p. 328.
[51]*Ibid.*, p. 335. *Ontario: Journals, 1912*, pp. 94, 161, 199, 200, 211. *Globe*, Mar. 26, 1912.
[52]N.C.W., *Year Book* (1913), pp. xxx-xxxi.

when the amendment was crushed a few minutes later.[53]

Late in 1913 Dr. Margaret Gordon, still serving as president of the Toronto association and now also vice-president of the national association, decided upon a new strategy. This would entail mountainous efforts, but results might compensate. Dr. Gordon first asked the mayor and the Council of Toronto if they would agree to send a resolution to the legislature in 1914 endorsing municipal suffrage for married women. This they obligingly agreed to do (for the fourth time), but with the usual result that nothing happened. Foreseeing this, Dr. Gordon also persuaded the Council to hold a referendum on the subject in the municipal election of January 1, 1914. Because of splendid organization, the women won the referendum by a vote of 26,516 to 12,606, more than two to one.[54] This gave Dr. Gordon the ammunition she needed for the remarkable campaign she conducted during the next three years. Writing to approximately 850 town and city councils throughout Ontario, she announced the satisfying score in the Toronto referendum and urged these municipalities to afford their voters similar means of registering public opinion. She also pleaded that they bombard the legislature with resolutions and petitions. The results of this effort were three-fold: thirty-three referenda were held, all favourable; about one hundred and sixty councils petitioned the legislature; the legislature remained unmoved.[55] Such were the tribulations of these earnest women who were asking only for what today is considered a common right.

The 1914 session found the legislature again confronted with three suffrage bills, those by Elliott and Johnson offering the municipal vote to married women with property, Studholme's, for the third time, bestowing both provincial and municipal franchise upon all women who were British subjects and twenty-one years of age. After the municipal angle had

[53]*Ontario: Journals, 1913:* McDonald bill, pp. 27, 211-12; Elliott bill, pp. 66, 213; Studholme bill, pp. 107, 214; Macdiarmid amendment, pp. 368-70. *Globe*, Feb. 21, April 2, 1913.
[54]City Clerk of Toronto to the author, July 15, 1946.
[55]N.C.W., *Year Book* (1915), pp. xxxviii-xxxix, 35-6. H. Ridley, *Woman Suffrage*, p. 13. I. Harper *et al.*, *Woman Suffrage*, VI, 759-60.

been disposed of by a straight party vote, the East Hamilton member spoke at length on his much broader bill and warned the government that if it did not play fair with the women, it might find itself confronted with militancy. This threat failed to disturb the complacency of Acting Premier Foy who observed that the House had already defeated the municipal proposal and that the bill under consideration was much worse. The customary blow was then administered.[56]

At the close of the year another change took place in the presidency of the Canadian Suffrage Association: Mrs. Denison resigned and was succeeded by Dr. Gordon.[57] The Association took this occasion to honour the work of its great founder, Dr. Emily Stowe. A bronze bust of Dr. Stowe was presented to the city and placed in the main corridor of the City Hall.[58]

A new premier, Sir William Hearst, led the Conservative forces in the Ontario legislature in 1915. Ever hopeful that a change in leadership might produce some advantage, a deputation interviewed Premier Hearst on February 24. They reminded him of the favourable referendum on municipal voting in 1914 and pleaded that he submit the question of full suffrage to a provincial referendum. Sir William's reply immediately ended all hope that the change in Conservative leadership marked a change in policy. He pointed out that such a referendum, if held, would only reflect the wishes of men, whereas he desired an expression of opinion from women. (It should be noted that this was the first and last occasion on which Sir William seemed troubled about women's opinions.) He did not believe that women wanted the franchise and was not even convinced that their influence would be good if they had it.[59] The temperature inside the premier's office matched the wintry gusts outside as the women retired from the encounter.

That suffrage still had its supporters in the thin Liberal

[56]*Ontario: Journals, 1914*, pp. 15, 155, 213. *Globe*, Mar. 31 and April 7, 1914. *Canadian Annual Review* (1914), pp. 382-3.
[57]I. Harper *et al.*, *Woman Suffrage*, VI, 760-1.
[58]H. Ridley, *Woman Suffrage*, p. 14.
[59]*Ibid.*, p. 14. *Canadian Annual Review* (1915), pp. 482-3.

ranks of the legislature was clear, however, when J. C. Elliott again introduced his bill for municipal franchise. In the four days of debate devoted to the measure, the overwhelming majority of speakers were in favour. When Attorney-General Lucas argued in the face of numerous petitions presented during the session, that women did not want suffrage, Studholme referred to his remarks as "side-stepping baby-talk and fairy stories."[60] N. W. Rowell also stepped into the debate on the women's side; but despite the silence of the opposing forces, the bill went down 66 to 20 at the snap of the party whip. On the last day of the session, William McDonald vainly pleaded for second reading of his very mild provincial franchise measure, a bill which would have extended the vote only to unmarried women with property.[61] Studholme brought in no more bills, apparently feeling that antagonism to his sweeping measure and to himself personally made it advisable to throw his support to the milder measures of others.

In the opening days of 1916 the women won a thrilling victory in Manitoba, and in Alberta and Saskatchewan they seemed virtually assured of success in the spring sessions of their legislatures. Encouraged by the rising star of liberalism in the West, a delegation again appeared before Premier Hearst on March 1, only to meet with another disheartening reply.[62] McDonald and Elliott saw their perennial measures suffer the usual stinging defeat and in the course of the debates, Premier Hearst appeared at his reactionary worst. Remarking that Conservative and Liberal women were working side by side in war work, he thought it would be a serious mistake to introduce any measure which might serve to sow discord between them. (Premier Hearst saw no incongruity, however, in the strange phenomenon of Liberals and Conservatives fighting side by side on the fields of France.) "Now

---

[60]*Globe*, Mar. 11, 1915.
[61]*Ibid.*, Mar. 9, 11, and 16, April 2, 1915. *Canadian Annual Review* (1915), p. 483. *Ontario: Journals, 1915*, pp. 26, 128, 192, 231. For petitions see *Ibid.*, pp. 26, 34.
[62]*Globe*, Mar. 2, 1916.

is not the time to pass an act of this kind, not even in my opinion the time to debate it."[63] In the face of such unalterable reaction, small wonder that, while the women of Ontario loyally rejoiced over the victories of their prairie sisters, they felt some bitterness. Only bigotry, injustice, and defeat faced these women who had pioneered the suffrage movement, who had "borne the burden and heat of the day for a longer period than the women of any other province."[64]

Victory was approaching, however. The Liberal party officially endorsed woman suffrage shortly before the opening of the legislative session in 1917. Although N. W. Rowell had frequently spoken in favour of it, he had always done so in a private capacity, never as the leader of the party. The change in the party's official attitude was manifested in the very first few days of the session, after the speech from the throne made it obvious that the government had no intention of introducing a suffrage bill. On February 15 Rowell, as leader of the Opposition, moved an amendment to the address, calling for such a measure. This move seemed to catch Premier Hearst off guard and he sought refuge in an appeal to the speaker to declare the motion out of order. When, five days later, the speaker ruled in Sir William's favour, Rowell carried an appeal to the House which upheld the speaker's ruling by a straight party vote of 58 to 27.[65] Sir William was still in the saddle; but, within a week, he turned his horse's head and rode off furiously in the opposite direction.

Bills for provincial franchise had been introduced on February 15 by William McDonald and J. W. Johnson, a Conservative private member and new convert to the cause. These measures were scheduled for second reading on February 27. The appointed day found the House galleries crowded with suffragists, assembled, as they supposed, to witness another blow dealt to their hopes. As Johnson's bill was called, Sir William rose to speak. One can almost imagine

[63]Quotation is from H. Ridley, *Woman Suffrage*, p. 14.
[64]I. Harper *et al.*, *Woman Suffrage*, VI, 761.
[65]*Ontario: Journals, 1917*, pp. 26-7. *Globe*, Feb. 16 and 21, 1917.

the looks of incredulous surprise followed by smiles of intense satisfaction as the women in the gallery heard the premier express his complete conversion to their cause. Sir William paid eloquent tribute to the war work of women and said it was on this account he now believed they should be taken into partnership with men in the councils of the nation. He re-iterated his belief that the majority of women still did not wish the vote and tried to convey the impression that by backing such a measure, the Conservative party was far in advance of public opinion. This was too much for Rowell, who pointed out that the Liberals had been supporting suffrage measures since the introduction of the first McDonald bill in 1912. Then, setting party animosity aside, the Opposition leader congratulated the premier on his change of heart and said he hoped the two parties would join forces to make the passage of second reading unanimous, which they did.[66]

This same day the McDonald bill and two bills to give the municipal franchise to married women passed second reading. As the walls of conservative opposition fell with a loud crash on February 27, a small voice cried out, protesting that one rampart still remained. The veteran Labourite from Hamilton complained that the bill would not permit women to sit in the legislative assembly; but in the midst of the joyous uproar and confusion, his cry went temporarily unheard.[67]

It is difficult to believe that Sir William's conversion was the result of any sudden appreciation of women's heroic role in the Great War. The explanation must be sought elsewhere. As already noted, Manitoba enfranchised its women in January 1916. Saskatchewan, Alberta, and British Columbia followed shortly after, forming a solid block of suffrage territory west of Ontario. Beginning in 1910 the number of states which had granted suffrage to women rose rapidly in the neighbouring republic; and Lloyd George's accession to power in 1916 was a fairly sure indication that before long,

[66] *Ibid.*, Feb. 28, 1917. *Journal-Press* (Ottawa), Feb. 28, 1917. *Ontario: Journals, 1917*, pp. 14, 51.
[67] *Ibid.*, p. 51. *Globe*, Feb. 28, 1917.

women would be enfranchised in the mother country. As an astute political leader, Sir William could not continue indefinitely to ignore this rising tide of liberalism. Better to steer his bark with the onrushing current than be swamped trying to combat it.

Hearst's abrupt reversal of his previous stand might also have been influenced by pressure from the Conservative administration in Ottawa. Sir Robert Borden's government was faced by 1917 with the necessity of resorting to conscription in the not far distant future, a policy which was anathema to the great majority of French Canadians, as well as to many foreign-born citizens residing in the West. It is not unreasonable to assume that the dominion government was already giving some thought to a plan for securing a carefully selected electorate in preparation for the approaching federal election, which would be certain to hinge on the conscription issue. (Such a plan did materialize in the complicated Wartime Elections Act of September 1917.) Why then destroy the goodwill of a potential body of voters in Ontario, where Conservatism had flourished since 1905 and where the idea of conscription was generally warmly received, when support might be needed so desperately to offset those sections of the country opposing conscription?

Whatever his reasons may have been, Premier Hearst was suddenly unwilling that credit for such an innovation as woman suffrage should go to a Liberal or even to a private member of his own party. On March 30 he had his attorney-general introduce an Ontario Franchise Act and on April 5 an Ontario Elections Act "to make assurance doubly sure."[68] Both these measures were rushed through, and received royal assent on April 12, the last day of the session. Also passed at the same time was J. W. Johnson's bill conferring the municipal franchise upon married women, marking the successful culmination of a struggle lasting three decades.[69]

[68]Allan M. Dymond, *The Laws of Ontario Relating to Women and Children* (Toronto, 1923), p. 175.
[69]*Ontario: Journals, 1917*, pp. 188, 203, 242, 253, 257-8, 268, 270. *Statutes of Ontario, 1917*, ch. 5; ch. 6; ch. 43.

Unexpected and gratifying as were these victories of 1917, they still left women ineligible for office in either the provincial or municipal field. At the height of the excitement over enfranchising women, N. W. Rowell had introduced a bill to make it possible for women to be elected to the legislative assembly, but Premier Hearst spoke at length against the measure. Certainly, he was not opposed to the principle, but he felt that they had gone far enough for the present, and so the matter was dropped.[70] A similar attempt by J. C. Elliott in 1918 was defeated when Sir William announced that since provincial elections had been postponed, there was no need to "rush into" this proposition! Even the veteran supporter of the women's cause, William McDonald, opposed it on the ground there was no demand for it.[71] As though in answer to the latter, on June 13 the National Council of Women petitioned the Ontario government to give to women these final political privileges.[72]

By 1919, with elections looming ominously ahead, Sir William appears to have felt that the time had come. Now there was no deputizing of the disagreeable assignment to an understudy. On March 26 Premier Hearst boldly introduced bills to make women eligible for both the provincial assembly and municipal office-holding, and with a final dash of generosity, sponsored a measure to make farmers' wives and daughters eligible to serve as school trustees.[73] When these bills became laws on April 4, the women of Ontario reached the end of their long struggle.

Ontario, which bore the brunt of pioneering for women's rights, appropriately sent the first woman member to the dominion parliament. This was Agnes Macphail, who was elected in 1921 and re-elected four times thereafter. Though Ontario has sent no woman to the House of Commons since

---

[70]*Globe*, Mar. 8, 1917. *Ontario: Journals, 1917*, pp. 32, 80.
[71]N.C.W., *Year Book* (1918-19), p. 58. *Globe*, Mar. 22, 1918. *Ontario: Journals, 1918*, pp. 50, 174.
[72]N.C.W., *Year Book* (1918-19), p. 102.
[73]*Ontario: Journals, 1919*, pp. 71, 99, 104, 190, 194, 237, 239, 240. *Statutes of Ontario, 1919*, ch. 8; ch. 47; ch. 76. It should be remembered that the school franchise had previously been limited to women property owners.

1940, it led all provinces in the number of women candidates in the federal election of June 27, 1949. Of the six candidates, three had the endorsement of a major party—a boon not commonly conferred upon women.

At the provincial level, however, Ontario has exhibited greater conservatism. Not until 1940 were any women elected and then only two, one of them Agnes Macphail. The provincial election of 1945 returned a solid male contingent; but Miss Macphail won a seat in the provincial House for a second term on June 7, 1948.

# *3*

# THE PRAIRIE PROVINCES

## *Democracy's "Grass Roots"*

THE PRAIRIE PROVINCES, which were the first to achieve woman suffrage, had the shortest and easiest campaign to wage.   Only in Manitoba was there any considerable activity prior to 1910, or a struggle with an unfriendly government. In Saskatchewan and Alberta it was only necessary to arouse enough general interest in the issue to ask for and receive the franchise from governments that never denied the justice of the request.   Manitoba again was the only one of the three in which final victory was mainly attributable to the efforts of a well-organized suffrage society.   In the other provinces, the prime agitators were powerful farmers' organizations and their women's auxiliaries.

Throughout the prairie campaign the women received staunch support from their men.   This presents an interesting parallel with the United States where pioneer communities were invariably the first to enfranchise women.   On both sides of the border the feeling generally prevailed that women as well as men had opened up the country, had shared the experiences of settling a new land, and were therefore entitled to a voice in making the laws.   Reporting to the Provincial Equal Suffrage Board of Saskatchewan on the results of a delegation to Premier Scott in 1915, Mrs. S. V. Haight, the vice-president, said, "It is splendid the way our men stand behind us and back us up as they do in our work for the franchise."[1]

The men of the prairies gave their most effective support to woman suffrage through three powerful farm groups: the Grain Growers' Associations of Manitoba and Saskatchewan, and the United Farmers of Alberta. All had officially endorsed woman suffrage as early as 1912 (Manitoba in 1911) and all invited women to participate in their activities, either directly as members or through women's auxiliaries. This gave women the opportunity to organize for discussion of common problems and to feel a sense of partnership with men in both the economic and political spheres. Moreover, no prairie suffrage delegation ever set out for the Legislative Buildings without a strong supporting phalanx of men. When Premier Sifton of Alberta promised the introduction of a suffrage bill in 1916, he first made the pledge to James Speakman, president of the United Farmers.[2]

An effective role in the history of woman suffrage in these provinces was played by the *Grain Growers' Guide*, the weekly which was the official organ of the three prairie farm organizations. From its start in 1908 the paper had a woman's page where items on suffrage frequently appeared, but the real crusade of the *Guide* began in 1911 when George F. Chipman became editor-in-chief. Chipman discussed the movement in feature editorials and published scores of letters to the editor on the subject. In June 1912 he placed an ardent suffragist, Miss Francis M. Beynon, in charge of the women's page, which from that date became a forum for the dissemination of suffrage news and ideas. Attempting to prove that public opinion endorsed women's enfranchisement, the *Guide* held referenda on the question in 1912 and 1913, both of which were overwhelmingly favourable.[3] After final victory had been won in 1916, Chipman wrote a reminiscent editorial. He re-

[1]*Grain Growers' Guide* (Winnipeg), Nov. 19, 1913; June 30, 1915.
[2]*Ibid.*, Sept. 22, 1915.
[3]*Ibid.*, Feb. 12, 1913; Feb. 4, 1914. The 1912 referendum included only men and resulted in a vote of 2,957 in favour and 965 opposed. The referendum of the following year included both men and women with more satisfactory results: 6,121 in favour, 553 opposed.

called having received a letter from an irate Saskatchewan farmer in 1913, part of which ran: "If you don't stop advocating woman suffrage in your paper you can cancel my subscription. My wife gets the *Guide* and reads your articles to me at the supper table and it makes things very unpleasant in my house." The editor had replied that his paper stood for a fair deal for women as well as for men and that the farmer was at liberty to cancel if he wished. Chipman concluded the story: "Evidently he saw the light because he is still a subscriber and the women have the vote."[4]

The suffrage movement on Canada's prairie frontier, as in other parts of the dominion, was noticeably affected by foreign influences, but less swayed than any other section by developments in the British Isles. Stories of British suffragette atrocities never were given as much prominence in the prairie press as in Maritime and British Columbia papers. Mrs. A. V. Thomas, one of Manitoba's outstanding feminists, commented: "We resented very keenly the fact that some English women came out and tried to stampede us into taking violent methods. We had not yet used peaceful methods and we refused to do anything violent until we had. We did not need anything like that."[5]

From 1911 to 1916 the *Grain Growers' Guide* teemed with stories of progress in the United States. Roughly, nine out of every ten items of news about woman suffrage printed by this paper had their origins in the republic. The greatest of all prairie newspapers, the *Manitoba Free Press*, while not crusading with the *Guide's* intense zeal, found most of its foreign suffrage news in American sources. When in 1914 the Manitoba Liberals endorsed votes for women, their published campaign platform drew heavily upon reports of progress made in the United States as a justification for the position they took.[6]

In spite of whole-hearted support from farmers' organizations and from influential sections of the press, political

[4]*Ibid.*, Mar. 29, 1916.
[5]This was in 1912. Letter from Mrs. A. V. Thomas to the author, April 21, 1944.
[6]*Platform of the Manitoba Liberals, 1914* (Winnipeg, 1914), p. 53.

democracy did not come to the women of the prairies without a struggle. The real foe was a traitor within the camp— woman herself, through ignorance, indifference, or actual hostility. Ignorance was the chief affliction and that was fortunate, for it was the most easily cured. Having been shown the way, women of the prairies generally displayed marked enthusiasm. The work of education was complicated in these regions by the vast distances to be covered. With the zeal of missionaries, however, the pioneers of the movement rode and drove across the broad, flat wheatlands carrying their message and winning converts.

Manitoba was the first province of Canada to grant full political privileges to women. This action, typical of western progressiveness, made it much easier to overcome reactionary forces in other provinces.

The movement in Manitoba began early. For the first faint stirrings, it is necessary to go back to the beginning of the 1890's when a group of Icelandic women founded the pioneer suffrage organization in the province, and for that matter in the entire West. While the actual date of the society's birth is unknown, it seems to have grown and prospered, and was followed later by other Icelandic suffrage groups including both men and women. Although they sometimes collaborated with English-speaking groups in delegations to the government, they carried on their own campaign for a quarter of a century by frequent petitions to the legislature and through articles in the Icelandic press. Their outstanding leader and editor was Mrs. M. J. Benedictsen, who carried on a sporadic correspondence with Dr. Stowe-Gullen and other Toronto suffragists.[7]

The first English-speaking organization to espouse the suffrage cause in Manitoba was the W.C.T.U., through its committee on legislation and franchise. The earliest available report of its activities is for 1893, but from that it is evident

---

[7]*Grain Growers' Guide*, July 7, 1920.  This issue contains a valuable article by A. A. Perry, "Winning the Franchise."  N.C.W., *Year Book* (1910), p. XXVII. A. S.-G., Scrap Books, VI, 30.

that the group had already been carrying on active suffrage work for a year or two. At its annual meeting in 1893, the W.C.T.U. adopted a very forthright suffrage resolution and petitioned the legislature that "the rights of citizens be not denied on account of sex."[8]

Included among the officers of the W.C.T.U. at this time were Mrs. E. A. Blakely, Mrs. J. A. McClung (mother-in-law of the much more famous Mrs. Nellie McClung), Mrs. B. Playfair, Dr. Amelia Yeomans, and Miss E. Cora Hind, all of whom played an important part in the movement in Manitoba.

Amelia Yeomans, an ardent temperance worker, was born in Montreal in 1842. She married Dr. Augustus Yeomans in 1860 and settled in Madoc, Ont. Widowed in 1878, she and her eldest daughter, Lillian, became interested in the study of medicine and graduated from the Ann Arbor Medical School in the early 1880's. Dr. Amelia, who was practising in Winnipeg by 1885, is thought to be the first woman physician of Manitoba. Interested in temperance before woman suffrage, she crusaded actively for both throughout the 1890's, but gradually gave up her earlier enthusiasms and even her medical practice to devote all her attention to evangelism. She died in Calgary in 1913.[9]

E. Cora Hind (whose initials were well known in agricultural circles throughout the dominion and around the world) won fame as a newspaperwoman during her long years of association with the *Manitoba Free Press*, but gained even greater renown as an agricultural expert. Her annual predictions on the size of the Canadian wheat crop (published in the *Free Press*) were phenomenal for their accuracy. Anxiously awaited by grain dealers and speculators across the country, they were also relayed to all parts of the world.

To place the equal rights question before the public, Dr. Yeomans and the W.C.T.U. staged a Mock Parliament in the Bijou Theatre, Winnipeg, on the evening of February 9, 1893.

[8]E. Luke, "Woman Suffrage," p. 335. A. A. Perry, "Winning the Franchise." *Manitoba: Journals, 1893,* pp. 20, 23.
[9]Information supplied by Mrs. Constance K. Sissons, niece of Dr. Yeomans, and relayed to the author by Miss Aileen Garland of Winnipeg, Jan. 13, 1947.

NELLIE L. McCLUNG

EMILY FERGUSON MURPHY

Unlike most such performances, this parliament was completely serious, with five speakers presenting arguments pro and con, and Dr. Yeomans herself gravely enacting the role of premier. Two days earlier, the legislature had received a petition from Dr. Yeomans suggesting that it adjourn for the evening to permit its members to attend. Although there was no adjournment, the *Manitoba Evening Free Press* counted twenty members in the audience and concluded its report of the very successful undertaking: "There is little doubt that wiser and better men left the house than entered it during the early part of the evening."[10]

More than a year elapsed between the Mock Parliament and the founding of the Manitoba Equal Franchise Club in November 1894. In the meantime the W.C.T.U. had presented a second petition bearing two thousand signatures and had witnessed the humiliating debut of the first provincial franchise measure in the 1894 session of the legislature.[11] Introduced on February 22, the bill was to have received second reading the next day. Many women were in the galleries on this occasion, hoping to hear a spirited plea for their enfranchisement. However, the *Manitoba Evening Free Press* of February 24 reported: "When the Speaker called the order for Second Reading of the bill, the promoter, Mr. Ironside, condensed his thoughts on the subject in the brief observation, 'Not printed.' "

This unhappy experience persuaded Dr. Yeomans that the time had come for an out-and-out suffrage society. Moreover, at a recent gathering of the National Council of Women in Ottawa, Dr. Yeomans had been appointed provincial president of the Dominion Women's Enfranchisement Association, which made her the logical leader to take the initiative in this matter. Following a meeting of the Central W.C.T.U. in Winnipeg on November 23, Dr. Yeomans asked those interested in suffrage to remain for a special meeting. Her address to this group set forth the justice and commonsense of her cause, and at its

[10]*Manitoba Evening Free Press and Sun* (Winnipeg), Feb. 10, 1893.  A. A. Perry, "Winning the Franchise."  *Manitoba: Journals, 1893*, pp. 10, 15.
[11]*Ibid., 1894*, pp. 62, 68, 88.

conclusion, Cora Hind made the motion which resulted in the formation of the first English-speaking suffrage organization west of Ontario. While men were welcomed as members, Dr. Yeomans urged that women should be chosen as officers to give them much needed practice in planning and organizing. Dr. Yeomans was elected president of the new-born suffrage group.[12] For about a decade this small band of feminists worked quietly, receiving little publicity, resorting to nothing spectacular, yet subtly moulding the opinions of those with whom they came in contact. After Dr. Yeomans moved away from Winnipeg, the Club expired for lack of leadership and the Icelandic groups were left to carry on by themselves.[13]

Manitoba women had received a small measure of their legislature's attention in the two closing decades of the nineteenth century and some slight progress in political status was made. Women property owners, whether married or single, were given the right to vote in municipal elections by an act of 1887, and the school franchise, including eligibility to serve as trustees, was granted to women ratepayers in 1890.[14] The inclusion of married women was an unusually generous gesture for those early days, most provinces regarding such a step an open invitation to domestic insurrection.

The path to provincial franchise, however, was thornier. During the discussion of a proposed plebiscite on prohibition in 1892, Kenneth McKenzie dared assert that the legislature "would never have the right sentiment of the country until the fair sex had the franchise." Though not disputing this gallant idea, the lawmakers were quite content to deny the province "the right sentiment" for the time being, as they demonstrated two days later by voting down James Huston's motion to extend the provincial franchise to women.[15]

Following the presentation of the first W.C.T.U. petition in 1893, expectations ran high that a suffrage bill would be

[12]*Manitoba Free Press*, Nov. 24, 1894.   A. S.-G., Scrap Books, V, 51, 59.
[13]A. A. Perry, "Winning the Franchise."
[14]*Statutes of Manitoba, 1887*, ch. 10; *1890*, ch. 38.
[15]*Manitoba Evening Free Press and Sun*, April 13, 1892.  *Manitoba Daily Free Press*, April 15, 1892.

introduced. Forecasting such a bill, the editor of the *Evening Free Press* conceded that many people had been converted by the recent Mock Parliament, but then launched into a bitter and unreasonable attack, concluding: ". . . the introduction of such a measure is to be deprecated. It is not seemly that the time of the Legislature should be wasted in such pleasant fooling as that would be, while if meant in all seriousness the objection to it is greater still and of a much graver sort." This forward-looking newsman doubtless felt considerable satisfaction when the proposed bill was watered down to a mere resolution and defeated 28 to 11 a few days later.[16]

The tone of this paper was remarkably changed a year later when the first provincial franchise bill was introduced by Robert Ironside. In an editorial entitled "Place Aux Dames," the editor took the most commonly used argument in opposition—that women did not want the vote—and suggested that the government hold a plebiscite among the women to let them "determine their own political fate."[17] In spite of this endorsement and the large W.C.T.U. petition, the Ironside bill died young, as previously noted, after its sponsor showed the white feather when second reading was called.[18] This ended all suffrage activity in the legislature for more than a decade.

During the first twelve years of the twentieth century, the Manitoba suffrage movement lay in the doldrums. Though there was quiet and unpublicized action by the W.C.T.U. and Icelandic groups, the issue on the surface appeared lifeless. An early generation of suffrage leaders had spent its force and a second generation had yet to gain its momentum.

Quite apart from the "breathing spell" theory, there is another hypothesis which may help to explain the inactivity of suffrage forces in Manitoba—and in British Columbia and the Maritime Provinces—in the first ten or twelve years of

---

[16]*Manitoba Evening Free Press and Sun*, Feb. 8 and 21, Mar. 1 and 3, 1893.
[17]*Ibid.*, Feb. 17, 1894. Mr. Molyneux St. John replaced Mr. William F. Luxton as editor of the *Free Press* in 1894. This probably accounts for the graceful editorial somersault.
[18]*Ibid.*, Feb. 24, 1894. A. A. Perry, "Winning the Franchise." *Manitoba: Journals, 1894*, p. 88.

the new century. Throughout the dominion this was an era of prosperity, and during good times agitation on all scores is likely to be less. Around 1912 money began to tighten up again, inducing people in all walks of life to seek remedies for their dissatisfaction through legislative reforms of one sort or another.

Then, too, this was a period of tremendous growth in western Canada. Canadian women who, with their families, were filling in the vast stretches of prairie land were busy getting adjusted to their new surroundings and had small opportunity to attend meetings or promote agitations of any sort. As Dr. Margaret McWilliams remarked in a letter to the author, "There were other work and other interests for everyone. Things were prospering and there was plenty to occupy their minds and hands. They did not see any necessity for the suffrage—the world was theirs anyway."

A faint stirring of interest was apparent in 1906 after the legislature took the reactionary step of barring married women from municipal voting.[19] Adopting the attitude that they had made a mistake which they were hastening to rectify, the lawmakers restored the privilege without debate in 1907[20] and for the next seven years were untroubled by the suffrage problem, except for an infrequent petition.

Although the legislature under the Conservative Roblin regime remained deaf and blind to the question, there were signs in 1910 of a renewed interest in other quarters. Two petitions from Icelandic groups were circulated through the province and found their way to the Legislative Buildings.[21] Readers of the *Grain Growers' Guide* could not fail to be affected by its contagious enthusiasm as it filled many of its columns with suffrage news from across the border. A Woman's Labor League which was formed in Winnipeg that year had for one of its avowed objectives the attainment of woman

[19]*Ibid.*, *1906*, pp. 13, 18, 164, 168. *Statutes of Manitoba, 1906*, ch. 51. *Manitoba Free Press*, Mar. 16, 1906.
[20]*Ibid.*, Jan. 18, 1907. *Statutes of Manitoba, 1907*, ch. 27. *Manitoba: Journals, 1907*, pp. 14, 28, 113, 116.
[21]*Ibid.*, *1910*, pp. 14, 22, 79, 91.

suffrage.[22] More important by far was the official endorsement of the movement by the powerful Grain Growers' Association of Manitoba in 1911.

Not until 1912, however, did suffrage once more attain its real stride. The cause for this renascence of the movement was the founding, during the early months of 1912, of the Winnipeg Political Equality League, one of the most enterprising and successful suffrage organizations in the dominion.[23] During the five short years of its existence, the League educated and agitated with such intelligent planning and intensity of purpose that the forces of reaction were routed.

Mrs. A. V. Thomas, founder and first president of the League, has explained its origin as a direct outcome of an unsuccessful attempt by a small group of Winnipeg women to secure from the Roblin government laws to better the social and economic status of women.[24] When peaceful overtures failed, the progressive forces were mobilized for a fight to the finish. With the willing co-operation of such groups as the W.C.T.U., the Grain Growers' Association, and the Direct Legislation League, the society was launched in the spring of 1912. From the start, men and women worked side by side in this group as officers and members, some of the most active being Mr. and Mrs. A. V. Thomas, Dr. Mary Crawford, Mr. and Mrs. F. J. Dixon, Miss Cora Hind, Mrs. Nellie McClung, Miss Francis M. Beynon, Mrs. A. G. Hample, Miss May Clendenan, Mrs. A. A. Perry, Mrs. Luther Holling, Mrs. C. P. Walker, Miss Kennethe Haig, and Mr. Percy Wilson. The favourable publicity invariably given to the League by the Winnipeg press was not surprising since at least ten

[22]*Grain Growers' Guide*, Nov. 9, 1910. The Labor Party of Manitoba had endorsed suffrage for women as early as 1902.

[23]Its name was changed to Manitoba Political Equality League in 1913 to indicate its provincial, rather than purely local, scope.

[24]Letter to the author from Mrs. A. V. Thomas, April 21, 1944. Nellie L. McClung, *The Stream Runs Fast* (Toronto, 1945), pp. 101-10. Mrs. McClung states that the seeds of a suffrage organization were planted at the weekly gatherings of the Canadian Women's Press Club. When it was found that the Local Council of Women refused to become "assoiciated with any controversial subject," a full-fledged suffrage association was deemed essential.

members were journalists.[25] Mrs. Thomas was the wife of a prominent newspaperman and had won recognition in her own right as Lillian Laurie of the *Manitoba Free Press*. (Her writing in more recent years has been done under the name of Lillian Beynon Thomas.) It is a remarkable coincidence that Mrs. Thomas and her sister, Francis M. Beynon, were able to use a pronounced journalistic talent in the cause of political equality.

The Manitoba Suffrage League was never affiliated with any similar group outside the province, though overtures were made to it by the Canadian Suffrage Association in Toronto.[26] The League's attitude was that they had a peculiar problem of their own, that they knew how to cope with it, and that mingling with other groups might only serve to dissipate their energy.

In March 1913 Dr. Mary E. Crawford, a Winnipeg physician, was elected president, a position she filled until the disbanding of the League in 1917. Under her leadership a campaign to raise money and gain publicity was begun. The members voted to raise $2,500 to maintain a paid organizer, to print suffrage literature, and to conduct an educational programme. They appointed a literature committee under the chairmanship of Miss Winona Flett (later Mrs. F. J. Dixon) and directed the drawing up of a pamphlet explaining why Manitoba women desired the vote. Mrs. A. V. Thomas became chairman of a speakers' bureau which offered to furnish well-trained spokesmen for any organization in any part of the province. The president herself was assigned the task of preparing a pamphlet on the legal status of women in Manitoba, and this was published late in 1913.[27] The League planned to draw up a petition for presentation at the 1914 session

[25]A. A. Perry, "Winning the Franchise." Interview with Miss Beynon, April 27, 1944. Smaller Minute Book of the Political Equality League of Manitoba, Mar. 29, 1912-Mar. 31, 1914 (in the Provincial Library of Manitoba); has no pagination. Hereafter cited as P.E.L. Minute Book.

[26]*Ibid.*, June 1912.

[27]Mary E. Crawford, *Legal Status of Women in Manitoba* (Winnipeg, 1913). Dr. Crawford received her medical degree from the University of Toronto in 1900 and started practice in Winnipeg in 1901. She became president of the Women's University Club of Winnipeg in 1909.

and made an unsuccessful attempt to induce Dr. Harvey Simpson to introduce a suffrage bill at the same time. Clergymen, several of whom had shown friendliness to the cause, were requested to include woman suffrage in an occasional sermon. In November 1913 a Women's Civic League was organized under the auspices of the Political Equality League to gather together the women who held the municipal franchise, urge them to use their vote, and present to them issues of public concern. A hundred suffrage banners were printed to adorn Winnipeg street-cars. But the most ambitious and successful publicity project of the year was the booth at the Stampede in August. There the League handed out literature, sold souvenirs, made speeches, and secured hundreds of signatures for its petition.[28] The editor of the *Grain Growers' Guide* reported that visitors from the American states where women voted gave courage to the Canadian suffragists by expressing sympathy with their cause, whereas Canadians were more likely to be divided in their opinions. Miss Beynon went further and expressed indignation over the insults received by attendants at the booth from certain women. "I am ashamed to have to say it, but the rudeness of women has helped to win the sympathy of many men." Though a minority sneered, the great majority of visitors, both men and women, said they were much in favour of woman suffrage.[29]

Feeling that the time had finally arrived to come to grips with the reactionary government, a powerful delegation was organized to meet the premier, Sir Rodmond Roblin, on January 27, 1914. In this effort the League was joined by many other organizations including the Icelandic Woman's Suffrage Association, the Grain Growers' Association, the W.C.T.U., the Trades and Labor Council, the Canadian Women's Press Club, and the Y.W.C.A. The slate of five speakers (two women and three men) was headed by Mrs. Nellie McClung.

Born in Ontario in 1873, Nellie McClung travelled west

[28]P.E.L. Minute Book, 1913. *Grain Growers' Guide*, Nov. 19, 1913.
[29]*Ibid.*, Aug. 20 and 27, 1913. The quotation is from the latter.

with her pioneering family in 1880. She graduated from the Winnipeg Normal School and taught school until her marriage to R. W. McClung in 1896. Mrs. McClung became famous as the author of novels, sketches of prairie life, and two autobiographical works. Her unusual gift for public speaking brought her countless demands for platform appearances from one end of the country to the other. Deep-seated convictions about the necessity for prohibition and the justice of political equality led Nellie McClung into the Manitoba woman suffrage movement at an early age. After her family moved to Alberta in 1914, she divided her activities in the movement between her new home and the old. Apparently her energy was truly inexhaustible. On August 25, 1946 Mr. and Mrs. McClung celebrated their golden wedding anniversary, a cruel blow to the theory that feminism is certain to wreck happy home life.

In her first official encounter with the Conservative premier, Nellie McClung, as usual, made a top-flight address. Sir Rodmond listened attentively until all five speakers had finished and then in a lengthy reply, which at times verged upon a harangue, showed himself unalterably opposed to the movement. He charged that it would break up the home and "throw children into the arms of servant girls," that in Colorado where women had the vote "they shrank from the polls as from a pestilence." Replying to Mrs. McClung's charges of corruption in the government and goaded by frequently audible sounds of mirth among his audience, Sir Rodmond lost his temper completely and shouted: ". . . consequently, when you say things are corrupt, it is only the imaginations of a wicked and vile mind." At another point, after his listeners had protested with murmurs of "No! No!" the premier snapped back: "I say so. I did not dispute you when you were speaking. You will be good enough to listen to my reply." But the irrepressible Nellie McClung's parting salvo was, "I believe we'll get you yet, Sir Rodmond!"[30]

[30]*Ibid.*, Feb. 4, 1914. *Canadian Annual Review* (1914), p. 572. P.E.L. Minute Book, 1914. The quotations are from the very complete account of the delegation found in the *Manitoba Free Press*, Jan. 28, 1914. *Platform of the Manitoba Liberals, 1914*, p. 51.

On the next evening, January 28, the League packed the Walker Theatre to capacity. The entertainment began innocently enough with the singing of some songs and the presentation of the inevitable "How the Vote Was Won." Then came the highlight of the evening, the Women's Parliament, with Nellie McClung in the role of premier. Here was her great opportunity, and she made the most of it. To a delegation of suppliant males seeking the franchise, "Premier" McClung addressed a speech which was a devastatingly clever paraphrase of Sir Rodmond's words on the previous day. The flavour of Nellie McClung's wit is rich even in excerpts, a few of which follow:

We wish to compliment this delegation on their splendid gentlemanly appearance. If, without exercising the vote, such splendid specimens of manhood can be produced, such a system of affairs should not be interfered with. Any system of civilization that can produce such splendid specimens . . . is good enough for me, and if it is good enough for me it is good enough for anybody. Another trouble is that if men start to vote they will vote too much. Politics unsettles men, and unsettled men mean unsettled bills—broken furniture, broken vows and divorce.

It has been charged that politics is corrupt. I don't know how this report got out, but I do most emphatically deny it. . . . I have been in politics for a long time and I never knew of any corruption or division of public money among the members of the house, and you may be sure that if anything of that kind had been going on I should have been in on it.

The audience rocked in their seats, convulsed with laughter. As the curtain went down, a great bouquet of red roses was handed up to the star of the performance. The *Free Press* reported that it was a token of appreciation from two Opposition members who had escaped from a stuffy civic function to enjoy Mrs. McClung's barbed wit.[31]

Financially, success was overwhelming; enough was realized to finance all the rest of the campaign. But much more important were the intangible results. Overnight suffrage had become respectable and fashionable. People who had been indifferent and in some cases frankly hostile hastened to jump

[31]P.E.L. Minute Book, 1914. *Manitoba Free Press*, Jan. 29, 1914. Winnipeg *Free Press News Bulletin*, Jan. 29, 1914. The quotations will be found in these two press reports. Letter to the author from Mrs. A. V. Thomas, April 21, 1944. Nellie L. McClung, *op. cit.*, pp. 111-122. The latter gives to Mrs. Thomas the credit for originating the idea of the "Parliament."

on the bandwagon. The evening's ridicule was later considered in some quarters to have been a factor in the downfall of the Roblin government the following year.[32]

Success was tempered somewhat by a setback in the legislature on February 13, 1914. An Opposition motion, introduced by G. H. J. Malcolm, to give women the provincial franchise was voted down, 32 to 12, by a straight party vote after Premier Roblin announced he would regard its passage as "want of confidence." The galleries that day were crowded with women who at least had the satisfaction of hearing several Liberal members champion their cause.[33]

This disappointment was compensated for, however, when the Liberal party held its pre-election convention in March. Invited by the Liberals to appear before them at their final session, Mrs. McClung and Mrs. Thomas made addresses which brought the delegates cheering to their feet. Immediately thereafter the convention adopted by unanimous vote a plank promising an equal franchise measure "upon it being established by petition that this is desired by adult women to a number equivalent to fifteen per cent of the vote cast at the preceding general election in this Province."[34]

In the election campaign which ensued, Premier Roblin and the Conservatives took a strong stand against woman suffrage. A printed booklet entitled *Record of the Roblin Government* devoted two entire pages to a list of reasons why suffrage should not be granted to women, charging that it would degenerate true womanhood, emotionalize balloting, and be "illogical and absurd" as far as Manitoba was concerned. "Wifehood, motherhood and politics cannot be associated together with satisfactory results."[35] Provoked by such arguments, the League threw itself into the campaign on the Liberal side. As might be expected, the most trenchant

[32]Letter from Mrs. A. V. Thomas, April 21, 1944. Letter from Mrs. Violet McNaughton, Nov. 17, 1943. Interview with Miss Francis Beynon, April 27, 1944.
[33]*Canadian Annual Review* (1914), p. 584. *Platform of the Manitoba Liberals, 1914,* p. 52.
[34]*Ibid.*, pp. 3, 50. *Canadian Annual Review* (1914), p. 590. *Manitoba Free Press,* Mar. 28, 1914.
[35]*Record of the Roblin Government, 1900-1914* (Winnipeg, 1914), pp. 168-70.

stump-speaker was Nellie McClung, who, more than ever, was out to "get" Sir Rodmond. Large crowds assembled wherever she was scheduled to appear and were delighted with speeches which were masterpieces of logical argument seasoned with humour.[36] A week before election day the Political Equality League staged a "Suffrage Week in Manitoba" to place squarely before the voters' eyes what, to the League, was the paramount issue of the campaign. The *Grain Growers' Guide* also leaped into the fray, urging its readers to do justice to women and turn Roblin out.[37] When the votes were counted, the Conservatives had won, but by an uncomfortably slim majority of four. Hope was high in the ranks of Liberals and in the hearts of women that some means could soon be found to turn the tables completely.

As 1914 drew to a close the League was able to report a rapidly spreading membership, particularly in outlying districts of the province, which were their chief concern. A minor success in Winnipeg was the election of the first woman school trustee.[38]

The Manitoba Grain Growers' Association, which had been giving the women splendid support in their struggle ever since 1911, took a step towards greater democracy in their own organization at the Brandon convention in January 1915, when they offered full-fledged membership to women upon payment of half-fee. The women gladly accepted the offer, upon one condition—that membership dues be the same for all. This condition was accepted with cheers and laughter.[39]

A month later the League held its first annual convention, primarily for the purpose of stimulating the growth of branch associations throughout the province. To this end a provincial executive was elected, headed by Dr. Crawford, Mrs. Richardson, and Mrs. Thomas. Mrs. Richardson was particularly valuable in this work for she came from the remote little settlement of Roaring River and knew at first hand the

---

[36]*Canadian Annual Review* (1914), p. 604. *Manitoba Free Press*, July 7, 1914.
[37]*Grain Growers' Guide*, July 1 and 8, 1914.
[38]*Ibid.*, Dec. 23, 1914. The trustee was Mrs. J. K. Brown.
[39]*Ibid.*, Jan. 20, 1915.

problems of organizing in rural regions.⁴⁰ A highlight of the
two-day convention was another joint delegation to Premier
Roblin. The fireworks of the previous interview were missing—perhaps because Mrs. McClung had moved to Alberta.
Sir Rodmond complimented the delegation on the excellence
of their speeches and promised to take the matter "under
advisement."⁴¹ However, when T. C. Norris, the Opposition
leader, introduced a suffrage resolution a few weeks later, it
was narrowly defeated by the Conservatives who followed
their chieftain's bidding.⁴²

This proved to be Premier Roblin's last opportunity to
balk woman suffrage, for in May 1915 the news broke of a
scandal in connection with the construction of the new Parliament Buildings. Sir Rodmond was forced to resign and T. C.
Norris became premier, necessitating another provincial election in August. The Political Equality League now had two
big tasks: to secure the election of the Liberals and to get the
petition which the Liberals had asked for signed before the
next session of the legislature.

The campaign of those summer months was wild with
excitement. In July the Conservative party, reorganized
under Sir James Aikens, attempted to make a come-back by
adopting all the principal planks of the Liberals, including
woman suffrage, prohibition, and direct legislation. Nellie
McClung, who had returned from Alberta to take part in the
fight, acknowledged the belated recognition from the Conservatives in a speech at Portage la Prairie on August 3:
"Thank-you, gentlemen, for thinking of us, unworthy though
we be."⁴³ The *Free Press* attacked two French language papers
(*Le Manitoba* and *La Liberté*) because of their stand against

⁴⁰The Roaring River Suffrage Association, organized in 1913 in a community
so small it does not appear on most maps, was probably the earliest branch
association outside of Winnipeg. It was extremely lively and kept the outside
world informed of its activities through Miss Beynon's column in the *Grain
Growers' Guide.* (See April 8, 1914.)
    ⁴¹*Manitoba Free Press*, Feb. 20, 1915.   *Grain Growers' Guide*, Feb. 24, 1915.
    ⁴²*Ibid.*, May 26, 1915.
    ⁴³*Manitoba Free Press*, Aug. 14, 1915.   *Canadian Annual Review* (1915), p.
631.   *Grain Growers' Guide*, Aug. 4, 1915.

woman suffrage.[44] George F. Chipman used all his eloquence in the *Guide* to sway the rural ridings to the Liberals.

The balloting on August 6, 1915 gave Premier Norris an overwhelming victory, and hope loomed high on the horizon for Manitoba women. The industry of the League and other loyal volunteers in securing signatures for the petition was such that by October 1 they had reached the requisite seventeen thousand; but with two months still to go, they raised their goal to thirty thousand. On December 23 a delegation of sixty men and women presented two petitions to Premier Norris. The first official petition contained 39,584 names. A separate petition contained 4,250 names gathered by ninety-four-year old Mrs. Amelia Burritt of Sturgeon Creek. The new premier was most cordial to the delegates and promised the early introduction of a woman suffrage bill.[45]

In the midst of these amicable proceedings, a hitch occured of which no record can be found in the press of the time. A letter from Mrs. A. V. Thomas, in the author's possession, tells how just one day before the legislature was to meet she was permitted to see the draft of the proposed bill. She was chilled to discover that, while it granted enfranchisement to women, it was not framed to permit them to sit in the legislature. When Mrs. Thomas's protest over the omission did no good, she telephoned every member of the League to exert pressure on their provincial representatives. She also informed her sister, Francis Beynon, who was attending the Grain Growers' convention in Brandon. Miss Beynon's threat to bring the matter to the attention of the convention quickly brought results and the bill was changed. Mrs. Thomas concludes her story: "It was a long time before the Premier would speak to me. However, we made it up before he died."[46]

This incident did nothing to mar the rejoicing which accompanied the passage of the bill through the various legislative stages. Introduced by Premier Norris on January 10,

[44]*Manitoba Free Press*, July 28 and 29, Sept. 4, 1915.
[45]*Grain Growers' Guide*, Dec. 29, 1915; Jan. 5, 1916.  N.C.W., *Year Book* (1917), pp. 83, 84.
[46]Letter to the author from Mrs. A. V. Thomas, April 21, 1944.

1916, it passed second reading unanimously four days later. Third reading on January 27 was a historic occasion; the oldest member of the House declared he had never seen anything like it in his life. Galleries were filled to overflowing with eager and excited women. As a special mark of courtesy, eight members of the League occupied seats on the floor of the assembly. Third reading was moved by Acting Premier T. H. Johnson, son of an Icelandic suffrage pioneer. Johnson gave a lengthy supporting speech, followed by several others, many in a humorous vein. One lone member, Joseph Hamelin, said he would be untrue to his convictions if he did not state his belief that the bill would lead to domestic discord—but he was going to vote for it anyway. Then came the vote, which was unanimous, and the whole chamber broke into an uproar of desk-thumping, cheers, and laughter from legislators and spectators alike. The baritones of the lawmakers vied with the sopranos of the women in the strains of "For They Are Jolly Good Fellows." Next day, January 28,[47] royal assent was given, and for the first time in Canadian history women were granted the provincial suffrage.[48]

In some post-victory reflections, Francis Beynon gave a vivid picture of what this achievement had cost in effort and also some sound advice to the thousands of women still unenfranchised in other parts of the dominion.

"An easy victory," some people say, who, looking on from a safe distance, have no conception of the drudgery that has been undergone by the members of the P.E.L. during the four strenuous years of its life. Nor do they take into account the fact that this was merely a final outcropping of a sentiment that had been patiently fostered by one society after another for more than twenty years.

After mentioning some of the great milestones like the Stampede and the Women's Parliament, she added:

Between these brilliant episodes, these highlights of publicity which caught the imagination of the public, were long drab stretches of tedious detail and

[47]This was two years to the day after the celebrated Women's Parliament.
[48]The best account of the proceedings of January 27 is in the *Manitoba Free Press*, Jan. 28, 1916. See also the *Canadian Annual Review* (1916), p. 658. Victoria *Daily Times*, Jan. 28, 1927. *Grain Growers' Guide*, Feb. 2, 1916. *Manitoba: Journals, 1916*, pp. 11, 18, 25, 43, 47. *Statutes of Manitoba, 1916*, ch. 36.

drudgery. . . . Indeed, if there is any lesson in the success of the women of Manitoba for the less fortunate provinces of Canada, it is the necessity of getting a great body of people working for this reform. Every such movement will have its outstanding women, who by their force of character and platform ability will make a magnificent contribution to the cause. . . . But back of this there must be a great body of quiet workers who act like a leaven upon the solid mass of public opinion. . . . Their work is complementary and both are essential to the success of any great movement.[49]

The victory in Manitoba in January 1916 gave considerable anxiety to certain elements of the Roman Catholic press, not only in Manitoba but also in far-off Quebec. This reaction drew warm replies from the *Free Press*. Particularly did the *Free Press* resent a lengthy and reactionary editorial on suffrage appearing in *L'Action Catholique*, the unofficial organ of the Roman Catholic archdiocese of Quebec.

Samples of the dirges being chanted by the ultramontane press of Canada . . . have been given on this page. These clerical sighings are, of course, what one would expect. Clericalism and democracy are mutually exclusive terms. For clericalism implies that the mass of ordinary people possess insufficient wisdom to direct their own destinies and need the guidance of superior persons who, of course, are the clerics. Thus it comes that every extension of democratic government is gall and wormwood to clericalism.[50]

A few additional minor political concessions were granted women in succeeding years of the Norris administration. An act of 1917 made women eligible for all municipal offices, provided they had property qualifications,[51] and further measures were passed in 1918 and 1919 placing married women on a basis of complete equality with their husbands in both municipal and school affairs.[52]

The Political Equality League planned at first to continue as a Political Education League, to train women in the use of their newly acquired rights and to press for social and economic reforms. However, with the surging pressure of a great

[49]*Grain Growers' Guide*, Feb. 9, 1916. Yet nowhere but in the Prairie Provinces was there ever anything remotely resembling a "solid mass of public opinion" for woman suffrage.
[50]*Manitoba Free Press*, Feb. 16 and 21, 1916. This quotation was given at some length because it foreshadows the long and tedious struggle facing the women of Quebec.
[51]*Statutes of Manitoba, 1917*, ch. 57.
[52]*A Review of the Administration of the Provincial Government—Manitoba, 1915-1920* (n.p., n.d.), p. 5. *Statutes of Manitoba, 1918*, ch. 67; *1919*, ch. 59.

drive removed, interest diminished to such a point that the League disbanded in 1917.[53]

Performance in the field of practical politics has fallen short of the promise held out by Manitoba women in their zeal for political equality. The province has never returned a woman to the dominion House of Commons and has elected only two to the provincial legislature: Mrs. Edith Rogers (1920-32) and Miss Salome Halldorson (1936-41).

Alberta,[54] a pioneer community, has almost always displayed a liberal attitude towards women. Alberta was the first province to elect a woman to the legislature, the first to appoint a woman judge, and followed closely the example of British Columbia in bestowing cabinet rank upon a woman.

Judge J. Boyd McBride, long a resident of the province, attributes the relative ease with which Alberta women won political recognition mainly to public appreciation of their heroic pioneering qualities. In addition, many of the women who migrated to Alberta "by early environment, by university education, and because of interest in public affairs, were quite as fitted as men to take their part in the intellectual and administrative development of the new country."[55]

From 1885 to 1905 Alberta was part of the Northwest Territories. During this period there is no evidence of any suffrage agitation, though the Ordinances of the Northwest Territories do reveal some small advances in women's political status. While women were barred from municipal voting and office-holding by an ordinance of 1885, another ordinance of that year permitted unmarried women with sufficient real property qualifications to be both school electors and trus-

[53]*Grain Growers' Guide*, Feb. 23 and Mar. 1, 1916. Letter to the author from Mrs. A. V. Thomas, April 21, 1944.

[54]Technically, Alberta was the third province to enfranchise women. Although the legislature of Alberta was the second in the dominion to vote for woman suffrage (on Mar. 6), royal assent was not granted until April 19. The Saskatchewan legislature meanwhile passed its suffrage bill on Mar. 14 and royal assent was granted that same day.

[55]J. Boyd McBride, K.C., "Memorandum as to Women's Rights in Alberta" (Edmonton, 1943), p. 1. This was written by Judge McBride at the request of Senator Cairine Wilson and is now in the author's possession. Hereafter cited as J. B. McBride, "Memorandum."

tees.[56] This privilege was extended in 1888 to include all rate-payers.[57] The last advance made by women under territorial status came in 1894 when widows and spinsters were given the right to vote (but not to hold office) in municipal elections.[58]

In 1905 Alberta was organized as a province and separated from the eastern section of the Territories, which became the province of Saskatchewan. The first faint traces of what might be termed a movement for women's rights appeared at the birth of the province and arose in a controversy over the homesteading laws. The law which denied a wife all dower rights in her husband's estate was manifestly unjust to those pioneer wives who had struggled shoulder to shoulder with their husbands to establish themselves under the hardships of frontier conditions.

It was while the first provincial legislature was sitting that Mrs. Emily Murphy and her family moved to Alberta. Judge Emily Murphy, born in Cookstown, Ontario, in 1868, was educated at Bishop Strachan's School in Toronto. In 1904 she and her husband moved to Winnipeg where Mrs. Murphy conducted the literary section of the Winnipeg *Tribune* for a few years before moving to Alberta in 1907. In her new home Mrs. Murphy became very active in civic affairs, especially in the attainment of laws for the betterment of conditions for women and children. On June 13, 1916 she was appointed a police magistrate for the City of Edmonton, the first woman in the British empire to hold such a post. Under the pen-name "Janey Canuck," Mrs. Murphy wrote many books and articles mirroring western life, some of which found their way into both British and American publications.

The Rutherford government was framing a law to give women certain dower rights, and Mrs. Murphy disapproved of some of its provisions. Single-handed she went before the

[56]*Ordinances of the Northwest Territories, 1885*, No. 3, sects. 10 and 22. In spite of this generous provision, no woman appears to have served as trustee prior to 1917, according to the present deputy minister of education of Alberta.
[57]*Revised Ordinances of the Northwest Territories, 1888*, ch. 59.
[58]Henrietta Muir Edwards, *Women of Canada* (n.p., 1900). A brief pamphlet compiled at the request of the Canadian National Council of Women for the Paris International Exposition. I. Harper *et al.*, *Woman Suffrage*, IV, 1037.

committee on legislation and argued with such success that
the bill, when passed, was substantially as she wished. It was
on this occasion that Mrs. Murphy, most happily married to
the Reverend Arthur Murphy, received a letter from a grateful but misinformed pioneer woman who wrote: "God bless
you, Janey Canuck, I have a troublesome husband too."[59]

The movement for woman suffrage got under way about
1910, first as an effort to have the municipal franchise extended
to married women and then to obtain full provincial franchise.
As usual, it was the W.C.T.U. which inaugurated the crusade,
though its efforts were soon merged with and strengthened by
the more powerful Local Councils of Women, particularly that
of Calgary under Mrs. Alice Jamieson (later Judge Jamieson).
The brief six-year campaign which culminated in the legislative
victory of March 6, 1916 included no bitter tilts with hostile
governments nor skirmishes with an unfriendly press or public.
Campaigners had the less spectacular but tiring duty of travelling over the broad and often thinly inhabited expanses of the
province, bearing the message of political freedom and urging
their listeners to voice their desire for a share in the state, so
that an otherwise willing government might feel the pressure
of popular demand. Judge McBride recalls that wherever the
crusaders went they were well received, the frontier as always
proving to be fertile soil for the seeds of democracy. Conspicuous in these campaign years were the valiant Five (Mrs.
H. M. Edwards, Mrs. Nellie McClung, Mrs. Louise Mc-
Kinney, Mrs. Emily Murphy, and Mrs. Irene Parlby) whose
names adorn the handsome plaque which hangs in the senate
ante-chamber at Ottawa, commemorating their successful
struggle to have women called to the Upper House.[60]

Encouragement came to the small core of active workers

[59]*Maclean's Magazine* (Toronto), Nov. 1919, p. 34. Letter to the author
from Senator Cairine Wilson, Mar. 22, 1943. Undated article about Judge
Murphy from Toronto *Saturday Night* (1930) found in the Murphy Collection of
Papers, in the possession of Judge Murphy's daughter, Miss Evelyn Murphy of
Vancouver, B.C. Hereafter cited as Murphy Papers.

[60]J. B. McBride, "Memorandum," pp. 4-5. Also a typewritten paper included in A. S.-G., Scrap Books, VI. Letter to the author from Dr. Irene Parlby,
Mar. 22, 1943.

in 1912 when the United Farmers of Alberta adopted a resolution calling for equal political rights for women,[61] yet it was
not until 1913 that the first outright suffrage organization was
formed, the Equal Franchise League of Edmonton. This very
active little group in the provincial capital included men as
well as women members; in fact, its president was Dr. W. H.
Alexander of the University of Alberta. Dr. Alexander was a
man of courage, for he undertook to preside over an association
which included Mrs. Emily Murphy and Mrs. Nellie Mc-
Clung. In 1914 the Edmonton Franchise League affiliated
with the national organization of the same name in Toronto.[62]

In the 1914 session of the legislature the first woman suffrage petition was presented by the Edmonton Equal Franchise League and the Local Council of Women of Calgary.
For a first petition, this one was imposing, for it contained
some twelve thousand signatures and claimed to represent
forty-four societies. It requested simply the striking out of
the word "male" before "person" in the Alberta Election Act
of 1909. To the delegation which presented the petition on
October 9, the Liberal premier, Arthur Sifton, appeared both
friendly and sympathetic; but he showed no desire to sponsor
such a measure until a more widespread demand for the reform was evident among women themselves.[63] (The feminist
forces of Alberta doubtless considered themselves fortunate
to have escaped a governmental lecture on the Divinity's
unalterable opposition to ballots for women.) Progress obviously depended upon increasing exertions in the educational
field.

Almost at the very time the delegation was making its plea
to Premier Sifton, the city council of Edmonton made an
overture to women, only to have the provincial legislature
overrule it a few days later. The city fathers wished to amend
their charter to give the municipal vote to both men and
women on a mere residence qualification. The objection, which
caused the almost unanimous defeat of the proposed change,

[61]*Canadian Annual Review* (1912), p. 583.
[62]Edmonton *Journal*, May 3, 1934.  *Canadian Annual Review* (1913), p. 736.
[63]*Ibid.* (1914), p. 652.  *Alberta: Journals, 1914*, pp. 22-3.

was not to the enfranchisement of women, but to the innovation of placing a share in municipal affairs in the hands of
those possessed of no property or tax qualifications.[64]

As already pointed out, one of the biggest tasks in provinces as overwhelmingly agricultural as Alberta and Saskatchewan was that of creating some kind of effective organization among farm women, who lived in small and widely
scattered communities. At their Lethbridge convention in
January 1914, the United Farmers of Alberta not only reaffirmed their support of woman suffrage, but also extended
an invitation to women to become full-fledged members of
their organization. Encouraged by this gesture, those farm
women who accompanied their husbands to Lethbridge attempted to hold a convention of their own, but since it had
not been carefully planned in advance, it did not achieve the
same measure of success as the first women's convention
initiated in Saskatchewan in 1913, and no permanent association was set up at the time.[65]

Undismayed by this inauspicious beginning, the farm
women began to organize local units during the summer and
fall of 1914. When the United Farmers held their next annual
convention at Edmonton in 1915, Alberta women were ready.
Their Women's Parliament of that year was an unqualified
success, culminating in the formation of an effective Women's
Auxiliary of the U.F.A. The programme at Edmonton included an address by Dr. Alexander, president of the Equal
Franchise League. Dr. Alexander remarked that while the
number of signatures on the 1914 petition had been encouraging, there had been a disappointingly small percentage of
rural women, a fact which Premier Sifton had been quick to
point out to the delegation. The speaker urged his listeners
to accept the premier's challenge and make their new organization powerful enough to impress its views upon the government.[66] Thus was launched Alberta's closest equivalent to a
provincial suffrage association.

[64]*Daily Bulletin* (Edmonton), Oct. 9 and 16, 1914.
[65]*Canadian Annual Review* (1914), p. 658.   *Grain Growers' Guide*, Feb. 4, 1914.
[66]*Ibid.*, Oct. 7, 1914; Jan. 13 and 27, 1915.

The year 1915 found the province at last thoroughly alive to the suffrage question. When Mrs. McClung moved to Alberta in the fall of 1914 she continued her vigorous crusading efforts both for suffrage and prohibition. The United Farmers gave their customary staunch support, concentrating their efforts in 1915 upon obtaining for women the right to vote in a prohibition plebiscite. An impressive delegation to the government was organized on February 26. The twelve speakers included Alderman Rice Sheppard for the United Farmers, Mrs. Avery Smith for the Edmonton Equal Franchise League, Mrs. R. R. Jamieson for the Calgary Local Council, and Mrs. H. M. Edwards, vice-president for Alberta of the National Council of Women. But as always, it was Mrs. McClung who stole the show, her colourful and pertinent remarks drawing frequent bursts of applause and laughter from a crowded house. Though Premier Sifton refused the women participation in the referendum, his attitude was courteous and his reply raised hopes that a suffrage bill might be introduced at the next session.[67]

Not content with vague anticipation of benefits to be conferred in some shadowy future, Mrs. McClung and Mrs. Murphy joined forces to call upon Sifton on March 2 and ask that a suffrage bill be introduced at that very session. Other cabinet members were also interviewed. The local press account does not reveal how the gentlemen fared at this meeting but the premier's comment upon its conclusion was simply, "Mrs. McClung and Mrs. Murphy are very determined women."[68]

News of impending victory came early in the fall of 1915 and in a rather unusual manner. On September 22 the *Grain Growers' Guide* published a letter from the premier to James Speakman, president of the United Farmers.

Dear Sir:—Your letter in regard to Woman Suffrage received. This matter has received the serious consideration of the government and I have given instructions for the preparation of a statute placing men and women in Alberta

[67]*Ibid.*, Mar. 10, 1915. *Daily Bulletin*, Feb. 27, 1915.
[68]*Ibid.*, Mar. 3, 1915.

on a basis of absolute equality so far as provincial matters are concerned. This bill will be presented at the next meeting of the legislature as a government measure.

Yours very truly,

A. L. SIFTON.

This letter, which made the public pledge of an equal franchise measure first to an organization of men rather than women, is testimony of the power of the United Farmers and of the loyal support which the men of the prairies gave to women.

The farmers' convention at Calgary in 1916 met in an atmosphere of jubilation over the imminent triumph. In their annual report, the directors mentioned the successful termination of their negotiations with the government and announced their determination to examine thoroughly the proposed bill before it should be introduced to the legislature. Apparently nothing was to be left to chance where this measure was concerned. The editor of the *Guide* was particularly enthusiastic in his report on the women's section of the convention, complimenting them on the wide range of subjects discussed and the evidence they displayed of political maturity.[69]

As the opening day of the 1916 session approached, interested organizations placed in Premier Sifton's hands a petition bearing approximately forty thousand signatures, the fruit of unremitting toil by hundreds of nameless workers.[70] It was the unquestionable proof of the widespread popular demand for the reform.

True to his word, Sifton announced in the speech from the throne on February 24 the intention of his government to introduce an equal franchise measure, and the very next day he brought forth the bill in his own name.[71] The bill was gener-

---

[69]*Grain Growers' Guide*, Jan. 26, 1916. It is of some interest to note that Chipman predicted that the granting of provincial suffrage would automatically include the federal franchise, a view which Sir Robert Borden's government failed to share in 1917.

[70]H. Ridley, *Woman Suffrage*, p. 15.

[71]*Alberta: Journals, 1916*, pp. 8-9. On the same day Premier Sifton introduced a prohibition bill, whose course through the legislature paralleled that of the suffrage measure, indicating a close tie-up between the two subjects. A similar connection is also discernible in several other provinces, especially Manitoba and British Columbia.

ous and concise, affording women a status of complete political equality with men in all provincial, municipal, and school matters. In introducing the measure the premier paid tribute to the women of his province: their heroic pioneering activities had given them "an unalterable right by eternal justice to be placed on an equality with men." At the second reading of the bill on the first of March there was a joyous outburst of enthusiasm by as many interested spectators as could crowd into the galleries. Only one legislator ventured to cast his vote against the bill. Third reading came just five days later, making the Alberta legislature the second in Canada to grant political equality to women.[72]

The newly enfranchised half of the Alberta electorate has vindicated to a considerable extent the faith that was placed in it on April 19, 1916. Alberta women have worked consistently for the passage of social legislation to protect women and children, with the result that some of the most enlightened and liberal laws in the dominion are imbedded in the province's statutes. Included among them are factory acts, child protection acts, generous dower and mother's allowances acts, and the Sex Disqualification Removal Act of 1930. In 1917 many women who had been barred from participation in school matters by a ratepaying requirement, were permitted to use their talents in this sphere, so close to their interests, when a law was passed allowing wives, daughters, and sisters of ratepayers to vote for and serve as trustees.[73] Alberta and British Columbia are the only Canadian provinces in which women are permitted to serve on juries.[74]

Only a few months after the passage of the enfranchisement act, the Sifton government appointed Mrs. Murphy and Mrs. Jamieson to act as police magistrates, thereby creating the first women judges in Canada and probably in the British

[72]*Ibid.*, pp. 9, 13, 16, 18, 135. *Statutes of Alberta, 1916*, ch. 5. *Canadian Annual Review* (1916), p. 742. *Daily Bulletin*, Mar. 1, 1916.
[73]J. B. McBride, "Memorandum," pp. 5-7. *Statutes of Alberta, 1917*, ch. 43; *1930*, ch. 62. Henrietta Muir Edwards, ed., *Legal Status of Women of Alberta* (2nd ed., n.p., 1921), preface and p. 49. Dr. Irene Parlby speaking on a CBC Forum, *The Position of Women in Canada*, Dec. 11, 1938.
[74]*Gazette* (Montreal), Jan. 19, 1945.

empire.[75] In the provincial elections of June 1917, Mrs. L. M. McKinney and Miss Roberta Macadams emerged successfully to take their places as the first women lawmakers of the dominion. Miss Macadams's election was particularly significant in that she, a nurse with the forces overseas, was chosen by a purely male constituency, having been elected as one of the soldiers' representatives in this wartime contest at the polls.[76] Nellie McClung served a term in the legislature beginning in 1921.[77] In all, Alberta has had nine women in her provincial assembly; and is one of the very few provinces which has sent a woman delegate to the federal House of Commons—Mrs. Cora Casselman of Edmonton. The Greenfield government called the Honourable Irene Parlby to the cabinet as a Minister without Portfolio in August 1921, a post she filled with distinction for fourteen years.

The passage of time and the exercise of political power whetted rather than dulled the appetite of Alberta women. Marshalled by Judge Murphy, five veterans of the suffrage campaign faced the conservative stronghold of the Red Chamber at Ottawa, the Supreme Court of Canada, and even the august Privy Council in London to prove that women are "persons" in the eyes of the law, and consequently entitled to membership in the federal senate. The Alberta government, alone of the nine provinces, loyally supported the women in this eventful struggle, sending its attorney-general, Hon. J. F. Lymburn, to London to assist Hon. N. W. Rowell in pleading their cause. For the further emancipation which was an outcome of the successful termination of the Persons Case, the women of all Canada owe a debt of gratitude to

[75]*Maclean's Magazine*, Nov. 1919, pp. 34-5. *Daily Bulletin*, Oct. 27, 1933. *Journal* (Edmonton), Oct. 28, 1933. J. B. McBride, "Memorandum," p. 2. Letter to the author from Judge J. B. McBride, July 27, 1945. Mrs. Murphy was appointed in June and Mrs. Jamieson in December.
[76]N.C.W., *Year Book* (1918-19), p. 56. I. Harper *et al.*, *Woman Suffrage*, VI, 755. Mrs. Louise McKinney was a staunch temperance worker and later, one of "The Five" who signed the petition in the Persons Case.
[77]There were eight women candidates in this election, two of them successful. Mrs. McClung's victory in that year was significant of the general esteem in which she was held, for she ran on the government (Liberal) ticket and the government was badly defeated. *Canadian Annual Review* (1921), p. 853.

those of this prairie province who wove reality out of a dream of complete political equality.[78]

The story of the movement for woman suffrage in Saskatchewan parallels closely that of the movement in Alberta. Conditions were similar in the two provinces, governmental attitudes were the same; and in each the main problem was that of education.

One small bit of evidence, a petition for municipal franchise for married women, exists to prove that some thought was being given to the question of political equality in 1909.[79] Suffrage agitation, however, did not get off to a real start until the following year when several petitions were addressed to the legislature also requesting the municipal franchise for married women with property. More important in the long run than this shower of miscellaneous petitions was the foundation of several Homemakers' Clubs in the autumn of 1910 under the leadership of Mrs. A. V. Thomas of Manitoba. These clubs, destined to become hives of suffrage activity, were a project of the Extension Service of the young and active University of Saskatchewan. Following Mrs. Thomas's successful preliminary organizational work, Miss Abbie DeLury was made permanent Director of Homemakers' Clubs, a position she filled with conspicuous success for many years.[80] Miss DeLury came from an academically distinguished family and was herself a personality. Small, determined, and quick of apprehension, she travelled about Saskatchewan for many years organizing and encouraging the Homemakers' groups. Each year in June the University invited delegates from the

[78]In Feb. 1939 the Local Councils of Edmonton and Calgary presented the portraits of the five petitioners to the government of Alberta. These portraits were hung in the Legislative Buildings to commemorate the valiant fight of Judge Murphy and her four associates. Only Mrs. McClung and Mrs. Parlby were alive at the time. *Daily Bulletin*, Feb. 24, 1939. (The Persons Case is treated fully in Chapter V.)

[79]*Saskatchewan: Journals, 1909*, reveals a lone petition for municipal franchise for married women by "F. N. Darke and others."

[80]Saskatchewan, Department of Agriculture, *Homemakers' Clubs 1910-1920* (Saskatoon, 1920), pp. 8-9. The *Grain Growers' Guide* performed valuable service, especially through Miss Beynon's column in 1913, in helping its readers to form these clubs.

many local clubs throughout the province to a four-day conference on the campus at Saskatoon. The subjects of the addresses and demonstrations covered a wide field of topics of interest to women, but inevitably woman suffrage had a place of honour on the programme. Living in the handsome residence halls of the University, where physical comfort was combined with companionship and intellectual stimulation, made the convention a never-to-be-forgotten experience in the lives of pioneer women. Better still, it gave the women practice in organizing for specific aims, got them thinking about problems which closely affected their interests, and gave them confidence in their own abilities. Although Homemakers' Clubs were organized in all three Prairie Provinces, they were most numerous and most successful in Saskatchewan.[81]

Two events of 1912 indicated the increasing interest in woman suffrage in the province. Following the path already marked out by the organized farmers of both Manitoba and Alberta, the Saskatchewan Grain Growers' Association endorsed an equal rights resolution at the annual convention in February.[82] And as the year drew to a close, J. E. Bradshaw rose in the legislature (December 16) and offered a suffrage resolution for the approval of the House. In the discussion which ensued almost all members declared they were in favour of the principle, but were simply not convinced that women themselves wanted it. After this polite but cool recognition, the resolution was allowed to die without a vote. G. F. Chipman of the *Guide* chided the legislators' weak excuse for delay; then turned to the women and advised that they be not backward in making their wishes known.[83]

That women were eager to follow Chipman's counsel was shown in 1913 by the rapidly growing number of letters from women to the *Guide* seeking advice on formation of clubs, sources of suffrage literature, proper procedure in drawing up petitions, etc. It will be remembered that Francis M. Beynon had become women's editor of the paper in the previous year.

[81]*Homemakers' Clubs, op. cit.*, pp. 55-63.
[82]*Canadian Annual Review* (1912), pp. 550-1.
[83]*Ibid.*, p. 573. *Grain Growers' Guide*, Jan. 1, 1913.

The women's column became almost exclusively a suffrage column as Miss Beynon struggled to project her own vast experience and unflagging devotion to women in hundreds of little hamlets and on lonely farmsteads across the prairies. Interspersed between such bits of factual information as the address of the National Women's Suffrage Association in New York or a technical point on parliamentary procedure could be found fragments of homely philosophy and good sound common sense like the following:

> Be as moderate as possible and be careful not to promise the millennium as soon as women get the vote, because it is too big an order for us to live up to. Also there is nothing to be gained by railing at men. . . . They are, in the main, mighty decent people and if they are approached reasonably and the subject presented to them sanely are amazingly easy of conversion.[84]

The growing interest took concrete shape early in 1913. While the Grain Growers assembled in annual convention and again gave hearty endorsement to a suffrage resolution, many of their wives gathered on the grounds of the University and held a congress of their own. The well-planned sessions included among their speakers such veterans from Manitoba as Mrs. A. V. Thomas, Nellie McClung, May Clendenan, and Cora Hind. Woman suffrage was endorsed unanimously and the convention closed with the delegates agreeing that the meetings must be repeated annually. The final act was a vote to organize permanently as an auxiliary of the men's association at their 1914 gathering. They thus became the first such organization in Canada. The success of the convention so impressed G. F. Chipman that he predicted the coming session of the legislature would enact woman suffrage in Saskatchewan.[85] But victories were not won so lightly, even in the progressive West.

Interest in the question remained keen throughout the year. Local farmers' units and their women's auxiliaries, which were rapidly being organized, sent ninety-one suffrage petitions containing three thousand signatures to Premier Scott

[84]*Ibid.*, Jan. 29, 1913.
[85]*Ibid.*, Feb. 19 and 26, 1913.

before the legislature convened in November: a very credit-able record when it is recalled that there was as yet no suffrage organization in the province. Apparently impressed by the spontaneity of this demonstration, the lawmakers passed unanimously a resolution favouring equal franchise, but Premier Scott refused to clothe this expression of opinion in the necessary legal garb. In a letter to Miss Beynon the pre-mier explained his reluctance on the ground that this legis-lature had not come into office pledged to woman suffrage and that its hands were therefore tied until it should receive a direct mandate from the constituents. The vigorous little lady thereupon told her readers the hour had struck not only for the formation of local suffrage organizations, but also for the creation of a strong provincial association with enough power behind it to make its influence felt in political circles.[86]

Notwithstanding this excellent advice, suffrage associa-tions as such were slow in taking root in prairie soil, perhaps because of the preference of women in this part of the country for carrying on suffrage activities through the rapidly spread-ing local units of the Women Grain Growers' Association. Contrary to the general pattern in other provinces, it was a small town, Moosomin, which fostered the first Political Equality League in Saskatchewan. This little group was launched in February 1914 with about fifty members. Miss Beynon was on hand to insure the success of the initial undertaking.[87] Although several other local franchise clubs were formed in the same year, it was not until 1915 that an attempt was made to weld them together into an effective provincial force.

Meantime the Women Grain Growers held their second annual convention in February. While retaining full-fledged membership in the men's association, a privilege accorded them in 1913, they voted to set up a permanent organization of their own and elected an extremely capable slate of officers: Mrs. Violet McNaughton, president; Mrs. S. V. Haight, vice-

---

[86]*Ibid.*, Dec. 17, 24, and 31, 1913.
[87]*Ibid.*, Mar. 25, 1914.

president; and Miss Erma Stocking, secretary. The delegates set two main objectives as their goals for the year: a concentrated effort to organize locals in every remote corner of the province and an intensive campaign to secure suffrage petitions to melt, if possible, the reluctance of Premier Scott. As early as July, Mrs. McNaughton reported to her executive committee that these efforts alone would not suffice and that a federation should be formed of Women Grain Growers' locals, the small political equality leagues which were springing up, the W.C.T.U., and any other sympathizing organizations. Mrs. McNaughton laid the groundwork for the federation herself by attending the W.C.T.U. convention in the fall of 1914 and firing the delegates with such enthusiasm for the project that representatives for the proposed provincial suffrage board were elected on the spot.[88]

The third annual convention in 1915 of the now flourishing Women Grain Growers' Association was optimistic over the past year's successes and plans for a new offensive. The annual report of the president noted the formation in little more than a year of sixty-two local branches, which were beyond question the real "suffrage societies" of Saskatchewan. Mrs. McNaughton was able to announce that uniformly favourable replies had been received from organizations to which she had broached the subject of a suffrage federation, and that an organization meeting would be held in Regina immediately following their own convention. That the convention discussed chiefly equal rights may be inferred from the list of the four principal speakers: George F. Chipman, Mrs. A. V. Thomas, Francis Beynon, and May Clendenan. The latter, who wrote regularly in the *Farmer's Advocate* as "Dame Dibbin," came right to the core of the matter when she remarked succinctly: "If democracy is right, women should have it. If it isn't, men shouldn't.''[89]

The much-discussed Provincial Suffrage Board was actually created that same month (February) by delegates repre-

[88]*Ibid.*, Feb. 18, July 22, Oct. 28, Nov. 25, 1914.
[89]*Ibid.*, Feb. 17 and 24, 1915.

senting the provincial W.C.T.U., the Women Grain Growers' Association, and a half-dozen local political equality leagues. Under the leadership of Mrs. F. A. Lawton of Yorkton, president, and Mrs. S. V. Haight of Keeler, first vice-president, the new group decided to press for the parliamentary franchise immediately rather than seek municipal privileges first, as older suffrage organizations in other provinces often did. For the duration of the war, however, it was deemed advisable to confine their campaign to nothing more spectacular than raising funds for literature and speakers, and continuing the tedious but essential work of securing signatures to petitions.[90]

The youthful Suffrage Board departed somewhat from the path marked out for itself in February by organizing the first suffrage delegation to the government in May. (One may argue, of course, that this still came under the heading "educational.") The delegation of about one hundred presented a petition containing between ten and fifteen thousand signatures[91] and backed it up with a verbal plea by six outstanding delegates including W. E. Cocks of the Trades and Labor Congress and J. B. Musselman of the Saskatchewan Grain Growers' Association. Premier Scott's reply was the essence of courtesy. He admitted that the educational campaign had changed his mind about the necessity of referring the matter back to the voters, but said he still felt he must consult his colleagues about the wisdom of acting immediately. Meanwhile, he urged that the women secure more signatures—a refrain which must have sounded a little more than familiar to his listeners.[92]

Though no legislation for the parliamentary franchise was forthcoming at the 1915 session, the legislature did amend the Municipal and Town Acts, to grant married women property owners the privilege of voting in civic elections. Office-holding,

[90]*Ibid.*, Mar. 24, 1915.  H. Ridley, *Woman Suffrage*, p. 16.  N.C.W., *Year Book* (1915), p. 124.
[91]The *Morning Leader* (Regina) with a newly developed interest in the suffrage question backs the larger figure.  The sturdy old friend of the movement, the *Grain Growers' Guide*, quotes the more conservative estimate.
[92]*Leader*, May 21 and 28, 1915.  *Grain Growers' Guide*, June 2 and 30, 1915.

however, was maintained as an exclusively male prerogative even in that limited field.[93]

Very early in January of 1916, Premier Scott wrote a letter to Mrs. McNaughton promising that equal suffrage would be granted in the forthcoming session; at the same time he requested a further influx of petitions.[94] A last call went out to the women's clubs and locals from Miss Erma Stocking, through the columns of the *Guide* (January 19), urging the return before February 1 of such an impressive array of petitions as to overcome any lingering doubts the government might have about whether the women of Saskatchewan really wanted the vote. Though the speech from the throne on January 18 mentioned the subject, there had been no suffrage bill introduced when, on February 14, another large delegation from the Provincial Equal Franchise Board presented their petition with the most imposing roster of signatures ever garnered in that province.[95]

Nor were the men's and women's farm organizations, assembled in convention at Saskatoon in February, going to let Premier Scott forget his promise. The men loyally passed their customary resolution endorsing woman suffrage, while the women sent the premier a telegram of thanks for his pledged word. There were two hundred and thirty women present at the 1916 Women Grain Growers' convention— forty-eight had launched the organization three years earlier. The spirit, energy, and cohesive drive of this group of prairie farm women might well have aroused pangs of envy in the women of older provinces where unity of either purpose or effort seemed impossible to achieve.[96]

At last on March 1, Attorney-General W. F. Turgeon introduced the bill. At no stage of its progress through committee or the various readings is there evidence in the press of any undue excitement on the part of the legislators or public. Only after third reading and royal assent had been bestowed

[93]*Statutes of Saskatchewan, 1915*, ch. 16, ch. 17.  *Leader*, May 27, 1915.
[94]*Canadian Annual Review* (1916), pp. 701-2.
[95]*Grain Growers' Guide*, Feb. 23, 1916.  *Canadian Annual Review* (1916), pp. 701-2.          [96]*Grain Growers' Guide*, Feb. 23, 1916.

on the very last day of the session (March 14) did the province's leading newspaper, the Regina *Morning Leader*, give the first indication that it was aware a measure of such far-reaching importance had been under discussion. In summing up the session's work, the *Leader* graciously but very briefly commented: "Easily first in importance is the conferring of the franchise upon the women of the Province. What this will mean for the future of Saskatchewan no person can foretell, but that it will make for moral uplift, for a better tone in political discussion, and cleaner politics is almost certain."[97] The unspectacular reception given woman suffrage in Saskatchewan, technically the second province in the dominion to embark upon this experiment in political equality, can be attributed only to the twin facts that the campaign was brief and without rancour, and that prairie men and women almost universally were convinced of the justice and rightness of the principle of equality.

The act itself took the form of a simple revision of the Saskatchewan Election Act. Unlike the comprehensive Alberta statute, this one applied only to provincial office-holding and voting.[98] Indeed, through some oversight, the government neglected to amend the Legislative Assembly Act which remained worded so as to permit only males to be elected to the legislature, while the new Election Act of 1916 expressly declared women eligible. This anomaly was rectified by a revision of the act in 1917.[99] Municipal office-holding privileges were extended to women with property qualifications by separate acts in 1916 and 1917.[100] The principle of equality was completely established in Saskatchewan in 1920 when wives and husbands of property owners were made eligible for municipal and school franchise and office-holding.[101]

[97]*Saskatchewan: Journals, 1916*, pp. 142, 169, 183.  *Leader*, Mar. 15, 1916.
[98]*Statutes of Saskatchewan, 1916*, ch. 37.
[99]The Government of the Province of Saskatchewan, *Some Saskatchewan Legislation Affecting Women and Children* (Regina, 1920), p. 6.  Further confirmed by a letter to the author from the deputy attorney-general of Saskatchewan, July 27, 1945.  The revised Legislative Assembly Act may be found in *Statutes of Saskatchewan, 1917*, ch. 7.
[100]*Ibid., 1916*, ch. 16, 26; *1917*, ch. 12.
[101]*Some Saskatchewan Legislation*, pp. 8-10.

Encouraged by the successful culmination of their own campaign, Saskatchewan suffrage leaders launched, in June 1916, a very short-lived attempt to form a Federal Franchise League to secure the federal ballot for women in all parts of the dominion. In this venture they were aided and abetted by Mrs. Nellie McClung. It was hoped by the delegates, who met on June 23 and 24, that a merger might be effected between the two rival "national" suffrage associations in Toronto and that the resulting unified body might lead to the formation of suffrage societies in provinces which still lacked such organizations.[102] Since no more is heard of this group after these two preliminary gatherings, one can only conclude that the enterprise foundered on the petty jealousies of two "national" associations within the confines of one city, or the indifference exhibited by women themselves in several provinces of the East.

Mrs. M. O. Ramsland became, in 1919, Saskatchewan's first woman lawmaker. After her defeat in 1925, no other woman entered the provincial legislature until 1944, when Mrs. B. J. Trew was successful. Saskatchewan's assembly reverted to the all-male tradition as a result of the election of June 24, 1948.

In the wider sphere of dominion politics, Mrs. Dorise Nielsen, running as a United Progressive, was elected to the House in 1940: the only woman in Canada to win a federal seat in that election. Mrs. Nielsen was defeated in 1945, but again Saskatchewan sent the sole woman member to Ottawa. In a three-cornered race, Mrs. Gladys Strum, an adherent of the Co-operative Commonwealth Federation, defeated the veteran campaigner, E. E. Perley, and General A. G. McNaughton. Not even this demonstration of political ability, however, was sufficient to keep Mrs. Strum from being overwhelmed by the Liberal spring tide of 1949.

[102]*Leader*, June 24 and 26, 1916.

# 4

# BRITISH COLUMBIA

## *The Individualist*

THE BRITISH COLUMBIA equal rights movement began in the middle 1880's, only a few short years after Dr. Emily Stowe had planted the seeds of feminism through her Toronto Women's Literary Club. Its course parallels to some extent that of its eastern counterpart: numerous petitions and delegations to the legislature, meeting a strongly entrenched and definitely unsympathetic Conservative regime during many of the pre-war years,[1] and strenuous efforts by small groups of women to wear down the opposition of a masculine electorate, and more difficult by far, to rouse their own sex from inertia and apathy.[2]

Yet two quite striking differences were apparent. The Ontario movement was noticeably inclined towards "missionary work" in other provinces, while the British Columbia contingent was largely "isolationist" in its endeavours. Moreover, the coastal suffragists had to contend with a type of press campaign, especially in 1913, which disturbed their eastern sisters very little, if at all. This was a tendency on the part of some west coast newspapers to play up stories of British militant suffrage activities. Between 1912 and 1914,

[1]Under Premiers McBride and Bowser, the Conservatives remained in power from June 1, 1903 to Nov. 23, 1916.
[2]Writing in the *British Columbia Federationist* of June 11, 1915, Miss Helena Gutteridge, a frequent contributor on the subject of women's rights, chided: "The backwardness of the suffrage movement in British Columbia is not due . . . to the desire of men to dominate their women folk, but to the lack of interest displayed by the women themselves."

the influential Victoria *Daily Times* featured lurid items calculated to catch the reader's eye the moment he unfolded his paper. British Columbia felt a strong attachment to the mother country and naturally its newspapers featured British suffrage news, and took their cue from the attitude of the British press.

The British Columbia movement was led through more than thirty years of effort by Mrs. Gordon Grant of Victoria. Mrs. Grant was not only an early leader in Canadian feminist ranks, but also a pioneer in the more general sense of the term. As a young girl, she moved with her parents from Quebec City to Victoria in the year of confederation, 1867. In spite of the cares of bringing up a large family, Mrs. Grant always found time to be interested in matters pertaining to the welfare of women and children. Her special sphere of activity was the W.C.T.U., but she also took an active part in the work of the Victoria Local Council of Women, which she helped to launch. Largely through her efforts the first Children's Aid Home was established in Victoria; and her eagerness to serve young people was further manifested when she was elected to the Victoria school board, thereby becoming the first woman of her city to hold such a position.

Mrs. Grant headed a delegation to the legislature almost every year throughout the entire struggle and in some years appeared more than once.

Whenever sufficient funds could be raised, delegations went to the Government at Victoria. They slept or talked six or seven in two bed staterooms. They took babies and children when they could not be left, and one lady brought her dog because there was no one at home to feed it. Mrs. Spofford[3] and Mrs. Gordon Grant gathered up the women from Victoria and environs. They planned their speeches and drilled their speakers. The only occasion they ran over their allotted time was when they were induced to let some gentlemen join them, and the women had no means of putting on the brakes.

[3]This was Mrs. Cecilia McNaughton Spofford who was associated with Frances Willard in founding the British Columbia W.C.T.U. in 1883 and was also one of the founders of the Victoria Local Council of Women at the time of Lady Aberdeen's visit in 1893. She was president of the latter organization for many years and was president of the Provincial Council at the time of her death in 1938 (aged 78). A pioneer feminist, she served on the Victoria school board from 1919-1921 and was a member of the Social Welfare Commission and of the Minimum Wage Board.

Although British Columbia suffragists appear not to have placed as much reliance upon petitions as their Ontario sisters, the *Journals* of the legislative assembly contain several references to suffrage petitions in the 1890's, some of W.C.T.U. origin, others from the Local Councils of Women in Victoria and Vancouver, in both of which organizations Mrs. Grant was active. It was she who drew up the first woman suffrage petition and presented it, with backing from the W.C.T.U., to the legislature in 1885.[4]

While many provinces were untroubled by suffrage agitation in the 1880's and 1890's, British Columbia was kept aware of the issue and some notable progress was made. Eleven bills to bestow provincial political privileges upon women were introduced between the years 1884[5] and 1899. The five which appeared in the 1880's were brought in by Simeon Drake and Hon. John Robson,[6] while the six bills of the succeeding decade were sponsored by John C. Brown, Harry Helmcken, and Ralph Smith. None of these bills passed second reading: indeed, they were frequently voted down by an almost two to one majority, but Ralph Smith's bill of 1899 came close to survival when it was defeated on second reading by only seventeen to fifteen.[7] Although a few of these measures were treated with hilarity and contempt, it is a credit to the lawmakers of those early days that they considered most of them worthy of prolonged debate and serious consideration.

Another encouraging sign was the measure of attention given by the province's two leading newspapers to these debates in their news and editorial columns. It is interesting to find the Conservative *Weekly British Colonist*[8] wholeheartedly

[4]Victoria *Daily Times*, Sept. 16, 1916. The quotation is from Helen Gregory MacGill, "Story of Woman Suffrage in British Columbia" (n.p., n.d.), City Archives, Vancouver. In this four-page typewritten document, the author takes to task those who erringly assume that suffrage came to women on the west coast as a simple matter of course.

[5]This first "bill" was actually introduced by Mr. Drake on Dec. 24, 1883 in the form of an amendment to a regular voters bill. The amendment was cast aside on Feb. 6, 1884.

[6]Hon. John Robson was serving as provincial secretary at the time, but introduced the measure as a private member bill.

[7]B.C.: *Journals, 1889*, p. 74. *Daily Colonist* (Victoria), Feb. 25, 1899.

[8]The *Weekly British Colonist* (Victoria) became a daily paper in 1891 under the title *Daily Colonist*. This paper is very good for reports of debates down to 1908; thereafter rather poor.

endorsing woman suffrage from the very beginning, while the Liberal Victoria *Daily Times* was generally opposed. With certain exceptions it was the Liberal wing of the press which accorded Canadian suffragists sympathetic support, whereas the Conservative wing was more apt to take up the cause only when it perceived in such a policy a nuisance value against political opponents. Amusing, and typical, is an editorial which appeared in the *Daily Times* on February 28, 1891:

> The true woman who would make the most of her every God-given attribute asks not for the ballot, but for love and home, where the carols of babyhood are sung to the sweetest of babies, where home is heaven, and where the weary husband may find rest and aching hearts sympathy.

British Columbia had followed an enlightened policy with regard to the municipal franchise. As far back as 1873 this ocean-washed pioneer community gave women the right to vote in municipal affairs, and did not limit the privilege to unmarried women.[9] Commenting in 1895 upon this extremely early evidence of frontier democracy, Edith Luke queried:

> Is it not strange that no tales of dire domestic strife have come to us from the homes of the province upon the Pacific? Is it possible then, after all that has been asserted to the contrary, that a man may accompany his wife to the polling booth on election day, and allow her to record her personal opinion . . . without quarreling with her on the journey home! It would seem so, as we are not told that divorces are more frequent in British Columbia than elsewhere.[10]

The right to vote in municipal matters did not include the right to hold office, which was not secured until forty-four years later in the general triumph of the suffrage cause. This was, however, because the feminist agitation emphasized the provincial sphere, and neglected this curious omission in the municipal franchise.

During the two decades preceding the turn of the century the women succeeded fully in one small field—probably the one closest to the hearts of many of them, the local school

---

[9]This of course applied only to women (as to men) with sufficient property qualifications. *Statutes of B.C., 1873*, ch. 5, sections 1 and 2. A short article in the *Daily Colonist* of Aug. 1, 1937 claims that women first used their new privilege in Victoria on Jan. 12, 1875. ". . . in spite of the interest they seemed to be taking in municipal matters at that time only three exercised their franchise."

[10]E. Luke, "Woman Suffrage," p. 334.

elections. This was accomplished in four separate steps. The right of women with property qualifications to vote for school trustees was secured in 1884, and in the following year the right was extended to wives of men possessing property qualifications. A decade later, in 1895, women qualified as to property became eligible for election as school trustees, and in one year's time wives of duly qualified men were granted the same privilege.[11]

As in other provinces which had experienced a lively suffrage activity in the closing years of the nineteenth century, the opening decade of the new century was a period of stagnation in the equal rights movement of the far West. Although Mrs. Grant loyally kept on leading delegations and an occasional petition reached the legislature to remind it that the suffrage cause was dormant rather than dead, only two bills for provincial enfranchisement of women were introduced during this period. James H. Hawthornthwaite championed the cause on both occasions. In the debate on his 1906 attempt appeared a new argument which revealed the dawn of an industrial era in which more and more women were leaving their homes to enter the labour market. Hawthornthwaite, a Socialist, advanced his measure mainly on the ground that women must have some means of combatting the economic conditions of the modern world where man-made laws offered them small protection. Parker Williams supported the sponsor in the debate, but the opposing members held their fire until the vote was called. The Conservative members then crushed the bill, twenty-four to twelve.[12] The defeat of the measure introduced in 1909 was almost as completely overwhelming, though the *Daily Colonist* noted one slight change: "Only one man on the Conservative side, Mr. Garden, a bachelor by the way, voted for the second reading of the bill, and in so doing won some applause."[13]

---

[11]*Statutes of B.C., 1884*, ch. 27; *1885*, ch. 25; *1895*, ch. 48; *1896*, ch. 42.
[12]*B.C.: Journals, 1906*, pp. 5, 30, 34.   *Daily Colonist* (Victoria), Feb. 2 and 3, 1906.   *Canadian Annual Review* (1906), p. 494.
[13]*Daily Colonist*, Mar. 13, 1909.   *B.C.: Journals, 1909*, pp. 125, 128.   The vote was 23-13.

Signs of a reawakening of active interest in the movement were discernible in November 1908 when the Local Council of Victoria, under the presidency of Mrs. Cecilia Spofford, officially endorsed woman suffrage. It was the first Local Council in Canada to do so. In 1910 the Local Council staged a Mock Parliament. Both the lieutenant-governor and the premier were among the audience, and witnessed the revolution that might be expected were women to take the place of men in the lawmaking chamber.[14]

By the close of 1910 suffrage forces gave every indication of shaking off the lethargy of the preceding decade and organizing for more effective action. This again was symptomatic of a general trend throughout the dominion, but no doubt there was a special impetus on the west coast, because the neighbouring American state, Washington, in that year became the first state since 1896 to bestow the franchise upon women. The Victoria Local Council, early in the autumn of 1910, took the initiative by recommending the founding of a full-fledged political equality club, a type of organization which, rather oddly, had never existed in British Columbia.[15] Prior to 1908, the only organization upon whose consistent support ardent suffrage workers could rely was the W.C.T.U.[16] As already indicated, both Mrs. Grant and Mrs. Spofford were active in the prohibition cause even before they became captains of the feminist movement, and beyond a doubt they regarded woman suffrage as a potent lever in obtaining the reform to which they had first given their devotion.

The Victoria Local Council's suggestion fell upon willing ears. In November the Political Equality League of Victoria became the province's pioneer suffrage organization and chose Mrs. Gordon Grant as its president. Just one month later Mrs. Grant embarked for Vancouver and helped to found a similar league whose first president was Mrs. Lashley Hall. These two local suffrage organizations became in May 1911 the nucleus of a provincial Political Equality League whose

[14]I. Harper *et al.*, *Woman Suffrage*, VI, 756.  N.C.W., *Year Book* (1910), p. 95.
[15]*Ibid.* (1911), pp. 73, 74.
[16]H. G. MacGill, *op. cit.*, p. 2.

purpose was to attempt to make the basis of the suffrage movement provincial in scope. As in all other provinces, however, this broader aim was never much more than a plan which looked well on paper. The nerve centre of the movement remained in Victoria and Vancouver.[17]

From 1911 until final victory in 1917 the provincial Political Equality League, under Mrs. Grant's guidance, led suffrage activities in the province. It organized delegations, presented petitions containing as many as ten thousand signatures, and frequently held public meetings. It maintained one and sometimes more paid organizers, of whom Miss Dorothy Davis was the most effective. Occasionally it found its progress impeded rather than aided by minor suffrage groups which sprang up after 1911 and often worked at cross-purposes during their brief existences. Deploring their appearance, which indicated internal conflict among suffragists themselves, Judge MacGill wrote in her usual terse and incisive style: "Like other pests, they grew by segmentation."[18] However, no amount of government hostility, public indifference, internal quarrels, or press coolness,[19] was able to daunt this small but determined Equality League which gathered increasing momentum with every year of its existence.

Three events occurred in 1912 to give at least a small measure of encouragement to the suffrage forces. The first of these came in January when the British Columbia Federation of Labor, following the tradition laid down by the labour movement of Great Britain in earlier years, endorsed woman suffrage.[20] Further support came from an entirely different direction when in February the Local Option League, meeting in convention at Vancouver, declared itself in favour of equal rights "after a warm discussion."[21] The most unexpected boon,

[17] *Canadian Annual Review* (1910), p. 313; (1911), p. 369. N.C.W., *Year Book* (1911), pp. 73-5.
[18] H. G. MacGill, *op. cit.*, p. 2.
[19] The *Daily Times* was in a state of flux on the subject of suffrage around 1911-12 and frankly said so in its editorial columns. The *Daily Colonist* had retreated into editorial silence, brought on no doubt by finding its own views out of line with the ideas of the Conservative government which it supported.
[20] *Canadian Annual Review* (1912), pp. 273-4.
[21] *Daily Times*, Feb. 3, 1912.

however, came from the unfriendly Conservative regime. In January the British Columbia Court of Appeal had unanimously refused the appeal of Miss Mabel French to be admitted to the provincial Bar, basing its refusal upon the interpretation of the word "person" in the Bar Act. The government rushed through a new Bar Act in the closing days of the 1912 session, sponsored by Attorney-General William J. Bowser, reputed to be an implacable foe of the suffragists. The new act accorded women the privilege of practising law, both as solicitors and barristers.[22] Lest his fellow Conservatives accuse him of introducing some dreadful innovation, the attorney-general was careful to point out that women already practised law in both Ontario and New Brunswick.

Following these preliminaries, the province became really aware of the suffrage issue, and from the opening days of 1913 down to the attainment of complete victory in 1917 there was no time at which the question was allowed to rest. The Political Equality League (which included men as well as women) chose January 16, 1913, the opening day of the legislature, as the occasion for a one-day drive with the dual purpose of securing signatures to their suffrage petition and increasing their own membership. Success attended this one day's concentrated effort, credit for which seems to have been largely due to Miss Dorothy Davis, the League's paid organizer, who displayed tireless energy, skill, and diplomacy. No means of peaceful persuasion were overlooked, as the suffragists provided their open air audience with literature, courteous answers, and even cake and coffee! When the day closed, the League had added a thousand more signatures to its petition and two hundred prospective new members to its rolls.[23]

The League's most important activity for 1913 was the organization of a delegation to Premier McBride on February 14. Seventy-two women, headed by their veteran leader, Mrs. Grant, were ushered into the premier's presence late

[22]*Ibid.*, Jan. 9, 1912. *Statutes of B.C., 1912*, ch. 18.
[23]*Daily Times*, Jan. 16 and 18, 1913.

that day and presented to the government a petition bearing ten thousand signatures. Six of the women made brief addresses. Miss Davis urged the government to behave with generosity and chivalry, but warned that if the women were rebuffed they would wage a struggle—"a peaceful struggle" she hastened to add, to the probable relief of the ministers. In reply, Premier McBride spoke non-committally, promising a definite answer within four or five days. Any hopes he may have entertained that these delaying tactics would lead to a dispersal of the delegation (two-thirds of whom came from the mainland) were disappointed, for the great majority of the women decided to stay right there in Victoria until the die was cast.[24]

The League seized this period while the equal rights question was in the forefront of public attention to hold an open meeting in the Alexandra Club on February 17. A large audience of men and women heard not only some of the province's most eloquent speakers on the subject, but also Miss O'Meara of Seattle, who brought encouragement and advice from the recently enfranchised women of Washington.[25]

At last, on February 19, Premier McBride indicated that he was ready to give his answer. In a speech which started off so urbanely as to cause his listeners' hopes to soar, the premier ended by dashing them to the ground: he said that his government was still of the same opinion it had held ten years before on this proposition. Little solace could be derived from his postscript to the effect that he would have no objection to a private member's introduction of such a bill.[26] His audience doubtless recalled the fate of the Hawthornthwaite bills at the hands of the Conservatives in 1906 and 1909. From this day the suffragist forces wasted no more time on petitions or delegations to a government whose feet were evidently planted in concrete as far as progress towards woman suffrage was concerned. They began a less spectacular policy of public education on the suffrage question, combined

[24]*Ibid.*, Feb. 17, 1913.
[25]*Ibid.*, Feb. 18, 1913.
[26]*Ibid.*, Feb. 20, 1913.

with an effort to throw the McBride-Bowser regime out of office at the earliest opportunity.

Within twenty-four hours of Premier McBride's announcement, the women learned that a private member bill for woman suffrage had been given first reading by the legislature. Its sponsor was J. W. T. Place, Socialist member for Nanaimo. (The Socialist party, though small, staunchly supported the equal rights movement.) The Place bill received a full-dress debate on February 27, with its sponsor and Parker Williams ably supporting it. The longest speech against the bill came from a member of the government, Hon. A. E. McPhillips, who quoted Gladstone, Spencer, and Bright in support of his views and attempted to prove that the most evil aspects of the French Revolution were due to the influence of women. McPhillips prefaced his remarks, of course, by saying that he yielded "to no man in the love, honour, and respect I have for women." On March 1 the bill was denied second reading by a vote of 24 to 9, and thus the subject was officially laid to rest for that session at least.[27] A similar bill sponsored again by Place in 1914 received very little debate and fared almost equally badly in a vote which rejected it, 23 to 10.[28]

With the outbreak of the world war, British Columbia suffrage groups, like those in other parts of the dominion, channelled their efforts primarily into war work with the result that suffrage activities *per se* died down somewhat during late 1914 and throughout 1915. However, this was not indicative of any slackening of interest in the problem, but rather a matter of putting first things first. In the long run this policy paid excellent dividends, for when active suffrage agitation revived in 1916, former enemies of the cause vied with its friends in offering tribute to the services performed by women as partners in defence of the nation.

One quarter which was anything but quiet on the suffrage question during the first two war years was the radical weekly, the *British Columbia Federationist*, official organ of the British

[27]*B.C.: Journals, 1913*, pp. 55, 105, 115. *Daily Colonist*, Mar. 2, 1913. *Daily Times*, Feb. 12, Mar. 1, 1913.
[28]*B.C.: Journals, 1914*, pp. 27, 55, 83.

Columbia Federation of Labor. Apart from editorial comment favouring equal rights, the *Federationist* ran a weekly column devoted exclusively to suffrage topics, under the editorship of Mrs. J. A. Clarke. Items ranged all the way from simple notices of suffrage meetings, through news of activities in all parts of the world, to sharp exhortations to the women of the province to press their demands more aggressively. Above all, the *Federationist* warned women not to put their trust in the Liberal party, which in 1915 was beginning to court openly the support of the suffrage forces.[29]

Three factors were mainly responsible for turning the tide for the suffrage movement in 1916. The first of these was the triumph of the campaign for equal rights in the Prairie Provinces during the first three months of that year. Besides bringing encouragement to the active workers in the movement, this triple victory on their eastern flank rather piqued British Columbians, who have always gloried in their progressiveness.[30] Second on the list was the fact conceded on all sides, even by Premier Bowser,[31] who now headed the Conservative government, that the war work of women was magnificent and justly entitled them to a share in affairs of state. The last factor may be set down to nothing more elevating than political expediency. After more than a decade of confinement to the political hinterlands, the Liberal party began to see chinks in the Conservative armour. As hopes for a victory over their political opponents grew brighter, the Liberals looked about for possible allies in the coming test of strength. What could be more natural than to turn to woman suffrage groups, which had been so frequently rebuffed by the Conservatives? Here was a group of intelligent, well-organized, and politically minded (though disfranchised) citizens, who would doubtless welcome a working alliance with the Liberals. As 1915 waned and with it the fortunes of the Conservative party, the Liberal party and the suffrage workers began to find each other's society increasingly agreeable.

[29]*British Columbia Federationist* (Vancouver), June 11 and 18, 1915.
[30]*Ibid.*, Feb. 11, 1916. *Daily Times*, Mar. 1, 1916.
[31]*Daily Colonist*, April 14, 1916.

Doubtless individual Liberals were genuinely sincere in supporting woman suffrage, but certainly the Liberal party, as such, had not put forth any heroic efforts for the cause of equal rights prior to 1916.[32]

Evidence of the new partnership appeared in February 1916 when H. C. Brewster, leader of the Liberal party, in accepting the Liberal nomination for a by-election in Victoria, said:

Another injustice which the Liberal party will remove when it gets the opportunity is the political and legal inequalities existing between the sexes. I do not have to argue before a Liberal audience the unfairness of the present laws, . . . . It will be enough to say they are unjust, undemocratic and detrimental to our development, and will not exist any longer in British Columbia under a Liberal government than they did in the province of Manitoba.

The announcement brought cheers from his listeners.[33] Less than a week later, through the columns of the *Daily Times* of February 22, the Liberals issued a special invitation to women to attend all the campaign meetings preceding the by-election. It was eventually won by Brewster, who became a fearless champion of women's rights in the legislative chamber.

In the legislative session which opened on March 2, 1916, woman suffrage was a paramount issue, and jockeying for political advantage threw the whole situation into confusion. The drama began on March 21 when the veteran Socialist, J. T. W. Place, introduced his third woman suffrage bill. Speaking during the debate on second reading, Premier Bowser astounded his listeners by suggesting that Place withdraw his measure in view of the fact that the government had a plan of its own for dealing with the subject. Pointing out that the government intended to pass an elections bill which would permit soldiers to vote in the provincial election scheduled for late in the year, the premier announced his intention of adding

[32]After the Liberal victory in 1916, the *Daily Times* (Liberal) on Dec. 6 asserted that the Liberal party had adopted a woman suffrage plank at its Revelstoke convention in 1913, but if that be so, the fact certainly received no publicity at the time. In a letter to the author, dated April 19, 1944, Mrs. Laura Jamieson wrote: "The Liberal Party gave us the vote, not because it was progressive, but because it wanted the women's vote and could see that woman suffrage was coming anyway." At the time of writing Mrs. Jamieson was a C.C.F. member of the British Columbia legislature.

[33]*Daily Times*, Feb. 17, 1916.

an amendment to the bill providing that women would get the vote as of January 1, 1917—under one condition. The prerequisite was that a majority of the voters approve the project in a special referendum to be held at the time of the general election in 1916. The premier attributed the sudden reversal of his stand to his intense admiration for women's part in the war effort.[34]

Place refused to withdraw his bill and the cudgels were taken up and wielded without mercy by H. C. Brewster. He ridiculed the premier's statement about the cause for his change of heart and assailed the suggested referendum as unjust to the women who had already clearly indicated their desires, yet could have no voice in such a plan for measuring public opinion. In this attack he was joined by another Liberal, Malcolm A. Macdonald, who saw no reason why "the question should not be dealt with by the House now so that . . . women be given the opportunity to cast their ballots at the coming general elections." The tug-of-war between Conservatives and Liberals progressed through five days of bitter debate and harsh recrimination. Finally, on May 17, Premier Bowser snapped the party whip and the Place bill went down to defeat, 24 to 6, party discipline taking precedence over personal views for certain Conservative members who had voiced approval of woman suffrage on other occasions.[35]

During the tumultuous career of the Place bill, Premier Bowser received considerable abuse without as well as within the walls of the legislature. After passing through the phases of open hostility and cool indifference to the suffrage question, the *Daily Times* by 1916 had become a vehement and vocal champion of equal rights. With even less reserve than the lawmakers, the *Times* accused Bowser of promoting the government version of the suffrage bill in an effort to save his own skin. Charging that he was scared to death by the loss of two important by-elections in March, the paper claimed Bowser was now ready to make this devious concession to something

---

[34]*B.C.: Journals, 1916*, pp. 23, 139. *Daily Colonist*, April 14, 1916.
[35]*B.C.: Journals, 1916*, p. 139. *Daily Times*, April 14, May 12 and 18, 1916.

he really hated; whereas had he been sincere, he would have supported the Place bill.[36] That there was a measure of truth in these blasts is indicated by the studied silence of the Conservative *Daily Colonist*.

While dealing with the attitude of the press towards the subject of woman suffrage in the later war years, it is interesting and somewhat instructive to note the changed attitude of the *British Columbia Federationist*, once so vociferous in its support of the project. In an editorial of April 14, 1916, the *Federationist* pointed out that women by the thousands were invading jobs held by men before the war and would not willingly give up this newly acquired economic independence. The editorial concluded by asserting that the capitalist, anxious to exploit cheap labour, would see that women got the vote in order to keep men from getting back their jobs.[37] Whatever one may think of the soundness of such reasoning, the *Federationist* from that date on took no notice of the suffrage controversy, not even mentioning the passage of the Bowser and Brewster suffrage bills in 1916 and 1917.

Before the final vote on the Place bill had been taken, Mrs. Gordon Grant spoke at a meeting of the Victoria Local Council on May 8. The veteran suffrage campaigner, who had retired from nominal leadership of the Political Equality League in 1913 but continued to be the mainspring of the movement, expressed her opposition to Premier Bowser's referendum plan on two counts: the unfairness of submitting the question to a purely male constituency and the fact that it would mean women would neglect their war work to campaign for a favourable vote. She reminded her listeners that a delegation of thirty-six women representing all women's societies in British Columbia had gone to the premier late in April and expressed their unanimous opposition to his plan, apparently in vain. She concluded by urging her audience to organize an effective campaign, if the head of the government

---

[36] *Ibid.*, April 14, May 18, 1916.
[37] This argument was repeated in heavy type on the front page of the Aug. 11, 1916 issue of the *Federationist*.

insisted upon throwing down the gauntlet to the women.[38]

Just before the defeat of the Place bill, an emergency convention of the Political Equality League, presided over by Mrs. Grant, met in Vancouver on May 15 and 16. Their first action was to telegraph a final appeal to Premier Bowser for the passage of a straight suffrage bill, with no strings attached. When his reply was received, firm on the plan for referendum, the delegates laid the groundwork for a campaign to reach every voter in every ward of every city and town in the province.[39]

Undeterred by arguments, pleas, or abuse, the government went ahead late that month and pushed through the legislature two companion bills. One was known as "An Act for referring to Electors the Questions of the Expediency of Suppressing the Liquor Traffic in British Columbia . . . and the Extension of the Electoral Franchise to Women." The other, depending upon a favourable decision in the referendum provided for by the first, would grant women both the provincial franchise and the right to be elected to the legislative assembly. Both bills received royal assent on May 31.[40]

Passage of these two measures galvanized the recently organized Women's Suffrage Referendum League into feverish activity. Under the chairmanship of R. T. Elliott, K.C., the League appointed workers for every city ward, held weekly campaign meetings, and invited all sympathetic organizations, whether men's or women's, to send delegates to the central committee. Although more than half a dozen friendly societies responded to the invitation, the League's most active lieutenants during the ensuing months were the Provincial Political Equality League, the Local Council of Women, and the Women's Liberal Association, formed in 1915. Members of the latter frequently appeared on the platform with Liberal party candidates during the election campaign, officially

[38]*Daily Times*, May 9, 1916.
[39]*Ibid.*, May 20, 1916. The agency formed to carry out this objective became known as the Women's Suffrage Referendum League or Committee.
[40]*B.C.: Journals, 1916*, pp. 151, 156, 162, 166, 176. *Statutes of B.C., 1916*, ch. 50, 76.

launched by H. C. Brewster on July 4, 1916, and kept the referendum question in the spotlight. In spite of the valiant efforts of the women, it would be erroneous to infer that woman suffrage was more than a minor issue in the campaign as a whole. Such matters as the corruption of the Bowser administration, railroad and steamship policies, and development of natural resources received the lion's share of attention. Indeed, when the four Liberal candidates for Victoria issued a summary of their platform on August 11, woman suffrage was not even mentioned in the list! The support of the Liberal leader and of the party as a whole was unquestioned, however, and thus the Suffrage Referendum League threw its entire strength toward the dual goal of a Liberal victory and an affirmative vote on the woman suffrage referendum.[41]

The provincial elections of September 14, 1916 amply rewarded the suffrage forces for their exertions and for any neglect they may have suffered during the course of the campaign. Brewster and his Liberal followers routed the Conservative regime by a comfortable margin, and the suffrage referendum won by more than two to one.[42] In his message to the people, delivered in the first flush of victory, Premier-elect Brewster acknowledged the assistance rendered by the suffrage forces, particularly in the capital. "To the women of Victoria also, who soon will be granted the franchise as a matter of simple right, I desire to convey the thanks of the Liberal party for their invaluable aid."[43] Gratifying as victory in the political field must have been to Brewster, how much more soul-satisfying must the eventual triumph of a thirty-one year campaign for political equality have been to the veteran leader, Mrs. Gordon Grant. It is an index to the character of this great woman that in the hour of achievement no recriminations were uttered against a defeated foe, and no

[41]*Daily Times*, May 31, June 2 and 9, July 5 and 19, Aug. 12, 1916.
[42]The actual vote was 43,619 for, and 18,604 against the proposal. It is an interesting sidelight that the prohibition forces were victorious in their referendum held the same day, though their margin of success was not so impressive (36,392 for and 27,217 against). *Canadian Annual Review* (1916), p. 781.
[43]*Daily Times*, Sept. 15, 1916.

vain promises made about the imminent arrival of the millennium. Enough for her to point out the need henceforth for men and women to work together in perfecting laws, and to sum up her own emotions with eloquent simplicity: "It is good just to have lived to see this day."[44]

Through a technicality involving delayed election returns from overseas, the Bowser suffrage act of 1916 had never been proclaimed in force, with the result that when the new legislature met on March 1, 1917, the women of the Pacific province were still legally disfranchised despite their victories of the preceding year. Frankly avowing the desire to take credit for the enfranchisement of women, the Liberal party, through the speech from the throne on March 1, promised to rectify the anomaly with all due speed.[45] Introduced by Attorney-General Macdonald on March 27 in the form of an amendment to the Provincial Elections Act, the bill was designed to permit women both to vote and to be elected to the legislature. Second reading, once the stumbling-block of all suffrage bills, was hurdled with ease. Even ex-Premier Bowser spoke in favour of the bill at this juncture, repeating his profound admiration for women's war work and handsomely expressing the hope that Sir Robert Borden might see fit to do something for women in the federal field.[46]

Third reading and royal assent were both bestowed on April 5. A large delegation of women attended the session, bearing bouquets of lilies and roses which were placed on the desks of Premier Brewster and Attorney-General Macdonald. Not to be outdone in gallantry the premier extended to the suffrage leaders the unusual courtesy of occupying seats on the floor of the legislature. Nor did the festivities end there. Judge MacGill recalls that Brewster invited the leaders to a victory dinner that evening where cabinet ministers and suffragists joined to celebrate the happy ending.[47]

[44]*Ibid.*, Sept. 16, 1916.
[45]*Ibid.*, Mar. 1, 1917.
[46]*Ibid.*, Mar. 27, 28, and 30, April 4, 1917.   *B.C.: Journals, 1917*, pp. 42, 49, 57, 61.
[47]*Daily Times*, April 6, 1917.   H. G. MacGill, *op. cit.*, p. 3.   *Statutes of B.C., 1917*, ch. 23.

Two further minor legislative achievements in the 1917 session added to the victory. An equal guardianship law, symbolic of women's new status, was incorporated in the statutes;[48] and a Municipal Elections Act removed all disabilities from women in serving as city officials, thus complementing at last the privilege of municipal voting which had been given almost half a century earlier, in 1873.[49]

The women of British Columbia were not slow to demonstrate their willingness to assume the responsibilities of public office. The new Liberal government also manifested its faith in their capacity by making Helen Gregory MacGill judge of the Juvenile Court in 1917, and in appointing several women to posts as inspectors and censors.[50] But the most colourful figure by far among the women who entered public life following emancipation was Mary Ellen Smith. Wife of Hon. Ralph Smith, long a champion of the suffrage cause in the legislative assembly, Mary Ellen became British Columbia's first woman legislator when, following her husband's death, she won his seat in a by-election on January 24, 1918. For ten years she retained her place in the legislature and headed a drive for improved social legislation; indeed, in her very first session she succeeded in piloting through a minimum wage law for women. According to Mrs. Laura Jamieson (a later member of the legislative assembly), Mrs. Smith possessed good looks, a pleasing personality, and political astuteness. Honours were showered upon her. She was the first woman cabinet member in the British empire, being appointed as minister without portfolio in the Oliver government on March 24, 1921. In the same year she was offered the speakership by Premier Oliver, but turned down the honour on the ground that she could accomplish more as an ordinary member. She did, however, become the first woman in the empire to occupy the speaker's chair when she held it temporarily for one afternoon in 1928. The remarkable Mary Ellen was still active chairman of the provincial Liberal party

[48]H. G. MacGill, *op. cit.*, p. 3.
[49]N.C.W., *Year Book* (1917), p. 84.
[50]*Ibid.* (1918-19), pp. 54-6.

when death finally overtook her at the age of seventy-two on May 3, 1933.[51]

About concrete results of woman suffrage in improved legislation, two of British Columbia's daughters differ widely in their opinions. Mrs. Laura Jamieson contends that, after an early flurry of activity, the suffragists sat back and considered their work done.[52] On the other hand, Judge MacGill mentions with pride the passage of laws dealing with wages and hours, child labour, old age pensions, and the raising of the age at which boys and girls are permitted to marry.[53] This divergence in views may be partly attributable to the fact that Judge MacGill, of an earlier generation, remembers vividly conditions before any of the changes in women's status and in social legislation appeared on the horizon. To one of the pioneers, pride in accomplishment is but natural. Mrs. Jamieson, on the contrary, represents a party (the C.C.F.) and a small group of politically active women, who rebel at the conservatism of the country to such an extent that the halting steps which have been made in the direction of progress appear totally inadequate.

Mrs. Jamieson's judgment seems a little severe in view of the long stream of acts bettering conditions for women and children which flowed from the Pacific coast legislature during the decade following women's enfranchisement. Indeed, British Columbia is generally recognized throughout the dominion as a pioneer of social legislation and a model to other provinces in that respect. Moreover, the province, with Alberta, has passed two laws giving the women of those provinces a unique position in Canada. Since 1922 the women of British Columbia have been eligible for jury duty, and in 1931

[51]*British Columbia Federationist*, Jan. 18 and 25, 1918. H. G. MacGill, *op. cit.*, p. 4. Letter to the author from Mrs. Laura Jamieson, April 19, 1944. *Evening Journal* (Ottawa), May 4, 1933. Vancouver *Daily Province*, May 4, 1933. An excellent biographical sketch of Mary Ellen Smith may be found in Sir Charles G. D. Roberts and Arthur L. Tunnell, eds., *A Standard Dictionary of Canadian Biography: Canadian Who Was Who* (2 vols., Toronto, 1938), II, 421-3.

[52]Letter to the author from Mrs. Laura Jamieson, April 19, 1944. Mrs. Jamieson blames the inertia on the fact that most suffragists were Liberals, and thus, in her opinion, not likely to be advanced in their thinking.

[53]H. G. MacGill, *op. cit.*, p. 4.

they were granted complete civil equality with men by a Sex Disqualification Removal Act, retroactive to 1871.[54] The unusual status thus conferred may have more than a merely coincidental relation to the fact that these two provinces lead the rest of the dominion in the number of feminine lawmakers they have chosen to represent them in their provincial assemblies. Compared with the Maritime Provinces and Quebec, which have never elected a woman legislator, British Columbia's score of seven women members is impressive. Yet the province has never sent a feminine representative to the federal House in Ottawa.

In the provincial elections of 1945, the two older parties in British Columbia merged their forces to assure victory against the rising tide of Socialism. Three women legislators, all members of the C.C.F., were casualties of this strategy, which dealt a decisive setback to the fortunes of the Socialist party. The two survivors of that election, Mrs. Nancy Hodges and Mrs. Tilly Jean Rolston, were members of the older parties.[55] Repetition of this stratagem on June 15, 1949, secured identical results.

In the federal election of 1949, two seasoned C.C.F. campaigners—Mrs. Dorothy Steeves and Mrs. Grace MacInnis— gave their successful Liberal opponents some cause for anxiety. But British Columbia, exponent of progress in so many instances, remains paradoxically in the ranks of the provinces which have never experimented with feminine representation in Ottawa.

Liberals and Conservatives have not failed, however, to note that one source of strength within the ranks of the C.C.F. has been that party's willingness to practise as well as preach political equality. Women in the British Columbia wing of the Socialist party commonly serve on committees and in important managerial posts; in fact Mrs. Grace MacInnis told the author that at the 1946 provincial convention fully half of the delegates were women. It is not unreasonable to

[54]*Statutes of B.C., 1922*, ch. 38; *1931*, ch. 55.
[55]Charlotte Whitton, "Is the Canadian Woman a Flop in Politics?" *Saturday Night*, Jan. 26, 1946, pp. 6-7.

suppose that the older parties will before long follow suit and offer their women adherents a greater share in policy-shaping and office-holding.

If the invitation is offered, the pioneer spirit of the women of British Columbia will certainly rise to accept it.

# *5*

# OTTAWA INTERLUDE

## *Women's Political Rights as a Federal Issue*

WITH THE capitulation of the Hearst government in Ontario on April 12, 1917, all the provinces from the Ottawa River to the Pacific had yielded to the pressure for woman suffrage. The surrender of the four eastern provinces was more belated, and before it came about there intervened the campaign for women's rights in the federal area.

The opening salvoes in the federal struggle had been contemporaneous with the early phases of the suffrage movement in Ontario and British Columbia. In three successive sessions, in 1883, 1884, and 1885, Sir John A. Macdonald, the great Conservative prime minister and champion of the theory of strong central government, introduced suffrage bills whose main purpose was to establish a uniform dominion franchise,[1] but each of which also included a section that would give the federal franchise to widows and unmarried women.

The bill of 1883 was introduced on April 13 by Sir John himself. In discussing the bill the prime minister mentioned the inclusion of unmarried women with sufficient property qualifications but gave no explanation for his singular proposal. When Edward Blake, leader of the Opposition, rose to speak against the proposed measure, his indignation sought out other portions of the bill for attack; the woman suffrage

---

[1]From 1867 to 1885, the determination of the qualifications for voting in dominion elections was left in the hands of each province, just as this same question is placed under the jurisdiction of the individual states in the American republic.

section was apparently so insignificant as to be unworthy of notice. On the ground that the session was too near its close to permit proper consideration of the measure, Sir John moved on May 23 that it be set aside until the following session; but not before the House had received a petition from the Dominion Women's Enfranchisement Association in Toronto asking that *all* women with sufficient property qualifications be included in the bill.[2]

Some weeks before the suffrage bill was laid to rest, an Ottawa paper, the *Daily Free Press*, attacked the prime minister for limiting his proposal to unmarried women. In an editorial of April 19, 1883, it said:

> By what process of reasoning we should like to know, has the Premier arrived at the conclusion that an unmarried daughter should have a vote and her mother not? The idea is ridiculous. . . . There are no people in the community more thoroughly alive to political issues, more independent and accustomed to think, plan, execute and direct than the married women. Often, indeed, they are much wiser than their husbands, possessed of keener insight, truer sympathies and clearer perceptions of right and wrong. . . . The argument that it would disturb the concord of the home is bosh. . . . If Sir John really desires to make a name for himself among the great men of the world, he will abolish the restrictions in his bill and place all women, married or single, on the same level in the law of the franchise.

The franchise bill of 1884 was almost identical in its terms with the earlier measure, and although supported by three petitions from municipal bodies in Ontario, was allowed to drop from sight without debate and with no explanation for its demise by the government which introduced it.[3] Macdonald's party had been returned to power in 1882 with a comfortable majority of sixty in the House; he was probably in no haste to change the federal electoral system when there was no apparent need for it.

In 1885 Sir John determined to push through to a conclusion his project of a uniform federal franchise. The bill originally provided for the enfranchisement of unmarried

[2]I. Harper *et al.*, *Woman Suffrage*, IV, 1034-5. *Canada: H. of C. Journals, 1883*, pp. 206, 285, 432. *Canada: H. of C. Debates, 1883*, I, 593-6; II, 1387. *Canada: Bills of Commons, 1883*, No. 107.
[3]*Ibid., 1884*, No. 7. *Canada: H. of C. Journals, 1884*, pp. 20, 29, 60, 85, 455. *Canada: H. of C. Debates, 1884*, II, 1627.

women, but this clause was dropped by Sir John when he perceived that its retention might endanger passage of the measure. Nevertheless, in the many days of debate the subject of woman suffrage was given its first thorough airing on a national scale. At the start of the long and ofttimes bitter debate, Sir John represented himself as an enthusiastic supporter of female suffrage, yet was careful to point out that this one portion of the bill was an "open" question, whereas the rest was a government measure. The Opposition did not fail to taunt him on this score, saying that he was using it as a trial balloon and that he was obviously willing to desert the ladies at the first sign of danger.

Seven days of debate preceded the elimination of the woman suffrage clause from the measure. The loudest howls of anguish from the Opposition benches were caused by the threatened destruction of the rights of the provinces to regulate the federal franchise. However, when the question of female franchise held the spotlight, the major portion of the arguments was definitely in favour. But a careful listener in the House galleries would have noticed that the chants of praise for the ladies were delivered almost exclusively by members of the Liberal Opposition, while Sir John's own followers maintained an ominous silence. Where the Liberals did offer criticism on this aspect of the bill, it was generally on the score that all women were not to be enfranchised or that certain provinces, such as Quebec, were unready to take such a step and that the question should therefore remain with the provinces.

It must not be inferred that there were no spokesmen for the opposing view. A few members from both parties brought forth the stock arguments of the anti-suffragists: that the time was not ripe, that there was no general demand for it (which was quite true), that it defied Bible teachings, that it would degrade women, etc. Yet the astonishing thing in these speeches was the absence of any strong opposition. Apparently those opposed were so sure of their ability to defeat the measure that they felt they could afford the luxury of silence.

The *coup de grâce* was administered to the "open" section of the measure on April 28 when one of Sir John's own back-benchers, Charles J. Townshend of Nova Scotia, moved successfully that it be struck from the bill. Macdonald, who was well aware of the mutiny in the ranks of his party, made no last-minute effort to save that which he had earlier professed to favour so ardently. Indeed, when the Commons resumed their discussion of the measure on the following day, his first words were a cheerful acceptance of the decision of the House and a promise to delete from the bill "all portions . . . which relate to the female franchise."[4] Thus the great Franchise Act of 1885, which changed the basis of dominion suffrage from provincial to federal, defined a person as ". . . a male person, including an Indian and excluding a person of Mongolian or Chinese race."[5]

The reasons for Macdonald's brief flirtation with the woman suffrage issue are not easy to fathom. One biographer, G. Mercer Adam,[6] does not even mention the Franchise Act of 1885, while G. R. Parkin states erroneously: "To the enfranchisement of single women . . . he avowed himself personally favourable, but he did not introduce it into the bill."[7] John Lewis, one of the contributors to the monumental work *Canada and Its Provinces*, acknowledges that such a clause was in the bill originally and that its inclusion contributed "to the prolonged and obstructive discussion," but presents no explanation for its appearance so long before there was any concerted pressure for such a measure.[8]

[4]*Ibid.*, *1885*, II, 1444.

[5]*Canada: Bills of Commons, 1885*, no. 103.   The debates for these seven days will be found in *Canada: H. of C. Debates, 1885*, II, 1133-1204, 1241-77, 1340-85, 1388-1444.   *Canada: H. of C. Journals, 1885*, pp. 232, 308-14, 318-19, 341-3, 352-3. It is an interesting sidelight on this bill of 1885 that there was no woman's suffrage petition presented during the session; and for the three petitions presented in favour of the bill, there were over six times that number against it.

[6]G. Mercer Adam, *Canada's Patriot Statesman: The Life and Career of the Right Honourable Sir John A. Macdonald* (Toronto and London, 1891).

[7]George R. Parkin, *Sir John A. Macdonald* (Vol. XVIII in the Parkman Edition of *The Makers of Canada*, Toronto, 1908), pp. 258-60.   The quotation will be found on p. 259.

[8]John Lewis, "Canada under Macdonald, 1878-1891," in Adam Shortt and Arthur G. Doughty, eds., *Canada and Its Provinces* (Edinburgh Edition, Toronto, 1908), VI, 98-9.

However, some light is shed upon the problem in Macdonald's *Memoirs*, edited by his friend and former secretary, Sir Joseph Pope. The latter claimed that Sir John's idea of a franchise bill was one which would include two basic principles: (*a*) a uniform suffrage (to complete the work of confederation), and (*b*) recognition of a property qualification as establishing the right to vote. Sir Joseph believed that the prime minister favoured the extension of the franchise to single women primarily because to exclude them would be at odds with his basic theory of a property qualification. A second motive ascribed to Macdonald by Pope presents an interesting contradiction, for it proposed to cure the evils of democracy by a further extension of democracy. According to Sir Joseph, the prime minister would "welcome the advent of a new and powerful conservative factor in politics, whose tendency he believed would be to strengthen the defences against the irruption of an unbridled democracy."[9]

Certainly it seems unfair to assume, as Macdonald's Liberal opponents did, that the woman suffrage clause was political chicanery to win votes. With so little general demand for votes for women in the mid-eighties, it cannot be said that he was catering to popular opinion. It is surely possible that the prime minister, a man of truly great breadth of vision, was genuinely impressed by the justice of woman suffrage, at least for single women, and would gladly have enacted it into federal law were the cost not too high. As a practical statesman, however, he was not prepared to sacrifice either party unity or a bill he deemed very important in order to gratify a personal preference for a noble but unpopular principle.

From 1885 until 1898 control of the federal franchise remained in the hands of the dominion government. With interest in suffrage gaining increasing momentum in many parts of the country during these years, the small amount of attention given to the subject by the parliament at Ottawa is somewhat odd. More surprising was the scarcity of suffrage

[9]Joseph Pope, *Memoirs of the Right Honourable Sir John Alexander Macdonald, G.C.B., First Prime Minister of the Dominion of Canada* (2 vols., Ottawa, 1894), II, 246-8. The quotation is on p. 248.

petitions to the federal lawmakers. After the débâcle of 1885, suffrage groups appear to have lost even the courage to raise their voices in supplication, with the result that in the second half of the decade but one petition on the subject was presented to the House of Commons, that of the Methodist Church Conference in 1888.[10] Beginning in 1891 and continuing until 1896, the W.C.T.U., by an annual flutter of petitions, kept the subject from fading altogether out of the legislators' minds. All told there were eighteen such petitions in those years, fourteen of which originated with either the dominion W.C.T.U. or one of its branches.[11]

Not till near the end of dominion control of the federal franchise did the House of Commons trouble itself with the women's phase of the franchise question. On April 6, 1894 Robert B. Dickey, a Conservative member from Nova Scotia, attempted to persuade the House to incorporate a limited form of female franchise in a suffrage bill then under consideration, but could not arouse any debate on the question.[12]

A similar motion by Nicholas Flood Davin on May 3 of the following year accomplished nothing concrete for the feminist forces, but did at least produce the first full-dress debate on the question in ten years—and also the last until the period of the Great War. Davin, a Conservative from the Northwest Territories, supported his motion by a long and eloquent plea, using history and the Bible as well as common-sense modern arguments in an effort to forestall every objection that might be brought forth. In spite of this, more speakers opposed the project than in Sir John's time,[13] and Wilfrid Laurier, Liberal Opposition leader, further complicated the question by reintroducing the old problem of dominion versus provincial control. The Liberal statesman said he had no objection to woman suffrage if any province demonstrated that it wanted it, but his own province (Quebec) was firmly

---

[10]*Canada: H. of C. Journals, 1888,* p. 140.
[11]*Ibid., 1891,* pp. 84, 100, 109, 124, 155, 197, 210; *1892,* pp. 291, 294, 374; *1894,* pp. 64, 77, 85, 138, 159; *1895,* p. 49; *1896,* p. 167.
[12]*Ibid., 1894,* p. 61.   *Canada: H. of C. Debates, 1894,* I, 842.   I. Harper *et al., Woman Suffrage,* IV, 1035.
[13]Sir John A. Macdonald died in 1891.

opposed and he would object to having the issue forced upon any province. In contrast with such fair and understandable opposition was the speech of Guillaume Amyot of Quebec. Resorting to the well-worn theme that casting a ballot would remove women from their proper sphere, Amyot solemnly averred that women are "the point of connection between earth and Heaven. They assume something of the angel. . . . Let us leave them their moral purity, their bashfulness, their sweetness, which gave them in our minds so much charm. It ill becomes the community to change her sex and to degrade her by the exercise of the franchise." In a final blast he produced this gem: "You make men of women and you depoetize them."[14] After three days of debate, Davin's motion was lost by a vote of 105 to 47.[15]

Wilfrid Laurier became prime minister in July 1896. In view of the strenuous Liberal opposition to Macdonald's Franchise Act of 1885, it is not surprising to find that one of the matters to which the new Liberal prime minister early turned his attention was the restoration to the provinces of the control over the dominion franchise. This was accomplished by the Franchise Act of 1898.[16] During the debates on this important franchise measure there was no mention of woman suffrage, nor was there any woman suffrage petition to parliament in that year. With control of electoral lists once more in the hands of the provinces, the parliament at Ottawa was relieved of all responsibility for the enfranchisement of women for many years to come. The small but valiant bands of women found it necessary henceforth to concentrate their political efforts upon their provincial governments, and this undoubtedly militated against the successful formation of any truly nation-wide suffrage association.

Amid press reports of wild scenes in England where the

[14]*Canada: H. of C. Debates, 1895*, I, 730-4.
[15]*Ibid.*, *1895*, I, 702-19, 730-4, 1867-8, 2141-5. *Canada: H. of C. Journals, 1895*, pp. 61, 105, 119-20. I. Harper *et al.*, *Woman Suffrage*, IV, 1035. Henrietta Muir Edwards, *Women of Canada* (a pamphlet compiled at the direction of the National Council of Women in Canada for the Paris International Exhibition in 1900, has no pagination).
[16]*Statutes of Canada, 1898*, ch. 14.

militant suffragists were in full swing from 1908 until 1914, Canada generally maintained an almost unbelievable degree of apparent indifference to the suffrage question. Echoes of the distant strife naturally found their way to the dominion and isolated groups in the separate provinces exerted heroic (though peaceful) efforts to secure the franchise for women, but the editor of the *Canadian Annual Review* was close to the truth when he wrote in 1912: ". . . it must be said that the discussion in Canada was, in comparison [to England], weak upon both sides of the subject."[17]

Mrs. O. D. Skelton, commenting in 1913 upon the marked Canadian apathy toward the enfranchisement of women, in contrast with the keen interest exhibited in England, the United States, New Zealand, and Australia, attempted to offer some plausible explanations.[18] Her principal contention was that Canadian women had suffered few disabilities or hardships because of their lack of political power. Except for Quebec, Mrs. Skelton maintained that women in the dominion already possessed most of the social and civil rights which other women might hope to gain through possession of the ballot. Furthermore in Canada, where men outnumbered women in the ratio of 100 to 88, women were not as yet forced to compete with men in business and professions as they were in England. Turning to the United States, Mrs. Skelton found that the history and political doctrines of that country had aided the women's cause. Such milestones of freedom as the Declaration of Independence, the freeing of the Negro, followed by the granting of political rights to the ex-slave, were lacking in the more northern democracy. Since the struggle for political freedom had never been as drastic or spectacular in Canada, it had failed to leave as deep an imprint on the rank and file of the people.

On a very practical plane, Mrs. Skelton pointed out that in a predominantly agricultural world where thousands of new

[17]*Canadian Annual Review* (1912), p. 304.
[18]Isabel Skelton, "Canadian Women and the Suffrage," *Canadian Magazine*, XLI (Toronto, 1913), 162-5. It should be remembered that New Zealand women were enfranchised in 1893 and Australian women in 1903.

homes were being laid out every year, women were too busy with their personal and household problems to give much thought to outside affairs. The vast size of the country tended to isolate and hamper the active suffrage leaders. Canada was vast and transportation difficulties great, but Mrs. Skelton's reasoning, which was based on Canada's position as primarily a pioneering agricultural country, overlooks the fact that it was two such countries—Australia and New Zealand—which led the world in enfranchising women. In the United States, it was the pioneer communities of Wyoming, Utah, and Idaho which first conferred political equality upon women, and this before the close of the nineteenth century.

Canadians, however, were not antipathetic to the suffrage cause. Though they themselves spurned militant activity, it is a lesson in Canadian tolerance to note that prominent English suffragists (some having served jail sentences), who visited the country in 1911 and 1912 and went on lecture tours across the dominion, were invariably greeted by large audiences and listened to with respectful, if not always enthusiastic, attention. These visitors included Mrs. Emmeline Pankhurst, Miss Sylvia Pankhurst, Mrs. Forbes Robertson Hale, and Miss Barbara Wylie. The last, in an address at Montreal on November 4, 1912, attempted to arouse her audience to unwonted behaviour.

Don't be submissive. Don't be docile. Don't be ladylike. Don't dread being conspicuous. Now is the time for deeds not words. Remember you are fighting for liberty. . . . Concentrate all your efforts on the Dominion Parliament. Insist that the Federal Elections Act be repealed. . . . Go to Mr. Borden in your thousands and demand votes for women at this Session . . . not at some long distant future, but now.[19]

Robert Borden, who became prime minister of Canada in 1911 at the head of a Conservative government, had had a taste of English militancy before Miss Wylie's Canadian tour and found it not to his liking. While on a visit to England in 1912 he received a delegation of suffragettes who harangued him for an hour on the deplorable state of women in the country

[19]*Canadian Annual Review* (1911), p. 370; (1912), pp. 305-7. The quotation is from the latter, p. 305.

he represented, and ended by threatening to introduce violent methods upon the Canadian scene. With chilling brevity Borden replied: "Any suggestions as to methods in your campaign which may be introduced into Canada will not have the slightest influence upon me. If I am to be subject to methods which are to make my life unpleasant or inconvenient or even shortened, I frankly tell you these considerations will not govern my actions in the least."[20]

A suffrage delegation of a different kind met the prime minister on December 23, 1912 in the city of Toronto. As mentioned in Chapter I, Mrs. F. M. Denison and some of the officers of the Canadian Suffrage Association took the occasion of the premier's visit to their city to ask for a federal franchise act for women and to try to get from him a definite statement about his position on the question. Little satisfaction was gained from the vague promise that he would give revision of the franchise act his consideration at some unspecified time in the future.[21]

An equally indefinite statement was secured a few months later from the federal Opposition leader. Speaking in Toronto on the occasion of the organization of the Toronto Women's Liberal Association on May 5, 1913, Sir Wilfrid Laurier commented: "In every civilized country I see no reason why women should not have the franchise if they desire it."[22]

Probably neither Borden nor Laurier anticipated how soon after these incidents the question was to become an issue. In 1916, twenty-one years after the defeat of Nicholas Flood Davin's motion, the suffrage question returned at last to plague the federal parliament and more especially the government under Sir Robert Borden. Manitoba had already granted equal rights (January 27, 1916) and her two sister provinces of the prairies were moving rapidly in the same direction when a Liberal member from Saint John, N.B., rose on February 23

[20]*Evening Journal* (Ottawa), June 10, 1937. *Gazette* (Montreal), June 11, 1937.
[21]I. Harper *et al.*, *Woman Suffrage*, VI, 759. N.C.W., *Year Book* (1913), pp. XXX-XXXI. *Canadian Annual Review* (1912), p. 171.
[22]*Ibid.* (1913), p. 392. Mrs. Newton Wesley Rowell was president of the new organization.

to move an amendment to the Dominion Elections Act to the effect that women possessing the provincial franchise be also granted the federal franchise. Although the startled government succeeded in having William Pugsley's motion postponed until February 28, a full-fledged discussion of the vexatious subject could no longer be sidestepped.[23]

In making his motion the member from Saint John had two objects in view. First was the federal act which specifically barred women from voting in federal elections in the provinces of Alberta and Saskatchewan (also in the Yukon Territory). These were the only two provinces in the dominion to which the statute applied. Would it seem fair then, with the enfranchisement of the women of those provinces imminent, that they should find themselves debarred from federal voting privileges while their sisters in Manitoba, where no such federal disqualification existed, might exercise both the provincial and federal franchises? Pugsley thought not. Then, too, in spite of Sir Robert's statement to the women of Toronto in 1912 and notwithstanding the commonly held opinion that (outside of Saskatchewan and Alberta) provincial enfranchisement would automatically confer upon women the right to vote in federal elections, there was no proof that the courts would adopt that view and certainly the government had made no official pronouncement upon the question. Pugsley's motion would provide for this contingency, too, and see that complete justice was done to women.

In the debate which followed some eight or ten members were willing to place their views on record; they were divided almost equally on the question. Except for Pugsley himself, the advocates of the motion were from the West while those opposed were from the older sections of the country. G. W. Kyte of Nova Scotia delivered the longest and bitterest speech in opposition. The Nova Scotian used every weapon in the arsenal, not omitting divorce statistics from the United States where this plague of woman suffrage had been haunting the

---

[23]*Canada: H. of C. Debates, 1916*, II, 1185-1206. *Canadian Annual Review* (1916), pp. 427-8. *Daily Times* (Victoria), Feb. 29, 1916.

land for almost seventy years. On the other side a new note was sounded, along with the more time-worn arguments in favour of equal rights. This new note consisted of eloquent tributes to the heroic part Canadian women were playing in the Great War.

At length E. M. Macdonald, wearied of the talk which was accomplishing nothing, pleaded for some expression of opinion on the motion by the government. Unable longer to avoid the issue completely, Hon. Robert Rogers, minister of public works, tried to sidestep by stating that if Pugsley had only made his motion for a general dominion enfranchisement of women, he might have been disposed to support it. The motion's sponsor interrupted to ask how Rogers could reconcile this view with what Sir Robert Borden had told the delegation of women; but the minister simply ignored the interruption, made the entire question a party issue, and requested the Conservatives to support him in voting down the motion.

Apparently stung by Pugsley's reference to his reply to the delegation, Sir Robert rose and made a very lame attempt to justify his change of viewpoint. Yes, he had told the women it would be desirable for them ". . . *in the first place* [italics mine] to address themselves to the provincial authorities," but now the member for Saint John had raised certain issues which would make a review of the whole question of the federal franchise advisable at some future time. That would be the time also to consider the enfranchisement of women, but until then the prime minister opposed giving the federal franchise to some women and not others, and so would ask the House to defeat the motion. Pugsley probed into the wound once more.

My right honourable friend admits that he told those ladies that they had better go and address the Governments of the provinces and get them to promote legislation granting woman suffrage. What was the inference which these ladies had a right to draw from the statement . . .? Was it not that if any province enacted legislation giving women the right to vote for the Legislature they would also, as a matter of course, be granted the right to vote for the Dominion Parliament?

All to no avail. Taking their cue from Sir Robert and the

minister of public works, the Conservative majority turned the motion down soundly.[24]

Two other brief references to woman suffrage in the House during the 1916 session let the government know that the question could not be evaded indefinitely. On March 10 Frank Oliver of Edmonton read a telegram from the presidents of the Women's Institutes of Alberta and the Women's Industrial Association of Edmonton, in which they demanded to know whether the government had definitely decided against woman suffrage. Sir George Foster promised to give the telegram to the prime minister and suggested that Oliver send off a wire asking "the ladies to keep up their hopes until they get an answer."[25] Coming even more directly to the point on March 29, J. G. Turriff of Assiniboia queried: "Is it the opinion of the Minister of Justice that women who are on the voters' list in the province of Manitoba, which province has granted the franchise to women, will be entitled to vote for members of the House of Commons?" Hon. Charles Doherty's answer was brief and evasive. "It has never been the practice to answer questions of law."[26]

Meanwhile, outside the lower chamber of the federal parliament, some interesting and encouraging developments were taking place. Although the Liberal programme adopted by the National Liberal Advisory Council on July 20, 1916 contained no reference whatever to woman suffrage,[27] Laurier himself admitted that he had been won over to the cause. In a private interview late that spring with Professor Carrie Derick, one of the outstanding feminists of Montreal, he is reported to have stated that if returned to power in the next elections he would introduce an equal franchise bill.[28] This promise he reiterated publicly in an address before the Wo-

---

[24]*Canada: H. of C. Debates, 1916*, II, 1202-6.

[25]*Ibid., 1916*, II, 1608.

[26]*Ibid., 1916*, II, 2301.

[27]A summary of the programme may be found in the *Daily Times* for July 21, 1916.

[28]Entry of June 2, 1916, Minute Books of the League for Women's Rights, in the possession of the present League Executive, Montreal. These Minute Books, which have no pagination, cover the years from 1913 to 1919, and from 1922 to 1947. Hereafter cited as L.W.R. Minute Books.

men's Canadian Club at London, Ontario, on September 12, 1916.[29]

Borden, on the contrary, was not yet ready to make any commitments. Confronting the visiting prime minister in Winnipeg that December, Mrs. Nellie McClung put the matter before him bluntly. "We feel that we should have the franchise given to us without any further agitation, for we are too busy to fight for it, and we will greatly begrudge the time if we have to do so." The most famous of all western feminists, whose sharp wit and fierce jibes had made the premier of Manitoba lose control of his temper during an interview in 1914, extracted little more from the imperturbable Sir Robert than: "Certainly, the women of Canada have earned the right to consideration."[30]

That "consideration" soon followed. Undaunted by the government's treatment of his motion at the previous session, Pugsley returned to the attack on January 31, 1917 when he gave notice of motion of a resolution that either the federal vote be given to those women who had the provincial franchise or that the federal vote be extended to all women throughout the country. This "either . . . or" policy would indicate that although Pugsley preferred to adhere to the traditional Liberal course of permitting each province to control the federal electorate, he was willing to meet the objections expressed by the prime minister and Hon. Robert Rogers to his motion of February 28, 1916. The motion was allowed to stand for several months mainly because of Borden's absence from the country that spring, and then was eventually dropped on May 21, after debate on a similar motion by a Conservative private member had stolen its thunder.[31]

The entire afternoon and evening of May 16, 1917 had been given over to a full debate of the woman suffrage question as the result of a motion by the Conservative member for South Oxford, Donald Sutherland, that the question of en-

[29]*Daily Times*, Sept. 13, 1916.
[30]*Manitoba Free Press* (Winnipeg), Dec. 12, 1916.
[31]*Canada: H. of C. Debates, 1917*, I, 309, 672, 759; II, 1594, 1627-8.

franchising women "should engage the attention of the Government at the present session."[32] Of all the speeches made on this occasion, only one was in the slightest degree antipathetic to the subject under discussion, that of D. D. McKenzie (Liberal) of North Cape Breton. The Nova Scotian was promptly assailed by a western Liberal as an "old-fashioned Tory." Apart from this brief spat, Conservatives and Liberals both praised women's war work, cited records of women's progress in other democratic countries, and conceded the justice of their demands. R. B. Bennett, promising young Conservative of Calgary (later prime minister of the dominion), confessed that, though he had not been favourably disposed toward votes for women in pre-war years, women's heroic exertions in the national crisis had won him completely to their cause.[33]

The only factor which prevented this debate becoming a harmonious chorus was the seemingly inevitable conflict between Liberals and Conservatives over control of the federal franchise—whether it should remain with the provinces or be restored (at least partially) to the dominion government. Discussion on this phase of the question was precipitated early in the debate when the minister of justice, Hon. Charles Doherty, gave his opinion that granting the provincial franchise to women in the five provinces west of the Ottawa did not also include the federal franchise. His reasoning, based upon the common law interpretation of the word "person" and upon certain famous English franchise cases, appeared so abstruse and technical to at least one member of the House as to cause him to remark:

As to the legal arguments that we heard this afternoon from the Hon. Minister of Justice, if he had anything clear in his mind, or if he was able to make anything clear to the other legal lights in this House, he certainly was not able to make anything clear to the ordinary layman because when the honourable member was through it seemed to me that the matter was more muddled up than when he started.[34]

In a speech as remarkable for its lucidity as the justice

---

[32]*Ibid., 1917*, II, 1477. *Canada: H. of C. Journals, 1917*, p. 216.
[33]*Canada: H. of C. Debates, 1917*, II, 1515-20.
[34]*Ibid., 1917*, II, 1490-9, 1518. The speaker was J. G. Turriff (Liberal) of Assiniboia.

minister's was for its obscurity, Sir Wilfrid Laurier paid his warmest respects to woman suffrage, but argued for a continuance of provincial control and explained why he disagreed with the interpretation placed upon the Franchise Act of 1898 by Doherty.  Citing section 10 of the act, Sir Wilfrid pointed out that the law provided that the provincial lists be adopted for federal elections.  The fact that section 32, dealing with Saskatchewan and Alberta, specifically mentioned *male persons only* as qualified to vote, was further evidence that in other sections of the act, where no such restriction was included, the lawmakers had not necessarily meant males only.

I submit, not as a violent legal supposition, but as a matter of common sense, that, having chosen to accept the franchise created by the respective provinces, we decided to take the franchise not merely as it existed then, but as it might exist at any time in the future.   If therefore, the franchise of any province is different to-day from what it was in 1898, under the legislation then enacted, we take the franchise as it is to-day. . . . It seems to me that this is a reasonable interpretation of the statute.

The Liberal leader concluded, however, that if there were the slightest doubt about women being federally enfranchised in those provinces where they had recently received provincial political rights, the federal franchise law should be amended immediately to make certain that their newly won rights included the dominion franchise.[35]

This occasion marked the first appearance of Sir Robert Borden in the House after a visit to England, and the warm reception tendered to him by the lawmakers of all shades of political opinion must have heartened him considerably.  Following Sir Wilfrid in the suffrage debate, the prime minister began with an expected approval of Doherty's legal views and then sprang the surprise which was the sensation of that day's proceedings—his unequivocal endorsement of woman suffrage.  Deprecating the idea that voting rights should be bestowed upon women as a reward for service, Sir Robert claimed that in the national emergency ". . . they have showed themselves worthy to take a part in the government of this country and

[35]*Ibid., 1917,* II, 1503-4.

they have thereby made abundantly clear *what I believe was clear before* [italics mine], their right to a voice in the government of the country in which they live." The prime minister closed by saying he thought the question ought to be decided by parliament before any appeal was made to the people in a general election, and moved to amend Donald Sutherland's motion accordingly. Liberal members, like German of Welland and Turriff of Assiniboia, lost no time in pointing out that Sir Robert's amendment was either a bid for the extension of the life of parliament beyond October 7, 1917 or "a very quiet, smooth way of doing the women of Canada out of a vote for the next Dominion election." With nothing definite settled except the desirability of giving women the right to vote, and with some members clamouring for immediate action on the question, debate was adjourned that memorable evening upon Sir Robert's promise to resume it at some future date.[36]

The prime minister's unexpected endorsement of woman suffrage, coupled with his insistence that it be accomplished by an act of the dominion parliament, roused suspicions in the Liberal wing of the press. A New Brunswick reporter in the press gallery told his readers that as the debate proceeded interest waned in the women's problem, but waxed hot over transferring the voting lists from the provinces to the federal government. "That seven of the provinces of the Dominion which prepare the lists on which the federal franchise is based are at present Liberal may be one reason why the Government has in contemplation a dominion franchise act before it appeals to the people."[37] The *Manitoba Free Press*, on May 26, attempted to tear apart the legal arguments of the minister of justice and then informed its readers that an inner clique of the Conservative party, headed by Hon. Robert Rogers, had become anxious to revert to dominion control of the franchise as a means of keeping the party in power and distributing more patronage. Looking at this question from the calm perspective of more than a quarter of a century, one is led to

[36]*Ibid., 1917*, II, 1506-8, 1510, 1518.  *Canadian Annual Review* (1917), pp. 291, 433.  *Citizen* (Ottawa), May 17, 1917.
[37]*Daily Telegraph* (Saint John), May 17, 1917.

conclude that the sudden interest of the Conservative administration at Ottawa in the enfranchisement of women—*if
brought about by the enactment of dominion legislation*—was
undoubtedly prompted by the natural desire to win the forthcoming elections; but the lower motives attributed to the
government by the *Free Press* were scarcely warranted.

The opening wedge for women in the federal field was the
passage of the Military Voters Act in September 1917. The
act provided that all British subjects, whether male or female,
who had participated actively in any branch of the Canadian
armed services were to have the vote at any general election
held during the war or prior to demobilization. Its purpose
was primarily to enfranchise soldiers and sailors under twenty-
one years of age, but it also included nurses, most of whom
were women. What little debate there was on the measure
in Commons was on other than the woman suffrage feature
of the bill, although Pugsley found the opportunity to ask the
government if it were not high time they introduced a thoroughgoing woman suffrage measure.[38] The bill occasioned
considerable debate in the senate, during which there was no
reference to the enfranchisement of women: an indication of
the weight attached to this feature by the members of the
upper chamber.

The same month which witnessed the quiet passage of the
Military Voters Act also saw a measure pushed through parliament to the accompaniment of indignant roars of disap-
proval, both within and outside of the legislative gristmill.
The problem of compulsory military service had been troub-
ling Sir Robert's government as early as 1916, for there were
large sections of the country to which the idea was abhorrent.[39]

[38]*Canada: H. of C. Debates, 1917*, V, 4406-7, 4688-9. *Statutes of Canada, 1917*,
ch. 34. Henry Borden, ed., *Robert Laird Borden: His Memoirs* (2 vols., Toronto,
1938), II, 706-8. Hereafter cited as H. Borden, *Memoirs*.

[39]Especially in Quebec and in those areas of the Prairie Provinces where
there were large elements of foreign born, some of whom had left their native
lands partly to escape compulsory military service laws. For a comprehensive
and interestingly written account of the situation in Quebec there is Elizabeth
Howard Armstrong, *The Crisis of Quebec, 1914-18* (New York, 1937). The *British
Columbia Federationist*, mouthpiece of the labour movement on the west coast,
was vehemently anti-conscriptionist in its editorials. Voluntary enlistment was
so obviously a failure in Sir Robert's opinion that he went on a recruiting tour
all the way to the west coast in December 1916.

The growing conviction in Borden's mind that conscription was necessary, no matter what the cost, if the government was to be able to fulfil its military commitments, reached certainty during his visit to England in the early spring of 1917.[40] Further complications arose from the fact that the life of parliament (already extended for one year beyond its statutory limit in 1916) was due to expire in October 1917. The temper of the Liberals in the House did not seem to warrant the assumption that another such extension would be forthcoming, though there is evidence to indicate that as late as July 17 Sir Robert clung to the hope that a wartime election might not be necessary. On that date he introduced a motion to extend the life of parliament until October 7, 1918, with the promise that, unless the vote for the motion was practically unanimous, he would drop the idea. The vote of 82 to 62 by which the motion passed was far from unanimity.[41] An early election thus became inevitable and it was obvious to all parties that, coming in 1917, it must hinge mainly upon the conscription issue.[42]

As the summer months merged into early fall, bringing closer the inevitable appeal to the country at the polls, Borden resorted to two expedients in an attempt to have his government returned to power and to unify the country behind his programme for the critical war months that lay ahead. The first device was the formation of a coalition government with that wing of the Liberal party which was not averse to conscription. After months of negotiation, such a coalition was formed and installed in office under the title of the Union government on October 12, 1917, about two months before the federal elections.[43]

[40]H. Borden, *Memoirs*, II, 697. I. Harper *et al.*, *Woman Suffrage*, VI, 761-2.
[41]H. Borden, *Memoirs*, II, 713-19.
[42]Oscar Douglas Skelton, *Life and Letters of Sir Wilfrid Laurier* (2 vols., Toronto, 1921), II, 533. Hereafter cited as O. D. Skelton, *Laurier*.
[43]*Ibid.*, II, 512-13, 515-16. H. Borden, *Memoirs*, II, 720-53 *passim*. Between May 25 and June 6 Sir Robert attempted unsuccessfully to have Sir Wilfrid and the entire Liberal party join the coalition. Thereafter his efforts were directed toward those of the Liberals who would support a conscription policy, though that meant abandoning their leader. Throughout these trying months of negotiations both Sir Robert and Sir Wilfrid exhibited the tact, patience, and willingness for self-sacrifice of true statesmanship.

The other half of the stratagem lay in the passage of the bitterly assailed Wartime Elections Act, whose purpose, in the opinion of the Opposition and notwithstanding heated government denials, was the securing of an electorate which would favour the continuance in office of Sir Robert's administration. Designed to be in force only during the war and until demobilization, the act was double edged. The creation of a federal electorate almost certain to return a Conservative (or Unionist) government to power would be accomplished in part by denying the franchise to two classes of citizens whose aversion to conscription was known, or thought to be known. The first group would cover all conscientious objectors, including some religious groups like the Mennonites and Doukhobors. The second group would consist of all those born in enemy countries and naturalized since 1902. Having thus weeded out several hundred thousand possible dissenters, the bill would mould a new and favourable mass of voters by bestowing the franchise upon all women who, being British subjects and twenty-one years of age or over, had a close relative serving in the armed forces of Canada or Great Britain.[44] The bill carefully maintained provincial control over age, race, and residence qualifications for these prospective voters, doubtless in the hope of avoiding some of the deadliest fire from the Liberal batteries in the House.[45]

Illness prevented the prime minister from introducing the

[44]Skelton maintains that the great majority of people disfranchised under the act were Liberals and adds that it was ridiculous to suppose that Czechs, Slovaks, Ruthenians, and Poles had any love for Austria or Germany. The women singled out for enfranchisement would naturally throw their vote to conscription in order to bring relief to their men overseas. "It was frankly a stacking of the cards, a gerrymander on a colossal scale, an attempt without parallel except in the tactics of Lenin and Trotsky to ensure the dominance of one party in the state." O. D. Skelton, *Laurier*, II, 529-30.

[45]*Statutes of Canada, 1917*, ch. 39. The exact wording of section 33A, the crucial one from the women's point of view, is as follows: "Every female person shall be capable of voting and qualified to vote at a Dominion election in any province or in the Yukon Territory, who, being a British subject and qualified as to age, race and residence, as required in the case of a male person in such province or in the Yukon Territory, as the case may be, is the wife, widow, mother, sister or daughter of any person, male or female, living or dead, who is serving or has served without Canada in any of the military forces, or within or without Canada in any of the naval forces, of Canada or of Great Britain in the present war. . . ."

measure personally, as had been intended. The difficult task of launching and explaining a bill which, in Borden's own words, "precipitated vehement opposition and violent controversy" devolved upon the secretary of state, Hon. Arthur Meighen, on September 6.[46] Frankly admitting that "the necessity for the Bill arises out of the precipitation of an election in time of war," Meighen explained the difficulties of getting votes from large sections of the 300,000 young men, "the finest of Canada," in the overseas fighting forces, even with the aid of the Military Voters Act. Yet justice to them and to Canada demanded that their influence be felt in the coming general election. Since their direct vote would be difficult to obtain in many instances, the bill proposed to do the next best thing by enfranchising "such of their kin at home who can best be said to be likely to vote in such a way . . . as they themselves would do upon our shores. Consequently this Bill provides a measure of woman enfranchisement which endeavours to attain that end." For justice to men in the overseas forces and for justice to Canada Mr. Meighen showed deep concern, but as to the merits or justice of woman suffrage there was not a single reference in his entire speech.[47]

Conscious of the objections that would inevitably arise to the partial enfranchisement of women, Meighen explained that this was because "a very substantial portion of the women of the country," though British citizens now, had become naturalized simply by marrying British citizens. "Remembering this, it seems very plain, indeed, that it would be unfair and unreasonable at this time, and under the shadow of this war, that an unlimited woman suffrage should be granted."[48] In closing his explanation of this portion of the bill, Meighen was careful to stress the maintenance of the provincial franchise qualifications; but in the brief debate which followed, Sir Wilfrid Laurier immediately pointed out

[46]H. Borden, *Memoirs*, II, 708. George R. Locke, *Builders of the Canadian Commonwealth* (Toronto, 1923), p. 295.
[47]H. Borden, *Memoirs*, II, 708-9. *Canada: H. of C. Debates, 1917*, VI, 5415-16.
[48]*Ibid., 1917*, VI, 5416.

the inconsistency of this position by referring to the thousands of women in the five western provinces (which now subscribed to equal rights) who would not possess the federal franchise under this bill. The Liberal leader could not refrain from hinting at a broken pledge, too, when he remarked: "It was understood on this side of the House, when my honourable friend from Saint John [William Pugsley] drew attention to the matter, that, in the next election, the women would have the franchise."[49]

Notwithstanding Liberal cries of protest at the use of closure to limit debate and the haste with which the bill was rushed through its various stages, the government pressed on grimly to obtain the passage of the measure by the House on September 14. Four days were consumed in thrashing out the bill's controversial provisions with the debate often reaching unwonted heights of caustic bitterness as the Liberal minority fought the measure tooth and nail every inch of the way.[50]

Certain highlights emerged from the debate, in spite of the repetitiousness of several members' remarks. Opposition members claimed the bill was a diabolical scheme to set up a special military caste to perpetuate the power of the Conservative government. The measure was described as undemocratic, un-British, unjust, reeking of Prussian militarism, and a stratagem to win the election rather than the war. Government members, supported by Conservative backbenchers, continually urged the "service and sacrifice" theme as the justification for the bill. Sir George Foster, minister of trade and commerce, reached a pinnacle of rhetorical eloquence in trying to make clear the government's distinction (for voting purposes) between two kinds of service performed by Canadian women during the war. Acknowledging the splendid work done on the home front by these women, Sir

[49] *Ibid., 1917*, VI, 5421.
[50] H. Borden, *Memoirs*, II, 709. Sir Robert says closure was necessitated because of the Opposition's "fierce and protracted resistance." The entire debate, which consumes 217 double column pages of Hansard (the official record of the House debates), will be found in *Canada: H. of C. Debates, 1917*, VI, 5550-60, 5567-636, 5637-702, 5807-80.

George labelled it "the service and sacrifice of sympathy."

But there is a degree that is still higher, and these women would be the first to acknowledge it. That is the service and the sacrifice . . . which comes from heart strings wrung, which looks out of tear-bedimmed eyes, which comes from sleepless nights and anxious days, which comes from the part of flesh and blood and family that is far from them and which is exposed to constant danger. No one doubts that this kind of sacrifice and service is far higher than the other. This is the distinguishing line upon which we base this franchise Bill, . . . .[51]

Suffragists who followed the proceedings might have been chagrinned to find their particular phase of the measure engaging approximately only one third of the members' time, the rest being devoted to the injustice done to loyal naturalized citizens by the disfranchising clauses of the bill. They could, however, take comfort in the reflection that when the woman suffrage portions did occupy the spotlight, members' comments were overwhelmingly favourable. The splendid and heroic role of women in the war now superseded all other arguments for political rights and scarcely a speaker, on either side of the bill, failed to mention it. Only on third reading did a few French members summon the courage to say they heartily disapproved of equal political rights for women under any circumstances.

Liberals criticized the disfranchisement of women in those five provinces which had granted women voting privileges. Borden pointed out that, according to his government's view, they were not being *dis*franchised because they never had been *en*franchised federally. Representatives from Ontario to British Columbia were quick to retort that such an interpretation had not been intended by the provincial lawmakers and would not be accepted gracefully by the people of the affected provinces.

The Conservative side declared that the provisions of the bill met with the approval of the great majority of women, and cited a letter signed by the presidents of the National Council of Women, the National Equal Franchise Union, the Daughters of the Empire, and the Ontario W.C.T.U. The

[51]*Ibid., 1917*, VI, 5854-5.

letter was reported to have appeared in the Toronto *Journal-Press* of September 13, 1917, and to have said it was the considered opinion of these women that a limited female franchise was desirable for the duration of the war.[52] A Liberal member countered with an extensive quotation from the Montreal *Gazette* for September 14 in which the Equal Suffrage League of that city scored the bill as one of the most autocratic and unfair ever to be placed before the House.[53]

Two ghosts rose up to haunt Borden at intervals throughout the debate: his now famous and oft-cited reply to the women of Toronto in 1912 and his remarks on enfranchising women before the next election (made before the House only a few months earlier on May 16, 1917). These mutually contradictory statements were brought up by his Liberal tormentors who claimed that he had since adopted a third stand on the woman suffrage question, prompted by expediency. In reply the government made much of the necessity for changing the naturalization law before granting complete suffrage for women, and said this would be impossible to accomplish at the present session.[54] More than once in the course of the debate, however, Borden pledged that if continued in office as a result of the approaching elections, he would introduce a thoroughgoing woman franchise measure.[55] With this modicum of hope suffrage groups were forced to be content for the time being.

[52] *Ibid.*, *1917*, VI, 5832-3. The speaker was either confused or misquoted. The newspaper referred to was the Ottawa *Journal-Press*.

[53] *Ibid.*, *1917*, VI, 5866.

[54] As the law stood in 1917, alien women could marry British subjects and thereby immediately become British citizens. Conversely, Canadian women who married foreigners lost their British citizenship. This situation was not changed until 1946 (*Statutes of Canada, 1946*, ch. 15), in spite of all that was said about the necessity for revising the naturalization law for women both during the debates on this bill and on the 1918 franchise measure. Letter to the author from Hon. Paul Martin, Secretary of State for Canada, Oct. 10, 1946. See also *Saturday Night*, Sept. 7, 1946.

[55] *Canada: H. of C. Debates, 1917*, VI, 5578, 5648. H. Borden, *Memoirs*, II, 712. The *Canadian Annual Review* (1917), p. 434, printed a copy of a letter signed by Sir Robert Borden which appeared in the Vancouver press on Sept. 17, part of which read: "In case I am returned to power, it is my purpose to place upon the statute books a measure granting the franchise to all women of British birth and conferring upon women of foreign birth the right to seek and obtain naturalization on their own behalf; that they may become endowed with the same privilege. . . ."

The bill's path through the senate was also anything but smooth. Members of the upper house were no more sparing than those of the lower in attacking the unfairness of the measure both to naturalized citizens and to women in general. The Liberal senators described the bill as an unscrupulous attempt by a dying government to keep itself in power. Strangely enough, in this stronghold of conservatism, no word was spoken against the principle of woman suffrage; there was only indignation at the number of women left unenfranchised by the bill. Angry words availed as much in the senate as they had in the House—exactly nothing; and the bill emerged from the upper chamber on September 20, to receive royal assent the same day.[56] Thus was enacted into law one of the most bitterly debated and controversial measures in Canadian history, as a result of which more than 500,000 Canadian women soon exercised the federal franchise for the first time.

Reactions in the anti-Borden press were as violent as in parliament; rather more so, for freedom of the press offered more scope in vocabulary than the rules of conduct in legislative halls would permit. The *British Columbia Federationist*, never noted for moderation, snapped:

The Ottawa high priests of political depravity have nobly risen to the occasion by incubating a "War Times Election Act" that has anything in the line of impudent chicanery and clumsy cunning that was ever perpetrated, beaten to a standstill.[57]

The much more staid and respected *Morning Chronicle* of Halifax chimed in from the opposite side of the continent:

No more partisan measure than this freak scheme to corral votes for a discredited Government, has ever been presented to, much less passed by, the Parliament of Canada. It is subversive of the fundamental principles of democracy. . . . It is, in effect, Prussianism and not the British sense of justice and fair play which is the guiding spirit. The War Time Franchise Bill would more properly be described as a Win-the-Election Measure, regardless of good faith and national honor—win at any cost and any price.[58]

That this was the general view of the purpose of the measure,

[56]*Canada: Senate Debates, 1917*, pp. 1114-51, 1183-1222. *Canada: H. of C. Journals, 1917*, p. 698. *Statutes of Canada, 1917*, ch. 39.
[57]*British Columbia Federationist* (Vancouver), Sept. 14, 1917.
[58]*Morning Chronicle*, Sept. 13, 1917.

even outside Liberal and radical circles, may be inferred from the comment of the unimpassioned, factual *Canadian Annual Review*.

The War-times Franchise Act brought in a large electorate of women voters who would probably be friendly to the Government, and disfranchised a large Western element which was undoubtedly hostile to both Government and war policy.[59]

The same thought echoed from a distance of more than a quarter of a century when a writer in *Saturday Night* declared: "The 1917 coalition had to manipulate the voters' lists very heavily to be sure of winning its election. . . ."[60]

Whatever one may choose to think of the motives behind the Wartime Elections Act, the fact remains that the women's vote suddenly became a very important factor in the election campaign of November and December 1917. Estimates of the size of the new element in the national electorate range all the way from half a million to a million. Appeals for their votes were directed at women not only by both political parties, but by pulpit and press. Dr. Augusta Stowe-Gullen, veteran feminist of Toronto, noted "the humorous spectacle of our anti-suffrage friends making speeches on the necessity and importance of women voting; while other anti-suffragists took women to the polls. . . ."[61]

When the smoke of the campaign had cleared away and the union government had been returned to power, it was generally conceded that the government owed its victory in substantial measure to the votes of those women upon whom it had chosen to bestow the franchise.[62] The government itself acknowledged that debt and its realization of the new importance of women in the national picture by convening a Women's War Conference at Ottawa from February 28 to

[59]*Canadian Annual Review* (1917), p. 579.
[60]Anon., "Ministers Must Lead," *Saturday Night* (Toronto), Nov. 18, 1944.
[61]*Canadian Annual Review* (1917), pp. 630-1. "Annual Report of the Standing Committee on Citizenship," N.C.W., *Year Book* (1918-19), p. 54. The quotation is from the latter.
[62]I. Harper *et al.*, *Woman Suffrage*, VI, 761-2. H. Ridley, *Woman Suffrage*, p. 20. *Telegram* (St. John's, Newfoundland), June 10, 1937. O. D. Skelton, *Laurier*, II, 530, 541. The Union government achieved a majority of seventy-one.

March 2, 1918. Delegates from all outstanding women's organizations in Canada were addressed by the governor-general and prominent cabinet members on such subjects as national health and child welfare, and national registration and industrial activity. Resolutions passed by the delegates on several matters were cordially received by the administration and indicated a further cementing of the friendly relations which existed between the government and many important women's organizations at the time of the conscription election in 1917.[63]

That the Union government intended to carry out Sir Robert's full enfranchisement pledge to the women of Canada became evident on March 18, 1918, when, amid all the pomp and ceremony traditionally surrounding the opening of a new parliament, the Duke of Devonshire read the speech from the throne. Further evidence that there would be no more hedging came just two days later, as Sir Robert rose in the Commons to sponsor personally the introduction of Bill Number Three, a real woman franchise measure. In moving second reading on March 22, the prime minister spoke at last as a person thoroughly convinced of the justice of the principle which he would now make the law of the realm.

I do not even base it on the wonderful and conspicuous service and sacrifice which women have rendered to the national cause in the war. Apart from all these, I conceive that women are entitled to the franchise on their merits, and it is upon that basis that this bill is presented to Parliament for its consideration. It is our belief that the influence of women exercised in this way will be a good influence in public life. We believe that beneficial results have ensued wherever the franchise has been granted to them. . . .[64]

Even the Toronto *Globe*, long a proponent of woman suffrage and certainly no friend of Borden's, conceded on March 22 that the proposed bill was "eminently fair and just" and that

[63]N.C.W., *Year Book* (1918-19), p. 58. *Canadian Annual Review* (1917), pp. 630-1 (for evidence of support of Union government by many women's organizations); (1918), pp. 590-1. The reader is also reminded of the letter in the Ottawa *Journal-Press* of Sept. 13, 1917, cited during the debate on the Wartime Elections Act. I. Harper *et al.*, *Woman Suffrage*, VI, 762-3.

[64]*Canada: H. of C. Debates, 1918*, I, 89. H. Borden, *Memoirs*, II, 781. I. Harper *et al.*, *Woman Suffrage*, VI, 763.

the premier, though a late recruit to the suffrage cause, was "an out-and-out one."

Until the bill reached committee of the whole, there was little argument about the principle of woman suffrage. The quite lengthy discussion on second reading concerned itself mainly with technical provisions involving nationality and qualifications for voting. As the bill was originally introduced, it would have made one uniform suffrage for women throughout the dominion, while leaving the provinces to determine the qualifications for men. In Quebec, where a small property requirement still prevailed, this would have resulted in a broader franchise for females than for males. Certain members from Quebec immediately made it plain that, while they did not approve of woman suffrage under any circumstances, such a provision as this completely outraged their French-Canadian sense of propriety. Though at first inclined to retain the uniform franchise for women, Sir Robert soon moved to amend his own bill, making it necessary for women to fulfil the same qualifications as men in each province.[65] It was in this form that the bill was eventually passed.

Another technical difficulty arose when Lieutenant-Colonel William F. Cockshutt, a Conservative, inquired anxiously whether this bill would permit women to be elected to the House, at the same time indicating his own feelings by the terse observation: "I would rather run against two men than against one woman." With dry humour the prime minister spoke to reassure him. "It would require the amendment, I think, of another Act. This is merely a franchise Act. As far as the general principle is concerned, I shall imitate the prudent reserve of my honourable friend who has just spoken."[66] Evidently granting the vote to women was as much as Sir Robert cared to swallow in one dose, too.

Real debate on the principle of the measure came on April 11 while the House sat in committee.[67] Several French-Cana-

---

[65]*Canada: H. of C. Debates, 1918*, I, 98-9, 364-6.
[66]*Ibid., 1918*, I, 101-2.
[67]*Ibid., 1918*, I, 634-77.

dian members began a powerful attack on the bill at the very outset of the discussion. Their grounds of complaint were two-fold: the bill would largely remove from the hands of the provinces the determination of the qualifications for the federal franchise (always a sore point with the Liberals), and more to be condemned, the enfranchisement of women would be contrary to natural order. Some were generous enough to say that if certain provinces wished to fly in the face of Providence by giving women the vote, that was their own affair; but in their beloved Quebec, neither men nor women wanted woman suffrage, and they would oppose this measure with every ounce of energy they possessed.

A few quotations selected at random from the speeches made by the French-Canadian members will indicate the kind of opposition Quebec suffragists were to face in the twenty-two year struggle that still lay before them to win the provincial franchise. Charles A. Fournier paid a compliment to Canadian womanhood and then warned:

A country cannot, without paying the full price, act contrarily to the laws of God and nature. There is an essential distinction between man and woman. . . . And to keep up the birth-rate of Canada we must keep our women within their sphere; we must attract them towards the accomplishment of the duties of their sex, duties specified by the unchangeable laws of nature. . . . It [woman suffrage] is the antithesis of that highest and sweetest mystery, conviction by submission, conquest by sacrifice. I want no contest with women, Mr. Chairman.[68]

With a magnificently comprehensive sweep, Jean Joseph Denis summarized his objections to the bill:

I say that the Holy Scriptures, theology, ancient philosophy, Christian philosophy, history, anatomy, physiology, political economy, and feminine psychology, all seem to indicate that the place of women [*sic*] in this world is not amid the strife of the political arena, but in her home.[69]

In a speech which exhibited both eloquence and learning, Arthur Trahan quoted from Auguste Comte:

In general the true path of progress is this: to render the feminine life more and more domestic and to release it more and more from all outside occupation, the better to insure the accomplishment of its end: mating.

[68]*Ibid., 1918,* I, 637-8.
[69]*Ibid., 1918,* I, 644.

The same member also expressed fear for the birth-rate, for the increase of the spoils system with the enlargement of the electorate, and the immorality which would ensue "from promiscuity between the sexes."[70]

The best speeches in favour of the proposal were made by western members, though several eastern members contributed. The supporters claimed that women were needed in the body politic because of their interest in social reforms; that Great Britain by recently enfranchising her women had set a pattern which Canada would do well to follow; that the old argument, "inability to perform military service," had been buried deep by the splendid work of women on farm and in factory during the country's hour of trial. The speakers marshalled an impressive mass of statistics to prove that women did avail themselves of the franchise in large numbers in those countries and provinces where they possessed it. Two westerners reminded the House that chivalry was not preserved by denying women their just rights. They were immediately supported by an English-speaking member from Quebec who made the pungent observation: "There is the argument that woman is queen of the home. I often think she is more really queen of the dishpan or the wash-tub. The idea that a woman sits regally enthroned by the fireside is very pretty, but is not according to facts."[71] Captain Joseph Read of Prince Edward Island dealt the birth-rate argument, so favoured by the French Canadians, a shrewd blow by pointing out that in *la belle France*, where women were refused the vote, the birth-rate was declining so rapidly as to constitute a serious national problem.[72]

The franchise bill passed third reading on April 12 with no debate, the members apparently having exhausted themselves and all available arguments in committee of the whole. But Sir Robert's protégé still had to face the senate and there debate became so protracted, especially on technical matters, as to necessitate a conference between the prime minister and

[70]*Ibid.*, *1918*, I, 648-50.
[71]*Ibid.*, *1918*, I, 663.          [72]*Ibid.*, *1918*, I, 667-8.

Sir James Lougheed.[73] In his *Memoirs*, Sir Robert explains: "The Senate was challenging the provisions of the Women's Franchise Bill, and I sent for Lougheed who told me he could manage them."[74]

Before they were completely "managed," however, many senators had seized the opportunity to say something about the measure. It is interesting to find that the most gallant speech in favour came from Senator Raoul Dandurand of Quebec,[75] while the most violent in opposition was made by a British Columbian senator, Hon. H. J. Cloran. The latter marshalled together every old outmoded argument that had been heard in the previous forty years for a final parade, but stressed especially his fear that woman suffrage might lead to family disunity. It is to be hoped that the following fragment of the senator's oration is more eloquent than descriptive of the state of discipline in his own household. "I would not deprive my wife, or my mother, or my daughter of any right that would bring them comfort, or ease, or emolument. No, I love them too much for that; but I love them more by not exposing them to disagree with me. . . ."[76]

Three unsuccessful attempts were made by senators to amend the bill when it reached committee of the whole. Hon. Philippe A. Choquette would have limited the proposal to unmarried women. Branding woman suffrage as "one of the regrettable errors of our time," Senator Laurent O. David would have limited it to women over thirty.[77] A proposal of quite a different character came from an entirely unexpected

[73]Hon. Sir James A. Lougheed, a Conservative member of the Union government. He had also been responsible for steering the Wartime Elections Act through the senate and had accomplished it by a policy described by one senator as: "Don't argue, just vote."

[74]H. Borden, *Memoirs*, II, 804-5.

[75]Senator Dandurand proved himself to be a loyal friend of the feminist movement in his own province as well as at Ottawa. In 1909 he had presided with Dr. Grace Ritchie-England over a suffrage meeting in Montreal at which the principal speaker was Mrs. Philip Snowden. He was also present at the organization meeting of the Provincial Franchise Committee in 1922. Mme Dandurand was one of the vice-presidents of the National Council of Women in 1918.

[76]*Canada: Senate Debates, 1918*, p. 365.

[77]*Ibid., 1918*, pp. 411-13.

source.   Senator Cloran made a motion on May 3 to amend the bill by providing that married women and widows not only have votes for themselves, but an additional vote for each living child under twenty-one years of age![78]

After clearing the senate on May 3, the bill received royal assent on May 24 and with that final formality woman suffrage in the federal field became an accomplished fact in Canada. The act, which was to go into effect on January 1, 1919, provided simply that "every female person" who was a British subject, at least twenty-one years of age, and possessed of the qualifications which would entitle a male person to vote in the province in which she resided, could vote at a dominion election.   The last provision also included married women and unmarried daughters, if the husband or father had the necessary property qualifications in any province which might still make such a requirement.[79]

In all but two provinces (Ontario and New Brunswick), the right of women to vote for members of the provincial legislatures was accompanied by the complementary privilege of eligibility for election, either in the same act or in a separate act passed at the same session. As already noted, the question of making women eligible for election to the House of Commons had been broached while the Women's Franchise Act was under discussion in 1918; indeed, it had also been mentioned during the earlier debates on the Wartime Elections Act.   But no one appeared unduly concerned when the government adopted its policy of "one step at a time."

However, with no appreciable amount of pressure from any source, either inside or outside parliament, the right of women to be elected to the federal House was quietly inserted into the Dominion By-Elections Act of July 1919. The occasion for this act was not connected with political rights for women.   By government decree demobilization had been officially set for August 1, 1919.   This would, of course, automatically terminate the Wartime Elections Act.   As stopgap

[78]*Ibid., 1918*, p. 434.
[79]*Statutes of Canada, 1918*, ch. 20.

legislation between demobilization and the thoroughgoing revision of the federal election law which the government had in contemplation for the 1920 session of parliament, the by-elections bill was introduced very near the close of the 1919 session. Debate in both House and senate upon the measure was very brief, and in neither chamber was the slightest objection expressed to making women eligible for election to the House of Commons. From the feminist point of view interest centred in section 69 of the act which provided that: ". . . any British subject, male or female, who is of the full age of twenty-one years, may be a candidate at a Dominion election."[80]

Although this measure gave to women a valuable new political privilege, it also included a retrograde step. By requiring that the wife of a naturalized citizen have the qualifications necessary for naturalization as a *feme sole*, the act had the effect of disfranchising many women who had voted in the "khaki election" of 1917 under the terms of the Wartime Elections Act.

In 1920 the Union government put through parliament the Dominion Elections Act which reverted to the old principle established by Sir John A. Macdonald in 1885—that of uniform suffrage throughout the country for federal elections. Voting requirements for both men and women were simply British citizenship, attainment of the age of twenty-one years or over, and residence in Canada for twelve months and in the electoral district for two months prior to the election. This powerful act had three notable effects on the development of women's rights in the federal sphere. By continuing the naturalization clause for married women as set forth in the By-Elections Act of the previous year it also disfranchised some women who had been able to vote in 1917. But by taking control of electoral requirements out of provincial hands (where the Women's Franchise Act of 1918 had partially left it), the 1920 measure gave the vote to some women

[80]*Canada: H. of C. Debates, 1919*, V, 4533, 4621-59. *Canada: H. of C. Journals, 1919*, pp. 516, 538, 586. *Canada: Senate Debates, 1919*, pp. 934-6. *Statutes of Canada, 1919*, ch. 48. The act received royal assent on July 7.

who would not have been able to meet the property requirement demanded by Quebec, small though it was. Finally, the
Act of 1920 reaffirmed and made permanent the right of
women to be elected to the House of Commons.[81]

The end of the long road stretching over almost half a
century had now been reached. Years of disappointment,
neglect, and rebuff had followed that far-off day in 1883 when
Macdonald had astonished his contemporaries by proposing
the enfranchisement of women. But with the war years came
a new concept of woman's place in the community. A Conservative government which had yielded the first small measure of political equality to women under the pressure of
expediency, ended by admitting itself whole-heartedly converted to the principle of equal rights. It had made women
eligible both to vote and hold office. Now, in 1920, it was up
to those women to use their newly won political freedom wisely
in order to justify the trust that had been placed in them.

The first dominion-wide election in which all women
participated was that of 1921, when the Unionist government
of Arthur Meighen[82] was supplanted by a Liberal administration under W. L. Mackenzie King. That approximately
one and a quarter million women now possessed the weapon
of the ballot was reflected in the strenuous appeals made to
them by both sides: the Conservatives reminding them that
their party had bestowed dominion franchise upon them, while
the Liberals, no more bashful, pointed to the enfranchisement
of women in Manitoba, Saskatchewan, Alberta, and British Columbia under Liberal governments. Four women
attempted to storm the citadel of the House of Commons, but
only one, Agnes Macphail of Ontario, who ran as an independent, succeeded in gaining admission.[83] For Miss Macphail
this marked the beginning of a parliamentary career nineteen
years long, during which her constituents showed their satisfaction with their representative by re-electing her four times.

[81]*Ibid., 1920*, ch. 26.
[82]Mr. Meighen had succeeded Sir Robert Borden as leader of the Unionist
government on July 10, 1920, when the latter retired because of ill-health.
[83]*Canadian Annual Review* (1921), pp. 503-4.

In the rejoicing over women's first general venture at the polls and the accompanying hope that their influence would raise the general tone of national politics, a sombre, pessimistic voice warned from the Nova Scotian mists that no good could be expected from the innovation. Those who took to heart the words of W. E. Maclellan, written during the 1921 campaign, must have been little cheered:

... few mature women really desired the franchise. What good, then, has been done by this fine and radical extension of the franchise? It has simply doubled the electorate, without making it wiser or better or more discriminating. It has greatly complicated the election preparations. It has opened the door to far wider and more demoralizing corruption ... it has wrought prospective evil in this; while many of the better class of women will not vote, no such abstention is to be expected from a less desirable class. ... The thing does not look pleasant or commendable just now, but it may improve on acquaintance. Let us hope so. Everyone, however, may as well awake from the dream that women are going to "elevate politics" by their votes or otherwise.[84]

One last attack upon women's franchise privilege was made in the federal parliament. On May 9, 1922, Senator L. O. David, who will be remembered for his unsuccessful attempt to amend the women's franchise bill in 1918, moved that unmarried women below the age of thirty be disfranchised. The gist of his long-winded speech in support of the motion was that unmarried women before thirty know nothing of politics and, furthermore, should have their minds bent upon "preparing themselves to fulfil the duties of their noble mission." Why Senator David felt that political light would suddenly dawn upon women at their thirtieth birthday he did not bother to reveal, unless he felt that by that time there would be little further chance of "fulfilling their mission," in which case they might just as well mingle in sordid politics. The motion was defeated by a vote of 33 to 19[85]—but nineteen supposedly rational men were persuaded to vote for such a proposal!

While critics like Senator David and W. E. Maclellan were

[84]W. E. Maclellan, "Women and Votes," *Dalhousie Review*, I (Halifax, 1922), 419-20.
[85]*Canada: Senate Debates, 1922*, pp. 152-3.

unfair, it must be conceded that until the recent war, when several women assumed positions of great responsibility at Ottawa,[86] the participation of women in the federal government was very limited. The record reveals that in the quarter century after 1920 only five women sat in the federal House of Commons.[87] The second world war did not result, as some had supposed it would, in a new crop of feminine members in the lower house. On the contrary, in the federal election of June 11, 1945, near the close of the war, Mrs. Dorise Nielsen and Mrs. Cora Casselman, who were running for re-election, were defeated. Mrs. Gladys Strum of Saskatchewan, a new-comer, was the only successful woman candidate. A woman's handbag perched atop one lone desk in the Green Chamber was symbolic of the extent to which Canadian women were represented among federal lawmakers in the early post-war years. The federal contest of June 27, 1949 removed even that forlorn symbol, for all women candidates were defeated.

In view of the very limited number of women who have served in the House of Commons, it is not surprising to find that no woman has ever attained cabinet rank in the federal government. Prior to the elections of 1945 there were rumours that in the event of a victory for the C.C.F., Agnes Macphail would receive a minister's portfolio. Fate and the electorate decreed otherwise.

A high if somewhat empty honour was conferred upon Mrs. Cora Casselman on March 13, 1944 when, for a few hours, she held the speaker's chair. Members broke into applause as she took her place on the high throne-like seat at the north end of the chamber and Lieutenant-Colonel Arthur Ross, who was speaking, hastened to congratulate her. For the first time in Canadian history, the words "Madame

[86]To mention a few notable examples: Mrs. Rex Eaton, Director of the Women's Division of National Selective Service; Miss Byrne Hope Sanders, Director of the Consumers' Branch of the Wartime Prices and Trade Board; and Mrs. Phyllis Gregory Turner, Chief Research Economist to the Dominion Tariff Board and also Technical Adviser to the Oil Administrator of the Wartime Prices and Trade Board.

[87]They are Miss Agnes Macphail, Ont., 1921-40; Mrs. Martha Louise Black, Yukon Terr., 1935-40; Mrs. Dorise Nielsen, Sask., 1940-45; Mrs. Cora T. Casselman, Alta., 1941-45; Mrs. Gladys Strum, Sask., 1945-49.

Speaker" echoed through the House of Commons.[88]

Greater and more enduring honour came to Mrs. Casselman in the spring of the following year when the government asked her to serve as one of the Canadian delegation to the San Francisco Conference. In her person all Canadian womanhood received its tribute for the magnificent work it had performed during a second great national ordeal.

The senate resisted feminine invasion much longer than the lower house. However, Senator Cairine Wilson was "summoned" under a Liberal government in 1930 and Senator Iva Fallis under a Conservative administration five years later. The story of the heroic struggle waged by the five justly celebrated Alberta women to win for women the right to sit in the upper chamber is heartening evidence that, once aroused, Canadian women can make their influence felt in politics.

The Persons Case is the name commonly used to designate the valiant contest waged by Judge Emily Murphy and her four associates from Alberta to prove that women are eligible for appointment to the Canadian senate. The name is derived from the fact that eligibility hinged upon the legal interpretation of the word "person" as found in section 24 of the British North America Act. While in the minds of most women there never existed much doubt about whether or not they were persons, legal minds found this point highly contentious until that day in October 1929 when Lord Chancellor Sankey, reading the opinion of the highest tribunal in the British empire, concluded that women are "persons" in the eyes of the law and hence entitled to be summoned to the Canadian senate.

Although the spectacular and much publicized phase of the case occupied the years 1928 and 1929, the roots of the struggle actually reach back to Edmonton, Alberta, in 1916. As already noted in Chapter III, the Liberal Sifton government, which had very recently enfranchised the women of its

[88]*Globe and Mail* (Toronto), Mar. 14, 1944. *Canada: H. of C. Debates, 1944,* II, 1429.

province, showed its faith in its new body of active citizens in
June of that year by appointing Mrs. Emily Murphy police
magistrate to preside over the newly created Women's Court
in Edmonton. The honour of becoming the first woman police
magistrate in the British empire was not without its draw-
backs and heartaches as Judge Murphy was to discover the
very first day she presided over her court. Enraged by a stiff
sentence which the judge imposed upon his client, counsel for
the defendant gave vent to his spleen by telling "Her Honour"
that she was not legally a "person" under the British North
America Act and had no right to be holding court anyway.
The judge held her peace, relying upon the provincial government to prove, if necessary, that she was a "person."[89]

Annoyances of this kind continued, however, aggravated
by the appointment in December 1916 by the Sifton administration of another woman police magistrate, Mrs. Alice
Jamieson, for the city of Calgary. As far as the province of
Alberta was concerned, the "persons" question was settled
and further embarrassment removed from its female jurists
by the decision of Mr. Justice Scott, upheld by the Supreme
Court of Alberta, in the case of *Rex* vs. *Cyr* (1917). With a
breadth of vision characteristic of the new West, the judge
opined: ". . . that applying the general principle on which the
common law rests, namely of reason and good sense, as applied
to new conditions, there is at common law no legal disqualification for holding public office in the Government of this
country arising from any distinction of sex. . . ."[90] For a
woman of Emily Murphy's make-up, however, it was not
enough to have the matter settled for Alberta only. The relatively brief tribulations suffered by her and by Magistrate
Jamieson, though satisfactorily concluded as far as the province was concerned, set this public-spirited citizen to thinking

[89]Emily F. Murphy, "History of the Movement" (Edmonton, c. 1928), has
no pagination. This is a brief memorandum written by the judge herself, shortly
after the unfavourable decision of the Supreme Court of Canada in 1928. May
be found in the collection of Judge Murphy's Papers, now in the possession of
her daughter, Miss Evelyn Murphy, Vancouver, B.C. Hereafter cited as E. F.
Murphy, "History." *Evening Telegram* (Toronto), June 18, 1938. *Citizen* (Ottawa), June 18, 1938. *Bulletin* (Edmonton), Apr. 25, 1928.
[90]E. F. Murphy, "History."

deeply about the whole question of women's position under the B.N.A. Act, and its possible implications with regard to their eligibility for the senate.

The matter was first called to public attention as the result of a resolution adopted by the first conference of the Federated Women's Institutes of Canada in 1919. With Magistrate Emily Murphy presiding over the conference and imparting her own boundless enthusiasm, it is not surprising that the delegates from all eight of the provinces represented unanimously endorsed a resolution requesting Prime Minister Borden to appoint a woman to the senate. Many other women's organizations soon followed suit, including the powerful National Council of Women.[91]

In January 1921 the Montreal Women's Club, under the leadership of Mrs. John Scott, abandoned the vague request for appointment of "a woman" and asked Prime Minister Arthur Meighen point-blank to name Mrs. Emily Murphy to the senate as soon as there should be a vacancy. Mr. Meighen courteously said no, for the law officers of the Crown had advised him that the nomination of a woman was impossible. Notwithstanding the rebuff, Mrs. Murphy was pleased that she, a westerner, had been singled out as the candidate of a group of easterners.

We women here want you in the Senate because you are a woman and a worthy representative. In fact, in all of Canada, we feel there is no other to equal Judge Murphy for the appointment. . . . With very best wishes and trusting it will not be too long before you are notified that you are going to be 'laid on the shelf' with the other Senators, but hoping of course, that you will not be too quiet, I am,

> Sincerely and affectionately,
> Gertrude E. Budd.

So wrote the secretary of the Montreal Women's Club to Emily Murphy in January 1921.[92] Receipt of this tribute from afar seems to have been the spark that kindled Mrs. Murphy's determination to fight the question through to a finish, for

[91]*Ibid.* Byrne Hope Sanders, *Emily Murphy—Crusader* (Toronto, 1945), p. 218. Hereafter cited as B. H. Sanders, *Emily Murphy.*
[92]Gertrude E. Budd to Emily F. Murphy, Jan. 7, 1921, Emily F. Murphy Papers. Hereafter cited as Murphy Papers.

pinned to this letter is a tiny note in the judge's own hand-
writing saying that this was where the campaign started.
Over eight years were to pass before her careful strategy and
inexhaustible patience triumphed over legal technicalities to
remove another barrier blocking the political progress of
women.

The idea of having a woman in the senate evoked an interestingly large response from men's and women's organizations
across Canada. Judge Murphy's papers contain dozens of
letters from associations asking how they might help or telling
about resolutions passed and sent to the government. In spite
of his refusal to the Montreal Women's Club, Mr. Meighen
felt the pressure of public opinion sufficiently to promise during
the election campaign of 1921 that, if re-elected, he would
strive to secure the admission of women to the upper house.[93]
The results of the election relieved him of that responsibility
temporarily and when Mr. Meighen again became prime
minister for three turbulent months in 1926, weightier matters
apparently engaged his attention.

A third prime minister found himself involved in this
question when in February 1922 the death of an Alberta
senator brought a new flood of appeals to Ottawa for the
appointment of Emily Murphy. For the first time the stocky
little magistrate from Edmonton made an open effort to secure
the position for herself when she addressed a letter on the subject to the prime minister, Mr. W. L. M. King, on February
14. Mr. King's reply, though it promised nothing definite,
was friendly to the general idea. Indeed, the bachelor prime
minister said he was prepared, if necessary, to seek an amendment to the B.N.A. Act.[94] This, coupled with Senator Archibald McCoig's notice of motion for an amendment to the
B.N.A. Act to permit women to sit in the senate, on June 25,
1923, must have given Judge Murphy and her growing body
of supporters the hope of imminent victory. But Senator
McCoig, for some unexplained reason, failed to appear on the

[93]E. F. Murphy, "History."
[94]B. H. Sanders, *Emily Murphy*, pp. 219-20.

day his motion was called.[95] Mr. King also failed to make good, as year after year went by with no action initiated by the government to amend the Act nor even to test the question in the courts.

By 1927 the indifference and inaction of five administrations (Borden, Meighen, King, Meighen, and King) convinced Judge Murphy that nothing was to be gained from a Wilsonian policy of "watchful waiting." Action of some sort must be taken, even though it might entail a heavy burden of effort and expense. Her biographer tells of the deep interest shown by Mrs. Murphy's brilliant lawyer brothers in her years of patient research on the "Persons" question and says that it was one of them, Mr. Justice William Nassau Ferguson, who first called her attention to section 60 of the Supreme Court Act, which became the basis for the most important legal action ever undertaken by a Canadian woman.[96]

Mrs. Murphy first consulted the Department of Justice at Ottawa about the correctness of the Ferguson-Murphy interpretation of section 60. Was it true that any five interested persons could petition the government for an order-in-council directing the Supreme Court of Canada to make a ruling on a constitutional point arising from the interpretation of the B.N.A. Act? Was she correct in assuming further that the government would defray the legal expenses involved in such a suit, if the government believed the issue of sufficient importance to warrant the outlay? The Crown's legal advisers answered yes to both queries. Better still, the Department of Justice considered the question weighty enough to merit giving financial support to the appellants.[97]

In selecting her four co-appellants, Mrs. Murphy endeavoured to choose women who had not only attained some degree of prominence for their public service, but who would also be able to present the women's side of the case creditably before the justices, should the need arise. Of one name there

[95]*Ibid.*, p. 220. Emily F. Murphy to Estelline Bennett, Aug. 4, 1924, Murphy Papers.
[96]B. H. Sanders, *Emily Murphy*, p. 222.
[97]*Ibid.*, p. 224.

could be not an instant's doubt. Mrs. Nellie McClung had won recognition across the dominion as an author, public speaker, and feminist. With the attainment of equal rights, she had served a term in the Alberta legislature; but more than all else, she had been a close personal friend of Judge Murphy for many years and had been actively engaged in promoting her candidacy for the senate.

Hon. Irene Parlby would, of course, be a valuable addition, having been both a member of the legislative assembly and a provincial cabinet member in Alberta since 1921. Mrs. Louise McKinney, who had been one of the first two women elected to any legislature in Canada, was also included. The fourth appellant was Mrs. Henrietta Muir Edwards, for many years convenor of laws of the National Council of Women and compiler of two short but painstaking works on the legal status of women in Canada and in Alberta.

In the late summer days of 1927, Judge Murphy received the petition form from the Department of Justice and circulated it among her co-appellants for their signatures. Generously, she insisted that the names appear in strictly alphabetical order with the result that Mrs. Edwards' name headed the list and the case was frequently referred to as "The Appeal of Henrietta Muir Edwards and Others." While this act of self-effacement turned the spotlight from the principal figure in the case, the four co-appellants have never failed to assert that all credit belonged to Judge Murphy.[98]

Signed, sealed, and on its way to Ottawa on August 27, the petition was officially incorporated in a request by the governor-general-in-council to the Supreme Court for a ruling on the question, "Does the word Persons in Section 24 of the British North America Act, 1867, include female persons?" Although the request was dated October 19, 1927,

---

[98]*Ibid.*, pp. 224-5.  A letter to the author from Miss Evelyn Murphy, July 3, 1943, states: "After the case was won in the Privy Council the four women each stated in addresses, interviews, etc., that the whole credit for the campaign from start to finish was due to Mother's sole efforts.  They were wholeheartedly generous in giving Mother this full recognition."

the case did not actually reach the Supreme Court for argument until March 14 of the following year.[99]

During the months that intervened between filing of the petition and pleading of the case the crucial matter of choice of counsel for the appellants had to be settled. The government's side of the question would be argued by the solicitor-general of Canada, Hon. Lucien Cannon, K.C. To face this formidable opponent, the five must, if possible, secure the finest legal talent available in the dominion. Judge Murphy's choice fell upon the eminent Toronto lawyer, Newton Wesley Rowell, K.C., who had won an enviable reputation among the legal profession on both sides of the Atlantic. This was the same N. W. Rowell, who, as leader of the Liberal Opposition in the Ontario legislature in 1916 and 1917, had ably supported woman suffrage. The government readily concurred in the appellants' choice and notified Rowell of his assignment.[100]

Two provinces were involved in the proceedings which got under way in the old Supreme Court Building at Ottawa on the morning of March 14, 1928. The government of Alberta had requested Rowell to represent it also in supporting the claim of the five. Helping to uphold the Crown's side was Charles Lanctot, K.C., special counsel sent by Quebec.[101]

Section 24 of the B.N.A. Act, the bone of contention, reads:

The Governor-General shall from time to time in the Queen's name, by Instrument under the Great Seal of Canada, summon qualified persons to the Senate; and subject to the provisions of this act, every person so summoned shall become and be a member of the Senate, and a Senator.

Mr. Rowell's factum supporting the theory that "qualified persons" included women was brief, direct, and easily understandable even to laymen. Essentially, counsel for the appel-

[99]B. H. Sanders, *Emily Murphy*, pp. 225-6. *Record of Proceedings in the Privy Council, No. 121 of 1928, On Appeal from the Supreme Court of Canada: In the Matter of a Reference as to the Meaning of the word "persons" in Section 24 of the British North America Act, 1867* (n.p., n.d.), pp. 3-5. Hereafter cited as *Privy Council Proceedings*. A copy of this document may be found at the Public Archives of Canada, Ottawa.

[100]Emily F. Murphy to W. Stewart Edwards, Deputy Minister of Justice, Feb. 1, 1928, Murphy Papers. Eugene Lafleur, K.C. and C. P. Plaxton, K.C. assisted in arguing the case for the Crown. *Canada Law Reports 1928: Supreme Court of Canada* (Ottawa, 1928), p. 278.

[101]*Ibid.*, p. 278. B. H. Sanders, *Emily Murphy*, p. 234.

lants argued that the word "persons" is as applicable to females as to males. There is but one limitation on the word "persons" in section 24 and that is the word "qualified" as defined in section 23. Section 23 lists the qualifications as British citizenship, attainment of the minimum age of thirty, and possession of four thousand dollars. Though it is true that the pronouns "he" and "him" are used in section 23, the Interpretation Act of 1850, known as Lord Brougham's Act, was in force at the time of the passage of the B.N.A. Act by the British parliament. Lord Brougham's Act stated that in all acts, words denoting the masculine gender should be deemed to include females, unless the contrary was expressly provided. Certainly there is nothing in the B.N.A. Act which provides the contrary.

Anticipating opponent's argument that women did not possess political privileges in any province of the dominion in 1867, Mr. Rowell stressed the fact that whereas the B.N.A. Act did leave qualifications for membership in the lower house in the hands of the provinces for an indefinite period, it expressly enacted qualifications for senators.

Moreover, when the dominion parliament made women eligible for election to the House of Commons in the Dominion Elections Act of 1920, it interpreted "persons" in section 41 of the B.N.A. Act to include females. There is thus no more justification for assuming that the imperial parliament limited the freedom of the governor-general to call women to the senate, provided they qualify under section 23, than for assuming that it limited the power of the dominion parliament to interpret "persons" in section 41 as including women.

In his concluding argument, Rowell referred to section 33 of the B.N.A. Act which declares that the senate itself shall be the judge concerning the qualifications of its own members, and submitted the interesting opinion that if the governor-general summoned to the senate a fully qualified woman and the senate accepted her, her position as senator could not be challenged.[102]

[102]*Privy Council Proceedings*, pp. 6-8.

Now it was the turn of the Crown to place its views before the Court. In a factum six times as long as Rowell's and bristling with learned references to legal cases, laws, and customs from as far back as the Roman empire, the solicitor-general advanced five main arguments against the eligibility of women for the senate. To begin with, any interpretation of the B.N.A. Act must have regard to the period when the act was passed and no new liberal ideas should be allowed to colour the interpretation. Nowhere in the dominion did women hold offices of any kind in 1867.

In spite of Lord Brougham's Act, the B.N.A. Act clearly did not have any intention of including women for it uses masculine pronouns throughout its entire length, and in the crucial sections does not once use the word "senatress," but only the masculine form "senator."

Women, under the common law in 1867, were under every conceivable form of legal incapacity and definitely barred from public functions. How then could it be possible to suppose that the drafters of the B.N.A. Act had meant to include women? Furthermore, since women were (and still are) barred from the House of Lords, would it be reasonable to assume they were intended to sit in the Canadian upper house?

The Crown concluded with an exhaustive examination of the situation of women in the provinces which confederated in 1867. Nowhere was there evidence to indicate that women had ever held office in any of them. In only one, Quebec, had there been isolated instances of women voting and even that had been forbidden by an act of 1849. New Brunswick in 1848 and Nova Scotia in 1851 had passed similar acts. With this lesson in history the Crown rested its case,[103] but the Court listened further while the attorney-general of Quebec concurred with the dominion counsel's view that neither in the common law nor in the context of the B.N.A. Act itself at the time it was passed, was there the slightest justification for women's participation in public functions.[104]

[103]*Ibid.*, pp. 9-28.
[104]*Ibid.*, pp. 28-38.

Weeks passed while Justices Anglin, Duff, Mignault, Lamont, and Smith pondered the matter. Then on April 24, 1928, Chief Justice Anglin, robed in the scarlet and ermine of his high office, delivered his opinion.[105] Favouring the historical view that the Court must construe the B.N.A. Act in the light of what was intended in 1867, and impressed by the disabilities of women under the common law at the same period, "The question being understood to be 'Are women eligible for appointment to the Senate of Canada,' the question is answered in the negative."[106] A laconic telegram from Rowell conveyed the disappointing news to Emily Murphy in Edmonton.

Neither bitterness nor surrender in defeat was possible to one of Mrs. Murphy's character. Her reaction, as expressed in a letter which she circulated among the four co-appellants a few days after receipt of the decision, seems to have been a mixture of quiet disappointment, good sportsmanship, and steady determination to fight the case through the one step remaining. The Supreme Court Act, which had furnished the basis for the unsuccessful action just taken, also provided that appellants might, through an order of the governor-general-in-council, carry an appeal from the Supreme Court of Canada to His Majesty's Privy Council in Great Britain. That Judge Murphy had contemplated the possibility of defeat and the consequent necessity for further action is also evident from her letter.

Be it understood that this appeal must not be construed as in any way expressing a lack of confidence in the determination of the Honourable the Minister of Justice and his colleagues of the Cabinet to devise means whereby the B.N.A. Act may be amended to permit of women sitting in the Senate

[105]All five justices were against the appellants, but two of them chose to write a separate opinion.
[106]The quotation is taken from a galley proof of the decision found among the Murphy Papers. *Privy Council Proceedings*, pp. 38-9. *Canadian Annual Review* (1927-28), p. 95. The *Manitoba Free Press*, in a sarcastic and bitter editorial on April 25, 1928, expressed the wonder whether the Supreme Court knew what it was doing in that day and age. It also predicted difficulties in both the senate and the provinces to block the path of an amendment to the B.N.A. Act. The Ottawa *Citizen* of the same date had no editorial condemnation for the decision, but rightly predicted that Mr. Justice Anglin's pronouncement would not be the last word on the subject.

of Canada, but only that we, as petitioners, can have no certainty that the exigencies of politics, or the dissent of one, or more, of the provinces, may preclude the possibility of such an amendment. . . . While we regret that the decision of the Supreme Court of Canada was not favourable to our cause, I am sure we are agreed that their decision was a sincere one, and should not be adversely criticized by any of us. Of the ultimate results, I have not the slightest doubt. Nothing can prevent our winning.[107]

For the duration of the 1928 session of parliament, however, the appellants bided their time in the hope that government action might make their appeal unnecessary. On the day that Chief Justice Anglin read his decision, Hon. Ernest Lapointe, minister of justice, rose in the House to reply to a question by A. W. Neill and stated that the government would take immediate steps to have the B.N.A. Act amended in order to permit the appointment of women to the senate.[108]

This was encouraging. But even if the government did try to move, there were still two stumbling blocks which might prevent such action. One of them Judge Murphy mentioned in her April letter to the co-appellants: the very strong possibility that Quebec or some other province might object strenuously to such an alteration of the Act. Inasmuch as the B.N.A. Act was considered (especially in Quebec) as a kind of treaty among the provinces at confederation, the imperial parliament might hesitate to make an alteration which would conflict violently with the wishes of one of the original members. Then, too, while there was no doubt that the King government could have put the proposed amendment through the House of Commons, there was the possibility that substantial opposition in the senate might prevent the necessary joint address of both Houses in Canada to the parliament of the United Kingdom.[109]

The constitutional problems did not arise. The federal lawmakers at Ottawa closed their 1928 session without doing anything to implement the proimse made by the minister of justice on April 24. Now, fortified by the advice and en-

---

[107]B. H. Sanders, *Emily Murphy*, p. 239.
[108]*Ibid.*, p. 238. *Canadian Annual Review* (1927-28), p. 95. *Canada: H. of C. Debates, 1928*, II, 2311.
[109]J. B. McBride, "Memorandum," p. 9.

couragement of Rowell and J. Boyd McBride, K.C., a lawyer
friend in Edmonton, Emily Murphy was ready for the last
stage of her fight.

Again the Department of Justice co-operated to the fullest
extent, agreeing to defray the further expense involved, ap-
proving the choice of Rowell as appellants' counsel, and drawing up the petition form. That Judge Murphy's confidence in
the legal ability of her Toronto lawyer was not diminished by
the Supreme Court's decision is evident from a letter which
she dispatched to him in mid-summer of 1928.

We hope as previously suggested, that you will consent to act as our counsel
in this appeal to His Majesty in Council and that you will take immediate
steps to this very desirable end so that a decision may be reached before
the next session of the Canadian Parliament. [Of lawmakers Mrs. Murphy
had evidently had enough.] . . . We are much gratified that the Government
is not opposing our application and have consented to become responsible
for the costs thereof. We are presuming that you will nominate counsel in
England for special leave to appeal but hope you may arrange that you
argue the case personally. . . .[110]

On November 20, 1928 the order-in-council was issued
granting the five appellants leave to appeal to the Judicial
Committee of the Privy Council,[111] but more than half a year
elapsed before the last act of the drama was played in London.
Meantime in Canada some backstage scene shifting was in
progress. The government of Alberta once more threw the
full weight of its support behind its daughters, going so far as
to delegate its own attorney-general, Hon. J. F. Lymburn, to
assist Rowell. The appellants were also pleasantly surprised
when on June 15, 1929, Premier Taschereau of Quebec withdrew his province from the contest.[112]

In a lofty book-lined chamber at No. 1 Downing Street

[110]Emily F. Murphy to Hon. N. W. Rowell, K.C., Aug. 15, 1928, Murphy
Papers.
[111]*Privy Council Proceedings*, pp. 60-1.
[112]For this development, Mlle Idola Saint Jean, one of Quebec's outstanding
feminists, takes the credit. Mlle Saint Jean claims that, after her failure to get
the National Convention of Liberal Women to protest Quebec's action in the
Persons Case, she appealed to various Labour Clubs in the province. These in
turn brought such pressure to bear upon Taschereau that he considered it advisable to withdraw from the case. *Women's Sphere*, official organ of the Canadian
Alliance for Women's Vote in Quebec (Montreal, 1937-38), p. 51.

proceedings began on July 22 and lasted throughout four days. Seated at a semi-circular table and dressed in ordinary business suits were His Majesty's five law lords, with Lord Chancellor Sankey presiding. Before them a group of lawyers, Canadian and English, clad in the traditional wigs and robes, argued for hours on end the fine point whether women could legally be considered "persons."[113] N. W. Rowell for the appellants and Eugene Lafleur, K.C., for the Crown used substantially the same arguments which had been set forth in the Supreme Court of Canada over a year earlier. Then, the pleading done, another waiting period of almost three months ensued while their lordships came to a conclusion.

There is a famous photograph of Lord Sankey at Temple Bar on October 18, 1929, on his way to deliver the historic "persons" decision (frontispiece). Preceded by the heavy mace of office and in full court regalia the stern Lord Chancellor looks as though prepared to pass sentence of death upon some poor scoundrel, rather than to read a decision which would bring joy and a new sense of dignity to thousands of women in the senior dominion.

Contrary to custom and perhaps out of deference to the importance of the occasion, Lord Sankey read the decision in full before the court. It was the judges' opinion that the Supreme Court's reliance upon Roman law and early English decisions was a mistake and that more weight should have been given to interpreting the B.N.A. Act itself. The British North America Act had "planted in Canada a living tree" capable of growth and expansion. All written constitutions are subject to development through usage and convention. The use of the word "persons" in the B.N.A. Act is ambiguous: some sections obviously use it to include both males and females, other sections use the words "male persons" where it is desired to confine the meaning strictly to males. The law lords further believed that the provisions of the Interpretation Act applied to the issue in question. Then came the vital words:

[113]The Right Honourable Sir Frederick Pollock, Bart., K.C., ed., *The Law Reports of the Incorporated Council of Law Reporting. House of Lords, Judicial Committee of the Privy Council and Peerage Cases* (London, 1930), p. 126. B. H. Sanders, *Emily Murphy*, pp. 243-4, gives an excellent description of the setting by a Canadian reporter who was an eye-witness.

". . . Their Lordships have come to the conclusion that the word persons includes members of the male and female sex, and that therefore the question propounded by the Governor-General must be answered in the affirmative; and that women are eligible to be summoned and become members of the Senate of Canada."[114]

The satisfaction with which the cabled news of victory was received by Emily Murphy can readily be imagined. Thirteen years had intervened since that day in a small Edmonton courtroom when she had been rudely told that she was not a "person" in the eyes of the law. Thoughts of all that the long struggle had involved must often have passed through her mind as telegrams and letters from all parts of the country expressing congratulations, joy, and gratitude, flooded the Murphy home. Appropriately, her four co-signers were among the first to salute her achievement; but it was a letter from the doughty Scottish feminist of Montreal which expressed the nationwide jubilation with characteristic zest.

Thrice-blessed and more than very honourable Janey,
    Well, alanna, you put it through.   Wonderful, wonderful woman!! . . . You should have been a Presbyterian because they have a doctrine known as 'the perseverance of the saints' and whether you believe in it or not you certainly exemplified it.   The women of Canada can never be sufficiently grateful. . . .
    I must say I did not expect it.   My faith was not of that robust nature which characterized yours. . . .
    Well, dearest and best, my bosom is bursting with perhaps sinful pride in you.   I am so proud of being your friend.[115]

Prime Minister King expressed himself as being "very pleased" at the outcome and added that, had the women lost the case, he would have submitted an amendment to the B.N.A. Act for the approval of parliament.[116]

Judge Murphy's biographer points out that in a long career of unselfish public service the one honour which the magistrate

[114]*Gazette* (Montreal), Oct. 19, 1929. *Times* (London), Oct. 19, 1929. W. P. M. Kennedy, *The Constitution of Canada* (rev. ed., London, New York and Toronto, 1937), p. 493.   This Canadian authority on the constitution states that the Privy Council's decision has been sharply criticized from a legal standpoint.
[115]Isabella Scott to Emily Murphy, Oct. 27, 1929, Murphy Papers.  Isabella Scott was Mrs. John Scott who, in 1921, had tried to have Judge Murphy nominated to the senate.
[116]*Gazette*, Oct. 19, 1929.

ever desired for herself was an appointment to the senate. That she deserved it, there can be no doubt; that she fully expected it, there is abundant evidence to prove. Yet Emily Murphy lived (until 1933) to see her obvious claims ignored twice. In 1930 the King government appointed the first woman senator in Canadian history, the Honourable Cairine Wilson—and Mrs. Murphy's intense disappointment was quietly covered up. Then in 1931 the death of an Edmonton senator appeared to indicate her certain appointment. But the Bennett government selected another, this time on religious grounds.[117] That ended the matter. For the brief remainder of her life, the subject was never mentioned.[118]

Today a bronze plaque at the entrance to the senate chamber in Ottawa commemorates the names of the five Alberta women who went all the way to the Privy Council to prove that women are "persons." As on the petition, so on the plaque, Emily Murphy's name is fourth. But in the ceremonies which accompanied the unveiling of the handsome tablet on June 11, 1938, no doubts were left in anyone's mind to whom full credit for the achievement belonged.[119]

Years have passed since the Bennett government called Mrs. Iva Fallis to the senate in 1935. No woman has since been so honoured. It was a male correspondent, however, who offered some advice on this point in a letter to the editor of *Saturday Night* in 1944. Pointing out that thirteen vacancies then existed in the senate and that the two women senators were both from Ontario, Mr. Morris Goodman of Montreal suggested it would be wise and generous if the prime minister were to appoint at least eight women senators, assigning one to each province. Such appointments would be a popular tribute to Canadian women for their services in the second world war.[120] However, the advice was not followed.

[117]Prime Minister Bennett claimed that inasmuch as the deceased senator had been a Catholic, he was morally obligated to replace him by one of similar faith.

[118]B. H. Sanders, *Emily Murphy*, pp. 249-59.

[119]*Christian Science Monitor*, June 11, 1938. *Citizen* (Ottawa), June 13, 1938. J. B. McBride, "Memorandum," pp. 10-11. Judge McBride, as friend and adviser to Emily Murphy, was one of the honoured guests in the senate antechamber on this occasion.

[120]*Saturday Night*, Feb. 5, 1944.

# 6

# THE MARITIME PROVINCES

## *Stronghold of Conservatism*

NOWHERE has the traditional conservatism of the Maritime Provinces been more apparent than in the securing of political rights for women. That statement does not reflect so much upon the liberality of the men of those sea-girt provinces as upon the attitude of the women themselves. One of Nova Scotia's most active feminists, Dr. Eliza Ritchie of Halifax, reported in November 1917 that there was little opposition but "a weight of indifference."[1]

It was natural that these provinces should exhibit varying shades of apathy. Of them all, New Brunswick was the most consistently active in the campaign, through a well-organized provincial W.C.T.U. and also through a very small but persistent group of women who maintained a suffrage organization in Saint John for a quarter of a century. Nova Scotia had two periods of fairly intense activity with a long period of torpor between them. In Prince Edward Island one searches almost in vain through the press and legislative records for any sign of interest or activity in the subject. What Mrs. E. M. Murray has written with particular reference to Nova Scotia seems generally applicable to the Maritime suffrage

[1]*Morning Chronicle* (Halifax), Oct. 27, 1917. Dr. Ritchie was Nova Scotia's first woman college professor, associated with Dalhousie University, and regarded as the intellectual leader of the women's movement in Halifax. She and Miss Mary Ritchie, both prominently identified with suffrage activities, were the daughters of Judge Thomas Ritchie of Halifax.

movement. "The so-called leaders of all organized work among women in those days were all women of outstanding intelligence and social leaders. It was never in any true sense 'a popular movement.' "[2]

Nor did indifference end with the acquisition of political rights. Although women of eastern Canada vote as regularly and conscientiously as in any other part of the country, they have shown no interest in holding anything more than purely local offices. Nowhere in Canada west of Quebec can it be said that women have never held a seat in the provincial legislature, and inasmuch as Quebec women have been entitled to this privilege only since 1940 the lack of women lawmakers in that province is less surprising than in the Maritime Provinces.

Illustrative of the "weight of indifference" which confronted those women who worked for many years in the Maritime Provinces to achieve their political rights is an anecdote related to the author by Mrs. Adam Shortt of Ottawa. Late one afternoon a campaigner entered a farm kitchen in Nova Scotia, prepared to do some educational work on women's rights. While the canvasser talked, the housewife bustled about, trying to attend to two or three chores at once. Her good husband sat by the stove doing nothing more strenuous than keeping warm. Sensing that her arguments were not having much effect, the visitor at length asked point-blank: "Don't you want the vote?"

"No," said the farmer's wife with emphasis, "If there's one thing John can do alone, for goodness' sake, let him do it!"

Maritime coolness to the suffrage question may also have been a result of isolation from the rest of Canada and from the United States. Even British suffragists, who visited Canada in some numbers during the six or eight years before the first

---

[2]Letter to the author from Mrs. E. M. Murray, Halifax, July 30, 1946. Mrs. Murray was a newspaper woman on the editorial staff of both the *Morning Chronicle* and its evening edition, the *Echo*, for many years. A leader in Halifax women's groups, she was also very active in the provincial W.C.T.U. Two protracted periods of residence in the United States (1888-1898 and 1905-1913) brought her into close contact with the much more active woman suffrage movement there. When she returned in 1913 to take up permanent residence in her native land, she carried with her a lively enthusiasm for the equal rights campaign.

world war and often captivated their audiences with their
zeal, generally by-passed the east coast, though their itiner-
aries at times led them to Victoria, on the other side of the
continent. Small groups of women like those of Saint John
eventually moved the mountain of indifference, almost un-
aided by external forces.

Although evidence exists that the women of Nova Scotia
were entitled to vote and even to hold office down to 1851,
there is no record that they ever took advantage of their
privileges.[3] From the time Nova Scotia was granted its
General Assembly in 1758 until the passage of the Franchise
Act of April 7, 1851, there was no express disqualification of
women. Whether some foreboding or simply a desire to bring
legislation into conformity with practice prompted the action,
it would be difficult to divine; but whatever the cause, Nova
Scotian lawmakers of the mid-nineteenth century included the
word "male" among the qualifications of their new franchise
measure.[4] The change in their political status wrought by the
inclusion of that one word in the act of 1851 passed unnoticed
by the women of the province.

A brief survey of the woman suffrage movement in Nova
Scotia indicates that it was sporadic and largely a by-product
of W.C.T.U. agitation for prohibition. Both Mrs. E. M.
Murray and Dr. Agnes Dennis, two of the province's leading

[3]*Canada: H. of C. Debates, 1885*, II, 1277. *Privy Council Proceedings*, pp. 6-7.
[4]*Revised Statutes of Nova Scotia, 1851*, Supplement, p. 59. The fact that
three provinces—Nova Scotia, New Brunswick, and Quebec—where franchise
privileges for women had existed in this negative form for many years, all took
the trouble specifically to deprive women of the right to vote between 1848 and
1851 leads one to speculate on the possibility that such action may have been an
outcome of the women's rights convention held at Seneca Falls, New York in
1848. Pioneer American feminists had there adopted a charter of women's rights
based upon the Declaration of Independence and topped their list of demands
with a clear call for women's enfranchisement. Publicized in the American press
for weeks, this innovation may well have prompted certain Canadian lawmakers
to insure that no such revolutionary nonsense should upset their own *status quo*.
The apparently retrograde character of this action, taken by three of the four
provinces which later confederated to form the dominion of Canada, becomes
more striking when one realizes that it was coincident with the establishment
of the principle of self-government in Canada under Lord Elgin's enlightened
administration.

feminists, concur in this view.[5] The only other organization which took any noteworthy interest in promoting equal franchise until the war years was the Halifax Local Council of Women, which became quite active around 1910 and continued to exert pressure until equality was achieved in 1918. Barring one abortive attempt to organize a suffrage society in 1895, there was no association exclusively devoted to that purpose until 1914. As one of the principal figures in the movement said:

It was never intensely widespread in the sense of agitating the whole Province at any one time. . . . Suffrage interest here spread slowly and for some years was practically confined to a small group in the capital city, with an occasional woman in the rural sections becoming more and more convinced that suffrage was essential for any progress in the affairs of women and children.[6]

Under the personal stimulus of Mrs. H. N. K. Goff of Philadelphia, acting as an emissary of Miss Frances Willard, the great American temperance leader and suffragist, a branch of the W.C.T.U. was formed in Halifax about 1878. Formation of other local units throughout the province warranted the chartering of a provincial W.C.T.U. in 1881. In view of the customary link between prohibition and equal franchise in the programme of this organization, it is not surprising to find the first traces of suffrage activity in the Nova Scotia legislature appearing during the formative years of the young and vigorous temperance society.

An attempt was made in 1884 to secure the right of unmarried women with property to vote in municipal elections and to act on school boards, but the measure was lost by the narrow margin of 12 to 11, when the speaker cast his vote to break a tie. A similar bill was defeated again in 1886 and finally passed in 1887, minus the school board provision. It is curious that this bill, which marks women's first political

[5]Letter to the author from Mrs. E. M. Murray, Halifax, April 19, 1943. Letter to the author from Dr. Agnes Dennis, Halifax, Nov. 7, 1943. Dr. Dennis, a native of Truro, after teaching for a brief period, married Mr. William Dennis, a newspaper owner and publisher of Halifax. Possessing quiet force and unusual executive ability, Dr. Dennis was for twelve years president of the Halifax Local Council of Women and for much longer periods president of the Red Cross and the Victorian Order of Nurses.
[6]E. M. Murray to the author, April 19, 1943.

advance in Nova Scotia, originated in the council or the upper house, for upper houses are traditionally the strongholds of conservatism. The 1886 measure, rejected by the assembly, likewise first saw light in the council.[7]

Although no woman suffrage bill for provincial matters was brought forward in the 1880's, there was some discussion of the subject during debate of a regular franchise measure in 1885. Much criticism of the bill under consideration was based upon the claim that it did not go far enough, and several eloquent pleas were heard for enfranchising unmarried women with property. At length William F. McCoy, a Liberal who had sponsored the municipal bill of 1884, moved for their enfranchisement. McCoy also met defeat by just one vote, for his motion was lost, 15 to 14. Nevertheless, feminists could derive satisfaction from the thought that more speakers had been favourable than opposed during debate, a few having even gone so far as to say they would like to see the ladies in the legislature.[8]

The few small flurries of legislative activities on suffrage matters in the eighties turned into a storm of fair-sized proportions in the nineties. Much of this action in the closing decade of the century was undoubtedly motivated by an increasing number of woman suffrage petitions beginning in 1892 and reaching a climax in 1895, when 34 separate petitions totalling more than 10,000 signatures were presented to the legislature. Many of these came from the W.C.T.U., others from various towns and municipalities, leading to the conclusion that, for a brief period at least, suffrage agitation was fairly province-wide in scope.[9]

---

[7]*Debates and Proceedings of the House of Assembly of the Province of Nova Scotia, 1884*, pp. 142-3, 238; *1886*, pp. 504-6; *1887*, pp. 376-7. Hereafter cited as *N.S.: Debates*. These *Debates* were not kept after 1916. Married women did not receive this privilege until 1920.

[8]*Ibid., 1885*, pp. 349, 352, 354-6, 359, 394-6.

[9]*N.S.: Journals, 1892*, p. 50; *1893*, pp. 78-80, 86-7, 95; *1894*, pp. 35, 55, 77, 89, 101, 108; *1895*, pp. 89-137 *passim*. Mrs. Charles Archibald was at this period and for many years president of the provincial W.C.T.U. For a number of years she was also president of the Halifax L.C.W. Possessing both intelligence and wealth, Mrs. Archibald turned her attention to all kinds of projects for the promotion of reforms. She was always a keen suffragist, first as a W.C.T.U. executive and later as one of the small group of Halifax women who formed the Equal Franchise League.

There were six attempts to enact bills for the provincial enfranchisement of women between 1891 and 1897.[10] Most would have limited the privilege to unmarried women, but those of Albert Hemeon in 1893 and Firman McClure in 1897 would have granted suffrage to women upon the same basis as men. All these bills produced some debate, but those of 1893 and 1895 elicited most excitement on the floor of the House, and also in the galleries, which were crowded with enthusiastic women on both occasions.[11]

In all these debates the most vocal in opposition was the attorney-general, Hon. J. W. Longley, who knew to perfection every argument in the repertoire. From the quotation of Scripture he would turn to the "woman on a pedestal" theme, and from that to the dreadful effect of votes for women upon the rearing of children—all with a force and eloquence which an opponent once termed "a brilliant pyrotechnic display."[12] One can picture without much difficulty the expressions on the faces of the women in those crowded galleries as they heard the attorney general deliver the following dictum on the true functions of women (with which voting, of course, would seriously interfere):

... first, the bearing and bringing up of children, and this is the highest. Second, the creating of home and the beautifying of home life. ... Third, to charm men and make the world pleasant, sweet and agreeable to live in. Fourth, to be kindly and loving, to be sweet and to be cherished, to be weak and confiding, to be protected and to be the object of man's devotion.[13]

The most consistent and persuasive upholders of the women's side in these debates were two Liberals and one Conservative, which indicates the non-partisan nature of these six private member suffrage bills.[14] With a persistence reminiscent of Waters in the Ontario legislature during the eighties, Hemeon, a Liberal, introduced four of the six measures and was stopped then only by death in 1895. Thomas B. Smith,

[10]1891, 1892, 1893, 1894, 1895, and 1897.
[11]*Morning Chronicle*, April 11, 1893; Mar. 14, 1895.
[12]*N.S.: Debates, 1893*, p. 205.
[13]*Ibid., 1895*, p. 140.
[14]The Liberal party was in power all through the period in which the struggle for woman suffrage was waged.

a Conservative, introduced the 1892 bill and gave generous support to the five which others sponsored. Though fathering no measure himself, William Roche (Liberal) was an ardent and eloquent advocate of the suffrage cause in every session. In contrast with the oratorical pyrotechnics of the attorney-general, the speeches of the three proponents were prosaic in style, but loaded with sound common sense, statistics, and illustrations drawn from the experience of others.

While some of these six measures were defeated by relatively small majorities (the 1892 bill by only 19 to 15), the last of the series in 1897 was rebuffed by a 26 to 6 vote.[15] The decisiveness of this setback froze legislative activity on the enfranchisement of women for many years. Between 1897 and 1916 there is not a single suffrage petition or bill recorded in the *Journals of the House of Assembly*. The only sign of recognition that women existed politically was an unsuccessful attempt in 1910 to make them eligible for appointment to school boards in cities and towns.[16]

One small advance effected by women in the 1890's must be noted. Women ratepayers, who had had the right to vote in school matters since 1881, were made eligible to act as school trustees in rural districts, where such positions were elective, by an act of 1895. In incorporated cities and towns, where these positions were filled by appointment, women did not become eligible until 1917.[17]

Apart from the well-organized petition campaigns and the educational work of the W.C.T.U., under Mrs. Charles Archibald's presidency in the last decade of the nineteenth century, there were a few other visible evidences of interest in the woman suffrage question. The *Morning Chronicle* of February 19, 1895 reported "a very successful drawing-room meeting" of between sixty and seventy at the Halifax home of Mr. and Mrs. Charles Archibald on February 16. Papers

[15]*N.S.: Debates, 1892*, p. 35; *1897*, p. 94.
[16]*Morning Chronicle*, Mar. 30, 1910.
[17]*Statutes of Nova Scotia, 1881*, ch. 7, s. 2; *1895*, ch. 1, s. 64; *1917*, ch. 26, s. 2. Mrs. Murray writes that all attempts to have a woman appointed to the Halifax school board were futile until the mid-1930's. Letter to the author, April 19, 1943.

on various phases of the suffrage question were read, prompting a discussion in which both men and women joined. The newspaper ended its report hopefully: "This initial gathering having proved such a success, it will doubtless be followed by others of the same kind, . . . ."

Another meeting was in fact held about a fortnight later, on the last day of February. This was an afternoon gathering, composed only of women, and definite action was taken. ". . . an association was formed, the object of which is to awaken, interest and qualify women to take a more active part . . . in all questions affecting their home duties, as well as in all public measures relative to their civic and state rights and obligations." Officers chosen were Mrs. A. H. Leonowens, president; Dr. Eliza Ritchie, vice-president; and her sister, Miss Mary Ritchie, secretary.[18] Then a curtain of silence fell and no more was heard of this unnamed organization, which made such a happy start. Mrs. E. M. Murray surmises that "the group simply suspended action because of public opposition to the idea. Men were dead against it here and few of our women had at that time ceased to be guided by man's opinion."[19]

The question of enfranchising women was considered of sufficient importance, however, to be chosen as the subject of the first intercollegiate debate in eastern Canada. Students of King's College challenged those of Acadia College to a verbal tilt, in which the latter took the affirmative side and won.[20] Two years later the Dartmouth Literary Association debated the same question before an audience of approximately one hundred men and women. In this instance the affirmative side lost by a poll of 45 to 43, and it was noted that the women of the audience largely voted in the negative. "This would indicate that the fair ones of Dartmouth are not so

[18]*Morning Chronicle*, Mar. 1, 1895. Mrs. Anna H. Leonowens, a woman of great talents and human understanding, is known familiarly to everyone today as "Anna" of *Anna and the King of Siam*. Although she was away travelling for extended periods of time, Mrs. Leonowens made her home in Halifax from 1878 until 1897.

[19]E. M. Murray to the author, July 30, 1946.

[20]*Morning Chronicle*, Mar 18, 1895.

desirous of entering politics as their male friends are to have them there."[21] This conclusion was borne out by the fact that in the Halifax municipal election of 1897 only 282 women voted out of approximately 1000 who were eligible to cast their ballots.[22]

Legislative apathy on questions pertaining to women's rights during the first decade and a half of the new century was fairly evenly matched by a similar disinterest among the general public. Even the W.C.T.U. appears to have largely abandoned its suffrage work to devote more concentrated effort to its main objective, which resulted in the passage of a province-wide prohibition act in 1910.[23] A brief flicker of interest was apparent in February 1908 when Mrs. Flora M. Denison of Toronto visited Halifax on an organizing tour of the Maritimes for the Canadian Suffrage Association. Mrs. Denison was well received and spoke three times in as many days before mixed audiences of men and women. At the close of her address in the Church of England Institute on February 10 she suggested that a suffrage organization be formed in Halifax. Without a dissenting vote, her listeners passed a resolution to that same effect—and there the matter rested.[24]

Reference has already been made to the historic declaration of policy adopted at the annual meeting of the National Council of Women held at Halifax in 1910. After five hours of debate, by a vote of 71 to 51, the Council endorsed the principle of enfranchisement of women. During discussion of the motion which had been made by the Canadian Suffrage Association, a delegate from Saint John expressed fear that adoption of such a contentious issue might lead to friction in the Local Council of that city. Dr. Eliza Ritchie said she had no fear of any such result in the Halifax Council, but the effect of this brave statement was largely nullified by another local

---

[21]*Ibid.*, Feb. 13, 1897.
[22]H. M. Edwards, *Women of Canada* (no pagination).
[23]The act is printed in full in the Appendix of *N.S.: Debates, 1910*, pp. 364-78.
[24]*Morning Chronicle*, Feb. 11 and 14, 1908. *Morning Herald* (Halifax), Feb. 10, 1908. A. S.-G., Scrap Books, V, 197 contains a clipping from an unidentified Halifax newspaper dated Feb. 11, 1908.

delegate who said she had belonged to the Halifax Local Council for four years and not once in all that time had she heard the subject discussed.[25]

Stimulated by the dominion-wide gathering of women, the Halifax Local Council became more politically conscious in the year that followed. Under the presidency of Dr. Agnes Dennis, it sent out questionnaires to prominent people in Canada, the United States, and Great Britain, asking the addressees to express themselves on the advisability of having women serve on school boards. The bulk of the replies was overwhelmingly favourable; but except for the publicity, no concrete result ensued. Dr. Dennis also urged the eligible women of the city to use their municipal voting privileges more conscientiously than they had in the past.[26]

With these two enterprises the energy of the Local Council appears to have spent itself. Except for an occasional debate on the subject and some short-lived enthusiasm whipped up at the 1911 and 1913 annual conventions of the provincial W.C.T.U.,[27] there was a complete dearth of suffrage activity between 1911 and 1914. The *Morning Chronicle*, which,though not antagonistic, had never shown itself over-friendly toward women's enfranchisement, gave considerable prominence in its news columns to the sensational activities of the English militants in 1912 and 1913, and this undoubtedly increased the caution of many Nova Scotians towards woman suffrage. Yet Mrs. E. M. Murray asserts that the very intensity of the struggle in England, coupled with the favourable impression created by visiting British suffragists, was one of the factors primarily responsible for reviving the Canadian suffrage movement just before the outbreak of the first world war.[28]

Partially offsetting the flood of unfavourable publicity

[25]N.C.W., *Year Book* (1910), pp. 97-104.  *Morning Chronicle*, July 6, 1910.
[26]*Ibid.*, Mar. 13, 20, April 21, May 8, 1911.
[27]*Ibid.*, Oct. 19, 1911; Sept. 13, 1913.  The W.C.T.U. had for many years maintained a standing committee on franchise.  Mrs. Ada L. Powers, president of the provincial W.C.T.U., and Mrs. M. R. Chesley, who became chairman of the standing committee in 1913, were both ardent feminists.
[28]E. M. Murray to the author, July 30, 1946.  This opinion was corroborated by Mrs. Allan L. Smith, for many years president of the Montreal Local Council of Women, during an interview in August 1946.

coming from abroad, was the action taken by the Anglican Synod which met in Halifax on June 4, 1914. Both votes for women and prohibition were discussed, and the Committee on Temperance reported strongly in favour of the extension of the franchise to women because this would tend to promote enactment of vital social and moral legislation. After some keen debate, the large majority of delegates voted in favour of a resolution supporting the principle, thereby bestowing upon it the approval of a conservative and highly respected organization.[29] Apropos of this instance of churchly benediction, it is worthy of note that, throughout the Maritime Provinces, the clergy were often far in advance of the general public in their stand upon the question of woman suffrage, doubtless impelled by their faith that women would be a powerful lever to pry much-needed reforms from slow or unwilling legislatures.

Hard on the heels of the Synod's action—perhaps as an outgrowth of that action, which placed suffrage activities on a thoroughly respectable plane—came the first attempt in nineteen years to organize an outright suffrage association. A few days after the Synod meeting, a group of women called on Mrs. E. M. Murray, recently returned from an eight-year residence in New York where she had been very active in suffrage circles, and asked if she would take the initiative in issuing a call for a meeting of all those interested in forming a suffrage club.[30] Mrs. Murray agreed to do so and issued the invitation in a letter to the women of Halifax which appeared in the *Morning Chronicle* on June 9. Pointing out that militancy and a belief in equal political rights were two separate matters, the letter described the rapid strides being made by suffrage forces in other parts of Canada and continued:

It seems a pity that Nova Scotia should be left out of this movement, and it is for this reason that a meeting has been called at the Women's Council House for next Thursday afternoon to form a Suffrage Club in this City. The meeting is open to all who are interested. It is not held under the

[29]*Morning Chronicle*, June 5, 1914.
[30]E. M. Murray to the author, April 19, 1943.

auspices of the Council, but is called by mutual consent of a few who believe in the extension of the franchise to the women of Nova Scotia. The purpose is to enlist all who are interested, and *the only campaign planned is a campaign of education.* [Italics mine.]

The meeting was held on June 11, 1914 and a fair-sized body of women attended, though the recognized suffrage leaders of the city (Dr. Eliza Ritchie, Dr. Agnes Dennis, and Mrs. Charles Archibald) were all absent. After a small group had unsuccessfully attempted to block organization until the fall, the gathering proceeded to elect officers, with Mrs. Murray heading the slate, and to draw up a constitution. In its report of the meeting, the *Chronicle* of June 13 wrote with an air of relief: "At any rate, it can no longer be said that Halifax has no suffrage club, and the prospects are that it will grow."

As on an earlier occasion (1895), the prediction proved over-optimistic. Mrs. Murray's action, taken without the approval of the veteran suffrage leaders, precipitated a factional quarrel among those friendly to suffrage, and nullified any action of importance for another two years at least.

I was soon made to understand I had committed the unpardonable sin of having attempted to form a suffrage organization before Dr. Ritchie thought 'the time was ripe.' I contended that one should not wait for time to be ripe, but do something to hasten the ripening. . . . The new society made little or no progress under the circumstances.

Shortly after the launching of this first suffrage group, Mrs. Murray left the city for several days to attend a convention of the National Council of Women. Imagine, then, her astonishment when she received a telegram at the convention notifying her that a suffrage society had been organized, time evidently having ripened quickly, that Dr. Eliza Ritchie had been made president, and that she (Mrs. Murray) was to be librarian! Subduing any ruffled feelings, Mrs. Murray wired that she would willingly serve with the newly chosen officers, provided the work went forward. But this ill-omened start proved to be only another flash in the pan. Halifax again found itself one of the very few provincial capitals in the dominion wich had not a suffrage organization.[31]

For two and a half years the suffrage movement slumbered in Nova Scotia. These were the years which witnessed the triumphant conclusion of the struggle in the three Prairie Provinces, and brought British Columbia to the threshold of victory. Then, jarred into consciousness, the suffrage movement in the Atlantic province awakened to face its most stirring year.

Signs of interest and activity came early in 1917 and were by no means confined to women's groups. At a nation-wide convention held in Halifax for a few days in January the first call to arms was sounded. Among the resolutions adopted by the Social Service Congress at its final session on January 26 was one expressing gratification at the enfranchisement of women in the West and urging the government of Nova Scotia to do likewise.[32] Not content with a resolution, the secretary of the Nova Scotia branch of the Social Service Council sent a letter to the provincial government and to all members of the legislature on March 5 calling attention to the resolutions adopted by the Congress (including that on woman suffrage) and adding:

It is my duty to call to your notice the following resolutions of the recent Social Service Congress held in this city. The importance and significance of the Congress must be so evident . . . as to make it unnecessary for me to urge that these matters receive your most careful attention. This Council will be glad to assist the Government, in any possible way, in making practical the suggestions of these resolutions.[33]

Another hopeful sign in 1917 was the changed attitude of the most powerful newspaper in the capital city—the *Morning Chronicle*. While never inimical to the suffrage movement in its editorials, the *Chronicle* had done the cause one serious disservice, as already noted, by featuring prominently the activities of the English extremists. Beginning with two vigorous editorials on February 14 and March 10 supporting equal

---

[31]*Ibid.* A further reference to this short-lived society may be found in the second Minute Book of the New Brunswick Women's Enfranchisement Association, pp. 92-3.

[32]*Herald*, Jan. 27, 1917.

[33]*Morning Chronicle*, Mar. 7, 1917.

franchise to the hilt, the *Chronicle* became the champion of the women's cause. While the suffrage bill was before the House in 1917, the *Chronicle* argued eloquently for its passage; and when the bill was rejected, largely because of the personal efforts of Hon. George H. Murray, the Liberal premier, the *Chronicle*, though Liberal in its own editorial policy, attacked the government in a manner to delight the stoutest Conservative. Like many others throughout the country, the *Chronicle* confessed that it was women's part in the war which had won it over.

Supporting the *Chronicle's* editorial enthusiasm was a series of four letters which appeared in its columns during February and March of this eventful year. Three of them were written by Judge Benjamin R. Russell, one of the best loved and most distinguished residents of Halifax, the fourth by Mrs. Ada L. Powers, president for many years of the Nova Scotia W.C.T.U.[34] These letters presented the case for woman suffrage with a lucidity of expression and force of argument which should have proved sufficient to demolish most of the old prejudices. In addition, Judge Russell's highly respected standing in the community weighed heavily in swinging the support of conservative Haligonians to the movement.

The happiest portent of all in this general stirring of progressive forces was the conclusive evidence presented by the women of the city that they themselves were at last united in their support of woman suffrage. Although for many years the Halifax Local Council had been deeply interested in projects of civic reform and had, as we have seen, made periodic attempts to arouse women to active citizenship, it had refrained from making any formal statement on the controversial subject of equal rights. All that was changed on February 22, 1917, when the Council, representing forty-one women's organizations with widely differing aims, voted unanimously to ask the legislature for "the extension of the parliamentary franchise to all duly qualified adults, without

[34] *Ibid.*, Feb. 14 and 21, Mar. 1 and 17, 1917.   Judge Russell was the brother of Mrs. Mary R. Chesley.

regard to sex." A copy of the resolution was placed on the desk of each member of the legislature on February 28—a tactful but pointed reminder that legislative indifference would no longer be tolerated.[35]

Storm warnings of an impending battle in the legislature appeared on the very first day of the 1917 session. While the speech from the throne on February 21 made no reference to the introduction of a franchise measure, it did at least pay tribute to the "unselfish devotion" of Nova Scotia women in the war years. But this was not enough to satisfy R. H. Graham, who moved the address in reply. After saluting in the warmest terms women's untiring war efforts and willingness to take on work that was once exclusively men's, he made a direct challenge to government action.

They have shown unexpected efficiency and reliability. They will never be satisfied with old conditions nor made to believe again in male superiority. The time is ripe to throw down the barriers to full political equality between the sexes, women having earned the right to a voice in public affairs. Other countries have gone far beyond us in this matter and we should not be behind the foremost.[36]

When three weeks had passed with no sign of the government's acceptance of the challenge, Graham introduced a bill on March 14 which would give women the provincial franchise on either their own or their husbands' property qualifications and would also extend the municipal franchise to married women who had property qualifications in their own right. In reality this bill was part of a well-engineered plan devised by the Halifax Local Council of Women before the legislature met. They had secured the services of Mr. Justice Russell in drawing up the measure they desired and had received assurance that Graham would sponsor it, should the government fail to act.[37]

Although there was no woman suffrage petition to the legislature during the 1917 session (those interested perhaps recalling how futile the petition campaign of the nineties had

[35]*Ibid.*, Mar. 1, 1917.   *Herald*, Mar. 9, 1917.
[36]*Morning Chronicle*, Feb. 22, 1917.
[37]*Ibid.*, Mar. 15, 1917.   *N.S.: Journals, 1917*, p. 56.   *Herald*, Mar. 15, 1917.

been), introduction of the bill brought temperance forces of the province staunchly to the side of the Local Council. A town meeting of approximately three hundred citizens of Wolfville, gathered under W.C.T.U. auspices, unanimously adopted a resolution backing the Graham bill and forwarded it to the legislature.[38] The officers of the provincial W.C.T.U., headed by Mrs. Ada Powers, sent a similar resolution to both the council and assembly a few days later. More impressive perhaps, since it came from a men's organization, was a supporting resolution forwarded to the lawmakers by the Nova Scotia Temperance Alliance, which was meeting at Halifax while the bill was under discussion.[39]

Second reading of the bill on March 21 brought many spectators to the galleries. The scenes of enthusiasm recalled those days in 1893 and 1895 when earlier suffrage ardour had prompted large numbers of women to attend the debates on the Hemeon measures. This time, however, there were no voices raised in opposition; the bill passed second reading unanimously and was sent on the committee on law amendments.[40] The editorial exultation of the *Chronicle* over what appeared to be certain victory was undoubtedly matched by the excited hopes of women spectators as they left the galleries.

Unwilling to leave anything to chance, even though success seemed assured, a delegation of eight women from the Local Council appeared before the committee on law amendments on the evening of April 11. Shepherded by Judge Russell, they presented their case with such brevity and skill that the attorney-general, Orlando T. Daniels, who presided over the hearing, felt impelled to congratulate them. Both the *Herald* and the *Chronicle* reported that the attitude of the committee

[38]*Ibid.*, Mar. 16, 1917. *Morning Chronicle*, Mar. 19, 1917. A letter to the *Chronicle* editor, appearing on Mar. 28, decried the press story of unanimity. This outraged citizen of Wolfville said the meeting was mostly composed of girls and women, and ended: "As far as my knowledge goes, the citizens of Wolfville are very indifferent on the question of Woman Suffrage."
[39]*Herald*, Mar. 29, 30, 1917.
[40]*Ibid.*, Mar. 22, 1917. *Morning Chronicle*, Mar. 22, 1917. In striking contrast to the editorial enthusiasm of the Liberal *Chronicle* was the editorial silence of the Conservative *Herald* on all phases of the suffrage question in 1917 and 1918.

was "most attentive and sympathetic." Opportunity was offered to any who opposed the measure to speak when the women finished, but no one took advantage of it. The hearing concluded with the attorney-general's promise that the matter would receive "most careful consideration," and the women retired, having every reason to feel that all obstacles were now overcome.[41]

A week passed and the bill was still in committee. As a gentle prod to the lawmakers, the Local Council at its monthly meeting on April 19, passed another resolution favouring the Graham bill and forwarded it to the committee.[42]

Five days later followers of the *Morning Chronicle* were greeted with large, bold headlines reading: "Suffrage Bill Slain in House of Assembly." The unexpected had happened. On recommendation of the law committee, the House had voted a "three months' hoist" for the Graham bill on April 23 by a margin of 12 to 8. Responsibility for this defeat, the more bitter because victory had seemed secure, lay directly upon Premier Murray. Efforts to avert the "hoist" had been stalled when he rose to his feet to declaim that although woman suffrage was inevitable, "the enactment of such a measure at the present time would serve no useful purpose." Party discipline was strong enough to do the rest. Even the very "sympathetic" attorney-general played "follow the leader."[43]

What the reactions of suffrage leaders were we can only imagine, but the repercussions from the editorial chair of the

[41]E. M. Murray to the author, April 19, 1943. *Morning Chronicle*, April 12, 1917. *Herald*, April 12, 1917. The delegation consisted of: Mrs. Archibald, Mrs. Chesley, Mrs. Powers, Dr. Ritchie, Dr. Dennis, Mrs. Murray, Miss Mary Fletcher, and Mrs. Clara B. Bligh. The inclusion of Mrs. Chesley and Mrs. Powers, both of Lunenberg and both officers of the W.C.T.U., represents the inevitable teamwork between the two groups which consistently did most to bring enfranchisement of women to Nova Scotia: the Halifax Local Council and the provincial W.C.T.U.

[42]*Morning Chronicle*, April 21, 1917.

[43]*Ibid.*, April 24, 1917. *Herald*, April 24, 1917. Though editorially silent about woman suffrage, the *Herald* was scrupulously fair in its news reports of suffrage activities. The "hoist" is a parliamentary manœuvre which kills a bill by voting to consider it at some later date when the mover of the "hoist" knows that the legislature will not be in session.

*Chronicle* on April 24 left nothing to guesswork. Throwing party allegiance to the winds, it thundered against the betrayal of liberal principles by the party which professed to sail under that name in Nova Scotia. In contrast with the Liberal administrations of the four western provinces, the Liberals of the Atlantic province were timid, unresponsive to modern trends. More to be condemned than Liberal conservatism was the government's perfidious handling of the Graham bill. "The manner of its defeat is small tribute to the courage and political sagacity, not to say the statesmanlike vision of those who voted or conspired to strangle it, but did not dare to utter a word against it."

Small comfort were two minor concessions made by that 1917 session of the legislature to irate feminist groups. Women were at last granted eligibility for appointment to school boards in incorporated towns, thus bringing to a successful conclusion the campaign waged quietly by the Halifax Local Council for almost two decades. Professional equality also moved one step closer to realization with the passage of a Barristers and Solicitors Act permitting women to study and practice law on the same terms as men.[44]

The débâcle of the Graham bill had at least one fortunate aftermath: it produced the only genuine suffrage organization the province ever had. The unexpected defeat was the cohesive force which bound into one association clubs and organizations in all corners of Nova Scotia which were friendly to the principle of equal rights. Petty quarrels and factional strife were forgotten as suffrage leaders rallied around Dr. Eliza Ritchie to form the Nova Scotia Equal Franchise League late in the spring of 1917. The organizers asked the Montreal Suffrage Association for a copy of its constitution—further evidence, if any were needed, that Nova Scotians had had very little experience with this type of organization.[45]

[44]*Statutes of Nova Scotia, 1917*, ch. 26, ch. 41. It may perhaps be deemed symbolic of Nova Scotia's general attitude towards feminism in any form to note that the only petition to the legislature in 1917 which concerned women at all was from forty barristers and solicitors of the Supreme Court of Nova Scotia praying that women be not enabled to practise law in the province. *N.S: Journals, 1917*, p. 75.

[45]L.W.R. Minute Books, entry of Aug. 16, 1917.

As finally constituted, the League was to include both individuals (men as well as women) and societies—any and all who believed in woman suffrage. Annual meetings were to be held in January, general meetings quarterly, and executive meetings once a month. The League's main work was to be educational, including the furnishing of trained speakers to any group in the province indicating a desire to hear them. Mrs. Murray was placed in charge of this vital phase of activity and an example of her work was promptly forthcoming. The *Chronicle* of July 21 reported that a forum and discussion on woman suffrage, held at the annual convention of Women's Institutes, evoked "intense interest and enthusiasm."

The first and only annual meeting of the League was held in Halifax on January 31, 1918. Officers chosen included Dr. Ritchie as president and many others who had been identified with the cause for years, but also some much needed new blood from outside the capital city.[46] Reports were made from various parts of the province, and many letters were read indicating at least a beginning of interest in the question over widely scattered areas. One serious setback to the League's plan of campaign was noted, however. The project of printing and distributing masses of literature was abandoned when the tragic shipping explosion occurred in Halifax harbour on December 6, 1917. Members rightly felt that their time and financial resources might better be used to relieve the suffering which followed the disaster.[47]

In the last few months of its existence the Franchise League carried on two quiet though effective forms of activity: a house-to-house canvas in the interest of the 1918 suffrage bill,[48] and a petition campaign which brought ten suffrage

[46]The complete slate was: Hon. Pres., Mrs. Charles Archibald; Hon. Vice-Pres., Mrs. William Dennis; Pres., Dr. Eliza Ritchie; 1st Vice-Pres., Mrs. J. A. Clark; 2nd Vice-Pres., Mrs. M. R. Chesley; 3rd Vice-Pres., Mrs. F. H. Sexton; Rec. Sec., Mrs. William Bligh; Corres. Sec., Mrs. William McNab; Treas., Miss Winifred Read; Convenor of Lecture Comm., Mrs. E. M. Murray; Convenor of Literature Comm., Mrs. W. T. Allen.
[47]*Morning Chronicle*, Feb. 2, 1918.
[48]N.C.W., *Year Book* (1918-19), pp. 56-7.

petitions from women's organizations before the legislature while the bill was under consideration.[49] But there was no evidence of excitement, no stirring scenes in legislative halls as the hour of victory approached. Whether prompted by painful memories or convinced that an attitude of decorous indifference would make a better impression upon the legislators, the women boycotted the House of Assembly at both second and third readings of the suffrage bill.[50]

A most eloquent tribute to the work of the League was the fact that the government in 1918 felt obliged to make the woman suffrage bill an administration measure and that W. L. Hall, leader of the Conservative Opposition, immediately gave his approval to the project. While it was true that Hall had tried to prevent Premier Murray's slaughter of the 1917 suffrage bill, the Conservative party had certainly never championed the suffrage cause but had rather ignored it. The government's change of heart may in small part be ascribed to developments in England where suffrage forces were standing on the threshold of victory.[51] Much more influential, however, was Premier Murray's sensing of the fact (like the rival suffrage group in 1914) that "time had ripened quickly."

Forecast in the speech from the throne, the equal franchise measure was introduced by the attorney-general on February 28 in the shape of "An Act to amend and consolidate the Acts in respect to the Electoral Franchise."[52] That the sponsor felt the incongruity of his situation was evident in his somewhat feeble explanation that the government had withheld support from the suffrage bill at the previous session so that other acts might be amended to enable women to enjoy the privilege of voting at all elections.[53]

[49] *N.S.: Journals, 1918,* pp. 42-3.
[50] *Morning Chronicle,* Mar. 21, 1918. *Herald,* Mar. 21, 1918. The latter reports that "there were only ten spectators in the galleries exclusive of two bored newspaper men who sit in the galleries day after day." One of the ten was Justice James W. Longley who, twenty years before, had so bitterly assailed the suffrage bills of the nineties.
[51] Mrs. E. M. Murray states that Premier Murray, after the defeat of the Graham bill, told a women's delegation that so long as he should be premier, the women of Nova Scotia would not have the franchise before the women of England. E. M. Murray to the author, April 19, 1943.
[52] *N.S.: Journals, 1918,* p. 20. *Morning Chronicle,* Feb. 22 and Mar. 1, 1918.
[53] *Ibid.,* Mar. 21, 1918. *Herald,* Mar. 21, 1918.

The bill, which would simply bestow voting and not office-holding privileges, passed first and second readings with no debate. Considerable discussion arose at a public hearing on March 26 while the measure was before the law amendments committee, though no opposition was expressed to the principle of votes for women. Hall, Opposition leader, felt that the bill should provide for universal suffrage without property qualifications. Present at the hearing were three members of the Franchise League. When invited to say what they thought about the bill, Dr. Ritchie and Mrs. William McNab expressed complete satisfaction, but Mrs. Murray concurred in the view of Hall and said she would prefer abolition of property qualifications. However, she was willing to accept the present measure as a step in the right direction.[54] With property qualifications maintained intact, the bill was recommended for passage and after a hasty trip through the Council, received royal assent on April 26, 1918. No women sat in the galleries that day.[55]

Apparently considered too insignificant for press comment, another bill which vitally affected women's rights also received royal assent on April 26. A simple amendment to the statute law, by deleting the word "male," conferred upon women the right to sit in the provincial legislature[56]—a right still waiting to be exercised.

A seventy-eight-year-old veteran feminist, looking back upon the important events of that year, deftly described the Nova Scotia suffrage movement in three short sentences:

At the end it came without struggle in recognition of women's services during the war. Things often work out that way I find. You struggle and struggle to no direct effect, and suddenly in a lull the whole thing snaps into place.[57]

[54]*Morning Chronicle*, Mar. 27, 1918. This is the last public reference to the League, which dissolved with the successful culmination of its objectives.

[55]*Ibid.*, April 27, 1918. *N.S.: Journals, 1918*, p. 260. *Statutes of Nova Scotia, 1918*, ch. 2, s. 3. (Property qualifications were, however, abolished by another act passed at this session. *Revised Statutes of Nova Scotia, 1923*, ch. 3.)

[56]*Ibid., 1918*, ch. 23, s. 1. Even the Statute Books maintain the tradition of Nova Scotian aloofness toward feminism. In this year which marked women's attainment of complete political equality, the index to the *Statutes* lists neither the word "Woman" nor "Female."

[57]E. M. Murray to the author, April 19, 1943.

Like a younger sister who often patterns her actions after those of an older member of the family, New Brunswick has frequently looked for guidance to the senior province lying eastward beyond Fundy's blanket of fog. Nova Scotia's acceptance of this gentle deference has been as matter-of-fact as an editorial in the *Morning Chronicle* of March 10, 1917 would indicate. With simple egotism the editor urged Nova Scotia to take its rightful place of leadership among the eastern provinces by enacting a suffrage measure, affirming that "it is but natural to expect that Nova Scotia will lead the way for the others to follow."

New Brunswick does, however, have definite opinions of its own. Although the development of the suffrage movement in the younger province has many close parallels with the movement in Nova Scotia, there are also differences. Public indifference to woman suffrage, though evident, was never quite the dead weight in New Brunswick that it was in Nova Scotia. The greater volume of petitions and the more frequent delegations to the government at Fredericton substantiate this. An influential press ally, the Saint John *Daily Telegraph*, appeared early on the scene to place the power of the printed word behind the suffrage cause in New Brunswick. Perhaps the most striking difference was that New Brunswick had a full-fledged suffrage organization as early as 1894. Though small and weak, at times little more than a symbol, the Enfranchisement Association at Saint John at least furnished a rallying point and a connecting link with the more vigorous organizations to the west.

When New Brunswick had been separated from Nova Scotia in 1784 and received its own governor and council, the fundamental act setting up the government for the new province had been so worded as to make it appear that women had both the rights of voting and office-holding. As in Nova Scotia, this assumption was based upon the negative premise that they were not forbidden these privileges. Although the Crown lawyers in the Persons Case claimed there was no evidence that women ever voted, Hon. H. R. Emmerson, ad-

dressing the New Brunswick legislature in 1894, stoutly affirmed that there were certain instances of women exercising
the franchise, at least until 1791.[58] At any rate all uncertainty
about these early and hazy manifestations of women's rights
was removed by an act of 1848 which confined political privileges exclusively to males.[59]

As happened so often in the older provinces, the earliest
stirrings of legislative activity came in the eighties. One
definite advance in woman's political status was made. After
receiving a total of six petitions from town and city councils,
and from small groups of women in various municipalities,
the legislature in 1886 put through a bill granting the municipal franchise to unmarried women who had the same property qualifications as were required of men.[60] The ease and
dispatch with which this matter was attended to by the lawmakers was perhaps conclusive proof of the sermon so often
preached by the *Daily Telegraph*—that the women of New
Brunswick had only to show conclusively that they desired
their political rights in order to attain them.

At the same session William Pugsley (who later gave Sir
Robert Borden so much trouble at Ottawa on the federal
franchise issue) introduced a measure to allow unmarried
women to vote and hold office in school elections. Although
the bill did not survive committee of the whole, the discusssion
which it provoked was highly favourable to women. Some
members believed the measure did not go far enough and
should include married women, while three (John V. Ellis, Dr.
Alfred A. Stockton, and Thomas Hetherington) were in favour
of giving women the provincial franchise immediately. Dr.
Stockton pointed out that the general principle of enfranchising women had been discussed by the legislative assembly
at the previous session (1885) and had received much favourable comment, though no definite action had been proposed

---

[58]*Privy Council Proceedings*, pp. 6-7.   H. M. Edwards, *Women of Canada.*
[59]*Statutes of New Brunswick, 1848*, ch. 65.
[60]*Ibid.*, *1886*, ch. 83.   For the petitions: *N.B.: Journals, 1886*, pp. 52, 79,
82, 91, 109.   For the bill: *Ibid.*, *1886*, pp. 82, 83, 98, 103, 129, 178.

at the time.[61] In spite of these surprisingly progressive remarks, no serious attempt to give women the provincial franchise was made before almost another decade had passed.

Suffrage activities in New Brunswick gained a momentum during the mid-nineties that was never surpassed at any later period, not even in those days at the close of the first world war when the goal was achieved. Although during the eighties the W.C.T.U. had formed many locals which were interested in suffrage, the first society dedicated exclusively to the attainment of women's enfranchisement was organized at Saint John in 1894. On March 30 eighteen women of that city met at the home of Mrs. Edward Manning and launched the small society which was to be the standard bearer of the New Brunswick suffrage movement for the next quarter of a century. Mrs. Manning became its first president, Miss Manning Skinner vice-president, and Mrs. W. F. Hatheway secretary-treasurer.[62]

At their second meeting on April 4, the society voted to become a branch of the Dominion Women's Enfranchisement Association and patterned the name of their own organization upon that of the larger body in Toronto, calling themselves first the Saint John, and then soon after, the New Brunswick Women's Enfranchisement Association. Apparently anxious to form ties with women's groups outside the Maritimes, the young society, whose treasury registered exactly nil, boldly voted to send Mrs. John Fiske as its delegate to the convention of the National Council of Women in Ottawa, and to pay her expenses. The secretary's explanation for the financial plunge was that "it would considerably strengthen our footing to be represented with the other portions of the Dominion in such an assembly, particularly as New Brunswick seems to be the least known of all the provinces, and it is not well to remain

[61]*N.B.: Journals, 1886*, pp. 21-2. *Daily Telegraph* (Saint John), Mar. 2, 1886. *Synoptic Reports of the Proceedings of the Legislative Assembly of New Brunswick, 1886*, pp. 22-3. Hereafter cited as *N.B.: Synoptic Reports.*
[62]Minute Books of the New Brunswick Women's Enfranchisement Association (2 vols. covering the years 1894-1903, 1908-1911, and 1915-1918), now in the possession of Mrs. W. Milner Wood, King's County, New Brunswick, I, 1-2. Hereafter cited as N.B. Minute Books.

in the background all the time." Another question of policy settled unanimously at this second meeting was "that moderation not malignity shall govern the members in the expression of their opinions."[63]

This small but energetic group of women carried on through the 1890's, always finding indifference rather than open hostility their principal foe. Their meetings, six to twelve a year, were seldom attended by more than fifteen or twenty members, and often by fewer. Programmes for these meetings were usually given partly to business and partly to educational features, including discussion of books and reading of papers prepared by members. Under the leadership of such faithfuls as Mrs. Fiske (who became president in 1898 and held the post until her death in 1914), Mrs. Hatheway, Miss Skinner, and Miss Mabel Peters, they twice initiated large petitions to the legislature for full parliamentary franchise. That of 1899 contained 3,700 signatures, indicating a tremendous amount of work by the tiny membership.[64]

The most striking of their publicity ventures was the holding of a public meeting on September 14, 1896 at which the principal speaker was Mrs. Julia Ward Howe. This "scoop" was possible only because the Association for the Advancement of Women (of which Mrs. Howe was president) was holding its convention at Saint John. The local society appealed to the famous American and a well-attended meeting heard feminism preached by a world-renowned expert.[65]

In contrast to this success was an episode in the fall of 1899. The Maritime Provinces convention of the W.C.T.U., meeting that year in Saint John, held a public meeting on woman suffrage. The programme committee had asked the Enfranchisement Association to participate, and Mrs. Edward Manning had been selected by the members to prepare and read a paper. The embarrassment of Mrs. Manning and the chagrin of the members can be readily imagined as one reads

[63] *Ibid.*, I, 4-5.
[64] *N.B.: Journals, 1895*, p. 20; *1899*, pp. 61-2.   N.B. Minute Books, I, 109.
[65] *Ibid.*, I, 67.

a forlorn little note in the Association's Minute Book: "We regret to add that on account of the lengthy and brilliant speeches that were made on that evening the W.C.T.U.'s forgot that our Suffrage Club had any part to perform."[66]

While little advance in the political status of women had been made by the close of the nineties, it was none the less a decade of great legislative activity on the question. Dozens of petitions descended upon the legislature, some containing several hundred signatures of both men and women. These petitions, often sponsored by the W.C.T.U., almost invariably sought full provincial enfranchisement for women.[67]

Spurred on by this display of public sentiment, Dr. Stockton sponsored a resolution in 1894: "That it is desirable to confer upon Women the right to vote for the election of Members to this House." The principal opponent was the attorney-general, Andrew Blair, who argued that most women did not want it and the mother country had not adopted it. After five hours of debate, the assembly sided with the attorney-general by a vote of 21 to 14. The *Telegraph*, which had thrown its full support to the suffragist cause, commented with unwarranted optimism: "There is no law to prevent the Attorney-General from changing his mind, and it is to be hoped he will see the subject more clearly before next year. The ladies may rest assured that they hold the winning cards if they are only ready to use them."[68]

Mindful of the fact that the petitions of 1894 contained a total of approximately 10,000 signatures, two members appeared to feel there was sufficient popular support for woman suffrage to warrant the introduction of enfranchisement bills in 1895. Dr. Stockton proposed a measure to bestow the provincial franchise upon unmarried women. Though he warmly supported the Stockton bill, Hon. H. R. Emmerson introduced a broader measure a week later, one which would

---

[66]*Ibid.*, I, 117-18.
[67]*N.B.: Journals, 1891*, p. 31; *1892*, p. 52; *1894*, p. XXXI; *1895*, pp. 20, 85; *1899*, pp. 61, 62, 84.
[68]*Ibid., 1894*, p. 122. *Daily Telegraph*, April 18, 19, 1894. Quotation in April 19 issue.

enfranchise all women. Emmerson, a member of the government, stated that his bill was in response to a request of the
Maritime W.C.T.U., which had not been satisfied with the
Stockton bill. In support of these bills eighteen petitions were
sent to the legislature, but in the end Blair, who evidently still
did not "see the subject more clearly," had his way. Both
measures were defeated by narrow margins: that of Dr.
Stockton by 15 to 14, the more generous one of Emmerson by
19 to 15.[69]

In a lengthy editorial of February 27, 1895, the *Telegraph*
distributed both praise and blame with a lavish hand. After
congratulating the women for the excellent showing they had
made in their petition campaign, the editor heaped scorn and
censure upon the heads of the attorney-general, John Sive-
wright, and others who had conspicuously opposed the bills.

... no opponent ... was able to put forward a single reason against their
bill which was worthy of serious consideration, or which rose above that
species of argument which is denominated as twaddle. The man who, in this
age ..., sets himself down seriously to the task of showing that women
should not be entrusted with the power of electing legislators, only proves
his utter incapacity for comprehending the signs of the times and the tendencies of the age. We consider that the cause of woman suffrage has made
an immense gain this year in New Brunswick, and that its triumph at an
early date is as certain as the rising of tomorrow's sun.

Events were to prove, however, that the attorney-general was
closer to "comprehending the signs of the times" than the
*Telegraph* editor, whose boundless enthusiasm for the suffrage
cause more than once made him a false prophet.

No bill for provincial enfranchisement of women appeared
at the 1896 session; indeed, even petitions were lacking. However, one advance was made, which proved to be the last
until 1915. The legislature in 1893 had passed a bill, sponsored
by none other than Blair, which permitted the appointment
of *one* woman to each board of school trustees in cities and
towns. Becoming a trifle bolder in 1896, the lawmakers de-

---

[69]*N.B.: Journals, 1895*, pp. 40, 41, 49, 80-3 (for the Stockton bill); pp. 62, 70
(for the Emmerson bill). *N.B.: Synoptic Reports, 1895*, pp. 81, 86-91. *Daily
Telegraph*, Feb. 20, 25, 26, 1895.

creed that all such school boards *must* have *two* women members.[70]

Two more attempts were to be made to enfranchise women before the nineties drew to a close, but both of these showed evidence of a mounting legislative hostility toward the equal rights question. Dr. Stockton, unsupported by petitions, introduced a mild measure for the enfranchisement of unmarried women in February 1897. While the bill was before the assembly the Enfranchisement Association wrote to each member of the House asking him to support it and to reply stating how he would vote. Only fourteen replies were received—considerably less than half the membership—and of these six were favourable, six opposed and two uncertain.[71] If this response be taken as a gauge of the importance attached to the question by members, it is not surprising that Dr. Stockton's measure elicited no debate and was allowed to die, unmourned, in committee.[72]

New hope mounted in the hearts of the suffragists when H. R. Emmerson became premier in January 1898. Hastening to congratulate him and to render thanks for past support, the Enfranchisement Association asked that he would again introduce a suffrage bill for them. Strategy appeared to dictate waiting for the 1899 session, in order that thorough preparations might be made for building up popular support of such a measure. Thus the chief activity of the little group for 1898 was the rounding up of signatures for a petition to dwarf all previous petitions. In this work they had the generous support of the provincial W.C.T.U., with the result that on April 7 and 12 the legislature was bombarded by twelve suffrage petitions, that of the Enfranchisement Association alone containing almost 4,000 signatures.[73]

[70]School trustees were appointed in cities and towns, elected in rural communities. (Note Pugsley's bill of 1886, which referred to rural communities.) *Statutes of New Brunswick, 1893*, ch. 18; *1896*, ch. 14. Hon. H. R. Emmerson sponsored the 1896 Act.

[71]N.B. Minute Books, I, 74-5, 80.

[72]*N.B.: Journals, 1897*, pp. 76, 77, 96. *N.B.: Synoptic Reports, 1897*, pp. 117-18.

[73]N.B. Minute Books, I, 88-90, 92-3, 95, 100. *N.B.: Journals, 1898*, pp. 61, 62, 84.

Fortified by this demonstration of popular sympathy with the project, Premier Emmerson introduced both a suffrage resolution and a bill for full enfranchisement on April 13, though he refused to make the bill a government measure. Considerable debate, mostly of an unfriendly nature, arose on the resolution. Recalling that William Pugsley stressed before the federal parliament in 1916 and 1917 his early support of woman suffrage, it is rather surprising to find the summary of his speech suggesting that he was not in 1898 as strongly in favour of the proposition as formerly.

> Before a change so radical, so permanent and so far reaching was adopted, the question should be submitted to the people. It followed as a logical conclusion that if the right to vote was given to the women the right to represent the people in the legislature would surely follow. It was because of these far reaching responsibilities that he shrank from hasty legislation.[74]

Despite an eloquent plea for support by the premier, the resolution suffered a thumping defeat of 34 to 7, after which the bill was immediately allowed to lapse.[75] Discouraged and irritated by the rough handling which the measure had received from the legislators, the Enfranchisement Association turned down a motion by one of its members that a letter of thanks be sent to Premier Emmerson and those few who had supported him. "The attitude of the Legislature towards our Petition did not commend itself to the Club," was the terse comment of the secretary.[76]

With the opening of the twentieth century the suffrage movement of New Brunswick entered upon a decade and a half of public indifference and legislative rebuffs. The goal seemed farther from attainment in 1914 than it had at the close of the nineties.

The small group of Saint John women who called themselves a suffrage society continued to function except from December 12, 1903 until November 9, 1907, when the weight of discouragement was evidently too much for them to bear. Many of their meetings were attended by fewer than ten

[74]*N.B.: Synoptic Reports, 1899*, p. 65.
[75]*N.B.: Journals, 1899*, pp. 100-1.
[76]N.B. Minute Books, I, 111-12.

members and their treasury was so small they could seldom send delegates to the annual meetings of the National Council of Women or the Canadian Suffrage Association, much as they desired to maintain their affiliations with these national bodies. The indifference, if not outright hostility, of women themselves to the Enfranchisement Association reached such a point in 1902 that the suffrage society felt compelled to withdraw from the Local Council of Women. This unfortunate experience in Saint John was in vivid contrast to such cities as Victoria, Calgary, and Montreal where the Local Councils were focal points for suffrage activities. With evident bitterness, Miss Mabel Peters addressed a letter to the Saint John *Evening Times* on February 19, 1908:

Knowing that the Woman's Clubs of Saint John are to be asked by the Suffragists to indorse their petition to the legislature for full parliamentary suffrage, and knowing, as I do, the avowed 'conservative' sentiment of some of the Women's organizations only too well, I feel that the following . . . is very appropriate to the situation.

She then quoted an article from an American newspaper which flayed those women who, with smug superiority, called themselves "conservative" and blocked the progress of other women much more effectively than men ever thought of doing.

The contacts of the suffrage society with the legislature during this period were as unhappy as an unpopular cause could make them. Two fairly large petitions, drawn up and presented to the assembly in 1908 and 1912 were ignored by the lawmakers.[77] An attempt in 1908 to have the legislators commit themselves openly on the enfranchisement question met with no greater success than their previous efforts in 1897.[78] But the bitterest doses to swallow were the very cool, sometimes even insulting, receptions which their delegations to the government or to the legislature were given.

The first of these delegations, consisting of Mrs. Fiske, Mrs. Hatheway, Miss Peters, and Mrs. Colby Smith, was to

[77]*N.B.: Journals, 1908,* p. 61; *1912,* p. 109.
[78]N.B. Minute Books, I, 173-4.

the new Conservative premier, Hon. Douglas Hazen, on May 13, 1908. The four women supported by two members of the legislature (W. F. Hatheway and J. E. Wilson) pleaded for a bill to enfranchise only unmarried women. Although the premier received them courteously, his reply was definitely chilling. Women would undoubtedly be enfranchised when enough of them wanted to be, but that time was not now. Furthermore, women might better cling to the lines of activity for which they were suited than be "burdened with the public work of the country."[79] A similar delegation to Premier Hazen on January 21 of the following year came away with no greater satisfaction.[80]

Contempt and open affront were the lot of those members of the Enfranchisement Association who journeyed to Fredericton in 1909, 1912, and 1913 to support the only three woman suffrage bills which appeared during the years of adversity. Although the Hatheway, Dickson, and Munro bills were of the mildest character, confining their enfranchisement proposals strictly to single women, the introduction of each in the legislature was the signal for some fresh outburst of legislative mockery.

W. F. Hatheway's bill in 1909, which received the fairest treatment accorded to any of these three measures, had passed second reading on April 23 and was before committee of the whole the following day, when seven of the Saint John suffragists appeared at the provincial legislative building to lobby for its passage. Their arrival was greeted by the gallant lawmakers with cries of "Help!" "Police!" "Sergeant - at - Arms!", followed by a loud clanging of the division bells. In spite of the unusual reception, the women managed to speak to several lawmakers and had the courage to remain at Fredericton until their measure was given the "three months' hoist" on April 27 by a vote of 24 to 14. With admirable restraint and brevity, the Minute Book of the Enfranchise-

[79] *Ibid.*, I, 180-1. *Daily Telegraph*, May 14, 1908. *Canadian Annual Review* (1908), p. 410.
[80] *Ibid.* (1909), p. 453. *Daily Telegraph*, Jan. 22, 1909.

ment Association closed the incident with the notation: "On this occasion we were treated with insult."[81]

Three years later Walter B. Dickson attempted to introduce a similar bill. Evidence of some popular support for the cause lay before the assembly in the shape of five suffrage petitions and eleven resolutions from branches of the W.C.T.U. and the men's Provincial Temperance Federation, yet the legislature refused to receive the bill on the flimsy pretext that it was a measure of a public character introduced by a private member.[82] Mrs. Hatheway, who had gone to Fredericton intending to support the bill, fared no better than its sponsor when she was prevented from speaking by the attorney-general who informed her that only members could address the whole House. This gentle, dignified woman, who had been the victim of a lewd joke circulated among members of the House at the time of the 1909 delegation, had her opportunity to put in print the well-merited rebuke she had intended delivering in person to the lawmakers before the attorney-general intervened.

How can we expect the country to turn toward anything moral and right when such men are sent as representatives and framers of its laws? When we realized that all but one of these men are still in the Legislature, we hardly expected that our bill would meet with any other treatment than it received last week. Such men may well dread the vote of every pure-minded woman.[83]

Knowing that he was heading for rough waters after the fate of the Dickson bill, Donald Munro moved for leave to introduce a women's franchise measure on February 21, 1913, claiming that it had the backing of the Saint John Branch of the Canadian Suffrage Association, the provincial W.C.T.U., and the Carpenters' and Joiners' Brotherhood of Saint John. Before galleries crowded with women, many of whom had loyally come all the way from Saint John for the occasion, a full-dress debate arose on the motion. Although supported

[81]*Ibid.*, April 9, 26, 28, 1909.  *Gleaner* (Fredericton), April 24, 1909.  *N.B.: Journals, 1909*, pp. 150, 153, 183.  *N.B.: Synoptic Reports, 1909*, pp. 158, 185-9. *Canadian Annual Review* (1909), p. 459.  N.B. Minute Books, I, 182.
[82]*N.B.: Journals, 1912*, p. 120.
[83]*Globe* (Saint John), April 18, 1912.

by the premier, James K. Flemming, it was noted that such speeches as those of Leonard Tilley and Colonel John Sheridan, which were vehemently opposed to the project, elicited the most enthusiastic applause from the members.   Thus no surprise was occasioned when Munro lost his motion by a vote of 21 to 10.[84] Waxing belligerent over the continuing succession of defeats, the *Telegraph* of February 22 rumbled editorially: "If we escape without a season of militant tactics we shall be lucky." But in that prediction it was as wide of the mark as ever.

At times small rifts appeared in the heavy clouds of disappointment.   Two trifling concessions by the legislature offered some evidence of progress towards a more liberal view of women's status.   Sponsored by Hon. William Pugsley, a bill to permit women to study and practice law went through the assembly in 1906 without any difficulty.[85]   Eight years later, after receiving a petition from the City and County of Saint John, the lawmakers passed an act to permit Saint John to hold a plebiscite on extending the municipal franchise to the married women of that city.   The heartening result was 3,175 in favour as against 2,260 opposed, which led to passage of the desired act at the following session of the legislative assembly.[86]

Outside the legislature, too, there were occasional signs of encouragement to stir the pulse of the faithful band in Saint John.   Temperance forces, which were well organized in New Brunswick, gave material aid whenever petitions or bills were to come before the assembly; indeed, the province-wide scope of the W.C.T.U., as compared with the purely local character of the Enfranchisement Association, often carried greater weight with the lawmakers at Fredericton.[87]   Much-needed editorial support from the press continued to stem from the *Daily Telegraph* during the lean years and was augmented

[84]*N.B.: Journals, 1913,* p. 60.   *N.B.: Synoptic Reports, 1913,* pp. 21-7.
[85]*Statutes of New Brunswick, 1906,* ch. 5.
[86]*Ibid., 1914,* ch. 80; *1915,* ch. 96.
[87]The New Brunswick Grand Division of the Sons of Temperance gave its official blessing to woman suffrage in 1910.

around 1908 by the friendly suffrage policy adopted by the editors of two other Saint John papers—the *Globe* and the *Times*. The old rift between the Saint John Local Council of Women and the Enfranchisement Association was finally closed in 1910 when the former adopted a much more friendly attitude towards woman suffrage, largely as a result of the decision reached by the National Council at the Halifax Convention of that same year.

Prompted perhaps by the very meagreness of fare in the Maritime Provinces during the early years of the twentieth century, the suffragists of Saint John evinced an amazing hunger for suffrage news from both Britain and the United States. More than once their minutes reveal them dipping into their scanty funds to send for suffrage literature from the United States. When one of their members went on a lengthy visit to the republic in 1909, she was instructed to send regular notes on suffrage progress there, and upon her return in 1911, the literature and news she brought back were eagerly devoured by the members.[88]

Militant tactics adopted in pre-war years by English suffragists, though not condoned or emulated, evoked broadminded sympathy and tolerance among the Saint John suffragists, the more refreshing because it was so unusual in the conservative atmosphere of the Maritimes. The minutes for their meeting of December 9, 1911 close with the words (written by Mrs. Hatheway): "Let us withhold our judgment upon the window-smashers until the quiet comes after victory and not condemn what must seem rude and mistaken methods to us who have had no experience with old country politics, but remember what these English women are fighting for."[89] Converting preaching into practice, the Enfranchisement Association sponsored a public meeting at the Opera House in Saint John on January 15, 1912 to hear Miss Sylvia Pankhurst. "The slight, fair English girl who looked almost frail" held a large audience spellbound for two hours while she de-

[88]N.B. Minute Books, I, 189, 209.
[89]*Ibid.*, I, 210.

scribed the reasons for the militant campaign and the methods used by the English suffragettes.[90]

The war years which brought suffrage activities to a successful climax in so many parts of Canada produced amazingly little stir in New Brunswick suffrage circles, at least until 1917. Two of the oldest and most active members of the Suffrage Association, Mrs. Emma Fiske and Miss Mabel Peters, died in 1914. This double loss occurred while the society was in the midst of its campaign to win the municipal franchise for the married women of Saint John. However, the project was successfully completed in the spring of 1915.

Under a new slate of officers headed by Miss Clara O. McGivern, the group sent a delegation to the city commissioners on February 10, 1915 with the request that the latter draw up the desired bill in conformity with the favourable 1914 referendum and present it to the legislature. In the presence of the delegation, the city fathers voted unanimously to accede to the request, and the bill itself, supported by a petition circulated by the Enfranchisement Association, went through the legislature with no debate on May 5.[91]

Though this achievement was small in comparison with the ultimate aims of the society, success of any sort was so unusual as to warrant a celebration, especially since this year marked the Association's twenty-first anniversary. A public meeting was held in the studio of the Saint John Art Club on May 6. The guests were regaled with musical numbers, a speech on woman suffrage by the Reverend F. H. Wentworth, and a playlet entitled "Miss Appleyard's Awakening." Proceeds of the evening netted the Association $33.90, the most substantial sum recorded in their treasury. Congratulatory messages were received from both of the national suffrage organizations in Toronto, evidence that the society's struggle against the mountain of public indifference in the Maritime

---

[90]*Telegraph and Sun*, Jan. 16, 1912. (The *Daily Telegraph* changed its name in 1910.)  Miss Pankhurst was the guest of Mrs. W. F. Hatheway during her visit to Saint John.

[91]N.B. Minute Books, II, 41-5.  *Globe*, Feb. 11, 1915.  *N.B.: Journals, 1915*, pp. 31, 32, 35, 155, 167.  *Statutes of New Brunswick, 1915*, ch. 96.

Provinces was being watched with sympathetic interest in other parts of the dominion.[92]

War work absorbed the energies of the members to the exclusion of all else during 1916, with the result that very few meetings were held and no legislative campaigns set under way. Inspired by the victories of the West, however, members came to the conclusion that patriotic work and franchise matters could well be combined without detriment to either. So it was with renewed energy that the ten or twelve faithfuls of the Enfranchisement Association gathered weekly, beginning in January 1917, to ply their needles and to plan an extensive campaign of education and agitation for that spring.

Under the leadership of Miss McGivern and Mrs. Hatheway (who still occupied the modest position of corresponding secretary) a tremendous amount of work was done during the spring months in preparation for the contemplated assault upon the lawmakers at Fredericton. Copies of suffrage acts from all provinces where equal franchise had been obtained were procured for study and a letter was forwarded to Hon. William Pugsley in Ottawa asking him to draft a suffrage bill for the women of his province. Letters were written to all forty-eight candidates for the provincial legislature before the spring elections of 1917 with the request for their stand on woman suffrage. Although many of the answers were non-committal, forty-one replies were received, an indication that the cause seemed worthy of more respectful consideration by would-be lawmakers than heretofore. After the Liberal victory in April, a letter was dispatched to the new premier, Hon. Walter E. Foster, requesting that he make woman suffrage a government measure in the forthcoming session of the legislature. The letter was followed by a personal call upon the premier in late April, when Mr. and Mrs. Hatheway and Mrs. Hooper (vice-president of the Enfranchisement Association) broached the subject of a suffrage bill. While they did not receive a flat denial to their request, the trio felt bound to report "a cold touch."[93]

[92]N.B. Minute Books, II, 53-5. *Globe*, May 7, 1915.
[93]N.B. Minute Books, II, 87-92, 103.

Recognizing the need for interest and support outside
Saint John, the association depleted its treasury in sending
out suffrage literature to all parts of the province. Several
newspapers were approached by Mrs. Hatheway in an effort
to secure wider news and editorial coverage. Most important
of all, a series of public meetings in various parts of the province was held under the Association's sponsorship in late
April and May to whip up interest in the pending suffrage bill
and to get people to sign petitions backing it. Mr. Hatheway
and Senator George G. King gave valiant support to the
women on these speaking trips, which exacted much in time,
energy, and courage.[94]

Other happy portents brightened those spring days of
1917. All nineteen local branches of the New Brunswick
W.C.T.U. stamped the project with their approval and threw
their weight into rousing favourable public sentiment for the
bill. Completely reversing its earlier antipathy towards
woman suffrage, the Saint John Local Council, representing
twenty-five women's societies, unanimously endorsed the
forthcoming bill and forwarded a resolution embodying its
stand to the Foster government. Many clergymen were now
openly ranged on the women's side and frequently used their
pulpits as sounding boards for spreading the tenet of political
equality. The press of Saint John added its voice to that of
the pulpit as the *Times*, *Globe*, and *Telegraph* continued to give
staunch backing to the suffrage cause.[95]

Yet there were signs that all might not be smooth sailing.
In a general report made before the Enfranchisement Association on May 2, Mrs. Hatheway warned that the defeat of
the Nova Scotia franchise bill on April 23 might have unfavourable repercussions in the New Brunswick legislature
because the latter so often "emulates their example." She
also recalled that the premier had been noticeably lacking in
cordiality to the suffrage delegation in April.[96]

[94]*Telegraph and Sun*, May 23, 1917.
[95]N.B. Minute Books, II, 96-101.
[96]*Ibid.*, II, 102.

The suffrage bill of 1917 was introduced by Dr. William F. Roberts, minister of health, as a private member's bill on May 29. More generous than earlier measures, it proposed to enfranchise all women on the same terms as men. A good-sized delegation from Saint John and six or seven other centres was present on June 6 when the bill passed second reading with no debate other than Dr. Roberts's speech supporting it, and was passed on to the committee on law practice.[97] Everything was proceeding with unbelievable smoothness. However, a treacherous reef on the course was pointed out by the *Telegraph* in an editorial on June 6, the very day the bill came up for second reading. Though backing the women to the hilt, the editor half lamented and half chided that the evidence that New Brunswick women really wanted the vote was not as clear as it should be.

On June 19 a delegation of both men and women from Saint John appeared at Fredericton to support the measure. The premier had consented to meet the delegation in the committee room, but such a large number came that nothing less than the assembly chamber would accommodate them, which forced the lawmakers into the unaccustomed regions of the galleries. The impressive turnout and the friendly reception accorded the speeches of the delegates appeared to insure favourable treatment of the measure in committee of the whole on the following day.[98]

Then: "Like a bolt from the blue . . . the next day they killed it." So the Association's Minute Book described the fate of the Roberts bill in committee on June 20. A three-hour debate preceded the vote of 24 to 15 which ended suffrage hopes for that session at least. As usual, high tribute was paid to women's war work, but opponents clung to their principal (and perhaps justifiable) contention that women in New Brunswick did not want the franchise. One of the highlights of the debate was the ardent support given the measure by

[97]*N.B.: Journals, 1917*, pp. 60, 96. *N.B.: Synoptic Reports, 1917*, pp. 44, 83-4. *Telegraph and Sun*, May 30, June 4, 7, 1917.
[98]N.B. Minute Books, II, 104.

two Conservatives who had formerly been vehement in opposition. James A. Murray, the former premier, who had moved
the "three months' hoist" in 1909, and Leonard Tilley, an
outspoken foe of the Munro bill in 1913, both claimed to have
been converted by the heroic efforts of women in the war.
But the thought persists that, while their about-face may have
been perfectly sincere, it became more attractive to the recent
converts as a source of annoyance to the party in power.
Among the fifteen votes in favour of the bill were those of the
premier and of the attorney-general, J. P. Byrne. Party lines
meant nothing, however, on a private member's bill and the
innate conservatism of the province asserted itself to anni-
hilate the Roberts measure.[99]

Holding a post-mortem, the *Telegraph* of June 21 commented that the defeat was only another postponement of the
inevitable, but with unwonted severity laid the blame for the
fiasco directly upon the women themselves.

Members of the House who were ready to admit that women are entitled to
vote might fairly expect that the great mass of women show at least enough
interest in the question to make their wishes known through petitions and
meetings to a greater extent than was done. With better management of
the campaign of education, or agitation, there should be no doubt of success
next session.

The year 1918 which logically should have produced a
vigorous follow-up campaign as advised by the *Telegraph*, was
actually one of disappointing inaction. The strenuous exertions of the previous spring coupled with an overwhelming
sense of failure appeared to induce a semi-paralysis among the
groups most vitally interested. To make matters worse, the
Saint John Suffrage Association found its weakened energies
further dissipated because of a political rift among its membership in November 1917. Miss McGivern, the president, and
Mrs. Hooper, the vice-president, both resigned when the
Association refused to vote an endorsement of Sir Robert
Borden's Union government.[100]

[99]*N.B.: Synoptic Reports, 1917*, pp. 156-61. *Telegraph and Sun*, June 21,
1917.
[100]N.B. Minute Books, II, 108-9.

The weakened remnant reorganized on January 11, 1918 under the presidency of Mrs. Hatheway for what proved to be the last year of its existence. With their able president off to the United States for a good part of the spring, the society took little effective action of any sort. They did discuss with Dr. Roberts the possibility of introducing another suffrage bill, but he asked to be excused for the 1918 session on the ground that his energies would be largely absorbed in pushing through a medical bill. To the lone member of the society who interviewed Premier Foster early that spring was given the advice that it would be just as well to postpone the introduction of a franchise bill for another session at least.[101] Meetings became less frequent as the year wore on and finally stopped altogether in January 1919. Not a word of explanation for the society's disappearance is given in the Minute Books, nor is there any evidence of a formal dissolution. Apparently the 1917 split in its small membership was more than it could survive and it gave up the ghost quietly, only a few months before enfranchisement for women became an accomplished fact in the spring of 1919.

The New Brunswick legislature seemed more aware of the suffrage question than the women themselves during the 1918 session, with the Conservative minority ever anxious to exploit its nuisance possibilities. On March 21 the leader of the Opposition introduced a resolution endorsing woman suffrage,which was seconded by Leonard Tilley. Party lines were again forgotten as members on either side of the floor praised the labours of women in war-time and pointed out that the principle of equal franchise was becoming common in western democracies. The premier was lukewarm. Though he announced that he would support the resolution and would eventually bring in a bill to implement it, he thought it better to wait another session. Wisdom might be gleaned from the experience of the dominion government, Great Britain, and Nova Scotia, all of whom had proposals to enfranchise women before them in 1918. The resolution passed without a division,

[101]*Ibid.*, II, 113-14, 118-21.

thus placing unanimous approval of the legislature upon the principle, if not the practice, of equal rights.[102]

Determined to follow up the advantage, the Opposition leader gave notice on April 8 that he would move for leave to introduce a woman suffrage bill two days later, but he changed his mind when Premier Foster hinted that he would advise the lieutenant-governor to disallow such a measure if it passed.[103] The premier was obviously putting off till the last possible moment something which was personally distasteful to him, yet which was admittedly bound to come. When the barriers were lowered, it would be the Liberal party which would do the lowering—not an upstart Conservative minority.

Woman suffrage came to New Brunswick in April 1919 mainly as a tribute to women's war work and because Nova Scotia had led the way a year earlier. No mass petitions aided the passage of the bill and no delegations of excited and enthusiastic women thronged the galleries to watch its progress. By 1919, "No lobbying was necessary, they'd said all they had to say, so the women stayed home, had an afternoon tea, shook hands all around, and with a 'Deo Gratias' dismissed the subject."[104]

Evidence that the Foster government was prepared to follow the general trend in suffrage matters came in the speech from the throne on March 6, 1919. By a happy twist of fate the man who read the portentous words on that occasion was Hon. William Pugsley, newly appointed lieutenant-governor, who had done so much to place the women's cause before the federal parliament at Ottawa in 1916 and 1917.[105]

The bill, which provided for the enfranchisement of all women in provincial matters on the same terms as men, was introduced by J. P. Byrne on March 21 and passed first and second readings without any discussion. Considerable debate arose in committee of the whole four days later, but none of it was opposed to the principle of the bill. Technicalities in-

---

[102]*N.B.: Journals, 1918*, p. 38.   *Telegraph and Sun*, Mar. 22, 1918.
[103]*Canadian Annual Review* (1918), p. 662.   N.B. Minute Books, II, 127.
[104]Letter of Mrs. J. V. Lawlor to the author, Jan. 10, 1947.
[105]*Telegraph and Sun*, Mar. 7, 1919.

volving what constituted citizenship for women occupied the bulk of the time, though one member, John R. Campbell, queried cautiously whether the bill would permit women to sit in the assembly. When Mr. Byrne assured him it would not, Frank Potts of the Conservative forces castigated the government for this ultraconservative omission, adding that the Liberals wouldn't be giving women the vote at all if the pressure of public opinion had not forced the unwelcome step upon them. Chivalry had its moment, too, when a gallant Irish member, Francis Sweeney, arose to suggest that now that women were going to cast the ballot, a special effort should be made to hold elections in good weather. All legislative hurdles were cleared by April 15. Two days later royal assent was bestowed by the lieutenant-governor, who congratulated the government on this enlightened piece of legislation and paid the final flowery tribute to women's part in the war.[106]

Fifteen years were destined to pass before New Brunswick granted the complementary political privilege of eligibility for the provincial legislature. If the women felt any disappointment or resentment over their exclusion from the assembly, they made no outcry about it either in 1919 or the years immediately following.

Meantime two small advances in the local political arena were made by women in the early 1920's. An act of April 16, 1921 bestowed upon all women the same municipal privileges enjoyed by men. Four years later married women who were wives of ratepayers were made eligible for voting and officeholding in rural school elections, on the ground that they were in a position to know better than any others what was best for the children.[107]

By 1934, the anomaly of being the only women in Canada who could vote yet not hold office stirred some of the women's organizations to action. After receiving many petitions, par-

---

[106]*Statutes of New Brunswick, 1919*, ch. 63. *N.B.: Journals, 1919*, pp. 34, 37, 135, 158. *N.B.: Synoptic Reports, 1919*, pp. 97, 124-5, 266-9, 292-5. *Telegraph and Sun*, Mar. 26, April 11, 15, 19, 1919.

[107]*Statutes of New Brunswick, 1921*, ch. 43; *1925*, ch. 8.

ticularly from the Women's Institutes,[108] the premier, Leonard Tilley, personally introduced the required bill, which slipped quietly through the various legislative stages, arousing no discussion either inside the assembly or out. It became law on March 9—evidently another instance of the *Telegraph's* old maxim, "Ask (in sufficient numbers) and it shall be given."[109]

On the day Premier Tilley introduced his important amendment to the Elections Act, the *Telegraph-Journal* spread this headline across its front page: "Women May Soon Sit in N.B. House." That was fifteen years ago. Shortly after passage of the act, one woman aspired to the honour in Northumberland and was roundly defeated. The lone woman candidate (C.C.F.) in 1948 fared no better. It seems that the women of New Brunswick are not yet politically minded. The comment of one of them is apt: "New Brunswick is the most conservative province in the Dominion, probably because the province was settled by Loyalists, and old standards, to a great extent, still prevail."[110]

Indifference to the question of women's political rights, which was generally so characteristic of the Maritime Provinces, reached its apex in the island province. Wrapped snugly inside its watery boundaries, Prince Edward Island built up a complete immunity to outside suffrage influences and was well content that no native variety of feminism took root in its soil. The women themselves were not interested. There simply were no *bona fide* suffragists within the borders of the province.

Prince Edward Island was the only province which never nourished a suffrage organization of any kind. The Local Councils of Women, which might have been important agen-

<hr>

[108]These organizations of women in rural areas had given loyal support to the suffrage delegations organized by city women in 1917. It balanced the score to have them become the key figures in obtaining for women the right to sit in the legislative assembly.

[109]*Statutes of New Brunswick, 1934,* ch. 22. *N.B.: Journals, 1934,* pp. 13, 16, 36, 38, 96. *Telegraph-Journal,* Feb. 9, 21, 1934.

[110]Letter from Mrs. Lillian M. B. Maxwell of Fredericton to the author, Oct. 28, 1943.

cies for moulding public opinion in the direction of equal rights, largely ignored the issue. Even temperance groups, the solid backbone of the suffrage movement in Nova Scotia and New Brunswick, carried on an almost negligible amount of agitation for the enfranchisement of women in this province where one of the earliest prohibition acts in Canada was passed (1900). Indeed, the only organization which ever seriously interested itself in the project was the Women's Liberal Club—and then not until all the provinces to the west of it, except Quebec, had granted women the right to vote.

The Island press and legislative annals naturally mirrored the apathy of the women. The attitude of the province's two leading newspapers, both of which were rabidly partisan, was one of complete indifference to the question, unless they perceived a chance to annoy the party they opposed. Island lawmakers were troubled by the barest minimum of suffrage petitions during those long years when provincial legislatures in some parts of the dominion found themselves confronted almost annually with petitions and delegations from active enfranchisement groups. Nor does a survey of the assembly's *Journals* reveal any lengthy series of bills for extension of the suffrage. The peace enjoyed by the Island's lawmakers where suffrage matters were concerned can best be gauged by the fact that the word "woman" never appeared in the index to the *Journals* from 1899 to 1917.

Before 1899, however, Prince Edward Island felt some mild echoes of the suffrage agitation which gripped other parts of the dominion in the late eighties and nineties. Acts of 1888 and 1892, entirely unsolicited by the women, gave unmarried women of Charlottetown and Summerside, the province's two large towns, the right to vote at municipal elections.[111] This was, of course, in line with similar action taken by the legis-

[111]*Statutes of Prince Edward Island, 1888,* ch. 12; *1892,* ch. 35. Not until 1927 was the same privilege extended to married women property owners. *Statutes of P.E.I., 1927,* ch. 9. Women's eligibility for municipal office holding appears to exist by default of any prohibition to the contrary. A letter from the office of the attorney-general at Charlottetown, dated Nov. 4, 1946, states that "it is presumed that when women were given the right to vote they would also be permitted to hold municipal offices."

latures of New Brunswick and Nova Scotia in 1886 and 1887.

The first and only serious discussion of voting rights for women, prior to 1918, came in the 1893 session. In that year Prince Edward Island passed an act consolidating its two-chambered legislature into one. During the discussions which arose over qualifications for voting, the Conservative Opposition put in a plea for woman suffrage, more for its nuisance value than anything else, one suspects. The subject was introduced by Angus McLeod on March 16 with the bold words: "I think the time has arrived when unmarried females, owning property in this Province, should have the right to vote." This was the signal for many other Conservative members to enter the fray, one going so far as to say that he should like to have women sitting in the new assembly. George Bentley, Opposition leader, added to the stir by making a formal motion to amend the bill that single women might be granted the franchise. In the midst of this demonstration, a Liberal supporter pointed out that the Conservatives had never suggested enfranchising women during their tenure of office down to 1891 and acidly demanded the reason for their present overwhelming interest. The verbal sport was ended and the motion lost after the premier, Hon. Frederick Peters, made the cogent observation: "We have not been asked for this amendment and therefore there is no reason for its adoption."[112]

Encouraged perhaps by the demonstration of Conservative support in 1893, but more probably stirred by the lively battles being waged during the mid-nineties in both the larger Maritime Provinces, the Island W.C.T.U. presented a petition for "full Parliamentary suffrages" for all women on May 2, 1894. An attempt by its sponsor, John Bell, a Liberal, to "explain the nature of the petition more fully" was ruled out of order by the speaker and there the matter rested for that session.[113]

[112]*The Parliamentary Reporter: Debates and Proceedings of the House of Assembly of Prince Edward Island, 1893*, pp. 136, 142, 156, 173-4, 180-4. These *Debates* were not published after 1893.

[113]*P.E.I.: Journals, 1894*, p. 174. *Daily Patriot* (Charlottetown), May 3, 1894.

Several petitions from women confronted the legislature in 1895, but these concerned property rather than political rights, and resulted in the passage of a very liberal Married Women's Property Act the following year. Two petitions seeking full enfranchisement for women were in fact presented in 1895, again by John Bell, but ironically enough, the petitioners were all men.[114]

The last legislative transaction dealing with women in this early period came in 1899. Following a petition from the Local Council of Women in Charlottetown, the Public Schools Act was amended to permit the appointment of women as school trustees in Charlottetown and Summerside.[115] The men of Prince Edward Island were apparently willing to give the women what they asked for, if they would only ask. We have already noted how petitions brought fairly rapid results in the Married Women's Property Act, and to that it should be added that the desired amendment to the Public Schools Act was accomplished just two weeks after the legislators received the Local Council's petition.

Following the mild agitation of the late nineteenth century, it can only be assumed that the Island women were perfectly content with their status, for silence on the subject of women's rights was as all-prevading outside of legislative precincts as it was within. The only record of any public discussion of the question prior to the war years was at a Maritimes W.C.T.U. convention held at Summerside in September 1913. The speaker at the session devoted to woman suffrage was Mrs. Deborah Livingstone of Rhode Island who told her audience plainly that she did not understand how the women of Canada could sit still and do nothing while guardianship laws were so manifestly unfair to them. Far from resenting this blunt speech from an outsider, the *Chronicle* of September 10 reported that Mrs. Livingstone "aroused much interest," but if she did, it was not the type of interest that led to action.

[114]*P.E.I.: Journals, 1895*, p. 31.
[115]*Statutes of P.E.I., 1899*, ch. 7. *P.E.I.: Journals, 1899*, pp. 48, 50, 60, 75-6, 84, 130. *Daily Patriot*, May 6, 1899. Outside of these two towns, in the rural districts, trustees were elected as in N.S. and N.B. In rural areas women did not become eligible for school trusteeship until 1917. *Statutes of P.E.I., 1917*, ch. 10.

For five more years the woman suffrage question lay dormant. Then, in the 1918 session of the legislature, with a Conservative government in power, the subject was brought to light without the women's having lifted a finger. On April 5, a Conservative private member, John A. Dewar, moved, seconded by Dr. A. A. McDonald, that:

Whereas the women of P.E.I. as well as women in other parts of the Empire, have taken a very active part in the various industries and War Charities, and by the good and useful work performed by them are materially assisting in winning the War:

And whereas in England, the U.S.A., in several provinces of Canada, the franchise has been extended to women and a Bill has now been introduced in the Canadian House of Commons to the same effect:

Therefore Resolved that in the opinion of this House An Act of the Legislature should be passed extending the franchise to the women of P.E.I.[116]

The reasons for this very generous and unsolicited gesture are plainly indicated in the language of the motion itself: a general desire to reward women's part in the war by acknowledging the justice of their political partnership in affairs of state, and a natural wish to have the province conform to the general trend towards woman suffrage in the English-speaking world.

The resolution was the subject of a very one-sided debate on the evening of April 24. The sponsors, aided by John Bell, now a leading figure of the Liberal Opposition, marshalled together all the well-known arguments in favour of equal franchise, while not one voice in the assemblage was raised against the proposal. Hon. Harvey McEwen was inclined to be slightly jocular and pertinently asked, "Why should the women be given the privilege before they asked for it?" The premier, Hon. Aubin Arsenault, also pointed to the apparent indifference of women, but both he and McEwen expressed their willingness to support such a measure and joined with other members to give the resolution unanimous passage.[117] No more was done at that session, the legislators feeling, quite justifiably, that the next move ought to be the women's. The Island women's failure to bestir themselves, even to the extent of submitting a suffrage petition, for four full years after this

---

[116]*P.E.I.: Journals, 1918*, pp. 80-1.     [117]*Island Patriot*, April 25, 1918.

open invitation by the legislature indicates their indifference to politics.

Press reactions to the resolution probably reflected the sentiments of the Islanders more faithfully than the legislators themselves. The *Island Patriot* (Liberal) made no editorial comment whatsoever. Prior to the debate on April 24, the Charlottetown *Examiner* (Conservative) of April 8 had questioned whether giving votes to women would benefit them and whether women were capable of "thinking Imperially." In a derogatory vein seldom encountered among English-language Canadian papers of the twentieth century, the *Examiner* reverted to nineteenth-century philosophy on woman's place when it queried: "Can women perform aright the multifarious duties of the home, follow the fashions closely, give time to social matters, take a lively interest in current news and gossip, etc., and also attend closely to matters and questions of political importance?" However, the editor exhibited a tolerant willingness to be converted to woman suffrage for he conceded that "the proposition . . . is, at all events, worthy of careful and serious consideration." That the process of conversion was not a speedy one was evident from the complete editorial silence which followed the unanimous passage of the suffrage resolution.

The 1919 session, which brought to an end a lengthy Conservative tenure of office, should logically have been the one to witness the enactment of a woman franchise bill, had there been the slightest demand for such a measure. The speech from the throne did actually mention a contemplated elections bill without specifying what type of change the government had in mind. Sensing an opportunity to embarrass the Conservative administration, the *Island Patriot* on April 3 jumped to the unwarranted conclusion that it was a woman suffrage measure and in a sudden conversion warmly espoused the cause. The *Patriot's* error was soon plain when an act to enfranchise all *male* veterans was put through the legislature, without so much as a mention of enfranchising women in the course of the debates.

In September 1919 the Liberals returned to power under
a new premier, John Bell. Although they had included a
woman suffrage plank in their platform during the campaign,
the government appeared in no great haste to redeem that
pledge. This again can be attributed to women's attitude
rather than to breach of promise by the Bell administration,
for if no suffrage bills appeared in the 1920 and 1921 sessions,
neither did any enfranchisement petition.

There is evidence that a quiet undercurrent of interest was
at last being developed among the women themselves, however, through the work of the Women's Liberal Club. In the
words of Mrs. Margaret Rogers Stewart, who was at that time
president of the association:

> As a club, we Liberal women decided we must have the suffrage, so in a quiet
> way we went to work contacting our local legislature by lobbying persis-
> tently. . . . We began by 'putting in a word' to all the women we met. A
> few of us . . . visited other parts of the province and held meetings for the
> women. There were few objectors so we had a good reception everywhere. . . .
> It was accomplished entirely by the work of our Women's Liberal Club.[118]

The fruits of this quiet campaign became evident on the
opening day of the 1922 session, when the speech from the
throne made a vague allusion to the possibility of an enfranchisement measure. S. S. Hessian, who moved the address in
reply, showed his contempt for the proposal by omitting all
reference to it, but B. W. Le Page, in seconding the address,
signified his cordial approval of the government's intention.[119]

More evidence of the Liberal Club's spade work came on
the second day when a petition was received, signed by
Margaret R. Stewart in the name of the Women's Liberal
Club of Charlottetown. This first and most important petition was followed by another on March 16 from the Women's
Institutes and a final petition on April 6 from a group of
women, whose organizational affiliation, if there was one, was
not set forth in the House *Journals*.[120] Although the petition

[118]Letter to the author from Mrs. Margaret R. Stewart, Charlottetown, Nov.
17, 1943.
[119]*Island Patriot*, Mar. 17, 1922.
[120]*P.E.I.: Journals, 1922*, pp. 16, 17, 56.

from the Institutes was signed by women of rural areas, the bulk of the signatures on the other two petitions were those of women residing in Charlottetown and Summerside. The *Patriot* of May 9 claimed, no doubt correctly, that the majority of women throughout the countryside had never been canvassed—one more bit of evidence to prove that in eastern Canada, at least, woman suffrage was obtained through the efforts of an exceedingly small minority.

Upon the introduction of the Stewart petition on March 15, Hessian changed his campaign of opposition from silence to obstructionary tactics. He first asked that the names on the petition be read and when told that there were three hundred signatures, demanded to know if they were "representative women." The speaker abruptly put an end to this strategy by refusing to have the names read.[121]

Some interesting light is thrown upon the weight attached to the suffrage question by the government in a little episode which occurred a few minutes after Hessian had been silenced by the speaker. In reply to the Opposition leader's query whether the government contemplated any important legislation for the session, the premier answered that there would be nothing "of a very serious kind." After making a few suggestions about what might be expected, he concluded, "In all probability there will be an act in accordance with the prayer of the petition just read giving the franchise to women."[122]

More than a month elapsed following these preliminary skirmishes and still the government made no move to implement its campaign pledge. Meantime the *Examiner*, which grasped every opportunity to taunt the Bell government, flayed the administration for its dilatory policy, if not downright faithlessness, on the suffrage issue. The issue of March 27 said:

The women's petitions for the voting franchise seem to have been treated with scant courtesy by the House. They were apparently too trivial for comment. . . . And opposition to the promised measure for giving women

[121] *Island Patriot*, Mar. 16, 1922.
[122] *Ibid.*, Mar. 16, 1922.

the right to vote has developed.   This has raised doubts in certain quarters as to whether the measure will be pressed. . . . To withhold the measure now would be adding another to the multitude of broken promises in the past, but what is one among so many? . . . it seems probable at this writing that the suffrage may be granted to take effect at the next general election . . . the present objectors being whipped into line before the vote is taken.

And again on April 6:

There is a whisper around the House and lobbies that the bill to give women votes in provincial elections may not be enacted at the present session, notwithstanding the Premier's promise to put it through at once, as made to prominent members of the Women's Liberal Club.  Some of the government's supporters are at heart opposed to it, others think it highly unpolitic, seeing what so many of the lady voters did in the federal election to the Conservative party which gave them votes.

At last on April 26, with but one week of the session remaining, Premier Bell introduced a resolution for the enfranchisement of women, and at the same time set forth his reasons for backing the proposal.  He claimed that it was supported by many petitions—a somewhat questionable premise.  It would also redeem a campaign pledge made in 1919. Women voted in federal elections; therefore it was but logical to make the franchise complete.  The sentiment of the world had changed on this question and the province "must recognize and keep pace with the march of public sentiment." Bell believed that the franchise would "broaden the subjects of conversation and study" for women.  The government would also benefit from women's advice on matters pertaining to health, morals, and the home.  And finally, it would be a mark of appreciation by a grateful province for the unselfish devotion of women during the recent war.[123]

A lively discussion followed the introduction of the resolution, with most of the comments highly favourable to the proposal.  As might be expected, however, Hessian objected to doing anything so drastic without first holding a plebiscite. Creelman McArthur attempted to soothe Hessian's fears by pointing out that the Liberals were not rushing into this matter blindly, that they had promised it to the women three

[123]*P.E.I.: Journals, 1922*, p. 82.   *Island Patriot*, April 29, 1922.

years ago and had then waited a decent interval of time because "it was thought well just to allow the women time to think it over."

Murdock Kennedy voiced his whole-hearted aversion to the entire idea of women in politics. "It is a wrong principle laid down. I tell you straight now and above board the wife's place and the women's place is in the home, in the kitchen looking after home affairs."[124]

Without further ado the resolution passed, whereupon Premier Bell immediately introduced a very generous measure which would permit women both provincial voting and office-holding privileges on the same basis as men. The only discussion at any stage of the bill's passage through the assembly was in committee on May 2, when the main argument was not over the principle of the measure, but rather whether women would have to have the $325 property qualification necessary to vote for councillors in their own name, or might qualify on their husbands' property. In a burst of generosity the assembly decided in favour of the latter, and in this form the bill passed third reading and received royal assent on May 3, 1922—the last day of the session.[125]

In the light of the Island's constant indifference to the entire question of equal political rights for women, it is not surprising that the events of that last week of the 1922 legislative session passed with no outward stir. Both the *Examiner* and the *Patriot* gave the progress of the bill the barest mention in their news columns and greeted the final passage of the measure with frigid editorial silence. If the Island women themselves felt any great elation over being freed from political disabilities, the rejoicing was of an inconspicuous nature.

According to Mrs. Stewart, Prince Edward Island women have been enthusiastic and conscientious voters, though no woman has ever offered herself as a candidate at a provincial

---

[124]*Ibid.*, May 9, 1922.
[125]*Statutes of P.E.I., 1922*, ch. 5. (The assembly is composed of 15 councillors and 15 assemblymen. To vote for the former a person has to own or lease real property of the value of $325.) *P.E.I.: Journals, 1922*, pp. 83, 88, 123, 126. Charlottetown *Examiner*, May 3, 4, 1922.

election. "I feel it is to be regretted that no woman has yet run in an election here. No one seems to have wanted to, with the result that the other sex guard their rights (?) very zealously and would not, I fear, welcome a woman in that field; but I think it will be a different story after the war, as through war work our women are becoming very public-minded."[126]

Prince Edward Island's post-war election on December 11, 1947, failed to bear out Mrs. Stewart's theory, however. Island politics remained as devoid of women as ever.

Great Britain's oldest colony[127] was granted its own legis-lature in 1833 and enjoyed the privilege of responsible govern-ment from 1855 until 1934. Due to overwhelming economic difficulties induced by the world-wide depression of the early 1930's, the island voluntarily relinquished self-government on February 16, 1934. For the next fifteen years Newfoundland was governed by a Commission of Government responsible to the Secretary of State for Dominion Affairs in the United Kingdom.[128]

War-born demand for the products of Newfoundland's forests, mines, and fisheries, as well as the island's develop-ment as a strategic allied base, created a return of prosperity in the 1940's and with it, a revived interest in the management of its own affairs. Accordingly, a national convention was assembled in 1946 to suggest alternative solutions for this new political problem. As the result of a referendum held in July 1948, Newfoundlanders chose (by a rather narrow margin) to

[126]M. R. Stewart to the author, Nov. 17, 1943.

[127]When Newfoundland became the tenth province of the dominion in the spring of 1949, it seemed advisable to include in this history a few salient facts about woman suffrage in the newest member of the Canadian family. The manu-script had been completed many months before and the author had no access to the types of source materials upon which the major part of the work is based. She is deeply indebted to Mr. R. A. MacKay, Department of External Affairs, Ottawa, to Mr. R. B. Herder, St. John's, and to Major R. H. Tait, Canadian Information Service, New York, for their generous cooperation in preparing this section.

[128]R. H. Tait, *Newfoundland: A Summary of the History and Development of Britain's Oldest Colony* (Harrington Press, U.S.A., 1939), pp. 59, 62-71.

confederate with Canada. Terms of union were worked out between the island colony and the dominion, the British parliament passed the requisite act of sanction, and on March 31, 1949 Newfoundland embarked upon the most recent phase of its political evolution.[129]

Although universal manhood suffrage prevailed in Newfoundland after 1889, there would appear to have been very little active interest in woman suffrage until after the first world war. Interest of a somewhat academic nature is discernible early in the twentieth century in the founding of a Ladies Reading Room and Current Events Club in St. John's, the capital city. (The name and activities of this pioneer group in Newfoundland bear an interesting resemblance to the precursor of all Canadian woman suffrage groups, Dr. Emily Stowe's Toronto Women's Literary Club of 1876.) Payment of one membership fee entitled all the women members of a household to use the clubrooms, read the magazines, and attend the lectures. Though not exerting a monopoly over the members' interests, the question of political equality was frequently their subject for discussions and debates. For many years Mrs. A. G. Gosling was president of the small circle, which later changed its name to the Old Colony Club.[130]

Not long after the end of the first world war, some of the bolder spirits of the Old Colony Club including Mrs. Gosling, Mrs. Hector McNeil, Mrs. T. B. Goodridge, and Mrs. Charles Hutton met at the home of Mrs. J. B. Mitchell to discuss the problem of securing the municipal vote for women. Out of this preliminary rose the determination to form a woman suffrage club dedicated to the attainment of full political equality, rather than just the municipal franchise. Island women were doubtless strengthened in their resolution by the recent victories of suffrage forces in neighbouring Nova Scotia and New Brunswick, as well as by the more spectacular

[129]Canada, Department of External Affairs, Information Division, *Fact Sheets*, No. 17, "Canada: The Province of Newfoundland" (Ottawa, April 1949).

[130]Anon., "Current Events Club—Woman Suffrage—Newfoundland Society of Art," in J. R. Smallwood, ed., *The Book of Newfoundland* (2 vols., St. John's, 1937), I, 199-201. Hereafter cited as Anon., "Woman Suffrage."

national triumphs in Great Britain, Canada, and the United States. Indeed, the anonymous suffragist who wrote the article on woman suffrage in *The Book of Newfoundland* acknowledges that Mrs. Carrie Chapman Catt sent them encouragement and "quantities of suffrage literature."[131]

The new group, again under the presidency of Mrs. Gosling, was not long in winning the municipal franchise for women (1921), and since it was based upon ownership of property, "Every woman who could, tried to own a garage or shed."[132] The exercise of the municipal franchise is not actually very widespread among women in Newfoundland for the husband is usually listed as the owner or tenant of the property.[133]

When it came to the question of the wider franchise, however, island suffragists encountered heavier seas. Their campaign started on May 20, 1920 with the introduction into the legislature of a petition requesting the general franchise for women. Sponsored by a war veteran, F. W. Legrow, the petition contained the signatures of 1,700 women of St. John's and encountered no visible opposition. In the same year, C. J. Fox introduced a bill to give substance to the petition's request, but the bill was turned down on second reading by a straight party vote of 13 to 9. It was the Liberal party under the leadership of Sir Richard Squires which dealt this rebuff to the women's initial legislative venture.[134]

In 1921 suffrage forces returned to the assault, this time equipped with a petition bearing signatures of 7,485 women[135]

---

[131]*Ibid.* It is the author's guess that the anonymous writer was Mrs. Charles Hutton, one of the most active members of the St. John's suffrage club.

[132]*Ibid.* *Acts of the General Assembly of Newfoundland, 1921,* ch. 13. Attempts by Mrs. Hector McNeil and two other women to win seats in the St. John's municipal council were unsuccessful.

[133]Letter to the author from R. B. Herder, president of the *Evening Telegram* (St. John's), July 13, 1949.

[134]Letters from R. B. Herder, July 13 and 23, 1949. In the latter, Mr. Herder quotes extensively from the Newfoundland Hansard of 1925, on the occasion of Premier W. S. Monroe's speech supporting second reading of his own woman suffrage measure. Monroe took this opportunity to review previous efforts to get such a bill passed and also to berate his predecessor (Squires) for blocking its enactment. Sir Richard Squires (Liberal) was premier from 1919-1923; W. S. Monroe (Conservative) from 1924-1928.

[135]This figure is Hansard's. Anon., "Woman Suffrage," claims 20,000 signatures.

from all parts of the island. What this petition meant in terms of patient industry can only be fully appreciated when one reflects that even now Newfoundland has but four communities with a population of over 5,000—most of the 1,300 settlements having fewer than 200 inhabitants—and that the sea is still the principal means of communication between towns. Impelled, perhaps, by this evidence of fairly widespread popular support, Premier Squires introduced a bill for women's enfranchisement, only to refer it to a select committee where it died of neglect. "There ended the second lesson."[136]

Twice repelled by a Liberal administration, the movement's nucleus at St. John's appears to have decided upon building a more solid foundation of public support before embarking upon any further encounters with the lawmakers. The women turned their efforts to the unceasing drudgery of interviewing prominent people, writing to all parts of the island, holding public meetings, and engaging in debates. "For years we agitated gently," but it was "surprising to find otherwise delightful people fly into terrific rages and order us out of their offices, when they learnt what our mission was."[137]

Wholehearted support from the island's two daily newspapers helped immeasurably to counterbalance such vehement opposition. "Hon. John Alexander Robinson, M.B.E., owner of the *Daily News*, was our greatest friend and adviser. He published all we sent in and gave us many editorials as well. W. J. Herder . . . threw open the columns of his paper, the *Evening Telegram*, and did all in his power to help our cause."

The next general election turned the Squires administration out of office and brought into power a Conservative government under Hon. Walter S. Monroe (1924). Although labelling it a non-party measure, the new premier took personal charge of piloting a woman suffrage bill through the House of Assembly. The Monroe bill, which became law on April 13, 1925, also conferred upon women the right to be

[136]Monroe's summary in Hansard.
[137]Anon., "Woman Suffrage." The quotation in the next paragraph is from the same source.

elected.[138] Strangely enough, but probably reflecting the situation then prevailing in England, women were required to be 25 years of age or over to vote, men only 21 years.[139]

That this remnant of inequality did not offend Newfoundland women too seriously is apparent from the fact that the suffrage club disbanded in 1925. A combined victory celebration and farewell meeting was held in the Casino, at which Mrs. Gosling was specially honoured for her successful leadership. Unlike so many other suffrage groups which were constantly harassed by financial difficulties, the suffragists at St. John's wound up their affairs with all expenses paid and several hundred dollars in the bank.[140]

In the nine-year period between the women's victory and the renunciation of self-government by Newfoundland, Lady Squires, a Liberal, was the only woman elected to the House of Assembly.[141] After 1934, of course, the problem of being elected ceased to trouble both men and women.

The age requirement for women was reduced to 21 years on the first occasion when Newfoundlanders went to the polls again. This was to select the national convention in 1946.[142] By the *Terms of Union of Newfoundland with Canada, 1948* (Term 15), the age of 21 years was confirmed for women voters in connection with the election of the provincial legislature. The federal franchise in the new province is, of course, governed by the general dominion elections law which permits women to vote at the age of twenty-one. Thus, legally, the women of Britain's oldest colony have at last achieved complete political equality.

Shortly after Newfoundland's entrance into confederation

---

[138]*Acts of the General Assembly of Newfoundland, 1925*, ch. 7.

[139]The Representation of the People Act, 1918, gave the vote in the United Kingdom to those women who were 30 years of age and over. The right was extended to women of 21 years by an act of 1928.

[140]Anon., "Woman Suffrage."

[141]*Ibid.* R. H. Tait, *op. cit.*, p. 61. Lady Squires served from 1928-1932 and was not re-elected. It is interesting, as well as slightly ironic, to note that Lady Squires was the wife of Sir Richard Squires, who returned to the premiership in 1928.

[142]*Acts of the Honourable Commission of Government of Newfoundland, 1946*, no. 16.

on March 31, 1949, she was plunged into the excitement of two elections: provincial on May 27 and federal on June 27. The resultant provincial legislature is all male.  Mrs. Grace Sparks (Progressive Conservative), running in the newly created federal riding of Burin-Burgeo, suffered the fate which engulfed all fifteen women candidates in the 1949 dominion election.

# 7

# QUEBEC

## *The First Shall Be Last*

BY AN ODD turn of fate French Canada, where the campaign to win political rights for women was longest in yielding results and came nearest to being a real struggle, appears to have been the first part of the British empire in which women made practical use of the right to cast a ballot.[1] Abundant evidence exists that in certain parts of French Canada women occasionally voted during the early years of the nineteenth century.

The Constitutional Act of 1791, which established a representative assembly in Great Britain's recently acquired French-speaking colony, defined voters only as "persons" fulfilling certain property qualifications. Unlike Nova Scotia and New Brunswick where women may have had the right to vote at this same period but did not use it, the women of Quebec had broader notions of the ground covered by the word "persons" and put their convictions into practice by voting on numerous occasions, at least between the years 1809 and 1834.

The earliest example on record was the occasion described by Senator L. O. David in his volume, *Les Deux Papineau*. In the bitterly contested election of 1809 several women of Montreal voted for Joseph Papineau, the candidate favoured by the French Canadians—among them his widowed mother.

[1]William Renwick Riddell, "Woman Franchise in Quebec a Century Ago," *Transactions of the Royal Society of Canada*, 3rd series, XXII (Ottawa, 1928), section II, pp. 85-99, *passim*. Hereafter cited as W. R. Riddell, "Woman Franchise."

As oral voting was the practice in those days, the elderly woman announced her choice for all to hear: "For my son, M. Joseph Papineau, for I believe that he is a good and faithful subject."[2]

Evidence appears that voting by women in Three Rivers was quite commonplace in 1820. From a letter of Judge P. Bedard to J. Neilson, Esq., dated July 1 of that year, we learn that women property owners voted and that in the case of a married woman, if the property was hers she did the voting, not her husband. The judge humorously described the misfortune which had befallen one of his own servants who had been so indiscreet as to place his property in his wife's name. On election day the unhappy man appeared at the polling place, only to find himself doubly humiliated by being refused the franchise and then sent to get his wife to the polls because she was the qualified voter in that family.[3]

Until 1827 the assertion of political rights by women aroused no public controversy, but following the elections of that year the House of Assembly of Lower Canada received two petitions on December 4, 1828 with regard to the strange custom being practised in that part of His Majesty's domains. That the inhabitants of the province were not of one mind on the question is evident since the petition from Quebec City berated a returning officer for refusal to accept the vote of a widow, while that from the Borough of William Henry claimed the returns from their district invalid because women's votes had been included. After considerable legislative bickering, the petitions were eventually laid aside without any decision having been reached one way or the other.[4]

The derisive and humiliating treatment frequently accorded women by Quebec lawmakers in the twentieth century

[2]The quotation is W. R. Riddell's translation of Senator David's work. L. O. David, *Les Deux Papineau* (Montreal, 1896), pp. 27-8. On these same pages Senator David wrote: "Comme la loi ne défendait pas aux femmes de voter, plusieurs en profitèrent pour aller au poll enregistrer leur vote en faveur du candidat du peuple."

[3]Letter cited in *Privy Council Proceedings*, Joint Appendix, p. 70. ". . . ici les femmes votent comme les hommes indistinctement. . . . Lorsque le mari n'a pas de bien et que la femme en a c'est la femme qui vote."

[4]*Ibid.*, pp. 71-9. W. R. Riddell, "Woman Franchise," pp. 88-93.

contrasts strangely with some of the broad liberal sentiments
expressed in that old Quebec City petition of 1828.

> . . . Petitioners have not learned that there exist any imperfections in the
> minds of women which place them lower than men in intellectual power, or
> which would make it more dangerous to entrust them with the exercise of the
> elective franchise than with the exercise of the numerous other rights which
> the law has already given them. . . . That in respect of property, taxation
> and duties to the State, the Widow, duly qualified by our Election Laws, is
> in every essential respect similarly situated with the man: her property is
> taxed alike with that of the man: she is certainly not liable to Militia duties,
> nor is the man above forty-five: she is not called to serve on a jury, nor is a
> physician: she cannot be elected to the Assembly, nor can a Judge or Minister
> of the Gospel. It may be alleged that nature has only fitted her for domestic
> life, yet the English Constitution allows a Woman to sit on the Throne, and
> one of its brightest ornaments has been a woman. That it would be impolitic
> and tyrannical to circumscribe her efforts in society,—to say that she shall
> not have the strongest interest in the fate of her country, and the security
> of her common rights. . . .[5]

Nothing further was heard of the matter until 1834 when
the legislature passed an Elections Act which said in part:
"No female shall vote at any Election for any County, City
or Borough of this province. . . ." The act was later disallowed
on grounds that had nothing to do with woman suffrage, but
of course the disallowance carried away the crippling clause
along with the rest of the measure. Although women probably
thus continued to have the legal right to vote, there is no evidence that they ever did after 1834. Public opinion barred
them as effectively as any statute; but leaving nothing to
chance, the legislators passed an act in 1849 which disposed
of the question for many years to come.[6]

Both Professor Carrie Derick of Montreal and Judge Helen
Gregory MacGill of Vancouver, two of the country's outstanding pioneer feminists, agree that the progress made by women
in Quebec was closely associated with the improvement of
their educational opportunities. In 1875 a girls' high school

[5]Arthur G. Doughty and Norah Story, eds., *Documents Relating to the Constitutional History of Canada, 1819-1828* (Ottawa, 1935), pp. 519-23.

[6]W. R Riddell, "Woman Franchise," pp. 93-6. As previously stated in
Chapter VI, footnote 4, the activities of the Seneca Falls women's rights convention in 1848 may have reminded Quebec legislators of the propriety of such
a measure.

ELLA B. HATHEWAY                    *Climo*

CARRIE  M.  DERICK                    *Notman*

was opened in Montreal and in 1884 eight of its graduates applied for admission to McGill, two of them (Grace Octavia Ritchie and Rosalie McLea) having passed the matriculation examinations ahead of all the young gentlemen seeking admission that year. The principal of the University, Sir William Dawson, was not enthusiastic over such an innovation, but a generous gift of Sir Donald Smith made possible the opening of classes to women. Although almost to the end of their course in 1888 the young women were not sure they would be permitted to receive degrees, they won that struggle too. On the day of graduation, their slim young valedictorian, Grace Ritchie, arose before an impressive audience to deliver her valedictory remarks. Only three days before, a plea for the admission of women to McGill's medical school had been censored out of her speech by Sir William, but the young woman, who was to become the province's first woman doctor and one of its staunchest feminists, took a deep breath and then spoke the carefully deleted passage. Sir William's reaction was not recorded for posterity, but the governor-general, Lord Lansdowne, a few minutes later commented favourably upon the valedictorian's remarks in his commencement address. Judge MacGill points out that the eight young women of that first graduation class all became unwavering advocates of women's rights, thereby proving the wisdom of the nineteenth-century English wit who warned his contemporaries "that if females were educated they would want things."[7]

Women did start "wanting things," even before the eight graduates were fairly launched upon their careers. The first organization to demand woman suffrage in Quebec, as almost everywhere else in the dominion, was the W.C.T.U., of which a branch was organized in Montreal during the winter of 1883-84. Of course the suffrage plank in the W.C.T.U. plat-

[7]Helen Gregory MacGill, "Place Aux Dames," *Canadian Magazine*, April 1933, p. 6. An address by Professor Carrie Derick delivered to the League for Women's Rights in Montreal on Nov. 28, 1933, summarized in the *Daily Star* (Montreal), Nov. 29, 1933. Interview with Dr. Grace Ritchie-England on July 5, 1943.

form was, as always, only an auxiliary to their main purpose, but temperance forces in Quebec were ever a loyal ally to the more strictly feminist organizations which came later.[8]

The nation-wide impetus which Lady Aberdeen gave to the women's movement during her husband's term as governor-general bore fruit in the founding of the Montreal Local Council of Women in 1893. Under the presidencies of such resolute feminists as Lady Drummond, Dr. Ritchie-England, and Professor Derick, the efforts of this lively new organization were channelled into active work for the securing of laws which would improve the status of women, politically and otherwise. Thus, twenty years before there was any outright suffrage association in Canada's metropolis, there was an influential group of women laying the necessary groundwork of education and agitation.

An unexpected result followed the efforts of the Local Council to have a woman appointed to the Protestant Board of School Commissioners in 1899. As the law then stood, any voter might hold this office, and since the municipal franchise had been extended to unmarried women ratepayers in 1892, that class of women appeared eligible. The surprising answer of the Quebec Legislature was to pass an amendment to the Schools Act completely debarring women from the position— a disqualification not finally removed until almost half a century later (1942). Better fortune attended their attempt to block a reactionary proposal of the Montreal City Council in 1903. Joined by the W.C.T.U., the Local Council protested so vigorously the projected attempt by the city fathers to deprive women of the school and muncipal franchises which they had won in 1892 that City Hall rapidly gave up its retrograde idea.[9]

[8]H. G. MacGill, "Place Aux Dames," p. 6. Professor Derick's address of Nov. 28, 1933. An article by Mrs. John Scott in the *Gazette* (Montreal), Mar. 28, 1940. Mme Pierre Casgrain has also acknowledged the unobtrusive but steady support of the temperance forces.

[9]H. M. Edwards, *Women of Canada*. The Local Council of Women of Montreal, *Fortieth Anniversary Issue and Annual Report, 1933-34* (Montreal, 1934), p. 27. Hereafter cited as L.C.W. Montreal, *Fortieth Anniversary Report*. L. C. W. Montreal, *Sixth Annual Report* (Montreal, 1900), p. 13. I. Harper *et al.*, *Woman Suffrage*, VI, 765.

The legislature at Quebec was untroubled by bills and petitions relating to women's political rights until after the first world war. Indeed, no bill proposing to bestow the provincial franchise upon women was introduced into the legislature until 1927. As in other provinces, however, a few small gains in the local sphere were made in the later years of the nineteenth century.[10] A very thin opening wedge appeared in 1888, when widows and spinsters possessing property were granted the right to vote on municipal by-laws creating debt. Full municipal and school voting privileges were extended to this same class of women by a general act of 1892, although the measure was careful not to tread upon the sensibilities of any town or city opposed to such an innovation by providing that a municipality could, in its own particular charter, cling to an exclusively male electorate if it chose to do so.[11]

The 1892 bill provoked the first general discussion on women's rights in almost half a century. While the bill lay in committee of the whole on June 2 several members spoke, not only upon the municipal phase but also upon the entire question of female franchise. A Conservative member, Louis E. Panneton, objected to the contents of the bill on the ground that any political concession to women would lead them to demand full voting privileges. Many other speakers said that while they were not prepared to see women in politics, it was only just that unmarried women taxpayers should have a

---

[10]Quebec City appears to have far antedated her sister municipalities in permitting women to vote. Mrs. John Scott, in an article appearing in the 1940-41 issue of *Women' Sphere* (p. 53), claims that unmarried women voted after 1854. In a radio broadcast in 1939, Mlle Idola Saint Jean stated that all women owners have voted there for more than 60 years. E. Luke, "Woman Suffrage," p. 335, also says that women in Quebec exercised the municipal vote for years, with a notary often calling at their homes to take their votes, because in olden times many considered it improper for women to go to polling places. The Town Corporations' General Clauses Act of 1876 (*Statutes of Quebec, 1876,* ch. XXIX) in section 50 no longer uses the word *male* among the qualifications for electors as in previous acts, and in section 34 distinctly employs the word *male* in enumerating qualifications for municipal office-holding. This fact would tend to support Mlle Saint Jean's contention that women property owners in the capital city were granted the municipal franchise around 1876.

[11]*Statutes of Quebec, 1888,* ch. 30; *1892,* ch. 35. In Montreal the right to vote in municipal elections was further extended to wives "separated as to bed and board" by an act of 1903. *Ibid., 1903,* ch. 62. L.C.W. Montreal, *Ninth Annual Report* (Montreal, 1903), pp. 7, 9.

voice in municipal and school affairs. The whole tone of the debate, which, according to the *Gazette*, produced "gallantry on both sides," was in marked contrast to the legislature's hostile attitude toward women forty years later. The W.C.T.U. petition to the legislature on this occasion was the first notice served upon Quebec legislators that the women's rights question was astir in French-speaking Canada.[12]

Although there is evidence of the existence of a short-lived and ineffectual suffrage group under the leadership of Mrs. Bullock of Montreal from 1909 to 1911,[13] the principal agitator in the feminist field down to 1913 continued to be the Montreal Local Council of Women. In 1909, after submitting the question of women's enfranchisement to its affiliated societies, a majority of whom replied favourably, the Council put its official endorsement upon the principle of full political rights for women, thereby becoming one of the first Local Councils in Canada to do so. Complementing this action, the Montreal Council threw the weight of its influence behind the Toronto delegation at Halifax in 1910 in their successful effort to secure the National Council's approval of woman suffrage.[14]

Turning from the national to the local stage, the Montreal Council showed its zeal for political reform by co-operating wholeheartedly with the Citizens' Association, the W.C.T.U., and the Fédération Nationale Saint Jean Baptiste,[15] in their efforts to get out the women voters to support reform candidates in the municipal elections of 1910 and 1912. Their efforts had marked success, and not only gave organized women a valuable lesson in practical politics, but also made men conscious of what women were capable of doing in a political

[12]*Gazette*, June 3, 7, 1892. *Quebec: Journals, 1892*, pp. 147, 203, 220, 393 (for the bill); 128 (for the petition).
[13]*Canadian Annual Review* (1909), p. 246. N. C. W., *Year Book* (1910), p. XXVII; (1911), p. XXVII.
[14]L.C.W. Montreal, *Fortieth Anniversary Report*, p. 34. L.C.W. Montreal, *Twenty-first Anniversary, 1893-1915* (Montreal, 1915), p. 21.
[15]The Fédération is an organization of French Catholic women similar to the Local Council of Women in its purposes and activities. One of its founders and its guiding spirit for many years was Mme Henri Gérin-Lajoie, an author and lecturer at the University of Montreal. Mme Gérin-Lajoie was one of the very few French-speaking women identified with the early phase of the suffrage movement in Quebec.

campaign. After this, it must have been somewhat disquieting for the feminist forces to read the results of a poll on woman suffrage announced by the Montreal *Daily Star* on October 12, 1912. Claiming that it had canvassed representative parts of the city, the *Star* said it had found 88.2 per cent of the population opposed and only 11.8 per cent in favour of giving votes to women.[16]

Late in 1909 the Montreal Local Council embarked upon another significant and fruitful phase of its activities. Through the efforts of Professor Derick and Dr. Ritchie-England some of the most important English suffragists, from both the moderate and militant wings of the movement, were brought to Montreal and lectured before large audiences under Council auspices. This was the period when the militant movement was at its height in England and though Canadians as a whole heartily disapproved of its violent tactics, these Englishwomen were invariably received with enthusiasm by their Montreal audiences.

The first speaker in the series, on December 4, 1909, was Mrs. Philip Snowden of the non-militant wing. A large crowd at Stanley Hall heard her give a stirring account of the movement in Great Britain and urge Canadian women not to lag behind. Although the *Gazette* was inclined to be unfriendly to suffrage ideas at this time, it succumbed to the charm and eloquence of the English lecturer.

No abler or more alluring missionary of the suffrage movement could be found than Mrs. Snowden, whose eloquence would be hard to match in any parliament, while in point of humour, originality and magnetic qualities she is head and shoulders above previous visitors to these shores. From the first few sentences she uttered, the male part of the audience, if faces are a criterion, were at her feet. Her personality was irresistible.[17]

In December 1911, Mrs. Emmeline Pankhurst, renowned leader of the militants, spoke on "The Englishwoman's Fight

[16]H. G. MacGill, "Place Aux Dames," p. 6. N.C.W., *Year Book* (1910), pp. 95-6. L.C.W. Montreal, *Fortieth Anniversary Report*, pp. 33-4, 42. L.C.W. Montreal, *Twenty-first Anniversary, 1893-1915*, pp. 20-1. *Canadian Annual Review* (1912), p. 309.
[17]*Gazette*, Dec. 6, 1909. The *Daily Star* for the same date confirms the report of the overwhelming success scored by Mrs. Snowden.

for the Vote." She was followed in November and December of 1912 by Miss Barbara Wylie and Mrs. Forbes-Robertson Hale. This powerful stimulation from abroad determined the Local Council to form a thorough-going suffrage organization at the earliest possible moment. On the same evening that Mrs. Hale spoke in Windsor Hall a committee was appointed to draw up a constitution and nominate officers for a suffrage association to include both men and women.[18]

Preparatory to the official launching of the new society, the Local Council secured some effective publicity in February 1913. The Montreal Suffrage Exhibition, under the chairmanship of Mrs. Douglas McIntosh, lasted for two full weeks. Addresses by prominent speakers were featured; and cartoons, literature, souvenirs, and badges were displayed and sold. Apart from the propaganda value, concrete success showed in the eleven hundred signatures appended to a suffrage petition and a cash balance of $276, of which $150 was devoted to the establishment of a Suffrage Literature Bureau. Both these assets were turned over to the new franchise association when it was organized two months later.[19]

The Montreal Suffrage Association, which became the focal point of activities in Quebec between the years 1913 and 1919, was organized on a wave of enthusiasm at a meeting led by Dr. Ritchie-England in Stevenson Hall on April 24, 1913. Lady Drummond presented a distinguished slate of officers to the gathering, which included both men and women. Professor Carrie M. Derick became president, a position she continued to hold until the organization's demise six years later. Vice-presidential posts went to two prominent Montreal men who gave the women their capable support throughout those early years: Dean F. P. Walton of the McGill Law School, and Rev. Dr. H. Symonds, dean of Christ Church

---

[18]L.C.W. Montreal, *Fortieth Anniversary Report*, pp. 42-3.  H. G. MacGill, "Place Aux Dames," p. 6.

[19]*Ibid.*, p. 6.  L.C.W. Montreal, *Fortieth Anniversary Report*, p. 43.  Mrs. John Scott, "A Story of the Fight for Woman Suffrage," *Women's Sphere:* official organ of the Canadian Alliance for Women's Vote in Quebec (Montreal, 1940-41), pp. 49-51.  H. Ridley, *Woman Suffrage*, p. 18.

Cathedral. Mrs. John Scott, long active in the W.C.T.U. and the Local Council, became secretary.[20]

The organization's first year was its most active, inasmuch as war activities later tended to overshadow suffrage work. Sometimes it was found possible to make a successful combination of the two, as on the occasions when the popular suffrage play, "How the Vote Was Won," or Dr. Anna Howard Shaw's film, "Your Girl and Mine," were presented. The Suffrage Association reaped the benefit of publicity, while the financial rewards were turned over to such patriotic organizations as the Red Cross, the Khaki League, and the I.O.D.E.[21] Even during the war years, however, the volume and range of the association's activities were amazing.

Petitions, resolutions, and interviews with leaders of both the federal and provincial governments were fairly frequent and left no doubt in official minds where the organization stood on many important issues. Pleas for full provincial and federal suffrage were naturally forthcoming, but this was only one phase of the Association's interests. It gave full support to Sir Robert Borden's conscription policy, but with equal vigour opposed his government's Wartime Elections Act.[22] Prohibition appeared to it essential as a war measure and, in co-operation with the Local Council, it dispatched a delegation to Ottawa to tell Sir Robert so.[23] Even Rt. Hon. H. H. Asquith, prime minister of Great Britain, became the object of critical attention: a strongly worded motion was forwarded to him condemning forcible feeding of suffragettes in English prisons "as a revival of medieval torture and a contravention of the traditional principles of British justice."[24]

On its own home ground the Association continued the earlier policy of the Local Council by participating actively

[20]L.C.W. Montreal, *Fortieth Anniversary Report*, p. 43. *Daily Star*, April 25, 1913.

[21]H. G. MacGill, "Place Aux Dames," p. 37. L.W.R. Minute Books, entries for Aug. 19, 1914; May 1915.

[22]*Ibid.*, entries for Aug. 16, Sept. 4, 14, 1917. N.C.W., *Year Book* (1917), p. 83.

[23]L.W.R. Minute Books, entry for Jan. 9, 1917.

[24]*Ibid.*, entry for Feb. 2, 1914.

in civic elections and endeavouring to have the municipal franchise extended to married women.[25] Efforts were also made to have women become eligible to serve as school trustees, by approaching the Protestant School Board to enlist its support before the legislature.[26] When in 1914 a decision by Mr. Justice St. Pierre supported the Bar Association of Quebec in refusing Mrs. Annie Langstaff (B.C.L. from McGill) permission to practise law in the province, both the Local Council and the Suffrage Association were prompt to take up the cudgels on her behalf. Under their joint auspices on February 26, a large indignation meeting filled the Y.M.C.A. Hall and overflowed into the corridors to hear more than a dozen prominent men and women protest the narrow-minded action. At the meeting's conclusion a motion by Rev. Dr. Symonds that the provincial legislature be requested to enact laws permitting women to enter the learned professions on the same terms as men was carried overwhelmingly.[27] Bills to enable women to practise law were in fact introduced at the 1915 and 1916 sessions by Lucien Cannon, but met with the fate which might have been expected.[28]

The amount of educational and publicity work accomplished by the organization was prodigious, especially during the first two years of its existence. Under the chairmanship of Mrs. John Scott, booths and displays were set up at the fall fairs in various towns of the province and also at such national and provincial exhibits as the Autumn Exhibition in Ottawa, the W.C.T.U. Exhibit and Sale in Montreal, and the Made in Canada Exhibition. By mid-summer of 1915, however, the war had brought this popular phase of suffrage education to an untimely end.[29]

Care was taken to see that the Association's activities re-

---

[25]*Ibid.*, entries for Dec. 30, 1913; Jan. 26 and Apr. 17, 1914; April 4, 1916.
[26]*Herald and Daily Telegraph* (Montreal), Nov. 25, 26, 1915.
[27]L.C.W. Montreal, *Fortieth Anniversary Report*, pp. 44-5. L.C.W. Montreal, *Twenty-first Anniversary, 1893-1915*, pp. 69-70.
[28]*Herald and Daily Telegraph*, Feb. 10, 24, 1916. L.C.W. Montreal, *Annual Report 1915-1916*, p. 29; *Annual Report 1916-1917*, p. 16.
[29]L.W.R. Minute Books, entries for Sept. 26, Nov. 26, 1913; June 4, 1914; June 1, 1915.

ceived as much attention as possible in the press. It found the *Herald and Daily Telegraph* particularly co-operative, not only in its press notices but also in offering to turn over one entire edition of the paper to the women. Under the editorship of Mrs. Minden Colé a woman's edition did actually appear on November 26, 1913. On that day astonished Montrealers found their papers sold to them not only by the regular vendors, but also by some of the city's most distinguished women in the unaccustomed guise of newshawkers.[30] Suffrage articles prepared by the Association appeared quite regularly in the *Herald* in late 1915 and early 1916, while at the same time another paper's distinctly unfriendly tone was not allowed to pass unnoticed. A brief Minute Book entry of November 23, 1915 states that Miss Derick was appointed to interview Smeaton White about the antagonistic attitude of the *Gazette*, but fails to shed any light on the outcome.

From the very outset, the Association became a medium for the distribution and sale of suffrage literature. Before the organization was a month old it had circulated a considerable quantity of material at the annual convention of the National Council of Women held that year in Montreal, and as a direct result, requests poured in from every province of the dominion for additional supplies. Under the chairmanship of Mrs. Catherine Weller, a regular Literature Bureau was established with headquarters at the Edinburgh Café. (The Minutes for January 26, 1914 note that there was an especially heavy demand for Mrs. Pankhurst's book, *The Great Scourge*.) Members were on duty daily from three to six "to sell literature, give advice and explanations, and in every way possible further the interests of the Association."[31]

One of the publications of which the Bureau sold more than two thousand copies was a pamphlet on laws relating to women, compiled and edited by Dean Walton of McGill.

[30]*Ibid.*, entries for April 29, Sept. 26, Oct. 2 and 13, 1913. Anon., "Suffrage Féminin dans la Province de Québec" (Montreal, n.d.), no pagination. This is a typewritten paper on file in the office of the League for Women's Rights, Montreal. *Women's Sphere* (1937-38), p. 51.

[31]L.W.R. Minute Books, entries for April 29, May 20, Sept. 26, Oct. 13, 1913; Jan. 26, Feb. 2, 1914.

Dissemination of the facts about women's disabilities under the archaic legal system of Quebec not only provided a solid groundwork on which suffrage groups might base their campaigns in the years ahead, but also undoubtedly helped to bring about the passage of a minimum wage act for women in 1919.[32]

Occasional public meetings with excellent speakers opened up another avenue of education. Three prominent Montreal lawyers—C. M. Holt, K.C., Maxwell Goldstein, K.C., and W. D. Lighthall, K.C.—took part on October 13, 1913 in a discussion of the legal status of women, leading to the general conclusion that the position of women in Quebec was intolerable. Senator Helen R. Robinson of Colorado spoke the following January on "Where Women Legislate," showing that many beneficial laws had been passed since women had been enfranchised in her state. Undoubtedly the most popular speaker of all, however, was Mrs. Nellie McClung who captivated her audience on October 25, 1915 with her gift for seasoning important though sometimes dry facts with a generous sprinkling of wit.[33]

Much more nationally minded than suffrage groups in either the Prairie or the Maritime Provinces, the Montreal Association affiliated with the Canadian Suffrage Association in 1913 and with its rival, the National Equal Franchise Union, in 1914. By sending delegates to both, Montreal feminists could avoid the pitfalls of factionalism and at the same time keep themselves conversant with suffrage activities in all parts of the country.

After the passage of the federal woman's franchise act in 1918, the conviction grew rapidly in the minds of Professor Derick and other leading members of the Association that in a province, seven eighths of whose population was French, the provincial franchise could be obtained only through effective

[32]*Ibid.*, April 29, Sept. 26, Oct. 2, 1913. *Statutes of Quebec, 1919*, ch. 11. The act created a commission of three to examine industrial conditions for women and to have the power to set minimum wages for them. The act also magnanimously provided that "one of such members may be a woman"—section 2.

[33]L.W.R. Minute Books, entries for Oct. 13, 1913; Jan. 5, 1914. *Herald and Daily Telegraph*, Oct. 26, 1915.

*Garcia Studio*

IDOLA  SAINT JÉAN

*La Rose*

THÉRÈSE CASGRAIN

co-operation between French- and English-speaking groups. Since the Montreal Suffrage Association was almost exclusively an English-speaking organization, its day of usefulness appeared to be over. With characteristic forthrightness, the Association voted unanimously to disband at its annual meeting on May 22, 1919. In her presidential farewell, Professor Derick expressed the hope that the day of closer teamwork between the two language groups would not be very far distant.[34]

Between 1919 and 1922 the city had no full-fledged suffrage organization, though during this period (and for many years after) the Franchise Committee of the Montreal Women's Club, of which Mrs. John Scott was chairman, kept the issue alive. The Committee not only continued the agitation for extension of provincial, municipal, and school privileges to women, but also helped launch a campaign in 1921 to have Judge Emily Murphy made a senator.[35]

Two matters of interest to women came before the 1920 session of the legislature. A bill sponsored by Henry Miles to permit women to practise law met defeat on February 13 by a two to one vote (38 to 19). The principal speaker in opposition was Amédée Monet who expressed the fear that such a concession might eventually lead to women's receiving the vote, becoming eligible for office, and other dreadful possibilities. Among the nineteen supporters, however, were five cabinet ministers, including the Liberal premier, Sir Lomer Gouin. (Sir Lomer had always been courteous and sympathetic towards Montreal Suffrage Association delegations, though he steadfastly refused to advance the desired suffrage bill.)[36]

On the same day Joseph Ashby moved, seconded by Aurèle Leclerc: "That in the opinion of this House the time has

[34]L.W.R. Minute Books, entries for April 17, May 22, 1919.
[35]Mrs. John Scott, "A Story of the Fight for Woman Suffrage," *Women's Sphere* (1940-41), p. 55. *Gazette*, Mar. 28, 1940.
[36]*Ibid.*, Feb. 14, 1920. *Canadian Annual Review* (1920), p. 644. *Quebec: Journals, 1920*, pp. 91, 100, 124, 140, 171, 201, 225. Anon., "Suffrage Féminin dans la Province de Québec." Dr. Ritchie-England told the author that Gouin's civility was in sharp contrast with Premier Louis Taschereau's "sneering" attitude toward women's delegations.

arrived for considering the advisability of giving women the right to vote." The mover explained that he was not intending to introduce such legislation at present, but simply wanted to know what members thought of the idea. Although the motion passed, the manner of its passage was somewhat unsatisfactory. According to the *Gazette's* legislative reporter: "There was some confusion at the close of the speech, and there was doubt as to whether the motion had carried or not, but the Prime Minister remarked 'carried on division,' and that ended the matter, so there is no more light on the opinions of members than before."[37]

Late in 1921 a group of women, both French and English, met under the leadership of Mme Henri Gérin-Lajoie, president of La Fédération Nationale Saint Jean Baptiste, to consider plans for such a joint organization as Professor Derick had envisaged in 1919. This preliminary meeting bore fruit in the formation of the Provincial Franchise Committee on January 16, 1922. Approximately thirty-five people of both language groups were present, including many well-known supporters of the cause such as Professor Derick, Dr. Ritchie-England, Mrs. John Scott, and Mrs. Walter Lyman. One of the prime movers in the infant organization, however, was a newcomer: Mlle Idola Saint Jean, a language professor at McGill.

It was decided that the new organization should be set up under dual leadership. Mme Gérin-Lajoie became head of the French section, and Mrs. Walter Lyman head of the English group. It was determined that the Committee should be non-political and should concentrate on an educational campaign to persuade the public and the legislature that women did not desire the vote in order to change their sphere of action in life, but rather "to raise and ameliorate social life."[38]

At their first meeting the sending of a delegation to Quebec

[37]*Gazette*, Feb. 14, 1920.   *Quebec: Journals, 1920*, p. 227.
[38]L.W.R. Minute Books, entries for Jan. 16, 19, 1922.   *Gazette*, Mar. 28, 1940. Anon., *Brief History of the League for Women's Rights* (Montreal, 1941), p. 3. This is a pamphlet published under League auspices after their victory in 1940. Hereafter cited as *Brief History of L.W.R.*

was discussed, with one member asserting (over-optimistically as it turned out) that Henry Miles had informed her that the new Liberal premier, Hon. Louis A. Taschereau, was favourably disposed towards women suffrage and would welcome such a delegation. Plans were carefully laid and the co-operation of both the Local Council and the Franchise Committee of the Montreal Women's Club secured.

On February 9, 1922 a delegation of approximately four hundred Montreal women was introduced to Premier Taschereau by Henry Miles. Among the speakers were Mme Gérin-Lajoie, Professor Derick, Dr. Ritchie-England, Lady Drummond, Mlle Saint Jean, and Mme Pierre Casgrain. The latter had come to public attention in the federal elections of 1921 when she conducted a highly successful campaign for her husband, who was prevented by illness from waging his own political battle. Her ability as a public speaker led to an invitation from the Committee to accompany the delegation to Quebec.

Premier Taschereau listened attentively to what the women had to say, but at the conclusion of their addresses quickly removed their misconception of his attitude toward woman suffrage. With disconcerting frankness he declared that though women might some day get the vote, it would never be from him; and in that determination he remained steadfast so long as he held power (until 1936).[39] The delegation returned to Montreal, sadly disillusioned. But Quebec lawmakers were to learn that the women of their province were not easily discouraged. This was only the first of many delegations, sometimes several in a year, which continued to put their claims before unyielding governments until success came almost a generation later.

At the behest of various feminist groups, Henry Miles attempted in 1922 to make a plea for woman suffrage in the legislature, with the idea of introducing a bill later, should the

[39] *Ibid.* L.W.R. Minute Books, entries for Jan. 16, 19, 1922. H. G. MacGill, "Place Aux Dames," pp. 37, 41. *New World* (Toronto), June 1940, p. 10. *Le Devoir* (Montreal), Mar. 4, 1940. L.C.W. Montreal, *Annual Report 1921-1922*, p. 18.

reaction to his proposal appear to warrant it. While he spoke, the heckling was terrific. One of his tormentors, with an especially distorted sense of humour, removed his chair. As Mr. Miles sat down he fell, amid howls of laughter. The laughter quickly subsided when it was discovered that he was seriously injured.[40]

After 1922, the Provincial Franchise Committee went under a complete eclipse until 1926. Although the Minute Books of the organization give no explanation, it is possible to trace the break in activities to the trials of the society in that first year. Discouragement over the rebuff from the premier was deepened in November 1922 when Mme Gérin-Lajoie, under pressure from the Church, resigned as French president.[41] With her capable hand removed from the helm, the motive power of the Committee flagged.

In February and March of 1926 J. H. Dillon attempted to have the municipal franchise extended to married women in Montreal, and the Franchise Committee showed a flicker of life. The lion's share of the agitation over this proposal was carried on, however, by the Montreal Women's Club. A delegation from this Club had appeared before the legislative committee of the city council to request their support for the concession to married women while the Montreal bill was before the legislature at Quebec. The city fathers turned down their request by a vote of 9 to 5 on February 22. Despite this vote, Mr. Dillon (a bachelor) gallantly decided to support the women by introducing an amendment to the bill the very next day. The Dillon amendment, surprisingly enough, was passed unanimously by the assembly but killed two weeks later in the upper house. Before this sad dénouement on March 17, the Montreal Women's Club had twice sent small delegations

[40]H. G. MacGill, "Place Aux Dames," p. 41. *Daily Star*, Mar. 23, 1940. According to *Le Devoir*, Apr. 26, 1940, Sir Thomas Chapais pointed out during the debate on the Godbout suffrage bill (1940) in the legislative council that at the time of the Miles' suffrage plea in 1922, a petition opposing woman suffrage was signed by 44,259 women. The author has been able to find no verification for this statement in either the House *Journals* or the contemporary press.

[41]L.W.R. Minute Books, entry for Nov. 29, 1922. *Women's Sphere* (1937-38), p. 48. Both Mme Casgrain and Mlle Saint Jean agree on the cause for Mme Gérin-Lajoie's resignation.

to the capital to plead for passage of the amendment. The treatment accorded Mrs. J. Holmes McIntyre (president of the Club), Mrs. E. T. Sampson, and Mme Gérin-Lajoie, when they attempted to state their case before the private bills committee of the legislative council, was churlish. Kept waiting from nine-thirty in the morning until almost midnight outside the locked door of the committee room, they were ultimately refused permission to speak at all. Mrs. McIntyre and Mrs. Sampson agreed that it "was the most humiliating experience of our lives."[42] Actually, however, this proved to be only a mild foretaste of what some later delegations were to be called upon to endure.

The *Gazette*, which since 1922 had changed its colours and assumed a friendly editorial policy toward feminist aspirations, was paternal in its comments on March 19. "First attempts are invariably disappointing. Man may determine his position and assert his place. Woman still has hers to seek in the matter of the franchise in the province of Quebec. It will not be surprising if the movement which was initiated before the Legislature this year is revived on a broader basis at no far distant date."

Encouraged by the possibility that the province's first woman suffrage bill might be introduced at the 1927 session, the Provincial Franchise Committee sprang back to life early that year. Unfortunately, a split in the organization developed almost immediately. On January 24 Mrs. E. T. Sampson and Mme Arthur Léger were elected presidents of the English and French sections of the Committee. Embittered over the outcome of the election,[43] Mlle Saint Jean resigned and formed a separate organization under the somewhat cumbersome name, L'Alliance Canadienne pour le Vote des Femmes du Québec. Mlle Saint Jean's own version of the split was set forth in the official organ of her association some ten years after that time.

[42]L.W.R. Minute Books, entry for Feb. 26, 1926. *Gazette*, Feb. 19, 23, 24, Mar. 4, 18, 19, 1926.
[43]This view is supported both by Mme Casgrain and Dr. Ritchie-England, but opposed by Mrs. John Scott, who joined the Saint Jean forces.

The only activity of the said Committee during five years existence consisted in a few meetings and a reception given to Lady Astor. . . . In 1927 a group of women, mostly working women, came to me in a delegation and asked me to reorganize the Provincial Committee which had been really inactive and, absolutely independent from political party, to begin a propaganda for suffrage. It was then that the Canadian Alliance for Women's Vote was founded and that it undertook a militant campaign, being always alert and active in order to obtain more liberty for women and especially to defend the freedom already won.[44]

Whatever the reasons for the division, there is no doubt that Mlle Saint Jean's organization had its roots deeper among working-class people and was more strictly a French feminist organization. During the years of protracted struggle which lay ahead, this group worked sometimes alone and sometimes in co-operation with the parent organization, contributing materially to the advancement of the women's cause. It cannot be denied, however, that by causing duplication of effort, the split was a detriment to feminist forces.

In 1928 Mme Thérèse Casgrain became sole president of the Provincial Franchise Committee which in November 1929 adopted the broader and more meaningful name, the League for Women's Rights. For fourteen years this captivating and able woman, who commanded the respect of both French- and English-speaking groups, directed the League and more than any other, became the symbol of the feminist movement in Quebec.[45] As the wife of the speaker of the federal House of Commons from 1936 to 1940, she had many important political contacts in the national capital which did the cause no harm; and as the mother of four children, she deprived anti-suffragists of one of their stock weapons of attack. "This has always been a matter of bitter chagrin to professional detractors of the suffrage movement who have unfailingly endeavoured to represent all suffragists as old harpies, invariably childless and detesting babies."[46]

While Mlle Saint Jean lacked the resilience and gracious

[44]*Women's Sphere* (1937-38), p. 48.
[45]R. A. Benoît, clerk of the legislative council at Quebec, referred to her as "the soul of the suffrage movement in our Province" in a letter to the author dated Sept. 4, 1945.
[46]*Standard* (Montreal), Mar. 23, 1940, magazine section, p. 2.

personality of Mme Casgrain, she had deep sincerity and an array of talents which enabled her also to make significant contributions to the women's cause.[47] She was a serious student and thinker, and was thoroughly conversant with every angle of the suffrage question. She wrote innumerable articles on women's status in Quebec for magazines, newspapers, and *Women's Sphere*, the official publication of her own suffrage organization.[48] She was tireless and, to outward appearances at least, utterly fearless in her work. Yet she once admitted to the author that she was ill for days before and after each ordeal of annual pilgrimage to the legislature at Quebec.

A colourful comparison of the two leaders was made in the Montreal *Standard* on March 23, 1940.

These remarkable women have long been the spearhead of woman suffrage in Quebec. They are not of a sameness. Flexible, witty, and charming to her finger-tips, Mme Casgrain has been the suffrage rapier: grim, relentless, implacable as the rock of Adamant, Miss Saint Jean has been the suffrage saber.

Early in 1927 a new phase in suffrage activities began when Victor Marchand courageously signified his willingness to sponsor the first provincial woman's franchise measure. The Marchand bill was the first of fourteen such measures considered by the Quebec assembly before the rock of legislative resistance was worn down. In spite of the unfortunate split in its ranks made by Mlle Saint Jean's resignation in January, the Provincial Franchise Committee joined with five other Montreal women's groups in sending a delegation to the legislature on February 19 in support of the bill. Pointing out that cars and radio were bringing women into public life and making them more fully aware of public issues, the delegation declared that women did want the vote, and if they had it

[47]Mlle Saint Jean died in 1945. Writing in 1938, Madeleine G. Huguenin made the flat (but debatable) assertion that if Mlle Saint Jean alone had been conducting the suffrage campaign, votes for women would have already been won. Madeleine G. Huguenin, *Portraits de Femmes* (Montreal, 1938), p. 167.
[48]Referring to a series of suffrage articles which Mlle Saint Jean wrote for the Montreal *Herald* in 1929, the *Standard* says that: "The campaign met with a phenomenal response and letters poured in." *Standard*, Mar. 23, 1940. *Women's Sphere* (1937-38), p. 51.

would use it for the promotion of social and humanitarian legislation. The impact of their arguments upon the law-makers may readily be calculated from the 51 to 13 vote by which the bill was refused second reading.[49]

William Tremblay's suffrage bill of 1928 suffered almost as heavy a defeat when the "six months' hoist" was imposed by a vote of 39 to 11.[50] Nevertheless, the women of the Franchise Committee faced Premier Taschereau later that year with other issues in which they were interested. Journeying to Quebec in October, Mme Casgrain and Mrs. Sampson pleaded for a Bar bill to enable women to practise law. Two months afterwards they cornered the premier at the Montreal City Hall and asked for certain specific changes in the civil code where women were concerned.[51]

Outside help was received for a project undertaken by the Franchise Committee of the Montreal Women's Club in 1929. A "sandwich-board campaign" was inaugurated in both Montreal and Quebec City, with women volunteers pacing the streets bearing vivid suffrage posters both fore and aft. Funds for this campaign and other related projects were furnished by the American suffragist, Mrs. Carrie Chapman Catt. Writing in the *Gazette* for March 28, 1940, Mrs. John Scott stated that Mrs. Catt had sent her one check for $500 in July 1927 and another for the same amount about a year later. This money enabled the Franchise Committee "to carry on a vigorous campaign in printing leaflets, arranging meetings all over the province and informing the public generally."

Although the Provincial Franchise Committee received several favourable replies to letters which it had sent to members of the legislative assembly in January 1929, it was twice severely rebuffed by that year's session of the legislature. The public bills committee of the assembly threw out without discussion a bill to permit women to become chartered accountants, though the Society of Chartered Accountants itself had

[49]*Quebec: Journals, 1927*, pp. 217, 237-8. L.W.R. Minute Books, entry for Feb. 19, 1927.
[50]*Quebec: Journals, 1928*, pp. 107, 147-8. *Gazette*, Feb. 24, 1928.
[51]L.W.R. Minute Books, entry for Dec. 21, 1928, and Annual Report(1928-29).

requested it.[52] Then, on February 27, the assembly rejected the second Tremblay suffrage bill by a vote of 50 to 16 before galleries filled with women and amid such scenes of derisive laughter and disorder on the floor of the House that the speaker had to call for order several times. The vote was on non-partisan lines and two cabinet members voted against the "hoist," but it was to be observed that both the premier and Maurice Duplessis, a future premier, ranged themselves among the majority.[53]

Less than a year after Mme Casgrain and Mrs. Sampson had appealed to Taschereau for reforms in the civil code, the premier set up the Dorion Commission to investigate the question (November 1929). Several women's groups of the city sent delegates to plead before the Commission, among them Mme Casgrain and Eugène Lafleur, K.C., for the League of Women's Rights; Mlle Saint Jean and Mme A. Levaque for l'Alliance; Mlle Irène Joly for the Association of Women Property Owners; and Mme Gérin-Lajoie (who had been agitating for this since 1915) for La Fédération Nationale Saint Jean Baptiste. Some of the telling points made by these speakers were that women could not bring law-suits without their husbands' consent, that the husband alone need consent to the marriage of minor daughters, and that women did not have the right to their own earnings.[54] Evidently this formidable array of speakers made a favourable impression upon the Commission, for it forwarded sixteen specific recommendations for changes in the civil code to the government in 1930, a few of which were enacted into law by the 1931 session of the legislature.[55]

Late in 1929, after the celebrated victory of the Alberta women in the Persons Case, Mme Casgrain discovered that

[52]L.W.R. Minute Books, entry for Feb. 15, 1929.
[53]*Quebec: Journals, 1929*, pp. 96, 168-9. *Gazette*, Feb. 28, 1929.
[54]*Ibid.*, Nov. 16, 23, 28, 1929. L.W.R. Minute Books, Annual Report (1929-30).
[55]*Gazette*, Feb. 15, 1930. Information obtained from interview with Miss Elizabeth C. Monk in July 1943. Miss Monk, who was the League for Women's Rights' legal counsellor and active in its work for several years, was long denied the right to practise law in her own province although she had passed the Bar examinations in Nova Scotia.

the qualifications for the upper house in Quebec were the same as those for the Canadian senate. The League immediately started agitation to have a woman appointed to the legislative council and took pains to point out that inasmuch as women were now eligible for the upper house, it was no more than reasonable to expect that legislation would be promptly enacted granting them eligibility for the assembly.[56]

The year 1930 marked the beginning of a decade of stirring activity by both the lately rechristened League and l'Alliance, a decade of seemingly endless disappointments and very few actual gains until the final brilliant victory of 1940. The first legislative session of the ten-year span witnessed the defeat of two bills which meant much to the hearts of women, though not by such one-sided scores as in former years.

Not since 1920 had a bill to permit women to practise law been introduced at Quebec. As an aftermath of a brilliant plea[57] made for women by Eugène Lafleur, K.C., before the Quebec Bar Association on September 4, 1929, a Liberal member, Oscar Drouin, introduced such a bill on February 6, 1930. Two weeks later the bill was rejected, 37 to 29, with the cabinet itself divided 6 to 4. The *Gazette* said that the bill might have stood a very good chance of passing, had the women not insisted upon having a suffrage bill introduced at the same session. The latter gave opponents of the Bar bill a chance to link the two together and drag forth all the old bogies about divorce, broken homes, and destruction of the civil code.[58]

Undeterred by the defeat of the Bar bill, Irenée Vautrin, a prominent Liberal and deputy speaker of the assembly, sponsored the 1930 suffrage bill. He made an able speech in defence of his measure on March 5, followed by several others who also argued in its favour. The sole dissenting address was that of J. Ephraim Bédard, who was tormented by visions of countless shattered homes in the province, should women get

[56]L.W.R. Minute Books, Annual Report (1929-30). *Gazette*, Nov. 15, 28, 1929.
[57]A copy of the plea is on file in the office of the League for Women's Rights, Montreal.
[58]*Quebec: Journals, 1930*, pp. 32, 36-7. *Gazette*, Feb. 8, 20, 1930. This paper reports that Duplessis spoke strongly in favour of the bill, a surprising circumstance in view of his steadfastly inimical view of woman suffrage.

the vote. Replying to Bédard, Hon. Athanase David pointed out that changing economic conditions were effecting a far more drastic revolution in home life than mere possession of the ballot was ever likely to do, and suggested that the disquieted member "might recall that there were many women who left their homes each morning, leaving the children to the care of the oldest child, so that they might work in factories." Despite the preponderance of favourable speeches, the "hoist" was carried by 44 to 24, with the cabinet again divided 6 to 4 as on the Bar bill. Defeat was made more palatable to the suffragists by the serious consideration accorded their measure by the members and because the twenty-four votes mustered in its favour represented a considerable advance over any previous year. With good sportsmanship, the women of the League sent Premier Taschereau sixty-three roses for his birthday.[59]

A definite gain in the professional field was registered by Quebec women in 1930 when the Society of Chartered Accountants decided to ignore the legislature and by its own independent action voted to accept women into its membership. The first woman to join the Society was admitted in September of that year, thereby shoving back the age-long barrier of prejudice another fraction of an inch.[60]

Before the year closed, two further lines of activity were pursued by the two suffrage organizations of Montreal. In the federal elections of 1930, Mlle Saint Jean courageously broke all precedent by running as an independent candidate in the constituency of Dorion Saint Denis. With no hope of winning, she nevertheless managed to garner about three thousand votes and undoubtedly succeeded in doing what she set out to do, to "bring this question of women's political influence before the public."[61]

[59]*Ibid.*, Feb. 8, Mar. 6, 1930. L.W.R. Minute Books, Annual Report (1929-30). *Quebec: Journals, 1930*, pp. 128, 195-6.
[60]L.W.R. Minute Books, entry for Oct. 15, 1930. Letter from Elizabeth C. Monk to the author, Aug. 16, 1945.
[61]*Women's Sphere* (1937-38), p. 53. Canadian Newspaper Service, publ., *National Reference Book on Canadian Men and Women* (Montreal, 1940), p. 626. M. G. Huguenin, *op. cit.*, p. 167. Dr. Ritchie-England also entered this race as the Liberal candidate for Mount Royal.

Mme Casgrain, supported by Mlle Irène Joly of the Association of Women Property Owners, focussed her efforts upon the aldermen of Montreal, in the hope of getting them to recommend to the legislature a change in the city's charter which would enfranchise married women with property. In November 1930 the City Council did actually vote (17 to 15) to support the extension of the municipal franchise to married women, separate as to property,[62] but the legislature took no action until February 1932. Then, at last, the lawmakers revised the charter of Montreal, making this additional class of women eligible to participate in civic elections, at the same time disfranchising the husbands who had been making use of their wives' property qualifications to vote.[63] Another small wedge had been driven into the ramparts of entrenched conservatism.

History repeated itself in the 1931 session of the legislature, both a Bar bill and a suffrage measure being rejected. The fifth attempt to enfranchise women was again introduced by Vautrin, ably supported this time by two Conservative members, Martin Fisher of Huntingdon and General C. A. Smart of Westmount. All three laid stress upon the economic independence which women were rapidly winning and which undoubtedly entitled them to political consideration. The large numbers of women who turned out at federal elections refuted the common argument that women neither wanted the vote nor would use it if they had it. Waxing hot, Fisher described the position of women in Quebec as "degraded." The lone speaker in opposition was a young Liberal, Amédée Caron, a newcomer to the assembly. He doubted whether women wanted a vote and whether conditions would be any better if they had it. Citing the mild changes wrought by that session in the civil code for women, he was unable to understand what more they could want anyway. The customary "hoist" blocked second reading by a vote of 47 to 21 on March 25, indicating a

[62]*Gazette*, Oct. 25, 26, Nov. 27, 1930.  This would, of course, exclude women married in "community of property."
[63]*Ibid.*, Dec. 2, 1933.  L.W.R. Minute Books, Annual Report (1931-32). *Women's Sphere* (1940-41), p. 9.  *Statutes of Quebec, 1931-32*, ch. 105.

slight setback from the previous year's record. However, the cabinet was now split evenly on the question (5 to 5).[64]

On the day following the rejection of the suffrage measure, Drouin's second Bar bill also received its death-blow, but by the extremely narrow margin of two votes. Apparently determined to win a reputation as an implacable foe of women's rights, the youthful M. Caron moved the "hoist" amid cries of: "Not twice in two days," "Too bad, too bad," "And he is so young, too." His arguments in support of his motion certainly did not increase the member's stature as a statesman, one sample of his logic being that if women became lawyers they might become judges and have to mete out the death sentence, for which he feared they would be too soft-hearted. In contrast were the remarks of Hon. Athanase David who observed that the day was long past when girls were turned out of convents solely to go into the kitchen and the home. If modern economic conditions forced women to go into the working world, was it fair to limit them as to types of work?

A university turns out a girl as a lawyer, telling her she is inferior to none in her profession, and the Bar steps in and says she may not practice that profession, and must get into housework. It is a great injustice, and for the past ten years, I have protested on behalf of the women of my province that they be given work suitable to their intelligence. It is not for us to limit the barrier at which their intelligence must be exercised, and tell them they can go so far and no further.

A bouquet of flowers on David's desk was a token of the appreciation felt by the women in the galleries for his support.[65]

Knowing full well that hopes for ultimate victory must depend upon a far broader popular demand than the purely urban feminist forces of the two preceding decades, the League began a campaign of education in the early thirties which was designed particularly to reach the women of rural Quebec. If the women of this old-world province had a more gruelling struggle to win the franchise than their sisters in other parts of the dominion, they at least had available to them a powerful propaganda medium not at the disposal

[64]*Quebec: Journals, 1930-31*, pp. 251, 388. *Gazette*, Mar. 26, 1931.
[65]*Ibid.*, Mar. 27, 1931. *Quebec: Journals, 1930-31*, pp. 291, 403-4.

of earlier suffrage groups—the radio. Under the direction of Mme Casgrain, a quarter-hour programme known as "Femina" was sent out weekly over station CKAC.[66] The programme was greatly expanded in 1935 and continued until Mme Casgrain entered active politics in 1942. Broadcasts in both French and English featured news of interest to women, prominent speakers on various aspects of women's role in the modern world, plays, and musical interludes.[67] That the propaganda device was successful in achieving results almost immediately is evidenced by the large file of letters in the League's possession from all parts of the province. The Annual Report of the League for 1932-33 stated:

Once more the audience we sought to reach was a province-wide one and the correspondence we have received in ever-increasing volume during the past months proves that we have reached it. The radio has proven itself again our best and most consistent weapon. . . . It is, after all, the woman who listens to us as she prepares dinner in some distant Gaspé farm-house . . . , whose voice will be the one to give its orders to the Legislative Assembly, which founds its attitude of refusal on the belief that she does not care for the struggle that the women of the cities are chiefly waging.

The suffrage bill for the session of 1932 was introduced by Dr. Anatole Plante, a new sponsor secured through the joint efforts of the League and the Alliance. The debate which preceded the customary "hoist" was a travesty. The League Minute Books afterwards expressed particular resentment against the remarks of A. Bélanger, but it was J. Filion of Laval who offered "to lend his pants to Idola Saint Jean any time she wanted them."[68]

At its next meeting the League passed unanimously a resolution protesting the tone of certain speeches made on

[66]The League's Annual Report (1936-37) states that for five years the radio time on CKAC was a gift of *La Presse* (Montreal). In later years the "Femina" broadcasts were transmitted over CBF and CBM, the French and English networks of C.B.C. for the entire province. Mlle Saint Jean also conducted a weekly radio programme called "Actualité Féminine."

[67]L.W.R. Minute Books, Annual Report (1931-32). Interview with Mlle Marcelle Barthe, July 1943. Mlle Barthe, associated with the Canadian Broadcasting Corporation in Montreal, played an important part in putting on the "Femina" broadcasts.

[68]*Quebec: Journals, 1931-32*, pp. 151-3. The "hoist" was carried on Jan. 20 by a vote of 52 to 23. *Women's Sphere* (1937-38), p. 49.

January 20—as a source of humiliation to the entire pro-vince—and complaining about the levity with which almost every suffrage bill was treated. Both organizations agreed, however, that the disgraceful scene in the legislature had really helped their cause, for letters poured in from all over the province and the country expressing sympathy.

The women again induced Dr. Plante to introduce their suffrage bill in 1933, and although it went down to a 53 to 20 defeat on February 22, both the suffrage leaders and the *Gazette* agreed that the tone of the debate was on a consider-ably higher plane than at the two previous sessions. Dr. Plante's own speech, a fine mixture of logic and irony, was the ablest of the day. The women of Quebec could be sent to Geneva as delegates, could become members of the federal House and senate, were even eligible for membership in the legislative council of Quebec, he said, yet they were denied the elementary political right of voting in their own province. Quebec was out of step with the rest of the dominion. Dr. Plante remarked: "We French Canadians have a great fault. We are intensely satisfied with ourselves, and in thinking of our own perfections we sometimes forget to look about us, and see what is going on." As for women swamping the assembly, should they be made eligible, he simply did not think it would happen, but he did feel that a few of them might "brighten up the place" and perhaps "induce more of the male members to pay more attention to the sittings." In concluding, Dr. Plante said that only 77 per cent of the men entitled to vote had done so at the last general election, so what was the point of arguing that women would not use the vote?

Dr. Ernest Poulin, principal opponent of the measure, not only bore out in his remarks the charge of self-complacency levelled at French Canadians by Dr. Plante, but also shed some light on at least one reason why the enfranchisement of women was so unduly delayed in Quebec. Why imitate other provinces? Were they any better run than Quebec? Woman suf-frage had not been proven beneficial anywhere so "why make such an important social and political change to gratify the caprices of a few leaders of the movement? To give women the vote meant overturning the social order, and was *against the spirit of the Roman Catholic Church* [italics mine], and would bring no advantage." A. A. Legault added his fears for the social order: "It was premature, and tempestuous because of the difficult times in which we live."[69]

Reactions of the leaders in 1933 were definitely optimistic. Both Mme Casgrain and Mlle Saint Jean felt that interest in the suffrage question was growing throughout the province, and this would in time engulf legislative conservatism. The *Gazette* of February 24 published a feature editorial urging the women to persist in their efforts, and scoffing at the paucity and weakness of their opponents' arguments. In a statement as sweeping as its adversaries', the *Gazette* affirmed that "all the equity and logic is on the affirmative side."

A mountain of indifference to the question continued, however, to exist among Quebec women. This was indicated by an article entitled "Les Femmes de la province de Québec sont-elles en faveur du vote féminin?" which appeared in *Canada français* in February 1933. The writer, Mme E. Croff, who may be assumed to have been expressing an attitude common to thousands of French-Canadian women, declared most emphatically that they were not. Asserting that the female vote in dominion elections had made little or no difference in politics, the author went on to affirm that "La politique laisse la Canadienne française indifférente." In the midst of her domestic preoccupations she had neither the time nor the ability to study political affairs. If she were possessed with the idea of reforming or changing things, she might follow either or both of two courses: devote herself to works of charity and social reform (though Mme Croff found Quebec so generous in its care of the unfortunate that little improvement need be wrought on that score) or discreetly influence the men of her family whenever it should seem necessary. "Elle peut influer sur les décisions et les volontés de l'homme sans jouer

---

[69]*Quebec: Journals, 1933*, pp. 30, 117-8. The *Gazette* for Feb. 23, 1933, contains a very full account of the debate.

à l'homme." The former course she particularly recommended for single women who, not having any "soins domestiques" on their hands, might otherwise find time hanging heavily. In spite of all the disadvantages of woman suffrage, Mme Croff admitted that it was bound to come sooner or later but she hoped that the evil day might be postponed as long as possible.[70]

Horace Miner's excellent study of the social structure of the typical small French-Canadian parish of Saint Denis, made in the late 1930's, also throws some valuable light on the rural woman and on rural politics in Quebec. Expressing as it does the views of a trained sociologist and an impartial outside observer, it is perhaps of more value than Mme Croff's article; yet insider and outsider concur on more than one point. Miner found the general attitude in Saint Denis to be that politics was ". . . 'too dirty' for women, who should be occupied in their homes."[71] Since families generally behaved as units in all matters, including politics, married women showed no desire to vote, feeling that their husbands expressed their opinions for them on election days. Among unmarried women, however, Miner discovered a livelier interest in political rights, this group apparently being conscious of the lack of a male medium through which to give voice to their convictions.[72]

The influence of the Roman Catholic Church upon political matters in rural Quebec was found to be of considerable weight. Although elections were generally regarded as secular matters in which the curé ought not to interfere, "He does, nevertheless, wield a potent political hand through the indirect or direct support he can give from the pulpit." *L'Action Catholique*, unofficial voice of the Roman Catholic Church in Quebec, was another intermediary through which the clerical

---

[70]E. Croff, "Les femmes de la province de Québec sont-elles en faveur du vote féminin?" *Canada français*, XX (6) (Quebec, Feb. 1933) 536-40, 566.

[71]Horace Miner, *Saint Denis: A French-Canadian Parish* (Chicago, 1939), p. 59.

[72]*Ibid.*, pp. 59, 68. The same idea is expressed in an unsigned article, "Enquête sur la femme Canadienne-française," *Almanach de la langue française* (Montreal, 1936), p. 13.

point of view upon political questions was propagated.[73]

Despite the old-world character of rural Quebec with its deeply ingrained social customs, many of which militated against the political emancipation of women, the sociologist found certain significant forces operating upon the rural portion of the province, which would in time produce profound changes in its social and economic structure. Two of these give special promise of producing noticeable effects upon the status of women. The first is the fact that the number of unmarried women in the province is steadily increasing. At the time of writing (1939), Miner found that 68 per cent of the total population of Saint Denis was single and that 34.1 per cent of the women over forty were unmarried.[74] If the author of the survey was correct in his deductions about the interest in politics of the province's spinsters, the field of feminist recruits would thus appear to be constantly widening.

More important from the long-range viewpoint is the increasing dependence of the old French-Canadian rural economy upon the urban industrial community, dominated largely by English-Canadian (and American) capital and ideas.[75] Miner points out that as the ancient economy based upon farming has gradually forfeited its self-sufficiency, it has tended to lose its old folk character—an environment in which women played no political role. This process of change has been accelerated by two other forces: increasing penetration of the French-Canadian countryside by newspapers, period-

[73]H. Miner, *op. cit.*, p. 59. The Montreal *Gazette* of Nov. 29, 1933, reported that a formal request by the League of Women's Rights for the support of the Catholic Syndicates or trade unions in the equal rights movement had been flatly rejected. In view of the almost universal support for woman suffrage among labour unions, this incident can only be interpreted as evidence of the Church's opposition to political equality in Quebec.

[74]H. Miner, *op. cit.*, pp. 27, 88.

[75]As of 1941, 63.32 per cent of Quebec's population dwelt in urban areas, making this province the most urbanized of the entire dominion. Further detailed study of the impact of industrialization upon French-Canadian society has been made in: Everett C. Hughes, "Industry and the Rural System in Quebec," *Canadian Journal of Economics and Political Science*, IV (Toronto, 1938); and Everett Cherrington Hughes, *French Canada in Transition* (Chicago and Toronto, 1943). Though neither work makes any reference to French-Canadian women and politics, both portray graphically the revolutionary change being wrought within Quebec's social structure—a change certain to have important effects upon the status of women in French Canada.

icals, and radio programmes having their origins in the cities; and the exodus of rural French Canadians in search of employment to cities on both sides of the border. The return of these exiles on temporary visits, or permanently, as sometimes happened during the depression years of the thirties, has caused the infiltration of many new ideas.[76]

In 1934, however, these forces had yet to show their effect. The woman suffrage bill brought forward in that year appeared before the legislature on February 9 under the sponsorship of a new godfather, Dr. Gaspard Fauteux, Liberal member from Montreal. Discussion of the measure was serious and the usual delegation of women, which appeared at Quebec in its support, was treated with unwonted courtesy. The most eloquent plea for the bill on the floor of the assembly came from a recent convert to the feminist cause, Edgar Rochette. Yet eloquence failed to carry the day against ingrained prejudice and the eighth attempt to enfranchise women was shelved on February 21.[77]

The Executive Committee of the National Federation of Liberal Women took note of the plight of their Quebec sisters in February by adopting a resolution, sponsored by Senator Cairine Wilson, deploring the political disability under which the women of the French-speaking province continued to labour.[78] But sympathy from outside was not what was needed, comforting though it might be. The *Gazette* of February 23 came much closer to the core of the problem in commenting editorially upon the defeat of the Fauteux bill:

When it can be shown that the women of Quebec do want the vote, the majority of the legislators very soon will relinquish their set and negative attitude in relation to this issue, . . . . The mission of the proponents of reform, then, lies in the constituencies, there to develop a more assertive public spirit and make the demand for the feminine franchise more articulate.

[76]H. Miner, *op. cit.*, pp. 233-4, 240-1, 246-8. On p. 248 Miner states that in the ten-year period ending in 1931, 49 per cent of the more than 400,000 persons who left rural for urban areas in Canada were residents of Quebec.

[77]The vote was 52 to 25. *Quebec: Journals, 1934*, pp. 115, 166-8. *Gazette*, Feb. 21, 22, 23, 1934. *Canadian Annual Review* (1934), p. 211. L.W.R. Minute Books, Annual Report (1933-34). Until 1949, Dr. Gaspard Fauteux was speaker of the federal House.

[78]*Gazette*, Feb. 21, 1934.

The two Montreal franchise organizations turned their efforts in 1934 towards seeking improvements in the status of women along subsidiary lines. Mlle Saint Jean succeeded in having the MacMillan Banking Commission recommend removal of the disability of married women in Quebec to control their own bank accounts, a suggestion which was soon enacted into provincial law.[79] The League for Women's Rights meantime continued its struggle for a broadening of the Women's Minimum Wage Act and the inclusion of women school teachers under the terms of the act. Certainly the latter were sorely in need of a champion, for the League's investigation of their salary scale revealed that the range of salary for women teachers in rural districts of the province was from $150 to the munificent maximum of $300 per annum. This endeavour also produced fairly prompt results. In 1935 teachers' salaries were brought under the Minimum Wage Act and the minimum set at $300—not a sum calculated to produce any immediate overcrowding in the teaching field, surely, but still a definite advance over previous conditions.[80]

In many respects the year 1935 was one to try the patience of saints—and women. A campaign to keep women out of jobs, which had been mounting in tempo during the depression years, reached its climax in the 1935 session of the legislature. J. A. Francœur introduced a measure which would have denied women the right to work except in fields, forests, and housework. Premier Taschereau, to whom the idea of women in politics was still abhorrent, led the opposition to Francœur's bill, calling it impractical; he was "not ready to refuse them the right to make their living."[81] Though the bill was killed by a vote of 47 to 16, it is a cogent reflection upon women's status in Quebec that even sixteen members could be found to back such a preposterous suggestion.

Impressed by Rochette's able defence of their suffrage measure at the previous session, the two feminist societies

[79]L.W.R. Minute Books, Annual Report (1933-34). *National Reference Book on Canadian Men and Women* (Montreal, 1940), pp. 625-6.
[80]L.W.R. Minute Books, Annual Reports (1933-34, 1934-35, 1935-36).
[81]*Gazette*, Jan. 23, 1935.

prevailed upon him to present the franchise bill in 1935. The discussion was childish and cheap. Robert Bachand, for example, observed that since cigarettes and cocktails were no longer the exclusive prerogatives of men, women might at least leave the political field to them. Both Mme Casgrain and Mlle Saint Jean told reporters they would never again appear in the House (a promise which, fortunately, neither one remembered to keep). That the tempers of all the delegates were thoroughly frayed is evidenced by a newspaper report: "The ladies showed what they thought of it [the vote on the bill] by walking out en masse from the galleries with as little silence as they could manage."[82]

The women of Quebec in their humiliation turned next to the Throne itself. As the whole empire celebrated King George's silver jubilee in 1935, a petition containing ten thousand signatures was gathered, begging the monarch to take note of the plight of his female subjects in this corner of his far-flung domains. When the Quebec government refused to forward their petition, the women commissioned one of their own number who was bound for the empire's capital to deliver the bulky document. The Quebec courier made her way to Buckingham Palace and placed the petition in the hands of household officials to be presented to His Majesty.[83] What the good king thought of the unusual request, about which he was powerless to lift a finger, is not related; but in any case the entire performance was an interesting and ingenious piece of publicity.

At the last session of the Quebec legislature under the Taschereau government, the franchise bill was introduced by Frederick Monk of Montreal. He was the first sponsor since 1929 who was not affiliated with the Liberal party. To the distress of the women whose sponsor and champion he had been in 1935, Hon. Edgar Rochette, recently appointed minister of labour in the Taschereau cabinet, bitterly denounced

---

[82]*Ibid.*, Mar. 21, 1935. *Quebec: Journals, 1935*, pp. 151, 243-4. *Canadian Annual Review* (1935-36), p. 277. The Rochette bill was defeated on March 20 by a vote of 43 to 19.
[83]*Daily Star*, Mar. 23, 1940.

the measure during the debate on second reading on May 27. For the first time, the premier insisted upon making the vote on the question a matter of party loyalty. Not a Liberal deserted him under these circumstances, party discipline triumphing over personal preference. The Monk bill was laid to rest by a comfortable majority of nineteen votes.[84]

In the provincial elections of 1936 the Union Nationale forces overwhelmingly routed the Liberals, who had guided the destiny of Quebec for almost forty years. The new premier, Maurice Duplessis, called an emergency session of the legislature for October 7. One of the matters to engage the attention of the special session was a revision of the electoral law. Finding that the proposed modifications contained no reference to woman suffrage, a small delegation of women headed by Mme Casgrain appeared before the public bills committee on October 28 and appealed for an amendment to section 12 of the act—the simple elimination of the one word "male."[85] Such an amendment was actually moved by Dr. Camille Pouliot, seconded by his cousin, Frank Pouliot, both members of the party in power. Duplessis opposed the motion. Speeches were inclined to jocularity and the general attitude was that elections were now a long way off. It would be time enough to deal with this vexatious little problem at some later date when one might need to trim sails in the face of an approaching electoral storm. A vote of 49 to 21 disposed of the amendment.[86]

Following the setbacks of 1936, the directorate of the League for Women's Rights determined upon a different

[84]The actual vote was 43 to 24. L.W.R. Minute Books, Annual Report (1935-36). *Women's Sphere* (1937-38), p. 50. *Canadian Annual Review* (1935-36), p. 281. *Quebec: Journals, 1936*, pp. 56, 57, 137, 138.

[85]*Gazette*, Oct. 26, 29, 1936.

[86]*Ibid.*, Nov. 6, 7, 1936. *Canadian Annual Review* (1935-36), p. 287. *Daily Star*, Nov. 6, 1936. There is absolutely no reference to the Pouliot amendment in *Quebec: Journals, 1936 (2nd session)*. There also appears to be some confusion about the mover and the vote. A list of sponsors of bills among the League's papers gives the credit to Dr. Camille Pouliot, as do the *Canadian Annual Review* and the *Daily Star*. The *Gazette* names Frank Pouliot as sponsor. The *Gazette* has the amendment defeated by 49 to 21; the *Canadian Annual Review* by 44 to 21; while the *Daily Star* contents itself with recording that it was defeated "overwhelmingly," with 23 votes for the amendment and no mention of the opposing vote.

course of action for 1937. Instead of searching for another sponsor to carry them through another painful defeat, all idea of a woman suffrage bill was abandoned for that session. Efforts instead were concentrated upon the most ambitious financial and educational project in the League's entire career. Inviting the support of outside agencies and individuals as well as that of its own slender membership, the League set a goal of $20,000 to be raised and used for a more intensive radio campaign, greater publicity in the press, particularly the rural papers, and the publication of literature explaining the purposes of the League. Members were urged to distribute the latter in the rural areas of the province during their summer holidays, a commission which the organization's Annual Reports for the next three years would indicate they carried out faithfully. At last the League had set itself to overcoming the chief obstacle—the disinterest in politics of the women of rural Quebec.[87]

Financially, the campaign of 1937 was completely successful. Gratifying, too, was the League's increased membership, by-product of a newly aroused public interest in the organization's platform. It is virtually impossible, however, to assess the net results of the year's main endeavour, for ideas take time to germinate in the average human mind. No province-wide sampling of popular feeling on the suffrage issue was attempted then or later. The only test of any sort was held in Montreal in November 1937 and in all likelihood confined to a group of people who could in no sense be considered as representative of the province as a whole. A ballot box was installed in a suffrage booth maintained by the League and other women's organizations at the Canadian Manufacturers' Exhibit. Twenty thousand leaflets were distributed to visitors who were invited to express their opinions on the enfranchisement of women by dropping a ballot into

[87]L.W.R. Minute Books, Annual Report (1936-37). *Gazette*, Mar. 11, 1937. The *Gazette* had long and frequently urged this type of campaign upon the Montreal feminists and now gave the programme a cordial blessing. In Dec. 1937 the League decided to devote more radio time to French and less to English, because most English-speaking Quebecers were already in favour of the League's main objective. L.W.R. Minute Books, entry for Dec. 2, 1937.

the sealed box. At the League's general meeting on December 2, His Honour, the mayor, opened the seals and presided over the tally which revealed 8,149 in favour of the proposition as against only 294 negative votes.[88]

The defeat of the suffrage bill in 1938 would certainly indicate that no undue pressure was brought to bear upon the lawmakers by an aroused public opinion. The twelfth attempt to enfranchise women was introduced by Grégoire Bélanger of the Union Nationale on March 8 and met its Waterloo only nine days later. Almost harder to bear than the actual count of 48 to 16 by which second reading was negatived was the defection of two former champions of feminine political rights: Hon. William Tremblay who had sponsored the bills of 1928 and 1929, and Hon. Martin Fisher who had argued so eloquently for the measure in 1931. Apparently Premier Duplessis was a stern disciplinarian and would brook no nonsense from his cabinet ministers on this question. The *Gazette* went so far as to claim that he choked off general debate on the bill by demanding a vote before all who wished to do so had spoken.[89] The new premier was rapidly proving himself to be a strong opponent of the women.

Despite the severity of the defeat of the Bélanger suffrage bill, 1938 was in certain other respects a banner year for the women's cause. In the spring the Rowell-Sirois Commission was collecting material for discussions at a later Dominion-Provincial Conference on Economic Relations and was being memorialized by interested groups of citizens in all parts of the country. Both suffrage organizations in Montreal took advantage of this occasion to point out the political and economic plight of Quebec women. Mlle Saint Jean's appeal was brief and mainly in connection with the income tax, but closed with the inevitable appeal for women's rights.". . . our demand for political freedom is based on logic and justice.

[88]*Ibid.*, entry for Dec. 2, 1937.
[89]This was the worst setback since the Tremblay bill of 1929. *Gazette*, Mar. 18, 1938. *Quebec: Journals, 1938*, pp. 87, 112-3. *Canadian Annual Review* (1937-38), p. 232. L.W.R. Minute Books, Annual Report (1937-38).

The women of Quebec have the same obligations as men without enjoying any of their rights."[90]

The brief presented to the Commission in the name of the League for Women's Rights was actually the work of Elizabeth Monk, its legal counsel. With its powerful logic and array of statistics, this document was a brilliant exposition of the degraded position of Quebec women and a sharp warning against complacency in other parts of the dominion toward the intolerable conditions existing in that province. Pointing out that the disfranchisement of women in Quebec had had its inevitable economic repercussions, Miss Monk assailed, as unfair to Quebec women, the growing tendency of the dominion government to appropriate funds for the provinces to administer. Actual discriminations against women in provincial laws and local ordinances were cited. For one example, when the dominion government allotted $220,000 to the province for a youth training programme, only $25,000 could be secured (and with great difficulty) for the training of young women as household workers. By way of contrast, the neighbouring province of Ontario allotted more than double that amount for the same purpose.

It is submitted that the Dominion Government is never justified in using federal funds imposed on men and women alike to subsidize governmental services administered by provincial authorities unless it is assured that there will be no discrimination against women taxpayers in the use to which the subsidies are put.

Turning from injustices in the apportioning of subsidies, the author of the brief went on to argue that lack of the franchise power had permitted the payment of disastrously low wages and salaries to women in industry and school-teaching. This in turn tended to lower the wages paid to men and in its ever-widening eddies, affected adversely the standard of living in the province and even in the entire dominion. A grim illustration of Miss Monk's contention about Quebec's depressed living standard was to be found in statistics on infant mortality rates across Canada in 1935. Only eight cities in the

[90]*Women's Sphere* (1938-39), p. 64.

dominion had an infant death-rate of over 100 per 1000, and of these, seven were in Quebec.

The barring of Quebec women from political privileges had the further unfortunate result of making it practically impossible for the federal government to appoint any women of the province to the senate, to federal commissions, or to judicial positions. As a simple but effective antidote for all the political, social, and economic ills stemming from the antiquated position of women under Quebec laws, the League's brief closed by recommending the passage of an amendment to the British North America Act similar in scope to the Sex Disqualification Removal Acts already in force in Great Britain, Alberta, and British Columbia.[91] Such a remedy would not only remove at one stroke all civil and political disabilities of the women of Quebec, where inequalities between the sexes were most glaring, but also clean up a few ancient legal handicaps still resting in the cobwebbed obscurity of other provincial statute books.

Although no immediate effect of this effort to state the women's case before a nation-wide audience was apparent, it undoubtedly called, in a dignified and compelling manner, the attention of federal authorities to an urgent problem. That the League had also managed to penetrate some layers of public opinion was apparent from the unexpectedly large demand for copies of the brief from all parts of the country.[92]

Another milestone was reached in June 1938 when the Liberal party of Quebec shattered all precedent by inviting forty women delegates to attend its convention in Quebec City.[93] Just what prompted this step the Liberals did not say,

---

[91]The above summary of the League's brief was made from Miss Elizabeth C. Monk's personal copy, which she kindly loaned to the author in the summer of 1941.

[92]L.W.R. Minute Books, Annual Report (1937-38). Miss Rosa Shaw, former president of the Canadian Women's Press Club, once told the author that the Monk brief was generally considered one of the three most brilliant presented to the Rowell-Sirois Commission.

[93]*Brief History of L.W.R.*., p. 9. L.W.R. Minute Books, entry for May 30, 1938. *Daily Star*, May 10, 1938. Mmes Pierre Casgrain, Henri Vautelet, and Charles Rinfret, veterans all in the League's long campaign for political equality, were among the forty delegates.

but speculation points to any one of three theories or perhaps a combination of all three.

After their overwhelming defeat by the Union Nationale in 1936, the Liberals realized they must elect a new leader and map out a vigorous programme if they hoped to revive party fortunes at the next provincial election. In this revitalizing process it could certainly do no great harm to enlist the aid of the small but energetic group of feminists, especially if there were no more than forty women among a total of eight hundred delegates.

The second theory points to the probability of gentle but firm pressure exerted upon the provincial wing of the party by the Liberal administration in Ottawa. (Hon. Ernest Lapointe, Quebec's most distinguished statesman at the federal capital, had spoken in favour of woman suffrage long before 1938.) This speculation takes on added weight in view of the highly favourable impression created by the League's brief to the Rowell-Sirois Commission in May.

Then, too, one would be foolish to discount the influence of Mme Pierre Casgrain, whose husband was speaker of the federal House of Commons at this time. Skilled in the arts of statecraft in her own right, and possessing entrée into Ottawa's innermost political circles, this talented woman undoubtedly played her cards with dexterity.

The Liberal convention at Quebec on June 10 and 11 broke new ground in more than one way, for the forty women delegates had the satisfaction at last of seeing a woman suffrage plank nailed into the platform by the unanimous vote of the eight hundred delegates.[94] This action was especially noteworthy after the choice of Adélard Godbout as the party's new standard bearer, for he was the same man who, as minister of agriculture in the Taschereau administration, had voted

[94]L.W.R. Minute Books, entry for June 15, 1938. Mme Vautelet told the author in August 1947 that most of the male delegates were personally opposed to woman suffrage and that the inclusion of the plank was only brought about as the result of some very astute behind-the-scenes manoeuvring by the women delegates, especially Mme Casgrain, who was a member of the Resolutions Committee.

against enfranchisement bills with disconcerting regularity during the 1930's.

Mme Casgrain once told the author she was convinced that Godbout's conversion to woman suffrage was sincere and that he was big enough to admit the error of his past views. Mlle Saint Jean, on the other hand, frankly expressed the opinion that the conversion was brought about by pressure from Ottawa. No matter what the motive, once the new Liberal leader had publicly committed himself to the cause of women, he did not let them down.

In 1938 the League won a new ally in the rural districts. Mme Casgrain was invited to address the annual convention of the Women's Institutes of Quebec. She spoke with such telling effect that these groups of rural women voted their support to securing woman suffrage. Though this step would account for only a small proportion of the country women, it was encouraging as marking the first direct contact between urban and rural groups in the enfranchisement drive.[95]

Nevertheless, it must be realized that the struggle for women's rights in Quebec was from first to last essentially an urban movement and even within that restricted sphere, confined almost exclusively to Montreal. Granting that there were two suffrage associations in the metropolis, as well as a dozen or more women's societies which were friendly to the project, the figures on League membership supplied in the organization's annual reports give a graphic idea of the small number of women who generated enough steam eventually to set the cumbersome legislative machinery in motion. At the very hour of victory, in 1939-40, only forty-seven members were counted among the faithful![96]

The year 1939, which witnessed the outbreak of the second world war and, inside Quebec, the unexpected overturn of the Duplessis regime at the fall elections, began as usual with the

---

[95]*Brief History of L.W.R.*, p. 9.

[96]L.W.R. Minute Books, Annual Report (1941-42). During the intense excitement of the financial drive of 1937, membership rose temporarily to an all-time high of almost nine hundred. Again, following the thrill of victory in the spring of 1940, the League attained a membership of 272.

defeat of a woman suffrage bill in the Quebec legislature. Introduced by P.-A. Lafleur of the Union Nationale on March 23, the measure passed first and second readings that same day and was immediately referred to the committee on public bills in general. The premier explained to the House that this procedure had been agreed upon during a conference with some of the feminist leaders earlier that month in order to give the women an opportunity to be heard. What thus appears at first sight as an extraordinary concession by an inveterate foe becomes more readily understandable when one considers that Duplessis himself was chairman of the committee in question.[97]

On March 29 a small but distinguished delegation of women had their day in Quebec before the committee. Speakers included Mme Casgrain, Mlle Saint Jean, Miss Margaret Wherry (Montreal Business and Professional Women's Club), Mlle Irène Joly (Women Proprietors League), Mme Henri Vautelet (long active in the League for Women's Rights), and Mrs. John Scott, veteran feminist of eighty-four, who astounded and delighted her audience by addressing them in French. So effectively did the women present their case that one of the cabinet, Hon. T. J. Coonan, and the Liberal Opposition leader, T. D. Bouchard,[98] declared themselves converted to the cause. Even the premier congratulated the delegation. That was on March 29. The next day his committee killed the bill.[99]

With the onset of the European conflict in early September, women turned much of their energies to war work, but at the same time, Premier Duplessis' unexpected call for a provincial election in the fall of 1939 made them realize that their great opportunity was at hand. One last publicity drive was launched through press and radio and in the ensuing electoral campaign, both the League and the Alliance threw their

[97]*Ibid.*, entry for Mar. 20, 1939. *Gazette*, Mar. 16, 24, 1939. *Quebec: Journals, 1939*, p. 169.

[98]M. Godbout, though Leader of the party, had lost his seat in the election of 1936. M. Bouchard voted against the Bélanger bill in 1938.

[99]*Quebec: Journals, 1939*, p. 207. L.W.R. Minute Books, entry for April 18, 1939. *Gazette*, Mar. 30, 31, 1939.

whole-hearted support to the Liberals, who won overwhelmingly.[100] M. Duplessis' strategy of relying upon Quebec isolationist sentiment to return him to a five-year term of office had miscarried disastrously, thanks in part to those very women whose hopes he had been instrumental in destroying on three separate occasions.

Though a friendly premier was now in office and a legislature strongly committed to woman suffrage would soon be meeting in Quebec, the League kept a watchful eye on the progress of events in the three and one-half months between the election and the opening of the 1940 legislative session. Unable to obtain from Godbout a definite statement that woman suffrage would be mentioned in the speech from the throne, the League organized a telegram campaign in all parts of the province. One telegram which could scarcely fail to make an impression was signed by the forty women delegates to the Liberal convention of 1938. Whether the suspicion was unfounded or the campaign successful, only M. Godbout would be in a position to say. At any rate, when the session opened on February 20, woman suffrage was included in the speech.[101]

Immediately a campaign was set under way by certain forces, notably groups of women in rural districts and the Roman Catholic Church in Quebec, to prevent the introduction of a woman suffrage bill. Having kept its opposition to the women's movement in subterranean channels for many years, the Church now determined to make an eleventh hour stand in the open.[102]

---

[100]*Brief History of L.W.R.*, pp. 10-11.

[101]L.W.R. Minute Books, entry for Feb. 12, 1940. *Le Devoir* (Montreal), Feb. 21, 1940. This French language newspaper assumed a very liberal attitude toward the woman suffrage question in the final weeks of the campaign, in marked contrast with *L'Action Catholique* (Quebec) and *Le Droit* (Ottawa).

[102]It is only fair to say that the attitude of the Quebec wing of the Catholic Church did not reflect the position of the See of Rome on the question of women in politics. A report published by the League of Nations in 1938 on the attitude of the Catholic Church toward woman suffrage showed such a wide deviation from that of the local segment of the Church that Mme Casgrain had proposed the reprinting and distribution of the report among the Quebec clergy. L.W.R. Minute Books, entry for July 13, 1938. For some unexplained reason, the suggestion was never carried out.

On March 2 Rodrigue Cardinal Villeneuve issued an official communiqué expressing his unalterable opposition to woman suffrage upon four grounds: that it would militate against family unity; that it would expose women to all the passions of elections; that the great majority of women in the province did not want it; and finally, that social and economic reforms could be as well achieved by women's organizations operating outside the realm of politics. The Cardinal ended the document with the assertion that he was expressing the common sentiment of all the bishops of the province.[103]

For three days following the Cardinal's challenge, Premier Godbout would make no public utterance indicating whether the churchly blast had altered his stand. But any rising doubts the women may have entertained during the interval of silence were set at rest on March 5. To Maurice Duplessis' question on the floor of the House about the government's intentions, Premier Godbout made the reply which is still quoted in Quebec feminist circles:

I do not know exactly when the bill will be submitted to the House or in what form it will appear, but I can tell my honourable friend that in the present case, as in other legislation, we will not exploit elevated sentiments in this province for the benefit of petty politics, and, strange as it may seem to him, there are still some people, who, once they have given their word, keep it.[104]

The premier's retort drew loud applause from his followers in the legislature and warm praise from the English press in Montreal, but *Le Droit* coldly lectured him that it was better to go back on his word than pursue a mistaken course of action.[105]

This critical tone was typical of many letters from various farm women's societies which appeared in *Le Devoir's* columns during the last week of March.[106] Their sudden influx in a

[103]*Daily Star*, Mar. 23, 1940. *Le Devoir*, Mar. 2, 1940. *New World*, June 1940, p. 11. The latter, speaking of the Quebec situation, says: "Two great obstacles have been the indifference of women themselves, and the attitude of certain sections of the Roman Catholic Church."

[104]*Daily Star*, Mar. 23, 1940.

[105]A summary of press reactions in *Le Devoir*, Mar. 7, 1940.

[106]*Ibid.*, Mar. 25, 26, 28, April 3, 1940. According to *Le Devoir* of April 3, many more such letters appeared in *L'Action Catholique* than in its own columns, sometimes as many as seven or eight in one day.

relatively brief space of time suggests the possibility of some expert and rather thinly concealed prompting. Examination of the contents of the letters lends further credence to this view, for almost invariably they mention the opposition of "notre vénéré cardinal."

Introduced by Premier Godbout himself on April 9, "Bill No. 18" proposed to give women the dual rights of voting and office-holding in the provincial realm, by making a few simple deletions and changes in the old Elections Act of 1936. Despite his meagre following in the assembly, Duplessis made an attempt right at the outset to block the bill on technical grounds, but to no avail.[107]

The measure surmounted its most critical hurdle—second reading—on April 11 by the gratifying count of 67 to 9. For the first time since confederation the House galleries were open only to women, but even had this courteous gesture not been made, it is doubtful whether any son of Adam could have mustered the courage to invade the solid ranks of enthusiastic women. Listeners heard the premier make a lengthy plea for woman suffrage, laying special emphasis on the economic factors which now seemed to justify the step. The only speech in opposition came from Dr. Albiny Paquette, who still thought voting and successful home life could not be combined. Nor did Dr. Paquette neglect his excellent opportunity to twit Godbout on the latter's change of heart. With candour the premier replied that he had been just as sincere in his opposition of former years as he was at present in his support of the project. "I believe, however, that circumstances in the province of Quebec have changed so much in the last few years that the problem presents itself now in an entirely different light."[108]

Even in committee of the whole and on third reading, Duplessis did not omit a few last jibes at the premier. In this sport he was joined by Lorrain, deputy from Papineau, but

---

[107]*Quebec: Journals, 1940*, p. 67.  *Gazette*, April 10, 1940.

[108]The quotation is from the *Citizen* (Ottawa), April 12, 1940. *Gazette*, April 12, 1940.  *Quebec: Journals, 1940*, p. 75.  *Le Devoir*, April 12, 1940, points out that there will be 753,310 masculine voters as against 820,000 women.

Godbout was quick-witted enough to remind the latter that he, too, had gone through some mental convolutions after supporting woman suffrage in 1936. Lorrain's reply contained a significant clause:

En 1936 j'ai voté à la demande d'électeurs et d'électrices anglaises de mon comté. Cette année à la suite de la *déclaration d'une haute autorité morale* [italics mine], d'autres personnes m'ont écrit et m'ont demandé de me prononcer contre le vote des femmes. D'ailleurs je ne suis pas ici pour exprimer ma propre opinion, mais celle des électeurs qui m'ont élu.[109]

At the conclusion of these verbal clashes, the Godbout bill went through third reading on April 18 by the same large majority of 67 to 9.[110]

Since Quebec, alone among the Canadian provinces, maintains a bicameral legislature, the suffrage bill had to make its way through the legislative council before the victory celebration could be complete. Introduced by Hon. Philippe Brais at 3:15 on the afternoon of April 25, the measure was pushed through all legislative formalities in record time, before the eyes of the women delegates, who were seated around the Chamber as well as in the galleries. Despite the fact that the whole procedure consumed only two hours and forty minutes, two veteran suffrage opponents, Sir Thomas Chapais and Médéric Martin, seized the opportunity to sing the swan-song of the die-hards. As the vote of 13 to 5 was given on third reading, Sir Thomas was heard to groan: "Well, before the ladies sit here with us, I hope a new style of hats will have been introduced." To his lament the *Gazette* added parenthetically: "Keep an eye on this Mrs. Casgrain. She may well be the next deputy for some county or other and, incidentally, she wears the kind of hats that even Legislative Councillors couldn't object to."[111]

One last act of gallantry paid in full the Liberal administration's obligation to the women. Knowing how much it would mean to them to have the final formality of royal assent

[109]*Ibid.*, April 19, 1940.
[110]*Quebec: Journals, 1940*, p. 92. *Gazette*, April 19, 1940.
[111]*Ibid.*, April 26, 1940. *Le Devoir*, April 26, 1940. *Quebec: Journals, 1940*, p. 106. L.W.R. Minute Books, entry for April 25, 1940.

bestowed upon the bill in their presence, the government had arranged with the lieutenant-governor that the ceremony should be performed immediately following third reading. Thus it was shortly after six o'clock in the evening of April 25 when the pilgrims from Montreal heard the ancient Norman-French formula, *Le roi le veult*, convert their ardently desired measure into the law of the realm.[112] The League's secretary closed her account of the day's proceedings with the matter-of-fact comment: "At 8 p.m. all the members of the delegation had a private Thanksgiving Dinner and took the train for Montreal at 10 p.m."

Vastly different was that home-coming of 1940 from the return journey made by heart-sick and browbeaten delegates on thirteen previous occasions. Patience, persistence, and skilful generalship had at last triumphed over the forces of indifference and reaction to give the women of Quebec their political freedom. It was a full generation after the great equal suffrage tide had washed over all other parts of the dominion.

That neither of the Montreal feminist organizations considered its work done with the victory of April 25 is evident not only from statements of their leaders at the time, but also from the fact that both remained alive and vigorous; the Alliance until the death of Mlle Saint Jean in 1945, and the League until the spring of 1947. The vote was viewed primarily as a lever with which countless other reforms might be pried loose as fast as these organizations could educate public opinion and focus it upon the legislature. Difficult indeed it would be for such groups to seek rest or dissolution while women of Quebec continue to be barred by law from certain professions, to be treated as minors—so far as married women are concerned—by an outdated civil code, to lack representation on all provincial boards and commissions, and to see their province desperately in need of better health and living standards.[113]

---

[112]*Statutes of Quebec, 1940*, ch. 7. The act did not go into effect until Jan. 1, 1941.
[113]L.W.R. Minute Books, Annual Report (1939-40). *Brief History of L.W.R.*, p. 12. *Standard* (Montreal), Mar. 23, 1940.

Judge Helen Gregory MacGill summed up the Quebec situation in 1940 and made a prediction.

Quebec haloed with romance and antiquity, French, Catholic, and altogether lovely, retained her language and her laws under English rule. Alike with other antiquities, the old French legal system is an historic curiosity and a modern embarrassment. Child marriage, father's sole ownership of the children, consent of husbands necessary before wives may practice professions, or enter businesses, are irksome and smell a bit musty in this day and age. . . . The stories of woman suffrage in the sister provinces are straws in the wind from which may be gathered the probable trends of the Quebec woman's vote. If history repeats itself, the new voters are likely to be more interested in measures for the protection of women and children, the old and the helpless, rather than in the fate of political parties.[114]

Further legislative advances in women's status followed swiftly upon the heels of the major reform act in 1940. At the same session, Montreal's charter was revised to initiate a new and rather complex method of choosing city councillors. Of the three types of councillors provided for under the revised charter, one third were to be chosen by various civic and educational groups—an opening which gave women their opportunity. Launching a vigorous campaign that fall, the League succeeded in having three women councillors elected in the December municipal contest: Miss Elizabeth Monk, Miss Kathleen Fisher, and Mme Théodule Bruneau.[115]

Two important legislative gains were registered during the 1941 session, both settling matters for which women had never ceased to agitate since the days of the first world war. Amendments to the Cities and Towns Act and the Municipal Code made *all* women with sufficient property qualifications eligible to vote and hold office in the municipal sphere.[116] Elizabeth Monk has pointed out that although these changes produced surface equality between men and women in muni-

[114]Helen Gregory MacGill, "Women and Politics in Quebec" (Vancouver, 1940), a typewritten article loaned to the author by Judge MacGill in 1943.
[115]*Statutes of Quebec, 1940*, ch. 75. L.W.R. Minute Books, entries for Oct., Nov., and Dec. 1940. *Standard*, April 19, 1941. *Brief History of L.W.R.*, p. 11.
[116]*Statutes of Quebec, 1941*, ch. 41 (Cities and Towns Act), ch. 69 (Municipal Code). The latter governs small municipalities, while the former governs larger municipal units which have not their separate charters. The reader is reminded that unmarried women have exercised the municipal franchise in Quebec since 1892.

cipal affairs, in actual practice many women still do not exercise local political rights. This is because husbands usually sign leases (and thus fulfil the tenant qualification), and also because the property qualification refers to *real* property. Most women of wealth possess it in other forms.

That year brought also to fruition the effort to gain admission for women to the Quebec Bar, a struggle which began in 1914 with Mr. Justice St. Pierre's decision denying Mrs. Annie Langstaff the right to practise law in Quebec. Following a plea for support from Mrs. Langstaff, Mrs. Leslie Bell, and Miss Elizabeth Monk on January 9, 1941, the General Council of the Quebec Bar Association voted twice in March, by the narrow margin of 12 to 11, to urge the Quebec legislature to pass enabling legislation. Not since 1931 had this type of bill engaged the attention of the lawmakers; but the Godbout government, adhering to its liberal policy on matters affecting women, passed the measure on April 29. Hoary tradition received another damaging thrust the following January, when Miss Elizabeth Monk and Mme Suzanne Filion became the first two women in the province to win admission to the Bar.[117]

Reversing the pattern followed by her sister provinces where office-holding in school districts was ordinarily one of the first political concessions won by women, Quebec did not yield on this score until 1942.[118] Insignificant as the measure may appear after the more spectacular triumphs of 1940 and 1941, it will, in all likelihood, have more real meaning to the women of the province than their other office-holding privileges. Experience elsewhere in the dominion has demonstrated that school questions are of immediate concern to women; to such an extent that, notwithtanding the average Canadian woman's reluctance to seek public office, she has frequently been willing to render service in this distinctly local sphere.

By-elections in Huntingdon and St. Johns-Napierville on October 6, 1941 gave the women of those two constituencies

[117]*Statutes of Quebec, 1941*, ch. 56. *Daily Star*, Jan. 10, Mar. 3, 18, 28, 31, April 5, 1941. L.W.R. Minute Books, Annual Report (1941-42).
[118]*Statutes of Quebec, 1942*, ch. 20.

the opportunity of becoming the first to vote in a provincial election in more than a century.[119] Not until August 1944 did the women of the entire province have a chance to exercise the privileges accorded them by the Godbout suffrage act of 1940. The result of that election turned their benefactor out of office and restored Maurice Duplessis.[120]

Although no Quebec woman has yet been appointed to the legislative council nor elected to the assembly,[121] and Mme Casgrain failed in her attempt to win a seat in the federal House in 1942,[122] there is no reason to feel that the situation is hopeless where this late-comer to suffrage ranks is concerned. Allowance must, of course, be made for the political apathy of Quebec's rural women; but even inertia will succumb in time to such forces as press, radio, compulsory education (introduced in 1943), and the persistent efforts of groups like the League to carry through needed reforms.

As might be expected, the war years largely diverted women's efforts into channels connected with the "home front." Yet even in those months of tension, women never completely lost sight of the social and economic goals to which they had dedicated their newly won political power. Under the presidency of Mme Georges Garneau, who succeeded Mme Casgrain in 1942, the League continued faithfully to press for a child protection law, prison reform, appointment of women to government boards, and amendments to the civil code.

[119]*Daily Star*, Oct. 6, 1941. *The Canadian Parliamentary Guide* (Ottawa, 1943), pp. 609-10. The author's great-aunt, a resident of Huntingdon, sallied forth to the polls at the age of ninety-one.

[120]Some small satisfaction may have come to Godbout in the knowledge that the popular vote for his party was larger than for the Union Nationale. M. Godbout also polled heavily in Montreal electoral districts where women voted in larger numbers proportionately than in the rural districts of the province.

[121]A by-election in Huntingdon County on July 23, 1947 furnished the opportunity for the shelving of another Quebec tradition, when Mrs. Mae L. O'Conner, Liberal, became the first woman in the province to run for the legislative assembly. She was defeated by a score of 3402 to 2675. Huntingdon *Gleaner*, July 30, 1947.

[122]This was the Charlevoix-Saguenay by-election of Nov. 30, 1942, occasioned by Hon. Pierre Casgrain's acceptance of a federal judgeship. Although Mme Casgrain ran second in the five-man race, she secured more than twice the number of the combined votes of the last three candidates. *The Canadian Parliamentary Guide* (Ottawa, 1945), p. 349. Three women candidates appeared in the federal campaign of 1949, a record second only to that of Ontario which had six. The three in Quebec represented minor political groups and all were badly defeated.

While many of these objectives are still to be achieved, experience has taught Quebec's women leaders that social gains, like political successes, are not attained without long and patient groundwork.

A definite sense of accomplishment came to the League with the federal government's appointment of a Penal Commission to inquire into conditions in federal penitentiaries, as recommended by the Archambault Report. This was a step which the League had strenuously advocated and in which they had helped to stir up public interest by organizing a delegation of several Montreal men's and women's organizations to the federal minister of justice in 1944.

A truly striking success was scored by the women in 1945— and by the women alone. Payment of the new federal family allowance cheques was to be made to mothers in every province except Quebec, where fathers originally were designated as the recipients. Stung by the obvious reflection upon Quebec women, the League and several other women's groups, acting under the leadership of Mme Casgrain, raised sufficient uproar to persuade the federal government to change its mind.[123]

In no other province of the dominion is there a greater challenge facing women in the post-war years than in Quebec, for no other province is saddled with such a mountain of archaic legislation. To be sure, married women may vote, may be legislators, judges, or members of the federal House of Commons and senate; but in the eyes of the Quebec civil code they are classed with children and idiots.[124] Just how long they will be content with this unique position, once they really understand the power that is theirs to wield, remains to be seen. Political freedom is a mockery while social thraldom continues to exist.

[123]Letter from Mme Georges Garneau to the author, Sept. 26, 1946. Letter from Miss Elizabeth C. Monk to the author, Aug. 16, 1945. Mrs. Mostyn Lewis succeeded Mme Garneau as president of the League in the fall of 1946.

[124]On Feb. 1, 1947, a brief on the legal incapacities of women under the laws of Quebec was submitted to the Commissioner appointed in 1946 by the government of the Province of Quebec to conduct an inquiry on the Legal Status of Married Women. The brief, drawn up by Miss Elizabeth C. Monk and Dr. Jacques Perrault, was submitted by a joint committee representing the League for Women's Rights, the Civics League, l'Association pour l'avancement familiale et sociale, the Local Council of Women, and La Fédération Nationale Saint Jean Baptiste—all of Montreal.

# APPENDICES

# *A*

## WOMEN IN CANADIAN POLITICS

POLITICAL EQUALITY is a prize not to be lightly held. Though it came to Canadian women without the harshness and bitterness of the struggle in Great Britain, it was won by the hard work and heartaches of small groups of women throughout the dominion who had the courage and vision to seek it. They gave precious years of their lives to securing political equality for women, and they hoped their successors would assume the responsibilities as well as the privileges of enfranchisement.

How well have Canadian women lived up to the hopes of those who blazed the trail? For the purposes of this survey the author has chosen to let the women of Canada speak for themselves, on the assumption that they are in the best position to appraise their own situation. While a few magazine articles have contributed ideas, most of the thoughts were expressed in interviews with and letters to the author. The twenty-five or thirty women who have been good enough to vouchsafe their opinions include pioneers of woman suffrage, women in political life, professional women, and active participants in women's organizations. Geographically, they represent every province in the dominion. They also represent, it must be remembered, the minority which is keenly aware of its responsibilities, and correspondingly apt to feel frustrated by the inertia of the majority.

If public office-holding be made the yardstick for measuring Canadian women's awareness of their political obligations, the record is certainly disappointing, though few would probably subscribe fully to Dr. Charlotte Whitton's indictment: "We remain the most inert, in the consciousness or use of our power, of women in nations the world over."[1] As previously stated in Chapter V, there have been, until 1949, only five women members in the federal House and two in the senate, with no woman ever attaining cabinet rank at

[1]Charlotte Whitton, C.B.E., "Women the World Over," *Chatelaine* (Toronto), Sept. 1946, p. 58.

Ottawa. The federal election of June 27, 1949 was a blow to those who hoped that while women's political progress was slow, it was at least steady. Only fifteen women were nominated (three less than in 1945) and all fifteen were defeated. For the first time in twenty-eight years, no woman's voice was heard from the floor of the House.

Since 1916, when the first three provinces let down the barriers to public office, there have been only two women cabinet members (Mrs. Mary Ellen Smith of British Columbia and Dr. Irene Parlby of Alberta) and twenty-two members of provincial legislatures (twenty-three, if Newfoundland's Lady Squires is included). In 1949 there are five women members, only one east of Alberta: two in Alberta, two in British Columbia, and one in Ontario. This means that approximately 50 per cent of Canada's population has no female representation at all in the provincial legislatures; while Ontario, with almost one-third of the dominion's inhabitants, is content with one. As noted before, Nova Scotia, New Brunswick, Prince Edward Island, and Quebec have never returned a woman to their assemblies.

In municipal affairs, where women could probably be most helpful and where they have held office in Great Britain by the thousands, the situation is no better. Dr. Charlotte Whitton finds that out of 4100 units of local government in the dominion, but 46 had women office-holders in 1946 for a total of 48 positions. The numbers ranged all the way from seventeen in Saskatchewan and fifteen in Ontario down to one for Quebec and none at all in New Brunswick and Prince Edward Island. Even the progressiveness of Manitoba and British Columbia failed to produce more than three and two.[2]

Of the five women holding provincial office today, three are of the newer and less orthodox parties: the two Alberta members are Social Credit and the Ontario member is C.C.F. Further, of the five women who have served in the House of Commons, only two represented the traditional parties.

A clearer perspective of the situation may, perhaps, be gained if the record of Canadian women is contrasted with that of women in other representative countries where they enjoy political equality.

As of early 1949, there were twenty-one women M.P.'s in Great Britain, a slight drop from the record high of twenty-four elected in 1945. The twenty-one included eighteen Labour members. Since Lady Astor's election in 1919, the number of women members has

[2] Charlotte Whitton, "Is the Canadian Woman a Flop in Politics?" *Saturday Night*, Jan. 26, 1946.

fluctuated mildly, rising to fifteen in 1931 and falling to nine in 1935. There have been only two women cabinet members, the Right Honourable Margaret Bondfield, minister of labour from 1929 to 1931, and the Right Honourable Ellen Wilkinson, minister of education from 1945 until her death early in 1947. In the local sphere, where British women have always served in good numbers, they have made unusually heavy inroads, particularly in urban centres where the Labour party is strong.

From the memorable day of Jeannette Rankin's election to the House in 1916 (four years before the adoption of the woman suffrage amendment), there have been only forty-six women in the United States Congress. This includes seven senators, five of them appointed and one elected to fill unexpired terms. Nine women were elected to the eighty-first Congress (1949-51); eight representatives and one senator. The election of Senator Margaret Chase Smith of Maine in November 1948 (after eight years of service in the House) roused considerable interest because she is the only woman to have been elected to the upper chamber without first having been chosen to fill out the unexpired term of some other senator. Unlike Canada, where only one of the five women M.P.'s has been re-elected (Mrs. George Black did not try to be), nineteen of the forty American women representatives have been returned to office, six of them more than once.

Frances Perkins, who headed the Department of Labour under President Franklin D. Roosevelt, has been the only woman to achieve federal cabinet status. As of April 1949 there were 217 women serving in state legislatures, a reduction of 17 below the to date highest figure of 234 in 1946. Women have served as Governor of Wyoming, Secretaries of State in Connecticut and South Dakota, and State Treasurer in Idaho. In the United States women have equal representation on the national committees of both major parties and on most state committees, and it is estimated that they do about 80 per cent of the election district work, faithful wheel-horses that they are!

In Australia and New Zealand, where political equality was born, women have been conscientious voters, but have not sought office. There have been but two women in the federal parliament of Australia and three in New Zealand. In the Union of South Africa, where enfranchisement came late (1930), there have been just two.

After the elections of 1946, approximately one-fifth of the seats in the Supreme Soviet were held by women and women held about one-third of the local offices. Two of the republics which make up the U.S.S.R. had women presidents that year.

In France and Japan political equality came to women only after the second world war: to one group in the hour of liberation, to the other amid the despair of conquest. In spite of the disparity in the situations, the women of both countries have displayed an amazing degree of political consciousness in this brief period. Since 1944 the women of France have gone to the polls in good numbers on several occasions and as a result of the elections in January 1947 hold approximately one-tenth of the seats in the National Assembly and about the same proportion of mayoralties. Mmes Madeleine Braun and Germaine Peyrolle are serving as vice-presidents of the National Assembly.

Japanese women, in whom subjection to the male has been inculcated from time immemorial, ran 82 candidates in the first post-war election and succeeded in electing 39, not quite one-tenth of the Diet. The new feminine members showed a surprising degree of political astuteness when they promptly formed a club and agreed to vote as a bloc, regardless of parties, on such basic issues as food control, which they felt women were more capable of solving than men.[3]

These figures would seem to indicate that on the provincial and local planes especially, Canada has made a poorer showing than the two larger English-speaking democracies, even when allowance has been made for the disproportion in population. Contained in them, moreover, is a distinct challenge to the women of the three countries where political equality has held sway for more than a quarter of a century from the women of newly enfranchised areas.

[3]The information for the facts on women outside Canada has been culled from several sources: letter to the author from British Information Service, New York, Nov. 21, 1946; C. Whitton, "Women the World Over;" *Equal Rights* (official organ of the National Woman's Party, publ. bi-monthly at Washington, D.C.), Sept.-Oct. 1945; Page H. Dougherty, "It's a Man's Game, But Woman Is Learning," New York *Times Magazine*, Oct. 3, 1946; New York *Times*, Jan. 2, 4, 1947; Marie Alix Lamotte, "Effect of the Women's Franchise on French Elections Is Mixed," *Saturday Night*, Mar. 1, 1947; Lindsay Parrott, "Now a Japanese Woman Can Be a Cop," New York *Times Magazine*, June 2, 1946; *Herald-Tribune* (New York), Jan. 26, 1947; Mme A. H. Askanasy, "Women's Organization for World Order, No. 3" (a typewritten document of 7 pages, Lynn Creek, B.C., May 16, 1946), forwarded to me by Miss Agnes Macphail. The British Information Service, New York, furnished the figures on women M.P.'s in 1949. Facts concerning American women in Congress were derived from a mimeographed bulletin, "Record of Service of Women in the United States Congress," published by the Publicity Division, Republican National Committee, Washington, D.C., April 1949.

Though outstanding leaders among them frankly concede that Canadian women have been a disappointment where office-holding is concerned, they are divided on the question of whether the case ought to rest there or whether other factors should be taken into consideration. Broadly speaking, the prevailing view in eastern Canada is that while women have been fairly conscientious about going to the polls, they have shown a depressing lack of initiative about assuming a more active role in politics, have exhibited an alarming lack of concern over public questions, and know little about applying pressure upon slow-moving governments. Mrs. F. A. Lane, women's editor of the Halifax *Chronicle*, takes some exception to this viewpoint. She maintains that in pre-war days Halifax had very active Women's Liberal and Conservative Clubs and also many other women's organizations which, though non-political, took a lively interest in public affairs.[4] The situation in Halifax, however, appears to be a happy exception rather than a normal pattern in the East. Moreover, although all the larger cities of Canada have their quota of active women's organizations, in most cases the objectives of those organizations are not primarily the settlement of political issues nor do they often understand the techniques of effective political action.[5]

As opinion is tapped in the more westerly areas of Canada, a note of optimism appears in the reactions, along with the usual confessions of disappointment. Three pioneer feminists of the Prairie Provinces point with pride to the broad scope of social legislation enacted in Manitoba, Saskatchewan, Alberta, and British Columbia and find it directly traceable to the influence and balloting power of women.[6] Dr. Margaret McWilliams of Winnipeg not only subscribes wholeheartedly to this view, but also feels that women have done much to clean up political life throughout the dominion.

Another factor must be added to the credit side of the ledger, one which the author's Canadian correspondents were too modest perhaps to mention, for it appears in not one of their letters. The successful functioning of the dominion's Wartime Prices and Trade Board during the recent war was the envy of countries the world

[4]Letter of Mrs. F. A. Lane, Sept. 3, 1946. Mrs. Cecil Stewart of Charlottetown, P.E.I. writes (Nov. 17, 1943) that the Island has "an unusually intelligent electorate," but deeply regrets that no woman has ever even offered herself as a candidate.
[5]Letter of Mrs. George V. Ferguson, Montreal, Jan. 4, 1947.
[6]A. A. Perry, "Is Woman's Suffrage a Fizzle?" *Maclean's*, Feb. 1, 1928; Dr. Irene Parlby speaking on the CBC National Forum, *The Position of Women in Canada*, Dec. 11, 1938; letter of Mrs. A. V. Thomas, Winnipeg, Nov. 18, 1946.

over, especially in the United States where the operations of the comparable Office of Price Administration left so much to be desired. While there is no intention of detracting from the credit due Mr. Donald Gordon and his able assistants in the administration of the programme, it could never have functioned as smoothly as it did without the intelligent support of the women of Canada—an object lesson, surely, in good citizenship.

Granting, then, that it is a mistake to make office-holding the sole gauge for measuring women's political consciousness and activity, we still face the fact that the overwhelming weight of opinion among Canadians sitting in judgment upon their fellow Canadians is that the political performance of the dominion's women has thus far been a disappointment. Their methods of expressing this conviction range all the way from the frankness of Dr. Whitton to the oft-heard apology that political immaturity is a national failing. Mrs. Grace MacInnis wrote in 1946: "Neither men nor women are yet pulling their weight in politics."

Attempts to analyze this self-confessed lethargy yield a wide variety of musings, theories, and inward searchings. One of the most commonly expressed causes, which seems to have a substantial basis in fact, is the widespread economic dependence of women upon men in Canada. The number of families which can afford to maintain domestic help is not large; hence most married women (in a society still rather close to the pioneering stage in many places) are absorbed in the cares of home and family. In most cases they are not able to take an active interest in political matters until middle life and then it is frequently too late to acquire the necessary background. Miss Aileen Garland of Winnipeg adds that there are also many very capable married women more or less barred from political activity because of the adverse effect it might entail upon their husbands' positions.

Among unmarried women who earn their own living, very few are self-employed and even the minority who are self-employed in professions are busy "building up a business against odds." Miss Garland points out that men who go into politics are drawn largely from three classes: lawyers, who are their own bosses or are connected with a firm which recognizes the value of political connections; farmers, whose work is seasonal; and business men, who own their own businesses. Salaries paid to lawmakers, particularly at the local and provincial levels, do not permit employed women to give up their regular positions.

An explanation advanced, oddly enough, by two suffrage pioneers as well as by Dr. Whitton is that Canadian women got the vote too easily to appreciate it. Mrs. A. V. Thomas contends that a struggle for the franchise would have awakened women to the importance of the ballot, while Dr. Whitton over-simplifies the case with the flat assertion, "Canadian women got the vote as a gift rather than a reward." There is, however, a great element of truth in her charge that, "The women of this country, like the Canadian democracy as a whole, are but half-appreciative beneficiaries of rich legacies of freedoms, rights and privileges which have been bequeathed by greater, earlier crusaders in the two lands to which we are most closely allied—the United Kingdom and the United States."[7]

Several of the first generation of voters deplore the willingness of women to follow the male lead in politics or, in cases where they have been politically active, to be content in most instances with membership in ladies' auxiliaries of the parties rather than direct party membership. The latter has resulted in their doing much of the drudgery, with payment in the form of "window dressing" jobs and a gentle pat on the back. Writing in 1928, on the occasion of the tenth anniversary of federal enfranchisement, Mrs. A. A. Perry alleged: "Although we have been endowed with that magic tool,the vote, which only a few of us so ardently desired, and which most of us have used so inadequately for nearly a decade, we are still so lacking in vision and self-respect that we follow the male leaders selected for us, discount our own power and carefully refrain from trying to use it directly."[8] While conceding women's passive willingness to follow men's lead in politics, a younger generation of Canadian leaders is emphatic about saying that when women do enter politics it will be as *persons*, not *women*. Their contention is that the old idea of female against male died with the achievement of equal suffrage and that the body politic should ideally consist of a working partnership between men and women.[9]

[7]C. Whitton, "Is the Canadian Woman a Flop in Politics?" The other pioneer referred to is Dr. Grace Ritchie-England of Montreal.
[8]A. A. Perry, *op. cit.*
[9]Mrs. MacInnis and Mrs. Ferguson are strong proponents of this idea. Speaking at the annual meeting of the Y.W.C.A. in Montreal early in 1946, Miss Byrne Hope Sanders said: "It is only as partners that men and women can achieve anything stable for the national good." Quoted in the Royal Bank of Canada's *Monthly Letter* of July 1946.

The tradition that politics is a man's game is not lightly broken in the minds of either men or women, especially among a people as conservatively inclined as Canadians. Mrs. Florence Bird professes to be expressing the attitude of the average male when she writes that Canadian men "regard career women and women in politics with dark suspicion. They really think there are 'men's things' and 'women's things' in separate compartments." Canadian women, especially those of her own province, come off little better at the hands of Mme Georges Garneau. "There are always the same handful who show interest, but the majority of women seem quite indifferent—and in some cases, hostile. There are groups who still think it is unladylike, if not vaguely immoral, for women to be interested in politics."

Stemming directly from this nineteenth-century attitude toward women in politics is the fact that political parties in Canada, particularly the two traditional ones, do not encourage women to take an active political role. The large number of women who make this indictment against political parties is rather surprising, and, even more so, is the fact that the charge comes from the West as well as the East. The majority of those expressing this opinion attribute it to the debatable fact that men fear women's ability and take this method of preserving the sphere of politics for themselves. Indignant men may be gratified to learn, however, that some of their detractors are willing to admit that, while this attitude may have been true in the past, it is gradually changing (perhaps hastened by the recent war) and that men would now welcome women into political activities. The latter group admonishes women, moreover, that they must take the initiative, that political parties and the men who run them will not go out to seek women candidates. Writing in the New York *Times Magazine*, Page Dougherty amusingly theorizes that women have made the mistake of expecting to be wooed for office in much the same fashion as marriage traditions dictate. This has been a serious error in judgment, for men in politics operate on an entirely different set of principles from men in love.

Harking back for a moment to tradition as a barrier to women's entrance into politics, the theory of innate Canadian conservatism is one that appears to intrigue thinking Canadians greatly, for they offer a variety of explanations for it and an interesting assortment of corollaries related to it.   Miss Laila Scott finds it to be a psychological remnant of Victorianism, which dominates much of the thinking of Canada as far west as the Prairies.[10] Its forbears, according to Mrs. Mary Ferguson, are an outdated survival of the colonial frame of mind and "a reaction to the wealth and bustle of the United States." Whatever its sources, this conservatism manifests itself in an exaggerated cult of "gentility" which exerts pressure upon women even more forcibly than upon men. Waxing warm upon this thesis, Mrs. Ferguson continues: "Our hats are much milder than American hats and there are a thousand more indicators! We react against show and expenditure of any kind. Elaborate this idea further (it's one of my favourites), and you can see that politics at every level suffers under the socially acceptable standards of 'gentility.' "

The game of politics certainly requires aggressiveness from its aspirants; yet if there is any quality more universally despised in women by members of both sexes, it would be difficult to find. Closely related to the cultivation of "gentility" and the desire to avoid giving an impression of aggressiveness, are the dread of appearing conspicuous at public meetings and the fear of being "set right" before an audience by someone with greater knowledge, authority, or assurance. Canadian women (from innate modesty rather than conservatism—this is my own opinion) appear to believe that one must be a recognized authority on a subject before rising to speak, an impression no doubt intensified by the fact that so many English women who have come to the dominion as public personages have been exceedingly well informed. And with that we are back again to the colonial frame of mind.[11]

Many thousands of Canadian women, especially of the older generations, feel hampered in entering public life by the lack of sufficient educational background, both general and political. This

[10]A former Canadian, now an American citizen, in his presidential address to the Canadian Historical Association in 1940 gave added weight to the general theory of conservatism. "One last group of essential Canadian qualities . . . really amounts to conservatism—a canny, deliberate approach to questions of political, social, or cultural change. . . . This caution has the effect of a time lag . . . which often means that Canada gets around to some social reform long after other countries have tested it and found it good . . . . the women of Canada have every right to complain because their position in society has lagged behind what has been conceded to their sex in the British Isles and the United States. There is still a strong Canadian prejudice against women in the professions, re-inforced by an almost universal belief that no woman should keep up her work after marriage." J. B. Brebner, "Canadianism," *Canadian Historical Association Report*, Toronto, 1940, p. 13.
[11]While Mrs. Ferguson was responsible for the quotations used in this sortie into the realms of conservatism, Miss Garland, Miss Scott, Mrs. MacInnis, and Dr. McWilliams have ably seconded her, as well as adding observations of their own.

is variously attributed to curriculum deficiencies in social studies in the schools and universities of the dominion, absence of higher institutions of learning exclusively for women—such as the great American women's colleges of the East, and most of all to the lack of political study groups in all parts of the country. Although Mme A. H. Askanasy of British Columbia has had some degree of success in establishing citizenship schools for women in western Canada and individual civics groups are to be found in most of the larger cities, it is rather significant that the dominion has fostered no national women's organization for the education of voters comparable to the League of Women Voters in the United States. Moreover, the few attempts that were made to convert suffrage organizations into study groups after enfranchisement died young of malnutrition.

Totally unrelated to any theory for feminine political apathy advanced thus far is the speculation that women are more direct than men about going after the things they want and hence find politics, with all its devious ways, baffling and frustrating. Dr. Ritchie-England adds that there is so little difference in the issues presented to the electorate by the two old-line parties that women tend to lose interest anyway. Mrs. E. M. Murray, octogenarian suffrage veteran of Nova Scotia, approaches the theory from a slightly different angle, but reaches the same conclusion. "I am personally of the opinion that they [women] are somewhat appalled when they think of the task ahead—to try to make good on the errors men have made. Not only Canadian men but men everywhere, judging from the state the world is in."

Mrs. Ferguson has an interesting hypothesis that Canadian women's organizations themselves have exercised a debilitating influence upon women's political activities. As urbanization increases and women naturally look for groups with which to affiliate, they join church clubs, social groups, and welfare organizations, the types of associations most readily available. These organizations, to keep their membership intact, avoid politics like the plague and construe "politics" to mean almost any public question. It is Mrs. Ferguson's contention that the majority of clubs which constitute themselves as study groups prefer to investigate Italian Art or World Travel or almost anything rather than the problems and processes of Canadian government. While admitting that there are many women's organizations which do strive actively for community betterment, Mrs. Ferguson maintains that they frequently absorb the energies of their members to such an extent that the women fail to realize it is in the political arena, in the last analysis, that things really get done. To this entire hypothesis Mrs. F. A. Lane takes emphatic exception, citing the fact that Halifax, a city of approximately 100,000 population, supports 176 women's clubs many of which, though non-political, "wield considerable influence on questions of public interest."

Peculiar to Quebec has been the pronounced hostility of the Roman Catholic Church to women in public life, which Dr. Ritchie-England believes has not only had a deadening effect upon the political activities of French-speaking women, but has also shown a tendency to carry over into the English-speaking portion of the population. As pointed out in Chapter VII, this attitude of the Quebec segment of the Church does not coincide with the views expressed by the Supreme Pontiff in the past several years. As recently as October 21, 1945 the Pope issued a message encouraging women to exercise their political rights and to co-operate with men in working for the good of the state.[12]

Only Miss Scott, among all those expressing views for this survey, mentioned a factor which, though undoubtedly affecting men more than women, could possibly shed some light upon the problem. She refers to the steady draining off of Canada's most precious possession to the United States. Attracted by more glittering prospects than their native land appeared able to offer, thousands of the dominion's most promising young people emigrated to the United States in the decades between the two world wars, a process halted only by Canada's entry into the second world conflict. It is conceivable that among their number were many young women who, had they remained at home, might have been engaging in political action and furnishing that leadership, the lack of which their young country feels so keenly. In this viewpoint Miss Scott receives powerful reinforcement from Professor J. B. Brebner's monograph, *Scholarship for Canada*. Discussing Canada's failure to retain gifted Canadians, Professor Brebner opines that it was not only an economic magnet which caused the exodus. "Pioneering young Canadians must have found that the inertia of their entrenched elders had

[12]C. Whitton, "Women the World Over," p. 58. This advice was not tendered in any formal encyclical, but was proffered to a group of Italian women to whom the Pontiff had granted an audience. *The National Catholic Almanac, 1946*, (published annually by St. Anthony's Guild, Paterson, N.J.), p. 769.

drained Canadian life of color, zest, adventure, and the stimulation which comes from free-ranging experimentation in ideas, in material enterprises, and in the arts. It must have been because they could not feel in Canada the sense of sharing in something more than the defence of things as they are that they left their country seeking 'lots more of something else.' "[13]

What are the prospects that women will assume a more active role in Canadian public life in the post-war era?

Opinions differ widely among Canadian women whether the war itself has made any appreciable difference in women's outlook and status. Pessimism again is the keynote of women in the East as they assert that, to date, women have neither shown any brave new interest in national or world problems, nor have they achieved that lasting economic stability or independence which is the necessary concomitant of political activity. Except for Mrs. Thomas, however, the westerners (including Mrs. Bird and Mrs. Ferguson, who became easterners only in 1947) take a more optimistic view. They mention the important positions held by many women, both in government and industry, and believe that having tasted power, they found it good. They point out the new awareness of government that came to many women through the many warborn governmental controls over civilian life. Women working in recreation and salvage programmes and other "home front" activities often learned for the first time the value of exerting pressure upon the government when action is required. Mrs. Grace MacInnis puts the situation on a somewhat more idealistic plane when she writes: "They are taking hold because the idea of serving human welfare has taken such hold of them that they no longer think of being self-conscious or too busy about other things."

Whether one inclines to the darker or brighter view of the war-time picture, there are some facts and statistics which cannot be ignored. Certain it is that women were employed in positions of great responsibility as never before by both the federal and provincial governments. (See Chapter V, footnote 86, for some outstanding dominion appointments.) Apart from the relatively limited number of top positions, women by the thousands, both single and married, improved their economic status during the war, either by working for the first time or by changing to better paying jobs.

[13]John Bartlet Brebner, *Scholarship for Canada* (published by the Canadian Social Science Research Council, Ottawa, 1945), p. 8.

The number of women in the three branches of the armed services alone (non-existent, of course, before the war) reached a peak of 35,856 in December 1944 and still included 31,942 on V-J Day.[14]

While the number of women workers in agriculture remained relatively stable throughout the war,[15] the normal trend of employing an ever widening number of women in industry was greatly accelerated during the war years. The figures for women employed in non-agricultural industry rose from 689,000 on October 1, 1939 to 1,015,000 on October 1, 1945, with war industries registering an impressive increase from 6,000 to 64,000 during the same period, having reached their amazing peak of 261,000 in 1943. The proportion of married women in non-agricultural industry showed a sharp trend upward from 10 per cent of all employed women in 1941 to 23 per cent in 1946.[16]

Another direct outcome of the war was that women received considerably higher pay owing to the exodus from domestic service and influx into manufacturing. Certain industries, such as aircraft manufacturing and shipbuilding, paid women an average weekly wage of $31.81, whereas the highest average weekly wage for women in the pre-war period was $15.83, in the fur goods industry. The average weekly wage for all women workers in manufacturing industries rose from $12.10 in 1938 to $19.33 in 1943.[17] Finally, owing to the need of replacing men, the war greatly increased the occupational dispersion of women,[18] thereby opening new avenues of employment to them which will never be entirely relinquished, even in years of peace.

Facts and figures available for the reconversion period suggest that it is still a man's world and that women are far from achieving lasting financial independence. At the same time, they certainly do not warrant complete pessimism. Largely because of the sudden closing down of war industries, 90,000 women lost their jobs in less than one year, from V-J Day to May 1, 1946; yet the highest number of women ever registered as unemployed was 49,000. That was in

[14]Canadian Information Service, "Canadian War Data," *1946 Reference Papers Series, No. 4* (Ottawa, May 15, 1946), Table 9, p. 6.

[15]It was 805,000 on Oct. 1, 1939 and 810,000 on Oct. 1, 1945, though it dropped to 765,000 in October 1943.

[16]"Canadian War Data," *op. cit.*, Table 1, p. 3. Statistics Branch, Department of Labour, "Women Workers in the Reconversion," *Canadian Labour Market*, II, no. 6 (Ottawa, July 15, 1946), p. 1. The number of women in non-agricultural industry reached its peak of 1,060,000 on Oct. 1, 1943.

[17]*Ibid.*, p. 2.

[18]*Ibid.*, p. 1.

March 1946 and the number had dropped to 37,700 by June 30. The relatively low unemployment figures resulted from the withdrawal of many married women from the labour force. (Sixty-eight thousand women withdrew between November 1945 and February 1946.) "Women Workers in the Reconversion" (p. 3) makes the assertion that this "was partly voluntary and in part because both government and private industry adopted a policy of excluding married women from employment to provide positions for returning servicemen."

As though such a policy were not a strange enough reward to those who filled the breach on the home front so capably, the federal government discriminated severely against employed married women in the income tax for the fiscal year 1946-1947.[19] Whether directly affected by this discriminatory tax or not, women would scarcely need to have the Department of Labour point out that: "This policy [of discrimination against the employment of married women] is indicative of the extreme vulnerability of women in the employment field."[20] Both "Women Workers in the Reconversion" and the report of the sub-committee on *Post-War Problems of Women* clearly recognize the right of *all* women to work at whatever occupations they choose with "equality of remuneration, working conditions, and opportunity for advancement."[21] A far cry, these brave recommendations, from the actualities facing many women, especially those who are married, in post-war Canada!

Despite these discouraging factors, many women, married and single, who did not originally intend to remain, are staying on in the ranks of labour. The pleasure to be derived from an independent income vies with necessity in holding them there. More women are

[19]*Ibid.*, p. 4. Although the Minister of Finance, in a letter to the author dated July 17, 1947, emphatically denied any such intention on the part of the government, the terms of the act lead one to the inevitable conclusion that it was aimed directly at forcing married women out of employment. The law provided that a married man supporting his wife be granted an allowance of $1500, but that this allowance be reduced by the amount of any income which the wife received in excess of $250. The conclusion becomes more obvious when it is recalled that before 1942 a husband was allowed to claim the full married allowance of $1500 if his wife's income was under $750, and that during the war he was allowed to claim full exemption *regardless of the amount of his wife's earnings*. Were any further proof needed, this should confirm beyond dispute Professor Brebner's assertion that there is "an almost universal belief that no woman should keep up her work after marriage."

[20]"Women Workers in the Reconversion," *op. cit.*, p. 4.

[21]*Ibid.*, p. 4. The quotation is from the report of the subcommittee of the Advisory Committee on Reconstruction, *Post-War Problems of Women* (Ottawa, 1944), pp. 9-10.

employed today than ever before and at higher wages: two definite advances toward that economic independence which makes possible a broadening of interests and the emergence of women into wider fields of activity and usefulness.

While there has been no sudden blossoming forth of feminine candidates for office in either dominion or provincial elections within the post-war years, there is some evidence to indicate that political parties are becoming increasingly aware of the need to offer women something more in the way of political activity than to do party chores and to vote for their candidates (male, of course) on election days. This is doubtless due in good part to the fear that the C.C.F., which has paid more than lip-service to political equality in its activities, will come in time to exert too powerful an attraction upon women voters.

An important step forward was taken by the Progressive-Conservative Association at its annual convention in Ottawa in March 1946 when it adopted unanimously the following resolution:

> Whereas women constitute more than 50 per cent of the voting strength of the nation:
> And Whereas women have never been and are not now accorded the representation in Parliament and on Government commissions and authorities to which their number and proved capacity entitle them:
> And Whereas women, by their patriotic endeavours and executive functions during wartime have qualified themselves to take an ever increasing part in the Government of Canada:
> Therefore Be It Resolved that this Association recommend:
> a) The appointment of more women to the Senate of Canada
> b) The nomination of more women candidates in the next Federal election
> c) The appointment of women to Governmental commissions . . .
> d) The amendment of the Civil Service Act . . . to establish the eligibility of women to all positions in the civil service
> e) The appointment of women to the Board of Examiners for Civil Service appointments.[22]

It sounds almost like the millenium, but the acid test is "deeds not words." (In the federal electoral campaign of 1949, the Progressive-Conservative party placed *four* women candidates in the field.)

At the same convention a new party office was created, that of Director of the Progressive-Conservative Women of Canada. Miss Hilda Hesson, after her election to the post, asked for recognition

[22]*Evening Citizen* (Ottawa), April 1, 1946.

of women "as part and parcel of the organization, not to be known as auxiliaries."[23] Apparently some progress along this line was made, for in her letter of October 28, 1946 she states that a regulation of the Progressive-Conservative party requires that fifty per cent of the officers of the Association be women.

The national Liberal Association, with less fanfare and formality, adopted a similar policy of encouraging its women members to assume a more active role in party counsels when it revised its constitution in November 1945. The Liberals also antedated the Conservatives in the creation of a top executive party office to be held by a woman. Mrs. S. C. Tweed of Ottawa became assistant director of the National Liberal Federation of Canada when that position was created in 1943.[24] But if performance is again made the criterion for gauging the seriousness of these promises, the Liberal record in 1949 is worse than the Conservative. Only one of the fifteen women candidates carried the Liberal party's endorsement!

In attempting to forecast the degree of awakening to political consciousness that may be expected of Canadian women in the near future, two other indications of a somewhat hopeful nature should not be overlooked. One has been the formation of a women's organization at Montreal which its sponsors hope will become in time the equivalent of the American League of Women Voters. Plans for such an association were announced at a luncheon of the veteran League for Women's Rights in March 1947, at which Miss Anna Lord Strauss, president of the American organization, was guest speaker.[25] Bowing gracefully out of a situation which had grown too big for it, the League drew its affairs to a close and merged its identity with other women's organizations to form a Canadian Association of Women Voters two months later. Should this project succeed, one of the most compelling needs in the field of political education for Canadian women should be satisfied.

The other harbinger of future improvement lies in the fact that Canada's amazing wartime development should offer more attractive possibilities to outstanding young Canadians and encourage them to remain at home where their youthful courage and idealism are so much needed.

[23]*Ibid.*, April 1, 1946.
[24]Letter to the author from Mrs. S. C. Tweed, April 25, 1947; revised constitution enclosed. Mrs. Tweed died in 1949.
[25]*Gazette*, Mar. 22, 1947. Letters of Mme Georges Garneau, Mar. 23, 1947 and of Mme Pierre Casgrain, April 16, 1947.

Partly as the result of slowly maturing design and partly through the fortunes of shattering world conflict, Canada has at last emerged a full-fledged nation and one of the more important "lesser powers" of the world. Today Canada's voice is heard with respect in the councils of the nations and must be raised in support of sound and wise decisions. In a democracy, a nation's voice is only that of its collective people—all people, both men and women.

# *B*

## BIBLIOGRAPHICAL NOTES

### I. Unpublished Sources

In attempting to chart a pioneer course through a comparatively unexplored field, many of the most important bibliographical aids are, necessarily, "original sources." While in the natural course of events some of the earlier of Canada's prominent feminists were beyond reach at the time this history was undertaken, many of the second and third generation woman suffrage leaders are still very much alive. They have been, almost without exception, most gracious and helpful about answering questions. So generous, indeed, have they been, through the media of both interviews and letters, that the author feels under a tremendous debt of gratitude to them.

Many other Canadians, not directly connected with the woman suffrage movement themselves, have been subjected to a similar barrage of questions. They, too, have been prodigal of their resources: offering clues to the whereabouts of suffrage leaders, personal recollections of friends and relatives connected with the movement, legal assistance, and personal opinions on the progress of women in Canadian public life. Their contributions have been of inestimable value.

The following persons have aided the author by correspondence or personal interview; in many instances by both methods.

The Honourable Attorneys-General of the dominion of Canada, and of the provinces of British Columbia, Manitoba, New Brunswick, Ontario, Prince Edward Island, and Saskatchewan.
The Honourable Douglas C. Abbott, Ottawa, Ontario.
Mrs. A. Netlam Beer, Montreal, Quebec.
Miss Francis M. Beynon, New York.
Mrs. John Bird, Ottawa, Ontario.
Mrs. George Black, Yukon Territory.
British Information Service, New York.

Canadian Information Service, Ottawa, Ontario, and New York.
Mme Pierre Casgrain, Montreal, Quebec.
Mrs. Cora Casselman, Edmonton, Alberta.
Mrs. Carrie Chapman Catt, New Rochelle, New York. (Deceased.)
The City Clerks of Quebec City, Quebec, and Toronto, Ontario.
Miss May Clendenan, London, Ontario.
Mr. and Mrs. Merrill Denison, New York.
Dr. Agnes Dennis, Halifax, Nova Scotia.    (Deceased.)
Mrs. Rex Eaton, Ottawa, Ontario.
Miss Margaret Evans, Saint John, New Brunswick.
Mrs. George V. Ferguson, Montreal, Quebec.
Miss Avis Fyshe, Montreal, Quebec.
Mrs. Claude Gardiner, Victoria, British Columbia.
Miss Aileen Garland, Winnipeg, Manitoba.
Mme Georges Garneau, Montreal, Quebec.
Miss Jean M. Gill, Charlottetown, Prince Edward Island.
Mrs. George Goodwin, Montreal, Quebec.
Mr. Robert M. Hamilton, Ottawa, Ontario.
Dr. D. C. Harvey, Halifax, Nova Scotia.
Alderman Hilda Hesson, Winnipeg, Manitoba.
Miss Marjorie C. Holmes, Victoria, British Columbia
Mrs. Laura Jamieson, Vancouver, British Columbia.
Mr. J. L. Johnston, Winnipeg, Manitoba.
Mrs. F. A. Lane, Halifax, Nova Scotia.
Mrs. J. V. Lawlor, Saint John, New Brunswick.
Mrs. Walter Lyman, Montreal, Quebec.
Judge Helen Gregory MacGill, Vancouver, British Columbia.
Mrs. Grace MacInnis, Vancouver, British Columbia.
Mr. E. Allison MacKay, Fredericton, New Brunswick.
Mr. R. A. MacKay, Department of External Affairs, Ottawa,
    Ontario.
Miss Agnes Macphail, Toronto, Ontario.
The Honourable Paul Martin, Ottawa, Ontario.
Mrs. Lillian Maxwell, Fredericton, New Brunswick.
Judge J. Boyd McBride, K.C., Edmonton, Alberta.
Mrs. Nellie McClung, Victoria, British Columbia.
Mrs. John McNaughton, Saskatoon, Saskatchewan.
Dr. Margaret McWilliams, Winnipeg, Manitoba.
Miss Marguerite Mitchell, St. John's, Newfoundland.
Miss Elizabeth C. Monk, Montreal, Quebec.

Miss Jessie F. Montgomery, Edmonton, Alberta.
Miss Evelyn Murphy, Vancouver, British Columbia.
Mrs. E. M. Murray, Halifax, Nova Scotia.   (Deceased)
Mrs. Dorise Nielsen, North Battleford, Saskatchewan.
Dr. Irene Parlby, Alix, Alberta.
Miss Annie Peters, Hampton, New Brunswick.
Dr. Grace Ritchie-England, Montreal, Quebec.   (Deceased.)
Mr. Edgar S. Robinson, Vancouver, British Columbia.
Mrs. Newton W. Rowell, Toronto, Ontario.
Mlle Idola Saint Jean, Montreal, Quebec.   (Deceased.)
Miss Byrne Hope Sanders, Ottawa, Ontario.
Mrs. John Scott, Montreal, Quebec.   (Deceased.)
Miss Laila Scott, Toronto, Ontario.
Miss Rosa Shaw, Ottawa, Ontario.
Mrs. Adam Shortt, Ottawa, Ontario.   (Deceased.)
Mrs. Allan L. Smith, Montreal, Quebec.
Mrs. Cecil Stewart, Charlottetown, Prince Edward Island.
Dr. Augusta Stowe-Gullen, Toronto, Ontario.   (Deceased.)
Mrs. Gladys Strum, Windthorst, Saskatchewan.
Major R. H. Tait, New York.
Mrs. A. V. Thomas, Winnipeg, Manitoba.
Miss Inga Thomson, Winnipeg, Manitoba.
Mrs. S. C. Tweed, Ottawa, Ontario.   (Deceased.)
Miss E. M. A. Vaughan, Saint John, New Brunswick.
Miss Ruth Vogel, Winnipeg, Manitoba.
Mrs. Olive Wells, Tunford, Saskatchewan.
Miss Margaret Wherry, Montreal, Quebec.
Dr. Charlotte Whitton, Ottawa, Ontario.
Senator Cairine Wilson, Ottawa, Ontario.
Mrs. W. Milner Wood, Woodman's Point, New Brunswick.

In addition to interviews and letters directed to the author, two very useful source collections were generously placed at her disposal. A year or two before her death in 1943, Dr. Augusta Stowe-Gullen of Toronto consented to lend her the six scrap books which had been compiled over a period of approximately half a century (from the late 1860's to 1917) by her grandmother, Mrs. Hannah Jennings, her mother, Dr. Emily Stowe, and by herself. These bulky volumes contain newspaper clippings, marginal comments by all three compilers, an occasional important letter, copies of petitions, and now and then an old programme detailing the order of events at some long-forgotten woman suffrage festivity. Unfortunately, many of the clippings in the collection are unidentified. The last book is better in this respect than the others, but still leaves much to be desired.

Through the kindness of Miss Evelyn Murphy and of Miss Byrne Hope Sanders, who was putting the finishing touches on her lively biography of Judge Emily Murphy at Ottawa in 1944, that portion of the judge's papers which deals with the Persons Case was placed at the author's disposal. There were dozens of letters written by and to her during the course of her thirteen-year struggle. The unpublished collection of Judge Murphy's papers is at present in the possession of her daughter, Miss Evelyn Murphy of Vancouver.

For certain special aspects of the suffrage question a few unpublished monographs have been useful. At the request of Senator Cairine Wilson in 1943, Judge J. Boyd McBride, K.C. of Edmonton drew up a short but informative"Memorandum as to Women's rights in Alberta," and forwarded it to the author. Because of his long personal friendship and close association with Judge Murphy in the Persons Case, Judge McBride's contribution to the historical background of the movement proved most helpful.

Two typewritten documents of a highly legal flavour are avail able for use in connection with the prolonged struggle of Quebec feminists. A copy of Eugène Lafleur's splendid, though unsuccessful, plea for the admission of Quebec women to the Bar, delivered before the General Council of the Bar of Quebec on September 4, 1929, is on file among the papers of the League for Women's Rights in Montreal. Copies of the brief presented to the Royal Commission on Dominion-Provincial Relations (the Rowell-Sirois Commission) by the League for Women's Rights in April 1938 are on file both in the League offices and among the personal papers of its author, Miss Elizabeth C. Monk of Montreal. There is also a complete file of the Commission's Briefs, Proceedings, and Recommendations in the Law Library of Columbia University, New York.

Three brief and undated articles, apparently prepared as addresses on some unspecified occasions by Judge Helen Gregory MacGill, may be found in the City Archives of Vancouver. Evidence that Judge MacGill maintained an active interest in suffrage matters so long as any Canadian women remained disfranchised is in their titles: "Story of Women Suffrage in British Columbia," "Quebec's New Women," and "Women and Politics in Quebec."

For only three provinces is there available a special source which yields unusually rich dividends for this subject, and for just one of these provinces is the record complete. This is the Minute Books or records of proceedings of certain of the provincial suffrage societies. The League for Women's Rights in Montreal has the complete file of Minute Books from the days of the parent Montreal Suffrage Association in 1913 right down to 1947. For the mid-West there is a Smaller Minute Book of the Political Equality League of Manitoba covering the period from March 29, 1912, through March 31, 1914, which may be found in the Provincial Library of Manitoba. Although there should obviously be at least one other volume to carry the record of the League's undertakings to completion in 1917, all efforts to unearth the hiding-place of such a volume have proven fruitless. The small New Brunswick Branch of the Dominion Women's Enfranchisement Association made its contribution to posterity in the shape of two Minute Books, now in the possession of Mrs. W. Milner Wood, Woodman's Point, King's County, New Brunswick. Mrs. Wood, daughter of Mrs. Frank Hatheway, one of the most active and faithful suffrage pioneers of the province, told the author that she thought there should be one other volume. Whether this is the explanation or whether several missing pages at the beginning of the second volume offer a clue, the records in the two available books cover only the years 1894-1903, 1908-1911, and 1915-1918.

## II. Published Sources

### A. *Statute Books*, *Legislative Journals*, and *Reports of Debates*

In dealing with a subject so closely associated with the development of remedial legislation, great reliance must obviously be placed upon an exhaustive examintion of sources which reveal the day-by-day activities of the federal and provincial legislatures. These volumes fall mainly into three classifications:

(1) *Statute Books:* which constitute a record of the complete contents of all legislation actually passed. They are available for the dominion and for each of the provinces.

(2) *Legislative Journals:* which are the daily reports of the action taken by the various legislatures upon bills, petitions, and motions presented for their consideration throughout each legislative session. In the bicameral federal parliament, separate *Journals* are kept for the senate and the House of Commons. Since seven provinces had

adopted the unicameral form of legislature by 1893, only two (Quebec and Nova Scotia) had double sets of *Journals* during most of the period covered in this history. Even in these two, reference to any significant action taken by the upper chambers is contained in the *Journals* of the lower Houses, which gradually came to supersede their upper counterparts in importance. (Newfoundland retained a bicameral legislature until 1934 and each chamber kept its own *Journals*. However, they were inaccessible to the author at the late date when it became advisable to add the brief section on Newfoundland.)

(3) *Reports of Debates.* A complete verbatim record of proceedings, commonly known as "Hansard," has been kept for the dominion parliament since the period of Confederation (1867) and is formally titled: *Debates of the House of Commons of the Dominion of Canada* and *Debates of the Senate of the Dominion of Canada.* The three Maritime Provinces, for a portion of the period under consideration in this history at least, kept reports of the proceedings of their legislatures; these are partly verbatim accounts and partly summaries of what took place at the sessions. New Brunswick publishes annually at Fredericton its *Synoptic Reports of the Proceedings of the Legislative Assembly of New Brunswick.* Nova Scotia issued *Debates and Proceedings of the House of Assembly of the Province of Nova Scotia* until 1916, while Prince Edward Island gave up publishing *The Parliamentary Reporter* as long ago as 1893. In the Parliamentary Library at Ottawa there is a series of volumes labelled *Ontario: Parliamentary Debates* for the period down to 1910. It consists of the Toronto *Globe's* fairly full accounts of speeches and proceedings in the provincial legislature, and is, of course, unofficial.

Before leaving the subject of available legislative source materials it should be mentioned that the King's Printer (Ottawa) issues annually a publication known as *Bills of the Senate and House of Commons* which gives the contents of bills which did not pass, as well as those that did. This was a helpful source of information in connection with Sir John A. Macdonald's suffrage measures in the 1880's.

B. *Newspapers*

Next in importance to legislative records among the printed source materials available for this study were newspapers from all sections of the country. These not only supplied general accounts of suffrage activities and meetings, but offered a forum for discussion of both sides of the suffrage question and, especially in those provinces where no *Debates and Proceedings* were kept, often threw valuable light on the progress of suffrage resolutions, petitions, and measures in the various legislatures.

(1) British Columbia.
    a. Victoria *Daily Times*.
    b. *Daily Colonist* (Victoria).
    c. *Daily Province* (Vancouver and Victoria).
    d. *British Columbia Federationist* (Vancouver).

(2) Alberta.    Edmonton *Bulletin*.

(3) Saskatchewan.    *Morning Leader* (Regina).

(4) Manitoba.
    a. *Manitoba Free Press* (Winnipeg).    After 1931 known as the Winnipeg *Free Press*.
    b. Winnipeg *Evening Tribune*.
    c. *Grain Growers' Guide* (Winnipeg).

(5) Ontario.
    a. *Globe* (Toronto).
    b. Toronto *Star*.
    c. Toronto *Star Weekly*.
    d. *Evening Telegram* (Toronto).
    e. Ottawa *Citizen*.
    f. Ottawa *Journal*.    Evening edition in 1918-19 known as Ottawa *Journal-Press*.
    g. *Le Droit* (Ottawa).

(6) Quebec.
    a. *Gazette* (Montreal).
    b. Montreal *Daily Star*.
    c. *Le Devoir* (Montreal).
    d. Montreal *Herald*—sometimes Montreal *Herald and Daily Telegraph*.
    e. Montreal *Standard*.
    f. *L'Action Catholique* (Quebec).

(7) New Brunswick.
    a. *Telegraph-Journal* (Saint John).    until 1910 known as *Dailp Telegraph;* from 1911 to July 1923 *Telegraph and Sun*.

    b. *Times-Globe* (Saint John). Until 1910 *Evening Times,* in 1911 *Evening Times and Star,* from 1912 to March 1927 *Times-Star.*

    c. *Daily Sun* (Saint John).

(8) Nova Scotia.

    a. *Morning Chronicle* (Halifax). After 1927 known as the Halifax *Chronicle.*

    b. Halifax *Herald.* Until 1910 the *Morning Herald.*

(9) Prince Edward Island.

    a. Charlottetown *Examiner.* Ceased publication in 1922.

    b. *Patriot* (Charlottetown). Between 1913 and 1925 title varied between *Island Patriot* and *Prince Edward Island Patriot.*

(10) Newfoundland. St. John's *Evening Telegram.*

C. *Pamphlets*

A relatively small amount of pamphlet material is available and of this much was originally issued for other purposes than woman suffrage. The most useful items in this classification are three series of annual reports issued by one national and two local women's organizations. The National Council of Women each year draws reports on women's activities from its affiliated organizations in all corners of the dominion and thus gives a wide general view of the progress of women's affairs in its publication entitled *Women Workers of Canada: The Reports of the Proceedings of the Annual Meetings and Conferences of the National Council of Women of Canada.* Known more commonly as *Year Books,* these reports have been published annually by the Council at Ottawa and Toronto since 1895, with the single exception of 1916. The Local Council of Women of Montreal has also issued *Annual Reports.* In addition, two special anniversary editions: the *Twenty-first Anniversary* and the *Fortieth Anniversary*(1915 and 1934)were published by the Montreal Council. These Montreal *Reports* were especially useful for this study because, unlike many Local Councils, the Montreal group early developed and continuously maintained an interest in woman suffrage. Mlle Idola Saint Jean's organization, l'Alliance Canadienne pour le Vote des Femmes du Québec, adopted the policy of publishing an official organ entitled *La Sphère Féminine.* These little booklets, published annually at Montreal from 1931 until Mlle Saint Jean's death in 1945 and written in both French and English, are open suffrage propaganda, but they contain useful summaries of Quebec women's progress in civil and political status year by year and also brief but well-written articles on feminism by several of the province's outstanding suffragists.

A miscellaneous group of pamphlets published by international, national, and local women's organizations, usually upon the observance of some special occasion, sheds some light on the progress of women in Canada. The international group includes: *The International Council of Women: Report of the Transactions of the Fourth Quinquennial Meeting Held at Toronto, Canada, June 1909*, edited by the Countess of Aberdeen and published in London, 1910; *The International Report of the Fifth Conference of the Woman Suffrage A liance* (London, 1909); and *Woman Suffrage in Practice* (London, 1913), published by the International Woman Suffrage Alliance. The two latter are in the English Pamphlet Collection of the Parliamentary Library (numbers 63 and 96) at Ottawa. On the national scale there are: Hilda M. Ridley, *A Synopsis of Woman Suffrage in Canada* (n.p., n.d.—though probably published in Toronto around 1937), and Dr. Augusta Stowe-Gullen, *History of the Formation of the National Council of Women of Canada* (Toronto, 1931). Miss Ridley's work is brief and not wholly accurate. The Saskatchewan Department of Agriculture issued *Homemakers' Clubs, 1910-20* (Saskatoon, 1920), a very useful short work on a type of woman's organization peculiar to the Prairie Provinces where political aspirations were largely forwarded through farm groups. For Quebec there is an anonymous pamphlet entitled *Suffrage Féminin dans la Province de Québec* (Montreal, n.d.) on file in the offices of the League for Women's Rights, and the more valuable *Brief History of the League for Women's Rights* (Montreal, 1941), published by the League as part of its celebration of the political liberation of the women of Quebec in 1940.

There are a few short publications available which try to show the political or legal status of Canadian women at various periods. Of national range are: Henrietta Muir Edwards, *Women of Canada* (n.p., 1900), published by the National Council of Women of Canada for the Paris International Exhibition of that year; and *Legal Status of Women in Canada* (Ottawa, 1924), published by the federal Department of Labour. Each of the three Prairie Provinces produced a summary of women's legal status within its own borders. These are: Mary E. Crawford, ed., *Legal Status of Women in Mani-*

*toba* (Winnipeg, 1913); *Some Saskatchewan Legislation Affecting Women and Children* (Regina, 1920), published by the government of the Province of Saskatchewan; and Henrietta Muir Edwards, ed., *Legal Status of Women of Alberta* (2nd ed., n.p., 1921).

In its Canadian Pamphlet Collection the Parliamentary Library at Ottawa has several short documents dealing with the woman suffrage question, two of them quite interesting because of their relatively early origin and the bitterness with which they attacked the proposition. The latter are: the Honourable John Dryden, *Womanhood Suffrage* (C.P.C. No. 1487), a speech of which the provincial minister of agriculture unburdened himself before the Ontario legislature in 1893; and Francis Parkman, *Some of the Reasons Against Woman Suffrage* (C.P.C. No. 3990), a remarkable essay by the noted American historian in which he predicted every manner of evil should the disastrous idea of equality ever gain a foothold in reality. An early champion of the project, James L. Hughes, spoke forth in vigorous rebuttal in a fifty-page pamphlet entitled *Equal Suffrage* (C.P.C. No. 756, Toronto, 1895). C.P.C. No. 1004 brings the question down to modern times with a complete report of a CBC National Forum discussion of *The Position of Women in Canada.* The participants in the forum, which was broadcast on December 11, 1938, were Dr. Irene Parlby, Mme Pierre Casgrain, and B. K. Sandwell. The attainment of the franchise by the women of Quebec in 1940 was the signal for an outpouring of newspaper and magazine articles commemorating struggles past and making bold predictions for the future. Four of these, all from the Montreal *Standard*, have been preserved in the Library's Pamphlet Collection: Walter Martin, *Quebec's Woman Warriors* (C.P.C. No. 1014), dealing particularly with the heroic efforts of the rival chieftains, Mme Pierre Casgrain and Mlle Idola Saint Jean; *Quebec Women Had Vote Over Century Ago* (C.P.C. No. 1020); *Quebec Women Look to the Future* (C.P.C. No. 1040); and *Quebec Women Plan for Future at Conference* (C.P.C. No. 1041).

Three political campaign documents from Manitoba shed considerable light on the campaign for woman suffrage in that province. All of them may be found in the Provincial Library of Manitoba: *Platform of Manitoba Liberals 1914* (Winnipeg, 1914), a 139-page pamphlet published by the Liberal party in anticipation of the 1915 elections, in which the Liberals flailed the Conservative Roblin government for its reactionary attitude toward women; *Record of*

the Roblin Government, 1900-1914, and the Criticisms and Pretensions
of Opponents (Winnipeg, 1914), a return broadside of 238 pages in
which the Conservative leader endeavoured to explain why he had
laboured to keep the blight of woman suffrage from his province;
and finally *A Review of the Provincial Government in Manitoba, 1915-
1920* (n.p., n.d.), in whose seventy pages the Liberal party set forth
its accomplishment of woman suffrage and other enlightened measures, unrestrained by false modesty.

Valuable indeed, is the *Record of Proceedings in the Privy Council,
No. 121 of 1928, On Appeal from the Supreme Court of Canada: In
the Matter of a Reference as to the Meaning of the word "persons" in
Section 24 of the British North America Act, 1867* (n.p., n.d.). Copies
of this document, which is indispensable for an understanding of the
Persons Case, are apparently very scarce, for not even the Parliamentary Library possesses one. There is one, however, in the Public
Archives of Canada at Ottawa. The document includes a very
comprehensive synopsis of legal arguments presented by both sides
before the Supreme Court of Canada and before the Privy Council
in London; also names of all people involved in the case and important dates.

There are a few good pamphlets dealing with the status of Canadian women in the post-war era, though they are largely statistical
(hence not very readable) and much more concerned with the economic problems of women than their political difficulties. In the
midst of the recent war, the federal government appointed an
Advisory Committee on Reconstruction, a subcommittee of which
was detailed to pay special attention to women's problems during
reconversion. Dr. Margaret McWilliams of Winnipeg was chairman of the group of ten representative Canadian women who made
their final and very excellent report on *Post-War Problems of Women*
on November 30, 1943. This was published at Ottawa in 1944 and
is obtainable from the King's Printer. For statistics on the astonishing number and types of jobs performed by women during the
war, Canadian Information Service, ed., "Canadian War Data,"
*1946 Reference Papers Series, No. 4* (Ottawa, May 15, 1946), is
helpful. An insight into what happened to those women war workers
during the first eleven months of peace can be obtained from a
mimeographed report put out by the Statistics Branch of the federal
Department of Labour entitled "Women Workers in the Reconversion," *Canadian Labour Market*, II, no. 6 (Ottawa, July 15, 1946).

The Royal Bank of Canada's *Monthly Letter* for July 1946, entitled simply "Canadian Women," is an entertaining prediction about the place women will assert for themselves in the future after their taste of war-born economic independence.

A mimeographed document, "Record of Service of Women in the United States Congress," issued by the Publicity Division, National Republican Committee, Washington, D.C., in April 1949, contains names, parties, and dates of service of all women members past and present. It was most useful in furnishing facts used for purposes of comparison in Appendix A.

### D. *Magazine Articles*

Because woman suffrage never became a burning issue in Canada, it failed to provoke periodical comment comparable to the outpourings in Great Britain and the United States. In milder and sparser fashion, however, Canadian periodicals, both popular and more weighty, devoted some space to the question. On the historical side two scholarly monographs make their contribution: the Honourable William Renwick Riddell, "Woman Franchise in Quebec a Century Ago," *Royal Society of Canada, Transactions*, 3rd series, XXII (Ottawa, 1928), section II; and W. L. Morton, "The Extension of the Franchise in Canada: A Study in Democratic Nationalism," *Canadian Historical Association Report*, 1943. The latter explores the subject of franchise extension in general, but makes some pertinent observations on the women's phase of the issue. More popular in style are: Helen Gregory MacGill, "Place Aux Dames," *Canadian Magazine* (Toronto), April 1933, which traces the progress of the suffrage struggle in Quebec to the time of writing; and Mrs. John Scott, "Fight for Woman's Suffrage," *Gazette* (Montreal), March 28, 1940, some interesting reflections of a Quebec woman suffrage veteran celebrating the victory.

Representative of articles which advocated political equality while the issue was still undecided are Edith M. Luke, "Woman Suffrage in Canada," *Canadian Magazine*, V (1895); R. E. MacNaughton, "A Plea for Woman Suffrage in Canada," *Canadian Magazine*, XXIX (1907); and A. H. F. Lefroy, "Should Canadian Women Have the Parliamentary Vote?" *Queen's Quarterly*, XXI (Kingston, 1913). W. E. Maclellan, "Women and Votes," *Dalhousie Review*, I (Halifax, 1922); and Mme E. Croff, "Les femmes de la province de Québec sont-elles en faveur du vote féminin?" *Canada français*, XX (Quebec, 1933), take a decided stand against the women; while Isabel Skelton, "Canadian Women and the Suffrage," *Canadian Magazine of Politics, Science, Art and Literature*, XLI (Toronto, 1913), attempts to explain the prevalent apathy of Canadian women toward the entire question.

Efforts to assess the value of women's contribution to the political scene after enfranchisement, both in Canada and on a broader plane, are found in: A. A. Perry, "Is Woman's Suffrage a Fizzle?" *Maclean's* (Toronto), February 1, 1928; Charlotte Whitton, "Is the Canadian Woman a Flop in Politics?" *Saturday Night* (Toronto), January 26, 1946; Charlotte Whitton, "Women the World Over," *Chatelaine* (Toronto), September 1946; and Page H. Dougherty, "It's a Man's Game, But Woman Is Learning," New York *Times Magazine* (New York), October 3, 1946. Mrs. Perry and Dr. Whitton do not show much mercy in describing the political shortcomings of their fellow Canadians.

E. *Books*.

Although, as previously stated, there are no books dealing directly with the woman suffrage movement in Canada, some information and certain side-lights on the subject were gleaned from the sources listed below.

Biographies of Canadian statesmen who were in any way involved in the suffrage issue are not plentiful and even in those available, very scant reference is made to the enfranchisement question: an all too obvious indication, no doubt, of the weight attached to the issue. Sir John A. Macdonald's long administration of dominion affairs is dealt with in the following: G. Mercer Adam, *Canada's Patriot Statesman: The Life and Career of the Right Honourable Sir John A. Macdonald* (Toronto and London, 1891); George R. Parkin, *Sir John A. Macdonald* (vol. XVIII in the Parkman Edition of *The Makers of Canada*, Toronto, 1908); Joseph Pope, *Memoirs of the Right Honourable Sir John Alexander Macdonald, G.C.B., First Prime Minister of the Dominion of Canada* (2 vols., Ottawa, 1894), the standard biography; and John Lewis, "Canada under Macdonald, 1878-1891," in Adam Shortt and Arthur G. Doughty, eds., *Canada and its Provinces*, VI (23 vols., Toronto, 1914).

However, it is only in the Pope work that Sir John's experiment in woman suffrage is mentioned particularly. Henry Borden, ed., *Robert Laird Borden: His Memoirs* (2 vols., Toronto, 1938), gives considerable attention to the Wartime Elections Act (1917) and a somewhat lesser amount to the exclusively female enfranchisement measure of 1918. Oscar D. Skelton, *Life and Letters of Sir Wilfrid Laurier* (2 vols., Toronto, 1921), throws valuable light upon the motives leading to the passage of the hotly disputed Wartime Elections Act; and George H. Locke's biographical sketch of Arthur Meighen in *Builders of the Canadian Commonwealth* (Toronto, 1923), contributes further to an understanding of the controversial measure of 1917.

Biographies of the leaders of the woman suffrage movement are practically non-existent and offer a promising field of exploration for Canadian historians and biographers. Within recent years, two worthwhile efforts have been made towards filling this gap. Byrne Hope Sanders, *Emily Murphy, Crusader* (Toronto, 1945), makes wide use of the Murphy Papers and is fascinating reading. Another pioneer feminist of the prairies has received well-merited attention in Kennethe M. Haig, *Brave Harvest: The Life Story of E. Cora Hind, LL.D.* (Toronto, 1945). It is as a pioneer woman journalist and agricultural expert that Miss Hind is presented to her readers, however, not as a champion of women's political rights. Nellie L. McClung, *The Stream Runs Fast* (Toronto, 1945) is autobiographical and, in spite of its modesty, occasionally casts a few beams of light on its author's endeavours to advance the cause of women; but what a golden opportunity awaits some potential biographer who would do full justice to that rich and turbulent career!

The monumental work of Ida Husted Harper *et al.*, eds., *The History of Woman Suffrage* (6 vols., New York, 1922), contains several sections on the progress of the movement in Canada, but unfortunately displays several glaring inaccuracies where the Canadian phase is concerned. Mrs. S. G. E. McKee, *Jubilee History of the Ontario Woman's Christian Temperance Union, 1877-1927* (Whitby, 1927), is useful because of the frequent linking of temperance and suffrage forces. Describing further the working partnership between the two groups is Nellie L. McClung, *In Times Like These* (Toronto, 1915), a collection of extremely witty and practical essays on women's position in the home and in society.

Five miscellaneous works dealing exclusively with the Quebec scene are helpful in clarifying the reasons why the suffrage struggle was so protracted in that part of the dominion. Horace Miner, *Saint Denis: A French-Canadian Parish* (Chicago, 1939), analyzes the social structure of rural French-Canadian society. Miner's work is supplemented by two further studies of the changing social and economic order in French Canada: Everett C. Hughes, "Industry and the Rural System in Quebec," *Canadian Journal of Economics and Political Science*, IV (Toronto, 1938); and Everett Cherrington Hughes, *French Canada in Transition* (Chicago and Toronto, 1943). Hughes does the same kind of analytical survey for the small industrialized town which Miner does for the rural parish.

Interesting sidelights on the French-Canadian woman's role in history, education, letters, and public life are available in *La femme canadienne française*, the title of the 1936 edition of La ligue des droits du français, ed., *Almanach de la langue française* (Montreal, 1916-1937). Madeleine G. Huguenin, *Portraits de Femmes* (Montreal, 1938), contains around one hundred and fifty brief biographies of Quebec's outstanding women past and present. Though two or three shed some light on the province's feminists, the omissions tell more than many pages of writing could about the average French Canadian's sentiments where woman suffrage is concerned. While stoutly commending Mlle Saint Jean's feminist activities, the author apparently thought Mme Casgrain, Professor Derick, Dr. Ritchie-England, and Mrs. John Scott unworthy of mention.

A short but useful work on the newcomer to the dominion is R. H. Tait's *Newfoundland: A Summary of the History and Development of Britain's Oldest Colony*, printed by the Harrington Press in the United States in 1939. Major Tait was the director of the Newfoundland Information Bureau in the United States from its inception in 1926 until its absorption by the Canadian Information Service in 1949. His book reflects its author's long practice in answering questions on this little-known part of the continent. In the first volume of J. R. Smallwood, ed., *The Book of Newfoundland* (2 vols., Saint John's, 1937), there is an anonymous article, "Current Events Club—Woman Suffrage—Newfoundland Society of Art." Although obviously written by one of Newfoundland's suffragists and containing some interesting personal recollections of their tribulations, it is rendered almost useless by its lack of dates and its disorderly arrangement.

Although it has no direct connection with the suffrage issue, Marcus L. Hansen and John Bartlet Brebner, *The Mingling of the Canadian and American Peoples* (New Haven and Toronto, 1940), is excellent for its description of the fluctuations of population across the international boundary which were characteristic of the midcontinent around the turn of the century and which go so far towards explaining the unusually heavy pressure of American suffrage influences upon the Prairie Provinces.

In the field of legal and constitutional works, Allan M. Dymond, K.C., *The Laws of Ontario Relating to Women and Children* (Toronto, 1923), is useful for the province concerned. Armand Grenier, K.C. and S. Edward Bolton, Reporters, *Canada Law Reports 1928: Supreme Court of Canada* (Ottawa, 1928), and the Right Honourable Sir Frederick Pollock, Bart., K.C., ed., *The Law Reports of the Incorporated Council of Law Reporting: House of Lords, Judicial Committee of the Privy Council and Peerage Cases* (London, 1930), were consulted for the Persons Case. Arthur G. Doughty and Norah Story, eds., *Documents Relating to the Constitutional History of Canada, 1819-1828* (Ottawa, 1935), yields some interesting documentary evidence on the strange urge to vote manifested by certain females in early nineteenth century Quebec.

## F. *Registers and Year Books*

As a guide-post in determining when and where important suffrage activities and measures might be expected, J. Castell Hopkins, ed., *The Canadian Annual Review of Public Affairs* (published annually at Toronto from 1901 to the present), was most helpful when this history was being mapped out. For a portion of the earlier period, Henry J. Morgan, ed., *The Dominion Annual Register and Review* (published annually at Montreal between the years 1878 and 1886 inclusive) was similarly useful.

For assistance in biographical material, the publications listed below were consulted and found to contain some information on figures connected with the woman suffrage movement; but it was again most evident that unless these people had some other ground for prominence, aside from woman suffrage connections, they were not ordinarily thought to be of sufficient importance for inclusion in standard biographical works. Various publishers have issued *The Canadian Parliamentary Guide* (Ottawa, 1862, annual, with a few exceptions), a work which is very useful in furnishing not only brief biographies of all members of Canada's dominion and provincial legislatures, but also dates of the rise and fall of governments, and the names of those who composed the various cabinets. Concerning persons outside of legislative precincts, an occasional morsel of knowledge was garnered from: Henry J. Morgan, ed., *The Canadian Men and Women of the Time: A Hand-book of Canadian Biography of Living Characters* (2nd ed., Toronto, 1912); Sir Charles G. D. Roberts and Arthur L. Tunnell, eds., *A Standard Dictionary of Canadian Biography: Canadian Who Was Who* (2 vols., Toronto, 1938); and Canadian Newspaper Service, publ., *National Reference Book on Canadian Men and Women* (6th ed., Montreal, 1940).

# INDEX

ABERDEEN, LADY, 32, 85n, 218; founder
of National Council of Women, 12;
endorses woman suffrage, 31
Acadia College, 163
Accountants, women, in Que., 234–5;
237
L'Action Catholique (Quebec City),
opposition of, to woman suffrage, 15,
256n, 257n; attacked by Manitoba
Free Press, 65; and clerical viewpoint
on politics, 243–4. See also Roman
Catholic church.
Acts of parliament
(Canada). See Dominion By-Elec-
tions Act, Dominion Elections Act,
Federal Franchise Act of 1885,
Federal Franchise Act of 1898,
Military Voters Act, Supreme
Court Act, Wartime Elections Act,
Women's Franchise Act.
(Great Britain) See British North
America Act, Constitutional Act of
1791, Interpretation Act, Lord
Brougham's Act, Representation
of the People Act of 1918, Sex
Disqualification Removal Act.
Acts of provincial legislatures. See
Alberta legislature, Quebec legisla-
ture, etc.
"Actualité Féminine," 240n
Adam, G. Mercer, 108
Aikens, Sir James, 62
Albany, N.Y., 24
Alberta, 40, 42, 58, 62, 66–75, 76, 102, 115,
117, 120, 138, 140n, 141, 146, 235,
268; ease of acquiring equality in,
46; premier's suffrage pledge to
U.F.A., 47; third province to enfranchise women, 66n; first women
judges in dominion, 66, 67, 73–4,
74n, 142; first women lawmakers in
dominion, 66, 74, 146; woman cabinet member, 66, 74, 146; women's
service in provincial legislature, 66,
74, 146, 268; organized as province,
67; dower legislation, 67–8; municipal rights for women, 73; school
rights for women, 73; influence of

women on social legislation in, 73,
271; woman member in House of
Commons, 74, 140n; government of,
and Persons Case, 74, 75n, 147, 152;
government of, defends its women
judges, 142; Supreme Court of, and
women judges, 142; United Farmers
of, see United Farmers of Alberta.
See also Alberta legislature.
Alberta legislature, acts of, Election
Act of 1909, 69, Election Act of 1916,
73, Sex Disqualification Removal
Act, 73, 252; delegations to, 69, 70,
71; suffrage petitions to, 69-70; 72;
municipal franchise and residence,
69-70; bills, for political equality, 72,
72n, 73, for prohibition, 72n; demonstration in, 73; second in dominion
to enfranchise women, 73; women
eligible for, 73
Alexander, W. H., 60, 70
Allen, Mrs. W. T., 174n
L'Alliance Canadienne pour le Vote
des Femmes du Québec, 231–2, 235,
236, 240; campaign for Liberals,
255–6; continues reform work, 260.
See also Saint Jean, Idola.
Allowances, mothers', in Alta., 73
American Association for the Advancement of Women, 20, 180
Amyot, Guillaume, 111
Anglican Synod, 166
Anglin, Chief Justice, opinion on "persons," 150, 150n, 151
Anna and the King of Siam, 163n
Anthony, Susan B., 16, 25
Apathy towards women's rights of
Canadian women, 3–4, 7, 18, 20, 32,
112–13, 272–8; of women in the
Maritime Provinces, 7, 83, 156-8,
163-4, 180, 185, 194, 198, 201–4, 207;
of Quebec women, 7, 83, 242–3, 257,
257n; of western women, 49, 84, 84n;
of public in general, 90, 177, 184, 190
Appellants, Persons Case, financial
support from government, 145; choice
of counsel, 147; arguments of counsel
for, 147–8; Supreme Court unani-